W9-BZD-444

# A Guide to Programming Logic and Design
## Comprehensive

Joyce Farrell

McHenry County College

ONE MAIN STREET, CAMBRIDGE, MA 02142

*an International Thomson Publishing company* I T P®

Cambridge • Albany • Bonn • Boston • Cincinnati • London • Madrid • Melbourne • Mexico City
New York • Paris • San Francisco • Singapore • Tokyo • Toronto • Washington

*A Guide to Programming Logic and Design—Comprehensive* is published by Course Technology.

© 1999 by Course Technology— I⊤P®

| | |
|---|---|
| *Associate Publisher* | Kristen Duerr |
| *Product Manager* | Jennifer Muroff |
| *Associate Product Manager* | Margarita Donovan |
| *Editorial Assistant* | Tricia Coia |
| *Developmental Editor* | Linda Falkenstein |
| *Production Editor* | Megan Cap-Renzi |
| *Marketing Manager* | Susan E. Ogar |
| *Text Designer* | Kim Munsell |
| *Cover Designer* | Efrat Reis |

For more information contact:

Course Technology, Inc.
One Main Street
Cambridge, MA 02142

International Thomson Editores
Seneca, 53
Colonia Polanco
11560 Mexico D.F. Mexico

ITP Europe
Berkshire House 168-173
High Holborn
London WCIV 7AA
England

ITP GmbH
Königswinterer Strasse 418
53227 Bonn
Germany

ITP Asia
60 Albert Street, #15-01
Albert Complex
Singapore 189969

Nelson ITP, Australia
102 Dodds Street
South Melbourne, 3205
Victoria, Australia

ITP Japan
Hirakawacho Kyowa Building, 3F
2-2-1 Hirakawacho
Chiyoda-ku, Tokyo 102
Japan

ITP Nelson Canada
1120 Birchmount Road
Scarborough, Ontario
Canada M1K 5G4

All rights reserved. This publication is protected by federal copyright law. No part of this publication may be reproduced, stored in a retrieval system, or transmitted in any form or by any means, electronic, mechanical, photocopying, recording, or otherwise, or be used to make derivative work (such as translation or adaptation), without prior permission in writing from Course Technology.

**Trademarks**
Course Technology and the Open Book logo are registered trademarks and CourseKits is a trademark of Course Technology. Custom Editions is a registered trademark of International Thomson Publishing.

I⊤P® The ITP logo is a registered trademark of International Thomson Publishing.

Some of the product names and company names used in this book have been used for identification purposes only, and may be trademarks or registered trademarks of their respective manufacturers and sellers.

**Disclaimer**
Course Technology reserves the right to revise this publication and make changes from time to time in its content without notice.

ISBN 0-7600-1177-X

Printed in Canada

5 6 7 8 9 WC 03 02 01 00

# Preface

*A Guide to Programming Logic and Design—Comprehensive* provides the beginning programmer with a guide to developing structured program logic. This textbook assumes that students have no programming language experience.

## Organization and Coverage

*A Guide to Programming Logic and Design—Comprehensive* introduces students to programming concepts, enforcing good style and logical thinking. General programming concepts are introduced in Chapter 1. Chapter 2 discusses the key concepts of structure including what structure is, how to recognize it, and, most importantly, the advantages to writing structured programs. Chapter 3 extends the information on structured programming to the area of modules. By Chapter 4 students can write complete, structured business programs. Chapters 5 and 6 explore the intricacies of decision making and looping. Students learn to develop sophisticated programs that use control breaks and arrays in Chapters 7 and 8.

In Chapter 9 students use arrays in more sophisticated ways, exploring sorting techniques. Chapter 10 focuses on the special issues involved in writing interactive programs that allow users to make menu selections from both single- and multiple-level menus. Chapter 11 covers the intricacies of sequential file merging, matching, and updating. In Chapter 12, students learn valuable modularization techniques, including the differences between local and global variables and how to pass variables to and from modules. Chapter 12 also provides clear explanations of the sometimes confusing terminology associated with object-oriented programming. In Chapter 13, students learn the vocabulary associated with event-driven programming and how to incorporate GUI objects into programs. Chapter 14 brings together all the concepts that students have learned by addressing issues of good program design—including reducing coupling and increasing cohesion.

*A Guide to Programming Logic and Design—Comprehensive* combines text explanation with flowcharts and pseudocode examples to provide students with alternative means of expressing structured logic. Numerous detailed, full-program exercises at the end of each section illustrate the concepts explained within the section and reinforce students' understanding and retention of the material presented.

*A Guide to Programming Logic and Design—Comprehensive* distinguishes itself from other programming logic language books in the following ways:

- It is written and designed to be non-language specific. The logic used in this book can be applied to any programming language.
- The examples are everyday business examples; no special knowledge of mathematics, accounting, or other disciplines is assumed.

- The concept of structure is covered earlier than in many other texts. Students are exposed to structure naturally, so they will automatically create properly designed programs.
- Text explanation is interspersed with both flowcharts *and* pseudocode so students can become comfortable with *both* logic development tools.
- Complex programs are built through the use of complete business examples instead of only segments of programs.
- Students learn the difference between local and global variables, and how to pass their values to and from modules.
- Object-oriented terminology is thoroughly explained. This feature is absent from many other programming logic books.
- Event-driven GUI programs are presented. Students enjoy working with the graphical objects. Few texts explore the logic behind them.
- Students gain an appreciation for good program design, and learn to recognize poor design.

## Features

New to this edition of the text is the inclusion of pseudocode—an important programming logic tool—to the flowcharts; greater clarity and refinement in the drawing and logic of the flowcharts; more end-of-chapter exercises; and the addition of cases that stimulate student interest and provide a context for learning in each chapter of the book. Discussion of object-oriented techniques and GUI programming is also new, and coverage of important design issues is expanded.

*A Guide to Programming Logic and Design—Comprehensive* is a superior textbook because it also includes the following features:

- **Case Approach** Each chapter begins with a short scenario to pique the students' interest in the topic. If students can see how each programming concept can be used, and why it is important, they will be more motivated to learn.
- **TIPS** These notes provide additional information—for example, an alternative method of performing a procedure, another term for a concept, background information on a technique, or a commonly-made error to watch out for.
- **Summaries** Following each section is a Summary that recaps the programming concepts and techniques covered in the section.
- **Terms and Concepts** Each section includes a list of key terms and concepts presented in the section.
- **Review Questions** Each chapter section concludes with meaningful programming exercises that provide students with additional practice of the skills and concepts they learned in the lesson. These exercises increase in difficulty and are designed to allow students to explore logical programming concepts.

## The Supplements

All of the supplements for this text are found in the Instructor's Resource Kit, which includes a printed Instructor's Manual and a CD-ROM.

- **Instructor's Manual** The author wrote the Instructor's Manual and it was quality assurance tested. It is available in printed form and through the Course Technology Faculty Online Companion on the World Wide Web at www.course.com. (Call your customer service representative for the specific URL and your password.) The Instructor's Manual contains the following items:

  - Suggested solutions to all of the programming problems presented in the text
  - Teaching notes to help introduce and clarify the material presented in the chapters
  - Conceptual and practical examination questions

- **Course Test Manager Version 1.1 Engine and Test Bank** Course Test Manager (CTM) is a cutting-edge Windows-based testing software program, developed exclusively for Course Technology, that helps instructors design and administer examinations and practice tests. This full-featured program allows students to generate practice tests randomly. The practice tests provide immediate on-screen feedback and detailed study guides for incorrectly answered questions. Instructors can also use Course Test Manager to create printed and online tests. You can create, preview, and administer a test on any or all chapters of this textbook entirely over a local area network. Course Test Manager can automatically grade the tests students take at the computer and can generate statistical information on individual as well as group performance. A CTM test bank has been written to accompany your textbook and is included on the CD-ROM. The test bank includes multiple-choice, true/false, short answer, and essay questions.

## Acknowledgments

I would like to thank all of the people who helped to make this book a reality, especially Linda Falkenstein, Development Editor, who worked diligently to make this a quality textbook. Thanks also to Kristen Duerr, Associate Publisher; Cheryl Ouellette and Jennifer Muroff, Product Managers; Megan Cap-Renzi, Production Editor; Margarita Donovan, Associate Product Manager; Tricia Coia, Editorial Assistant; and Beverly Jackson, Quality Assurance Tester.

I am grateful to the many reviewers who provided helpful and insightful comments during the development of this book, including Sandy Fabyan of Columbus State Community College, Donald Martin of El Paso Community College, Roy Foreman of Purdue University-Calumet, Missy Setzer of Blue Ridge Community College, Harry Rosenblatt of the College of Albemarle, Patty Loika Nunnally of John Tyler Community College, and John Humphrey of Asheville Community College.

Thanks, too, to my husband, Geoff, who acts as friend and advisor in the book-writing process. This book is dedicated to him and to my daughters, Andrea and Audrey.

*Joyce Farrell*

# Contents

## chapter 4

# WRITING A COMPLETE PROGRAM  91

## c h a p t e r   7

# CONTROL BREAKS *175*

## chapter 10

# USING MENUS AND VALIDATING INPUT  *273*

## chapter 13

# PROGRAMMING GRAPHICAL USER INTERFACES *367*

xx)<br>

Defining the Objects in an Object Dictionary 378
Defining the Connections Between the User Screens 379
Planning the Logic 380
Object-Oriented Error Handling: Throwing Exceptions 381
Terms and Concepts 385
Summary 385
Exercises 386

**chapter 14**

**PROGRAM DESIGN** 387

Section A: Program Design Issues 388
The Need for Good Design 388
Storing Program Components in Separate Files 388
Selecting Variable and Module Names 390
Terms and Concepts 392
Exercises 392
Section B: Coupling and Cohesion 393
Organizing Modules 393
Reducing Coupling 393
Increasing Cohesion 396
Functional Cohesion 396
Sequential Cohesion 397
Communicational Cohesion 398
Temporal, Procedural, Logical, and Coincidental
Cohesion 399
Maintaining Good Programming Habits 400
Terms and Concepts 400
Summary 401
Exercises 402

**appendix a**

**A DIFFICULT STRUCTURING PROBLEM** 403

**appendix b**

**USING A LARGE DECISION TABLE** 415

**index 422**

# An Overview of Computers and Logic

**case ▶** It's your first day as a computer programmer trainee at Solutions, Inc. "I'm so excited about learning to program," you say to Andrea Lake, Human Resources Director at Solutions. "I'm sure there's a lot to learn, and I'm ready to start. Show me to my computer and let me start typing!"

"You'll be learning a lot in the next few weeks," Andrea agrees, "but we're not showing you to a computer just yet. I'm going to introduce you to two of our best programmers, Boston Murphy and Lynn Greenbrier. They're going to explain that to be able to write good programs, you must first learn some basic computer terminology, and then you must gain a firm foundation in programming logic."

"But I want to start writing programs now!" you say. "I want to learn COBOL, C++, Java, and all the other languages I've read about."

"Simply learning those languages is like learning a few words of Russian or Japanese. Before you worry about using a language, we're going to train you to have something to say."

After studying Section A, you should be able to:

- Define basic computer terminology such as hardware and software
- Describe the data processing cycle of input, processing, output, and storage
- Explain the difference between syntax errors and logical errors
- List the steps involved in producing a computer program
- Describe the data hierarchy of file, record, field, and character

# Understanding Computer Programming

## Understanding Computer Components and Operations

The two major components of any computer system are its hardware and its software. **Hardware** is the equipment, or the devices, associated with a computer. In order for a computer to be useful, however, it needs more than equipment; a computer needs to be given instructions. The instructions that tell the computer what to do are called **software**, or programs, and are written by programmers. This book focuses on the process of writing these instructions.

Together, computer hardware and software accomplish four major operations:

1. Input
2. Processing
3. Output
4. Storage

Hardware devices that perform input include keyboards and mice. Through these devices, **data,** or facts, enter the computer system. Processing data items may involve organizing them, checking them for accuracy, or performing mathematical operations on them. The piece of hardware that performs these sorts of tasks is the **Central Processing Unit,** or **CPU.** After data have been processed, the resulting information is sent to a printer, monitor, or some other output device. Often, you also want to store the output information on hardware such as magnetic disks or tapes. Computer software consists of all the instructions that control when the data are input, how they are processed, and the form in which they are output or stored.

Computer hardware by itself is useless without a programmer's instructions or software, just as your stereo equipment doesn't do much until you provide music on a CD or tape. You can enter instructions into a computer system through any of the hardware devices you use for data: for example, a keyboard, disk drive, or magnetic tape unit.

You write computer instructions in a computer **programming language**. Just as some humans speak English and others speak Japanese, programmers write programs in different languages; some examples are BASIC, Pascal, COBOL, RPG, C++, Java, and Fortran. Some programmers work exclusively in one language; others know several and use the one that seems most appropriate to the task at hand.

No matter which programming language a computer programmer uses, the language has rules governing its word usage and punctuation. These rules are called the language's **syntax**. If you ask, "How the get to store do I?" in English, most people can figure out what you probably mean even though you have not used proper English syntax. However, computers are not nearly as smart as most humans; with a computer you might as well have asked, "Xpu mxv ot dodnm cadf B?" Unless the syntax is perfect, the computer cannot interpret the programming language at all.

Every computer operates on circuitry that consists of millions of on-off switches. Each programming language uses a piece of software to translate the specific programming language into the computer's on-off circuitry language, or **machine language**. The language translation software is called a **compiler** or **interpreter**, and it tells you if you have used a programming language incorrectly. Therefore, syntax errors are relatively easy to locate and correct. If you write a computer program using a language such as C++, but spell one of its words incorrectly or reverse the proper order of two words, the translator lets you know there is a mistake as soon as you try to run the program.

For a program to work properly, you must give the instructions to the computer in a specific sequence, you must not leave any instructions out, and you must not add extraneous instructions. This is called developing the **logic** of the computer program. Suppose you instruct someone to make a cake as follows:

```
Stir
Add two eggs
Add a gallon of gasoline
Bake at 350 degrees for 45 minutes
Add three cups of flour
```

Even though you have used the English language syntax correctly, the instructions are out of sequence, some instructions are missing, and some instructions belong to procedures other than baking a cake. If you follow these instructions, you are not going to end up with an edible cake, and you may end up with a disaster. Logical errors are much more difficult to locate than syntax errors; it is easier for you to determine if *eggs* is spelled incorrectly in a recipe than it is for you to tell if there are too many eggs or they are added too soon.

Just as baking directions can be given correctly in French or German or Spanish, the same logic of a program can be expressed in any number of programming languages. This book is almost exclusively concerned with this logic development process. We are not concerned with any specific language, so this book could have been written in Japanese or BASIC or COBOL. The logic is the same in any language. For convenience, we will use English!

Once instructions have been input to the computer and translated into machine language, a program can be **run** or **executed**. You can write a program that takes a number (an input step), doubles it (processing), and tells you the answer (output) in a programming language such as Pascal or C, but if you were to write it in English, it would look like this:

```
Get number
Compute answer as number times 2
Print answer
```

The instruction to `Get number` is an example of an input operation. When the computer interprets this instruction, it knows to look to an input device to obtain a number. Computers often have several input devices, perhaps a keyboard, a mouse, a CD drive, and two or more disk drives. When you learn a specific programming language, you learn how to tell the computer which of those input devices to access for input. For now, however, it doesn't really matter which hardware device is used as long as the computer knows to look for a number. The logic of the input operation—that the computer must obtain a number for input, and that the computer must obtain it before multiplying it by two—remains the same regardless of any specific input hardware device.

Processing is the step that occurs when the mathematics is performed to double the number; the statement `Compute answer as number times 2` represents processing. Mathematical operations are not the only kind of processing, but they are a very typical kind of processing. After you write a program, the program can be used on computers of different brand names, sizes, and speeds. Whether you use an IBM, Macintosh, or Unix system, and whether you use a personal computer that sits on your desk or a mainframe that costs hundreds of thousands of dollars and resides in a special building in a university, multiplying by two is the same process. The hardware is not important; the processing will be the same.

In the number doubling program, the `Print answer` statement represents output. Again, within a particular program this statement might cause the output to appear on the monitor, which might be a flat panel screen or a cathode ray tube, or the output might go to a printer, which can be laser or inkjet. The logic of the process is the same no matter what hardware device you use.

Besides input, processing, and output, the fourth operation in any computer system is storage. Storage comes in two broad categories. All computers have **internal storage**, probably referred to more often as **memory, main memory,** or **primary memory**. This storage is inside the machine and is the type of storage most often discussed in this book. Computers also have **external storage**, which is permanent storage outside the main memory of the machine on some device such as a floppy disk, hard disk, or magnetic tape. In other words, external storage is outside the main memory, not necessarily outside the computer. Both programs and data are sometimes stored on each of these kinds of media.

To use computer programs, you must load them into memory first. You might type a program into memory from the keyboard, or you might use a program that has already been written and stored on a disk. Either way, a copy of the instructions must be placed in memory before the program can be run.

Both internal memory and external storage are necessary. Internal memory is needed in order to run the programs, but internal memory is **volatile**—that is, its contents are lost every time the computer loses power. Therefore, if you are going to use a program more than once, you must store it, or **save** it, on some non-volatile medium. Otherwise, the program in main memory is lost forever when the computer is turned off. External storage (usually disks or tape) provides that non-volatile medium.

> Even though a hard disk drive is located inside your computer, the hard disk is not main, internal memory. Internal memory is volatile; a hard drive is permanent, nonvolatile storage.

Once you have a copy of a program in main memory, you must also place any data that the program needs into memory. For example, after you place the following program

```
Get number
Compute answer as number times 2
Print answer
```

into memory and start to run it, you need to provide an actual number—say, 8—that you also place in main memory. The number is placed in memory in a specific memory location that the program will call `number`. Then, and only then, can the `answer`, in this case 16, be calculated and printed.

> Computer memory consists of millions of numbered locations where data can be stored. The memory location of `number` has a specific numeric address, for example, 48604. Your program associates `number` with that address. Every time you refer to `number` within a program, the computer retrieves the value at the associated memory location.

## The Programming Process

A programmer's job involves writing instructions such as the three instructions in the doubling program in the preceding section. A programmer's job can be broken down into six **programming steps**:

1. Understand the problem.
2. Plan the logic.
3. Code the program.
4. Translate the program into machine language.
5. Test the program.
6. Put the program into production.

### Understand the Problem

Professional computer programmers write programs to satisfy the needs of others. Examples are the human resources department that needs a printed list of all employees, the billing department that wants a list of clients who are 30 or more days overdue in their payments, and the office manager who would like to be notified when specific supplies reach the reorder point. Since programmers are providing a service to these users, programmers must first understand what it is the users want.

Suppose the director of human resources says to a programmer, "Our department needs a list of all employees who have been here over five years because we want to invite them to a special thank-you dinner." On the surface this seems like a simple enough request. An experienced programmer, however, will know that he or she may not yet understand the whole problem. Do they want a list of full-time employees only, or a list of full- and part-time employees together? Do they want people who have worked for the company on a month-to-month contractual basis over the past five years, or do they want regular employees only? Do the listed employees need to be working for the organization for five years as of today, or as of the date of the dinner, or is some other date to be used as a cutoff? What about an employee who worked three years, took a two-year leave of absence, and has been back for three years? Does he or she qualify? The programmer cannot make any of these decisions; the user is the one who must address these questions.

Still more decisions are required. What does the user want the report of five-year employees to look like? Should it contain both first and last names? Social Security numbers? Phone numbers? Addresses? Is all this data available? Several pieces of documentation are often provided to help the programmer understand the problem. This documentation includes print layout charts and file specifications, which you will learn about in Chapter 3.

Really understanding the problem may be one of the most difficult aspects of programming. On any job, the description of what the user needs may be vague; worse yet, the user may not even really know what it is he or she wants. A good programmer is part counselor, part detective!

## Plan the Logic

The heart of the programming process lies in planning the program's logic. During this phase of the programming process, the programmer plans the steps to the program, deciding both what steps to include and how to order those steps. There are many ways to plan the solution to a problem. The two most common tools are flowcharts and pseudocode. Both tools involve writing the steps of the program in English, much as you would plan a trip on paper before getting into the car or plan a party theme before going shopping for food and favors.

**You may hear programmers refer to planning a program as "developing an algorithm." An algorithm is the sequence of steps necessary to solve any problem.**

**You will learn more about flowcharts and pseudocode in Section B of this chapter.**

The programmer doesn't worry about the syntax of any language at this point, just about figuring out what sequence of events will lead from the available input to the desired output. Much more will be said about this planning of the logic later; in fact, this book focuses on this step almost exclusively.

## Code the Program

Once the programmer has developed the logic of a program, then and only then can he or she write the program in one of more than 400 programming languages that exist. It is at this point that the programmer can worry about each command being spelled correctly and all of the punctuation getting into the right spots—in other words, using the correct *syntax*.

Some very experienced programmers can successfully combine the logic planning and the actual instruction writing, or **coding** of the program, in one step. This may work for very simple programs, just as you can plan and write a postcard to your friend in one step. A good term paper or a Hollywood screenplay, however, needs planning before writing, and so do most programs.

Which is the harder step, planning the logic or coding the program? Right now, it may seem to you that writing in a programming language is a very difficult task, considering all the spelling and grammar rules you must learn. However, the planning step is actually more difficult. Which is more difficult, thinking up the twists and turns to the plot of a best-selling mystery novel or writing a translation of an already written novel from English to Spanish? And who do you think gets paid more, the writer or the translator?

## Translate the Program into Machine Language

Even though there are many programming languages, all computers know only one language, their machine language, which consists of many 1s and 0s. Computers understand this machine language because computers themselves are made up of thousands of tiny electrical switches, each of which can be set in either the on or off state, which is represented by a 1 or 0, respectively.

Languages like Java or BASIC are available for programmers to use only because someone has written a translator program (a compiler or interpreter) that changes the English-like **high-level language** in which the programmer writes into the **low-level machine language** that the computer understands. If you use a programming language incorrectly, misspelling a word, using a word that doesn't exist in the language, or using illegal grammar, the translator program doesn't know what to do and issues an error message. The same situation occurs when you speak nonsense to a human language translator. Imagine trying to look up a list of words in a Spanish-English dictionary if some of the listed words are misspelled. Although making errors is never desirable, syntax errors are not a major concern to programmers because the compiler or translator catches every syntax error, and the computer will not execute a program that contains syntax errors.

If there were an English compiler to which you could submit the sentence The grl go to school, it would point out two syntax errors to you. The second word, grl, is illegal because it is not part of the English language. Once you corrected the word `girl`, the compiler would find another syntax error on the third word, `go`, because it is the wrong verb for the subject `girl`. This doesn't mean `go` is necessarily the wrong word. Maybe `girl` is wrong; perhaps the subject should be `girls`, in which case `go` is right. Compilers don't always know exactly what you mean, nor do they know what the proper correction should be, but they do know when something is wrong with your syntax.

## Test the Program

A program that is free of syntax errors is not necessarily free of **logical errors**. The sentence `The girl goes to school`, although syntactically perfect, is not logically correct if the girl is a baby or a drop-out.

Once a program is free from syntax errors, the programmer can test it—that is, execute it with some sample data to see whether or not the results are logically correct. Recall the number doubling program:

```
Get number
Compute answer as number times 2
Print answer
```

If you provide the value 2 as input to the program and the number 4 prints out, you have executed one successful test run of the program.

However, if the number 40 prints out, maybe it's because a logical error exists within the program. Maybe the second line of code was mistyped with an extra zero so the program reads:

```
Get number
Compute answer as number times 20
Print answer
```

The error of placing 20 instead of 2 in the multiplication statement has caused a logical error. Notice that nothing is syntactically wrong with this second program—it is just as reasonable to multiply a number by 20 as by 2—but if the programmer intends only to double the number, then a logical error has occurred.

It is always important to test a program with many sets of data. For example, if you write the program to double a number and enter 2 and get an output value of 4, it doesn't mean you have a correct program. Perhaps you have typed this program by mistake:

```
Get number
Compute answer as number plus 2
Print answer
```

An input of 2 results in an answer of 4, but it doesn't mean your program doubles numbers—it actually only adds 2 to them. If you test your program with additional data—say, a 3—then as soon as you see the answer 5, you know you have a problem.

Selecting test data is somewhat of an art in itself, and it should be done carefully. If the human resources department wants a list of names of five-year employees, it would be a mistake to test the program with a small sample file of only long-term employees. If no new employees are part of the data being used for testing, you don't really know if the program would have eliminated them from the five-year list. Many companies don't know that a problem exists with their software until an unusual circumstance occurs, for example, the first time an employee has more than nine dependents, the first time a customer orders more than 999 items at a time, or when, in an example that has been well documented in the popular press, a new century begins.

### Put the Program into Production

Once the program has been tested adequately, the organization can use it. Putting it into production might mean simply running the program once if the program was written to satisfy a user's request for a special list, or it might be a process that takes months if the program will be run regularly from now on, or if the program is one of a large system of programs being developed. Perhaps data entry people must be trained to prepare the input for the new program, users must be trained to understand the output, and existing data in the company must be changed to some entirely new format to accommodate this program. **Conversion** to using a new program or set of programs can sometimes take an organization months or years to accomplish.

## Understanding the Data Hierarchy

Some very simple programs require very simple data. For example, the number doubling program requires just one value as input. Most business programs, however, use much more data—inventory files list thousands of items, personnel and customer files list thousands of people. When data are stored for use on computer systems, they are often stored in what is known as a **data hierarchy**.

The smallest usable unit of data is the **character**. Characters are letters, numbers, and special symbols such as "A", "7", and "$". Anything you can type from the keyboard in one keystroke (including a space or a Tab) is a character. Characters are made up of smaller elements called **bits**, but just as most humans can use a pencil without caring whether or not atoms are flying around inside it, most computer users can store characters without caring about these bits.

Computers also recognize characters you cannot enter from the keyboard, such as foreign alphabet characters like $\Phi$ or $\Sigma$.

Characters are often grouped together to make up **fields**. A field is a group of characters with some meaning. For most of us, an "S", an "M", an "I", a "T", and an "H" don't have much meaning individually, but if the group of characters

"SMITH" makes up your last name, then as a group the characters have useful meaning. These characters might comprise a field that you choose to call NAME. Other fields with meaning to you might be called ADDRESS or SALARY.

Fields are often grouped together into **records**. Records are groups of fields that go together for some logical reason. A random name, address, and salary aren't very useful, but if they're your name, your address, and your salary, then that's your record. An inventory record might contain fields for item number, color, and price; a student record might contain ID number, grade point average, and major.

Records, in turn, are grouped together to make **files**. Files are groups of records that go together for some logical reason. The individual records of each student in your class might go together in a file called CLASS. Records of each person at your company might be in a file called PERSONNEL. Items you sell might be in INVENTORY.

Some files can have just a few records; others, like the file of credit card holders for a major department store chain or policyholders of a major insurance company, can have thousands or even millions of records.

In summary, you can picture the data hierarchy as shown in Figure 1-1.

---

File

  Record

    Field

      Character

---

**Figure 1-1:** The data hierarchy

A file contains many records. Each record in a file has the same fields; each record's fields contain different data. That data consists of one or more stored characters in each field.

As an example, you can picture a file as a set of index cards as shown in Figure 1-2. The stack of cards is the EMPLOYEE file. Each card represents one employee record. On each card, each line holds one field—NAME, ADDRESS, or SALARY. Almost all the program examples in this book will use files that are organized in this way.

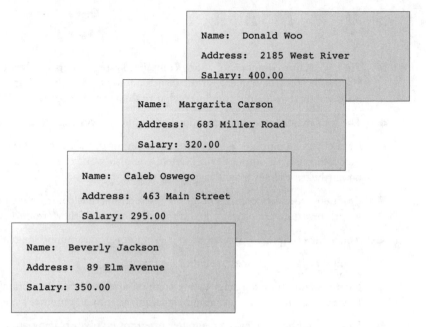

Name:   Donald Woo

Address:   2185 West River

Salary: 400.00

Name:   Margarita Carson

Address:   683 Miller Road

Salary: 320.00

Name:   Caleb Oswego

Address:   463 Main Street

Salary: 295.00

Name:   Beverly Jackson

Address:   89 Elm Avenue

Salary: 350.00

**Figure 1-2:** A file of employee records

# TERMS AND CONCEPTS

| | |
|---|---|
| hardware | main memory |
| software | primary memory |
| data | external storage |
| input | volatile |
| processing | programming steps |
| output | save a program |
| storage | code a program |
| Central Processing Unit (CPU) | high-level language |
| programming language | low-level machine language |
| syntax | logical errors |
| machine language | conversion |
| compiler | data hierarchy |
| interpreter | character |
| logic | bit |
| run | field |
| execute | record |
| internal storage | file |
| memory | |

# S U M M A R Y

- The two major components of any computer system are its hardware and software. Hardware is the equipment, or the devices, associated with a computer. The instructions that tell the computer what to do are called software.

- The four major computer operations are input, processing, output, and storage.

- Data enters a computer system through an input device, is processed by the CPU, and leaves through an output device. Often, you also want to store the output information on hardware such as magnetic disks or tapes.

- Computer software consists of all the instructions that control when the data are input, how they are processed, and the form in which they are output or stored.

- You write computer instructions in a computer programming language.

- Computer language rules are called syntax.

- Each programming language uses a piece of software, called a compiler or interpreter, to translate the specific programming language into a computer's machine language.

- Developing the logic of the computer program involves placing all necessary instructions in the proper sequence.

- All computers have volatile internal storage—probably referred to more often as memory, main memory, or primary memory—and external storage that is permanent storage outside the main memory of the machine on some device such as a floppy disk, hard disk, or magnetic tape.

- A programmer's job has six steps: 1. Understand the problem. 2. Plan the logic. 3. Code the program. 4. Translate the program into machine language. 5. Test the program. 6. Put the program into production.

- Using flowcharts or pseudocode involves writing the steps of a program in English.

- Writing instructions in a high-level programming language is coding; code is translated into low-level machine language for the computer.

- The compiler or translator catches every syntax error, and the computer will not execute a program that contains syntax errors.

- It is always important to test a program with many sets of data to ensure there are no logical errors.

- Putting a new program or system of programs into production is known as conversion.

- When data are stored for use on computer systems, they are often stored in what is known as a data hierarchy of file, record, field, and character.

# E X E R C I S E S

1. Match the definition with the appropriate term.

   1. Computer system equipment          a. compiler

   2. Another word for programs          b. syntax

   3. Language rules          c. logic

   4. Order of instructions          d. hardware

   5. Language translator          e. software

2. In your own words, describe the steps to writing a computer program.

3. Consider a student file that contains the following data:

   | LAST NAME | FIRST NAME | MAJOR | GRADE POINT AVERAGE |
   | --- | --- | --- | --- |
   | Andrews | David | Psychology | 3.4 |
   | Broederdorf | Melissa | Computer Science | 4.0 |
   | Brogan | Lindsey | Biology | 3.8 |
   | Carson | Joshua | Computer Science | 2.8 |
   | Eisfelder | Katie | Mathematics | 3.5 |
   | Faris | Natalie | Biology | 2.8 |
   | Fredricks | Zachary | Psychology | 2.0 |
   | Gonzales | Eduardo | Biology | 3.1 |

   Would this set of data be suitable and sufficient to use to test each of the following programs? Explain why or why not.

   a. A program that prints a list of Psychology majors

   b. A program that prints a list of Art majors

   c. A program that prints a list of students on academic probation—those with a grade point average under 2.0

   d. A program that prints a list of students on the dean's list

   e. A program that prints a list of students from Wisconsin

   f. A program that prints a list of female students

4. Suggest a good set of test data to use for a program that gives an employee a $50 bonus check if the employee has produced more than 1,000 items in a week.

5. Suggest a good set of test data for a program that computes gross paychecks (that is, before any taxes or other deductions) based on hours worked and rate of pay. The program computes gross as hours times rate unless hours are over 40. Then the program computes gross as regular rate of pay for 40 hours, plus one and a half times the rate of pay for the hours over 40.

6. Suggest a good set of test data for a program that is intended to output a student's grade point average based on letter grades (A, B, C, D, or F) in five courses.

7. Suggest a good set of data for a program for an automobile insurance company that wants to increase its premiums by $50 a month for every ticket a driver receives in a three-year period.

8. Assume a grocery store keeps a file for inventory. Each grocery item has its own record. Two fields within each record are the name of the manufacturer and the weight of the item. Name at least six more fields that might be stored for each record. Provide an example of the data for one record. For example, for one product the manufacturer is DelMonte, and the weight is twelve ounces.

9. Assume a library keeps a file with data about its collection, one record for each item the library loans out. Name at least eight fields that might be stored for each record. Provide an example of the data for one record.

**After studying Section B, you should be able to:**

- Identify and appropriately use the basic flowcharting symbols for input, processing, output, and decisions
- Explain the differences between flowcharts and pseudocode
- Define a variable
- Use a sentinel, or dummy value
- Use a connector symbol
- Recognize the proper format of assignment statements
- Explain the difference between character and numeric variables

# Introduction to Flowcharting and Pseudocode

## Using Flowchart Symbols and Pseudocode Statements

When programmers plan the logic for a solution to a programming problem, they often use one of two tools, **flowcharts** or **pseudocode** (pronounced "sue–dough–code"). A flowchart is a pictorial representation of the logical steps it takes to solve a problem. Pseudocode is an English-like representation of the same thing. *Pseudo* is a prefix that means false, and to *code* a program means to put it in a programming language; therefore *pseudocode* simply means "false code," or sentences that appear to have been written in a computer programming language but don't necessarily follow all the syntax rules of any specific language.

You have already seen pseudocode, and there is nothing mysterious about it. The following three statements constitute a pseudocode representation of a number doubling problem:

```
get NUMBER
compute ANSWER as NUMBER times 2
print ANSWER
```

Using pseudocode involves writing down all the steps you will use in a program. Some professional programmers prefer writing pseudocode to drawing flowcharts, because using pseudocode is more similar to writing the final statements in the programming language. Others prefer using flowcharts to represent the logical flow, because they can more easily visualize how the program statements will connect. Especially for beginning programmers, flowcharts are an excellent tool to help you visualize how the statements in a program are interrelated.

Almost every program involves the steps of input, processing, and output, as in the program

```
get NUMBER
compute ANSWER as NUMBER times 2
print ANSWER
```

Therefore most flowcharts need some way to separate visually these three steps. When you create a flowchart, you draw geometric shapes around the individual statements and connect them with arrows.

When you draw a flowchart, you use a parallelogram to represent **input** operations. You write an input statement, in English, inside the parallelogram, as shown in Figure 1-3.

**Figure 1-3:** Input symbol

Arithmetic operation statements are examples of **processing**. In a flowchart you use a rectangle to represent a processing statement as shown in Figure 1-4.

```
compute
ANSWER as
NUMBER
times 2
```

**Figure 1-4:** Processing symbol

To represent an **output** statement, you use the same symbol as you do for input statements—the parallelogram, as in Figure 1-5.

**Figure 1-5:** Output symbol

To show the correct sequence of these statements, you use arrows, or **flowlines,** to connect the steps. Whenever possible, most of a flowchart should read from top to bottom or from left to right on a page. That's the natural way we read English, so when flowcharts follow this convention, they are easier to understand.

To be complete, a flowchart should include two more elements: a **terminal** or START/STOP symbol at each end. Often, you place a word like START or BEGIN in the first terminal symbol and a word like END or STOP in the other. The standard terminal symbol is shaped like a racetrack ⬭. Figure 1-6 shows a complete flowchart for the program that doubles a number, and the pseudocode for the same problem.

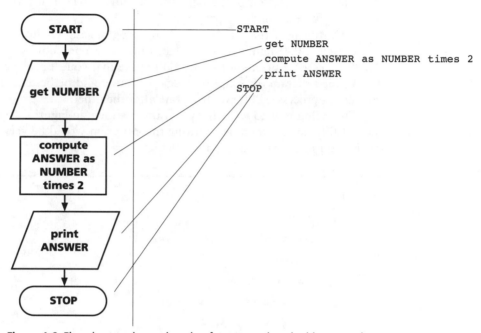

**Figure 1-6:** Flowchart and pseudocode of program that doubles a number

In the pseudocode in Figure 1-6, the words START and STOP start in the left margin; the actual program statements are indented. This style is not required when you write pseudocode, but as you develop more complex programs, indenting the program statements within the START-STOP pair will help you to see the beginning and ending points in program segments.

Programmers seldom create both pseudocode and a flowchart for the same problem. You usually use one or the other.

The logic for the program represented by the flowchart and pseudocode in Figure 1-6 is correct no matter what programming language the programmer eventually uses to write the corresponding code. After the flowchart or pseudocode has been developed, the programmer needs only to buy a computer, learn a language, code the program, compile it, test it, and put it into production.

"Whoa!" you are probably saying to yourself. "This is simply not worth it! All that work to create a flowchart and *then* all those other steps? For five dollars I can buy a pocket calculator that will double any number for me!" You are absolutely right. If this were a real computer program, it simply would not be worth all the effort. Writing a computer program would be worth the effort only if you had many, let's say 1,000, numbers to find the double of in a limited amount of time, let's say the next fifteen minutes. Then it would be worth your while to create a computer program.

Unfortunately, the number doubling program represented in Figure 1-6 does not double 1,000 numbers. It doubles only one. You could execute the program 1,000 times, of course, but that would require that you sit at the computer telling it to run the program over and over again. You would be better off with a program that could process 1,000 numbers, one after the other.

One solution is to write the program as shown in Figure 1-7: execute the same steps 1,000 times. Of course, writing this program would be very time consuming; again, you might as well buy the calculator.

```
START
    get NUMBER
    compute ANSWER as NUMBER times 2
    print ANSWER
    get NUMBER
    compute ANSWER as NUMBER times 2
    print ANSWER
    get NUMBER
    compute ANSWER as NUMBER times 2
    print ANSWER
    . . . and so on
```

**Figure 1-7:** Pseudocode for program that doubles 1,000 numbers

A better solution is to have the computer execute the same set of three instructions over and over again. This can be represented pictorially as shown in Figure 1-8. With this approach, the computer gets a number, doubles it, prints out the answer, and then starts over again with the first instruction. The same spot in memory, called NUMBER, is reused for the second number and for any subsequent numbers. ANSWER is reused each time to store the result of the multiplication operation.

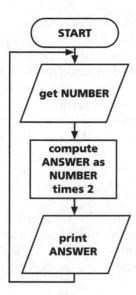

**Figure 1-8:** Flowchart of infinite number doubling program

## Using Variables

Programmers commonly refer to the locations in memory called NUMBER and ANSWER as **variables**. Variables are memory locations, the contents of which can vary. Sometimes NUMBER can hold a 2 and ANSWER will hold a 4; other times NUMBER can hold a 6 and ANSWER will hold a 12. It is the ability of memory variables to change in value that makes computers and programming worthwhile. Because one memory location can be used over and over again with different values, you can write program instructions once and then use them for thousands of separate calculations. *One* set of payroll instructions at your company produces each individual's paycheck, and *one* set of instructions at your electric company produces each household's bill.

The number doubling example requires two variables, NUMBER and ANSWER. These can just as well be named ENTRY and SOLUTION, or VALUE and TWICEVALUE. As a programmer, you choose reasonable names for your variables. The language interpreter then associates the names you choose with specific memory addresses.

Every computer programming language has its own set of rules for naming variables. Different languages put different limits on the length of variable names, although in general newer languages allow longer names. Some languages allow hyphens in variable names, for example HOURLY-WAGE. Others allow underscores, as in HOURLY_WAGE. Still others allow neither. Some languages allow dollar signs or other special characters in variable names, for example HOURLY$; others do not. For example, in some very old versions of BASIC, a variable name could consist of only one or two letters and one or two numbers. You could have some cryptic variable names like HW or A3 or RE02. In other languages, variable names can be very long. COBOL, for example, allows up to 30 characters in its variable names, so names like AMOUNT-OF-SALE and TOTAL-FOR-JANUARY are not uncommon. COBOL allows hyphens in its variable names for better readability. Another language, C, usually uses lowercase letters, doesn't allow hyphens, but does allow underscores, so you can use a name like price_of_item. Languages like C++ and Java are case sensitive, so HOURLYWAGE, hourlywage, and hourlyWage are three separate variable names, although the last example, in which the new word begins with an uppercase letter, is easiest to read. So that they stand out from ordinary words, variable names in this text will be shown in all uppercase letters.

Even though every language has its own rules for naming variables, when designing the logic of a computer program, you should not concern yourself with the particular syntax of any particular computer language. The logic, after all, works with any language. The variable names used throughout this book follow only two rules:

1.  *Variable names must be one word.* That one word can contain letters, numbers, hyphens, underscores, or any other characters you choose, with one exception—there are to be *no spaces*. Therefore R is a legal variable name, as is RATE, as is INTEREST-RATE. The variable name INTEREST RATE is not allowed because of the space. There is no programming language that allows spaces within a variable name, and if you see INTEREST RATE in a flowchart or pseudocode, you should assume that the programmer is discussing two variables, INTEREST and RATE, each of which individually would be a fine variable name.

**When you write a program, your compiler may show variable names in a different color from the rest of the program. This visual aid helps your variable names stand out from words that are part of the programming language.**

2.  *Variable names must have some appropriate meaning.* This is not a rule of any programming language. If you really were computing an interest rate in a program, the computer wouldn't care if you called the variable G or U84 or FRED. As long as the correct numeric result is placed in the variable, its actual name doesn't really matter. However, it's much easier to follow the logic of a program that has a statement in it like `compute TOTAL as equal to INVESTMENT times INTEREST-RATE` than one that has a statement in it like `compute BANANA as equal to J89 times LINDA`.

Notice that the flowchart in Figure 1-8 follows these two rules for variables: both variable names, NUMBER and ANSWER, are one word, and they have some appropriate meaning. Some programmers have fun with their variable names by naming them after their friends or creating puns with them, but such behavior is unprofessional and marks those programmers as amateurs.

> An additional general rule in all programming languages is that variable names may not begin with a digit, although usually they may contain digits. Thus in most languages BUDGET2001 is a legal variable name, but 2001BUDGET is not.

## Ending a Program by Using Sentinel Values

Something is still wrong with the flowchart for doubling numbers shown in Figure 1-8. It never ends! If, for example, the input numbers are being entered at the keyboard, the program will keep accepting numbers and printing out doubles forever. Of course, the user could refuse to type in any more numbers. But the computer is very patient, and if you refuse to give it any more numbers, it will sit and wait forever. When you finally type in a number, the program doubles it, prints the result, and waits for another. The program cannot progress any farther while it is sitting and waiting for input; meanwhile, the program is occupying computer memory and tying up operating system resources. Simply refusing to enter any more numbers is not a practical solution. Another way to end the program is to simply turn the computer off! That'll fix it! But again, it's neither the best nor an elegant way to bring the program to an end.

A superior way to end the program is to set some predetermined value for NUMBER that means "Stop the program!" For example, the programmer and the user could agree that the user will never need to know the double of zero, so the user could enter a zero when he or she wants to stop. The program could then test any incoming value for NUMBER and, if it is a zero, stop the program. Testing a value is also called making a **decision**.

You represent a decision in a flowchart by drawing a **decision symbol** or a diamond. The diamond usually contains a question, the answer to which is either yes or no. All good computer questions have two mutually exclusive answers like yes and no or true and false. For example, "What day of the year is your birthday?" is not a good computer question because there are 366 possible answers. But "Is your birthday June 24?" *is* a good computer question because for everyone in the world, the answer is either yes or no.

The question to stop the doubling program should be "Is the number just entered equal to zero?" or NUMBER = 0? for short. The complete flowchart will now look like the one shown in Figure 1-9.

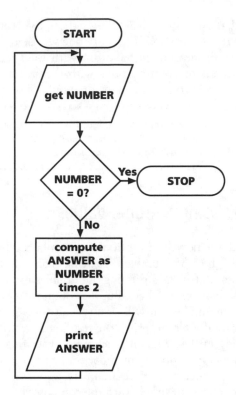

**Figure 1-9:** Flowchart for number doubling program with sentinel value of zero

One drawback to using zero to stop a program, of course, is that it won't work if the user *does* need to find the double of zero. Then some other data entry value that the user never will need, such as 999 or –1 could be selected to signal that the program should end. A preselected value that stops the execution of a program is often called a **dummy value** because it does not represent real data, but just a signal to stop. Sometimes such a value is called a **sentinel value** because it represents an entry or exit point like a sentinel that guards a fortress.

Not all programs rely on user data entry from a keyboard; many read data from an input device such as a disk or tape drive. When organizations store data on a disk or tape, they do not commonly use a sentinel value to signal the end of the file. For one thing, an input record might have hundreds of fields, and if you store a dummy record in every file, you are wasting a large quantity of storage on "non-data." Additionally, it is often difficult to choose sentinel values for fields in a company's data files. Any BALANCE-DUE, even a zero or negative one, can be a legitimate value, and any NAME, even "ZZ" could be someone's name.

Fortunately, programming languages can recognize the end of data in a file auto-matically, without a sentinel value, through a code that is stored at the end of the data. Many programming languages use the term **EOF** (for "end of file") to talk about this marker. This book therefore uses EOF to indicate the end of data, regardless of whether it is a special disk marker or a dummy value such as zero from the keyboard. Therefore the flowchart now looks like the one in Figure 1-10.

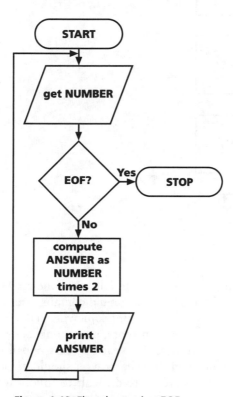

**Figure 1-10:** Flowchart using EOF

## Using the Connector

By using just the input, processing, output, decision, and terminal symbols, you are able to represent the logic for many diverse applications. This book uses only one other symbol, a **connector**. A connector will be used when limited page size forces you to continue the flowchart on the following page. If a flowchart has six processing steps and a page provides room for only three, you might represent the logic as shown in Figure 1-11.

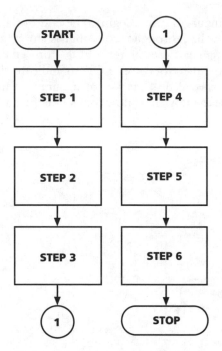

**Figure 1-11:** Flowchart using the connector

The circle at the bottom of the left column tells someone reading the flowchart that there is more to the flowchart. The circle should contain a number or letter that can then be matched to another number or letter somewhere else, in this case on the right. If a large flowchart needs more connectors, new numbers or letters would be assigned in sequence (1, 2, 3... or A, B, C...) to each successive pair of connectors.

When you are creating your own flowcharts, you should avoid using the connector if at all possible; flowcharts are more difficult to follow when they do not fit on a page. Your instructor or future programming supervisor may require that long flowcharts be redrawn so you don't need to use the connector. However, when continuing on a new page is unavoidable, the connector provides the means.

## Format of Mathematical Statements

When you create a flowchart or pseudocode for a program that doubles numbers, you can include the statement `compute ANSWER as NUMBER times 2`. This statement incorporates two actions. First, the computer computes the arithmetic value of NUMBER times 2. Second, the computed value is stored in the ANSWER memory location. Most programming languages allow a shorthand expression for these **assignment statements** such as `compute ANSWER as NUMBER times 2`. The shorthand takes the form `ANSWER = NUMBER * 2`.

In Pascal, the same expression is ANSWER := NUMBER * 2. You type a colon followed by an equals sign to create the assignment symbol. Java, C, BASIC and COBOL all use the equals sign for assignment.

According to the rules of algebra, a statement like ANSWER = NUMBER * 2 should be exactly equivalent to the statement NUMBER * 2 = ANSWER. To most programmers, however, ANSWER = NUMBER * 2 means "multiply NUMBER by 2 and store the result in the variable called ANSWER." Whatever operation is performed to the right of the equals sign results in a value that is placed in the memory location to the left of the equals sign. Therefore the statement NUMBER * 2 = ANSWER means to take the value of ANSWER and store it in a location called NUMBER * 2. There is a location called NUMBER, but there can't be a location called NUMBER * 2. For one thing, NUMBER * 2 can't be a variable because it has spaces in it. For another, a location can't be multiplied. Its contents can be multiplied, but the location itself cannot be. The statement NUMBER * 2 = ANSWER contains a syntax error, no matter what programming language you use; a program with such a statement will not execute.

When you create an assignment statement, it may help to imagine the word "let" in front of the statement. Thus you can read the statement ANSWER = NUMBER * 2 as "Let ANSWER equal NUMBER times two." The BASIC programming language allows you to use the word "let" in such statements.

Computer memory is made up of thousands of distinct locations, each of which has an address. Fifty years ago, programmers had to deal with these addresses and had to remember, for instance, that they had stored a salary in location 6428 of their computer. Today we are very fortunate that high-level computer languages have been developed that allow us to pick a reasonable "English" name for a memory address and let the computer keep track of where it is. Just as it is easier for you to remember that the president lives in the WHITE-HOUSE than at 1600 Pennsylvania Avenue, Washington, D.C., it is also easier for you to remember that your salary is in a variable called SALARY than at memory location 6428.

Similarly, it does not usually make sense to do mathematical operations on memory addresses, but it does make sense to do mathematical operations on the *contents* of memory addresses. If you live in BLUE-SPLIT-LEVEL-ON-THE-CORNER, you can't add 1 to that, but you certainly can add 1 person to the number of people already in that house. For our purposes, then, the statement ANSWER = NUMBER * 2 means exactly the same thing as the statement move NUMBER * 2 to ANSWER, which also means exactly the same thing as the statement multiply NUMBER times 2 resulting in ANSWER. None of these statements, however, is equivalent to NUMBER * 2 = ANSWER, which is an illegal statement.

# Types of Data and Variables

Computers deal with two basic types of data—character and numeric. When you use a specific numeric value, like *43*, within a program, you write it using the digits and no quotation marks. A specific numeric value is often called a **numeric constant**, because it does not change—a 43 always has the value 43. When you use a specific character value, or **string** of characters, like "Chris," you enclose the **string** or **character constant** within quotation marks.

▶ **tip**

Some languages require single quotes surrounding character constants; others require double quotes. Many languages, like C++ and Pascal, reserve single quotes for a single character such as 'C', and double quotes for a character string such as "Chris".

Similarly, most computer languages allow at least two distinct types of variables. One type of variable can hold a number and is often called a **numeric variable**. In the statement ANSWER = NUMBER * 2 both ANSWER and NUMBER are numeric variables; that is, their intended contents are numeric values such as 6 and 3, 150 and 75, or –18 and –9.

Most programming languages have a separate type of variable that can hold letters of the alphabet and other special characters such as punctuation marks. Depending on the language, these variables are called **character**, **text**, or **string variables**. If a working program contains the statement NAME = "LINCOLN" then NAME is a character or string variable.

Programmers must distinguish between numeric and character variables because computers handle the two types of data differently. Therefore means are provided within the syntax rules of computer programming languages to tell the computer which type of data to expect. How this is done is different in every language; in some languages there are different rules for naming the variables, but with others you must include a simple statement (called a **declaration**) telling the computer which type of data to expect.

Some languages allow for several types of numeric data. Languages like Pascal, C, and Java distinguish between **integer** or whole number numeric variables, and **floating-point** or fractional numeric variables that contain a decimal point. Thus in some languages the numbers 4 and 4.3 would have to be stored in different type variables.

Some programming languages allow even more specific variable types, but the character versus numeric distinction is universal. For the programs we develop in this book, we will assume each variable is one of the two broad types. If a variable called RATE is supposed to hold a value of 2.5, we will assume that it is a numeric variable. If a variable called ITEM is supposed to hold a value of "MONITOR," we will assume that it is a character variable.

**tip**

··················································································

Values like "MONITOR" and 2.5 are called constants or literal constants because they never change. A variable value *can* change. Thus ITEM can hold "MONITOR" at one moment during the execution of a program, and later you can change its value to hold "MODEM".

··················································································

By convention, character data like "MONITOR" is included within quotation marks to distinguish it from yet another variable name. Also by convention, numeric data is not enclosed within quotation marks. According to our conventions, then, RATE = 2.5 and ITEM = "MONITOR" are both valid statements. The statements ITEM = MONITOR is a valid statement only if MONITOR is also a character variable. In other words, if MONITOR = "COLOR", and subsequently ITEM = MONITOR, then the end result is that ITEM = "COLOR".

Every computer and every computer application handles text or character data differently from the way it handles numeric data. Every programming language requires that you distinguish variables as to their correct type and that you use each type of variable appropriately. (For example, you cannot perform arithmetic calculations with string data.) Identifying your variables correctly as numeric or character is one of the first steps you have to take when writing programs in any programming language.

# TERMS AND CONCEPTS

flowchart

pseudocode

flowlines

input-output symbol (parallelogram)

processing symbol  (rectangle)

terminal symbol (racetrack)

decision symbol (diamond)

connector symbol (circle)

variable

dummy (sentinel) value

EOF

format of mathematical statements or assignment statements

numeric constant

string or character constant

numeric variable

character, text, or string variables

declaration

integer

floating-point

 # S U M M A R Y

- A flowchart is a pictorial representation, and pseudocode is an English-like representation, of the logical steps it takes to solve a problem.

- When you draw a flowchart, you use a parallelogram to represent input operations, and you write an input statement in English inside the parallelogram.

- In a flowchart, you draw a rectangle around a processing statement.

- Output statements use the same symbol as input statements—the parallelogram.

- To show the correct sequence of these statements, you use arrows (or flowlines) to connect the steps.

- The standard terminal symbol is shaped like a racetrack.

- Variables are memory locations, the contents of which can vary. Because one memory location can be used over and over again with different values, you can write program instructions once and then use them for thousands of separate calculations.

- Every computer programming language has its own set of rules for naming variables.

- Variable names throughout this book follow only two rules: variable names must be one word, and variable names must have some appropriate meaning.

- Testing a value is also called making a decision. You represent a decision in a flowchart by drawing a diamond containing a question, the answer to which is either yes or no.

- A preselected value that stops the execution of a program is often called a dummy value because it does not represent real data, but just a signal to stop. Sometimes such a value is called a sentinel value because it represents an entry or exit point. When using data files, the term used for the end of the file is EOF.

- A connector is a circle you can use when the physical constraints of page size force the flowchart to continue on the following page.

- Most programming languages allow a shorthand expression for assignment statements using the equals sign. Whatever operation is performed to the right of the equals sign results in a value that is placed in the memory location to the left of the equals sign.

- Most computer languages allow at least two distinct types of variables, numeric and character.

- A statement called a declaration tells the computer which type of data to expect in a variable.

**E X E R C I S E S**

**1.** Match the term with the appropriate shape.

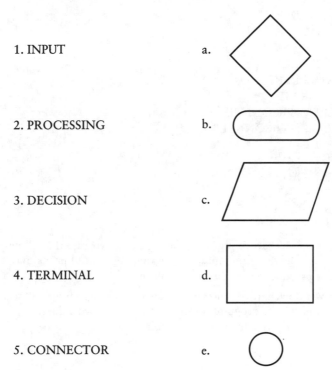

1. INPUT                a.

2. PROCESSING           b.

3. DECISION             c.

4. TERMINAL             d.

5. CONNECTOR            e.

**2.** Which of the following names seem like good variable names to you? If a name doesn't seem like a good variable name, why not?
   a. C
   b. COST
   c. COST-AMOUNT
   d. COST AMOUNT
   e. CSTOFDOINGBSNS
   f. COST-OF-DOING-BUSINESS-THIS-FISCAL-YEAR
   g. COST2004

3.  If AGE and RATE are numeric variables, and DEPT is a character variable, which of the following statements are valid assignments? If a statement is not valid, why not?

    a.  AGE = 23
    b.  AGE = RATE
    c.  AGE = DEPT
    d.  AGE = "DEPT"
    e.  42 = AGE
    f.  RATE = 3.5
    g.  RATE = AGE
    h.  RATE = DEPT
    i.  6.91 = RATE
    j.  DEPT = PERSONNEL
    k.  DEPT = "PERSONNEL"
    l.  DEPT = 413
    m. DEPT = "413"
    n.  DEPT = AGE
    o.  DEPT = RATE
    p.  413 = DEPT
    q.  "413" = DEPT

4.  a.  Draw a flowchart to represent the logic of a program that allows the user to enter a value. The program multiplies the value by 10 and prints out the result.
    b.  Write pseudocode for the same problem.

5.  a.  Draw a flowchart to represent the logic of a program that allows the user to enter two values. The program prints the sum of the two values.
    b.  Write pseudocode for the same problem.

# CHAPTER 2

# Structure

**case** ▶ "Are you ready to meet our best programmers?" Andrea Lake, Human Resources Director at Solutions, Inc, asks. "Boston Murphy and Lynn Greenbrier have both agreed to take you under their wings."

As if on cue, a grizzled character in jeans and a flannel work shirt emerges around the corner. "Boston!" Andrea says, "This is our new programmer trainee."

"Nice to meet you," Boston says. "I've been a programmer since the sixties, started on mainframes. I can show you the way things *should* be done."

"And this," Andrea says as she leads you to a nearby desk, "is Lynn Greenbrier."

"Hi. Welcome aboard! I've written quite a few programs for the latest microcomputer systems," Lynn says. "I *really* can show you the way things should be done."

"What programming lesson should I learn first?" you ask.

"You must learn how to use structure," Lynn replies.

"Hmmph," Boston grumbles. "She's right. Structure is crucial."

After studying Section A, you
should be able to:

■ Explain the difference between
structured and unstructured logic

■ Describe the three basic structures
of sequence, selection, and loop

■ Understand the priming read

■ Appreciate the need for structure

# Understanding Structure

## Unstructured Spaghetti Code

Professional computer programs usually get far more complicated than the number-doubling program from Chapter 1, shown in Figure 2-1.

```
get NUMBER
ANSWER = NUMBER * 2
print ANSWER
```

**Figure 2-1:** Number-doubling program

Imagine the program that NASA uses to calculate the angle of launch of a space shuttle, or the program the IRS uses to audit your income tax return. Even the program that produces a paycheck for you on your job is made up of many, many instructions. Designing the logic to such a program can be a time-consuming task. When you add several thousand instructions to a program, including several hundred decisions, it is easy to create a complicated mess. The popular name for snarled program statements is **spaghetti code**. The reason for the name should be obvious—it's as confusing to follow as following one noodle through a plate of spaghetti.

Suppose you are in charge of admissions at a college, and you've decided you will admit prospective students on the following criteria:

■ You will admit students who score 90 or better on the admission test your college gives as long as they are in the upper 75 percent of their high school graduating class. (These are smart students who score well on the admissions test. Maybe they didn't do so well in high school because it was a tough school, or maybe they have matured.)

- You will admit students who score at least 80 on the admission test if they are in the upper 50 percent of their high school graduating class. (These students score fairly well on the test, and do fairly well in school.)
- You will admit students who score only 70 on your test if they are in the top 25 percent of their class. (Maybe these students don't take tests well, but obviously they are achievers.)

Figure 2-2 summarizes the admission requirements:

| Test Score | High School Rank (%) |
| --- | --- |
| 90—100 | 25—100 |
| 80—89 | 50—100 |
| 70—79 | 75—100 |

**Figure 2-2:** Admission requirements

The flowchart for this program could look like the one in Figure 2-3. This kind of flowchart is an example of spaghetti code. Many computer programs (especially older computer programs) bear a striking resemblance to the flowchart in Figure 2-3. Such programs may "work," that is, they may produce correct results, but they are very difficult to read and maintain, and their logic is difficult to follow.

## The Structures

In the mid-1960s, mathematicians proved that any program, no matter how complicated, can be constructed using only three sets of flowcharting shapes, or structures. A **structure** is a basic unit of programming logic; each structure is a sequence, selection, or loop. With these three structures alone, you can diagram any event, from doubling a number to performing brain surgery.

The first of these structures is called a **sequence**, as shown in Figure 2-4. With a sequence, you do something, then you do the next thing in order. A sequence can have any number of events, but there is no chance to branch off. Once you start a series of events in a sequence, you must continue step-by-step until the sequence ends.

The second structure is called a **selection**, or a **decision**, as shown in Figure 2-5. With this structure, you ask a question and, depending on the answer, you take one of two courses of action. Then, no matter which path you follow, you continue on with the next event.

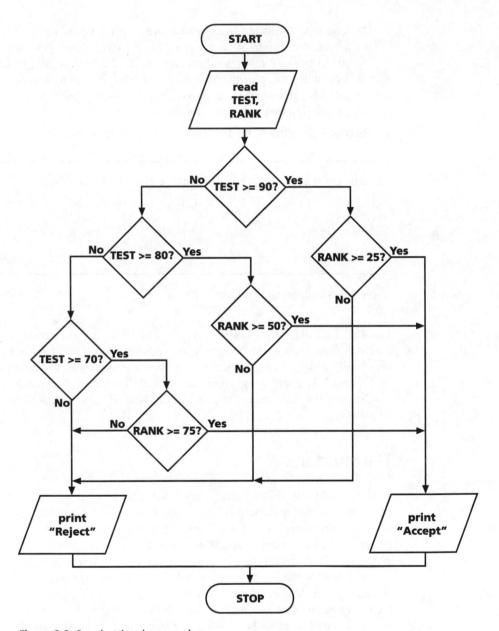

**Figure 2-3:** Spaghetti code example

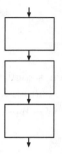

**Figure 2-4:** Sequence structure

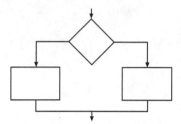

**Figure 2-5:** Selection structure

Some people call this structure an **if-then-else** because it fits the statement

```
if CONDITION is true then
   do one PROCESS
else
   do the OTHER
```

For example, while cooking you may decide:

```
if we have BROWN SUGAR then
   use BROWN SUGAR
else
   use WHITE SUGAR
```

Similarly, a payroll program might include a statement such as:

```
if HOURS-WORKED is more than 40 then
   calculate OVERTIME PAY
else
   calculate REGULAR PAY
```

Note that it is perfectly all right for one branch of the selection to be a "do nothing" branch. For example:

```
if it IS RAINING then
   take an UMBRELLA
```

or

```
if EMPLOYEE belongs to DENTAL PLAN then
    deduct $40 from PAY
```

These examples are called **single-alternative ifs**; their structure is diagrammed in Figure 2-6. In these cases you don't take any special action if it is not raining or if the employee does not belong to the dental plan. The case where nothing is done is often called the **null case**.

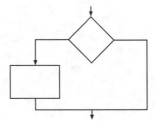

**Figure 2-6:** Single-alternative if structure

The third structure, shown in Figure 2-7, is called a **loop**. You may hear programmers refer to looping as **repetition** or **iteration**. In a loop, you ask a question. If the answer requires an action, you perform the action and ask the original question again. If the question's answer requires that the action be taken again, you take the action and then ask the original question again. This continues until the answer to the question is such that the action is no longer required; then you exit the structure.

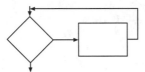

**Figure 2-7:** Loop structure

Some programmers call this structure a **do while** because it fits the statement

```
while TEST CONDITION continues to be true, do PROCESS
```

You encounter examples of looping every day as in

```
while you continue to BE HUNGRY
    take ANOTHER BITE OF FOOD
```

or

```
while PAGES remain in the READING ASSIGNMENT
   read another PAGE
```

In a business program you can write

```
while INVENTORY remains low
   continue to order MORE
```

or

```
while there are more PRICES to be discounted
   compute a DISCOUNT
```

All logic problems can be solved using only these three structures—sequence, selection, and looping. These three structures, of course, can be combined in an infinite number of ways. There can be a sequence of steps followed by a selection, or a loop followed by a sequence. Attaching structures end-to-end is called **stacking** structures. For example, Figure 2-8 shows a structured flowchart achieved by stacking structures and pseudocode that might follow that flowchart logic.

Additionally, you can replace any individual step in the preceding flowchart diagrams or pseudocode segments with another structure—any sequence, selection, or loop. For example, you can have a sequence of three steps on one side of a selection, as shown in Figure 2-9. Placing a structure within another structure is called **nesting** the structures.

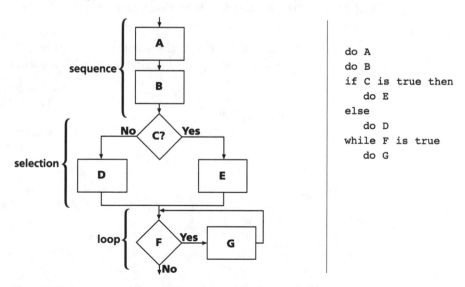

```
do A
do B
if C is true then
     do E
else
     do D
while F is true
     do G
```

**Figure 2-8:** A structured flowchart and pseudocode

When you write the pseudocode for the logic shown in Figure 2-9, the convention is to indent all the statements that depend on one branch of the decision as shown in the pseudocode. This shows that all three statements must execute if A is not true.

**tip**

Some programmers include a final statement for the pseudocode in Figure 2-9; they write `endif` to show that the `if` structure finishes at this point. Follow this convention if your instructor prefers this method.

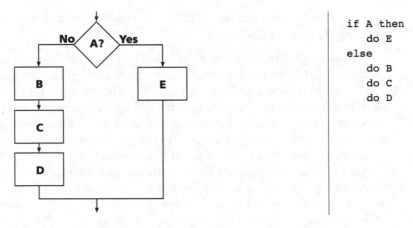

```
if A then
    do E
else
    do B
    do C
    do D
```

**Figure 2-9:** Flowchart and pseudocode for sequence in a selection

In place of one of the steps in the sequence in Figure 2-9, you can insert a selection. In Figure 2-10, Step C has been replaced with a selection structure.

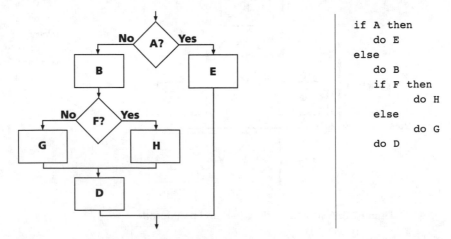

```
if A then
    do E
else
    do B
    if F then
            do H
    else
            do G
    do D
```

**Figure 2-10:** Selection in a sequence in a selection

In the pseudocode shown in Figure 2-10, notice that do B, if F then, else, and do D all are aligned vertically. This shows that they are all "on the same level." If you look at the same problem flowcharted in Figure 2-10, you see that you can draw a vertical line through the symbols with B, F, and D. The flowchart and the pseudocode represent exactly the same logic. The H and G steps, on the other hand, are one level down; they are dependent on the answer to the F question. Therefore the do H and do G statements are indented one level further in the pseudocode.

In place of Step H on one side of the new selection in Figure 2-10, you can insert a loop so it appears inside the selection that is within the sequence that constitutes the "no" side of the original A selection. See Figure 2-11.

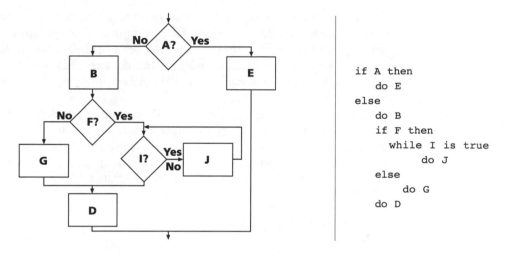

```
if A then
    do E
else
    do B
    if F then
        while I is true
                do J
    else
            do G
    do D
```

**Figure 2-11:** Flowchart and pseudocode for loop within selection within sequence within selection

The combinations are endless, but each of a structured program's segments is either a sequence, a selection, or a loop. Notice in Figure 2-12 that each structure has one entry and one exit point. One structure can attach to another only at one of these entry or exit points.

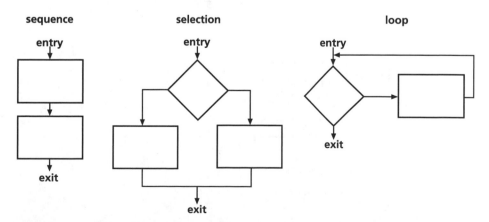

**Figure 2-12:** The three structures

In summary, a structured program has the following characteristics:

- It is made up of combinations of the structures **sequence**, **selection**, and **loop**.
- The structures are connected to one another only at their entrance or exit points.

## The Priming Read

For a program to be structured and also work the way you want it to, sometimes you need to add extra steps. The priming read is one kind of added step. A **priming read** or **priming input** is the first read or data input statement in a program. If a program will read one hundred data records, you read the first data record in a statement separate from the other ninety-nine. You must do this to keep the program structured.

At the end of Chapter 1, you read about a program that looks like the one in Figure 2-13. The program gets a number and checks for end of file. If it is not end of file, then the number is doubled, the answer is printed, and the next number is input.

Is the program represented by Figure 2-13 structured? At first it may be hard to tell. The three allowed structures were illustrated in Figure 2-12.

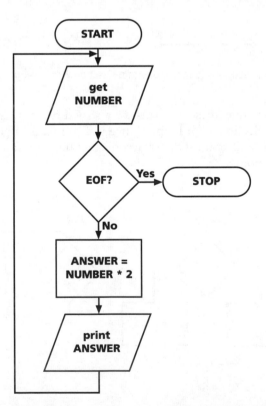

**Figure 2-13:** Flowchart of a number-doubling program

The flowchart in Figure 2-13 does not look exactly like any of the three shapes shown in Figure 2-12. However, because you are allowed to stack and nest structures and still retain overall structure, it may be difficult to determine whether the flowchart as a whole is structured. It's easiest to analyze the flowchart one step at a time. The beginning of the flowchart looks like Figure 2-14.

**Figure 2-14:** Beginning of a number-doubling flowchart

Is this much of the flowchart structured? Yes, it's a sequence. The next part of the flowchart looks like Figure 2-15.

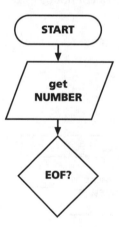

**Figure 2-15:** Number-doubling flowchart continued

The sequence is over. Either a selection is starting or a loop is starting. You may not know which one, but you do know the sequence is not continuing because sequences can't have questions in them. With a sequence, each step must follow without any opportunity to branch away. So what is starting with the question in Figure 2-15? Is it a selection or a loop?

With a selection structure, the logic goes in one of two directions after the question; then the flow comes back together. With a selection structure, the question is not asked a second time. In a loop, if the answer to the question results in the procedure executing, then the logic returns to the question that started the loop; the question is always asked again.

In the doubling problem, if it is not EOF (that is, if the end-of-file condition is not met), some math is done, an answer is printed, a new number is obtained, and the EOF question is asked again. So, the doubling problem is more like a loop than a selection.

It *is* a loop, but it's not a structured loop. In a structured loop, the rules are:

1. You ask a question.
2. If the answer indicates you should perform a procedure, you do so.
3. If you perform the procedure, then you must go right back to repeat the question.

The flowchart in Figure 2-13 asks a question; then if the answer is *no*, it does more than one thing: it does the arithmetic and it prints. Doing two things is acceptable because two steps constitute a sequence, and it is fine to nest a structure within another structure. However, when the sequence ends, the logical flow doesn't go right back to the question. Instead, it goes *above* the question to get another number. For the loop in Figure 2-13 to be a structured loop, the logic must return to the EOF question when the sequence ends.

The flowchart in Figure 2-16 shows the flow of logic returning to the EOF immediately after the sequence. Figure 2-16 shows a structured flowchart, but the flowchart has one major flaw—it doesn't do the job of continuously doubling numbers.

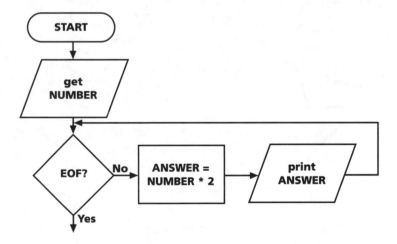

**Figure 2-16:** Structured, but nonfunctional, flowchart

Follow the flowchart in Figure 2-16 through a typical program run. Suppose when the program starts, the user enters a 9. That's not EOF, so the number is doubled and 18 is printed out as the answer. Then the question EOF is asked again. It can't be EOF because the sentinel (ending) value can't be entered. The logic never returns to the get NUMBER step. So 9 is doubled again and the answer, 18, is printed again. It's still not EOF, so the same steps are repeated. This goes on *forever*, with the answer 18 printing repeatedly. The program logic shown in Figure 2-16 is structured, but it doesn't work; the program in Figure 2-17 works, but it isn't structured!

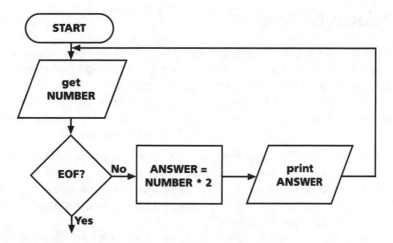

**Figure 2-17:** Functional, but nonstructured, flowchart

How can the number-doubling problem both be structured and work? Often, for a program to be structured, something extra has to be added. In this case, it's an extra get NUMBER step. Consider the solution in Figure 2-18. It's structured, *and* it does what it's supposed to! The program logic illustrated in Figure 2-18 contains a sequence and a loop. The loop contains another sequence.

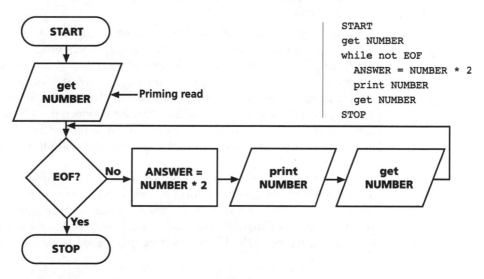

```
START
get NUMBER
while not EOF
    ANSWER = NUMBER * 2
    print NUMBER
    get NUMBER
STOP
```

**Figure 2-18:** Functional, structured flowchart and pseudocode

The get NUMBER step is typical in structured programs. The first of the two input steps is the priming input, or priming read. The term *priming* comes from the fact that the read is first, or *primary* (what gets the process going, as in "priming the pump"). The purpose of the priming read step is to control the upcoming loop that begins with the EOF question.

# Reasons for Structure

At this point you may very well be saying, "I liked the original doubling program just fine. I could follow it. Also, the first program had one less step in it, so it was less work. Who cares if a program is structured?"

Until you have some programming experience, it is difficult to appreciate the reasons for using nothing other than the three structures. However, staying with the three structures is better for the following reasons:

- Clarity—The doubling program is a small program. As programs get bigger, they get more confusing if they're not structured.
- Professionalism—All other programmers (and programming teachers you may encounter) expect your programs to be structured. It's the way things are done professionally.
- Efficiency—Most newer computer languages are structured languages with syntax that lets you deal efficiently with sequence, selection, and looping. Even older languages such as assembly languages, COBOL, and RPG, which were developed before the principles of structured programming, can be written in a structured form and are expected to be written that way today. Newer languages like C++ and Java enforce structure by their syntax.
- Modularity—Structured programs can be easily broken into routines that can be assigned to any number of programmers. The routines are then pieced back together like modular furniture at each routine's single entry or exit point.

Most programs that you purchase are huge, consisting of thousands or millions of statements. If you've worked with a word processing program or a spreadsheet, think of the number of menu options and keystroke combinations available to the user. Such programs are not the work of one programmer. The modular nature of structured programs means that work can be divided among many programmers, then the modules can be connected and the large program completed much more quickly. Money is often a motivating factor. A program that is written more quickly is available for use and making money for the developer sooner.

Consider the college admission program from the beginning of the chapter. It has been rewritten in structured form in Figure 2-19. Not only is it easier to follow now, but Figure 2-19 shows how the main module can be simplified even further through use of a structured module that can be plugged into the main module in several locations. Figure 2-19 also shows structured pseudocode for the same problem.

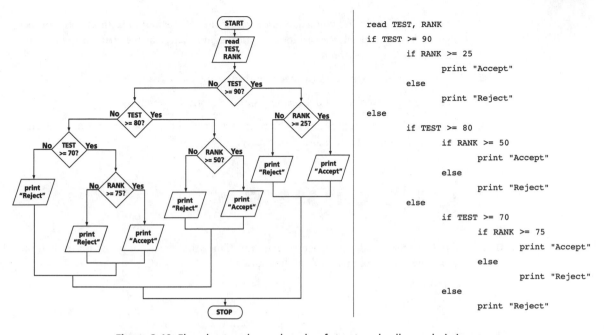

```
read TEST, RANK
if TEST >= 90
        if RANK >= 25
                print "Accept"
        else
                print "Reject"
else
        if TEST >= 80
                if RANK >= 50
                        print "Accept"
                else
                        print "Reject"
        else
                if TEST >= 70
                        if RANK >= 75
                                print "Accept"
                        else
                                print "Reject"
                else
                        print "Reject"
```

**Figure 2-19:** Flowchart and pseudocode of structured college admission program

# TERMS AND CONCEPTS

spaghetti code

structure

sequence

selection or decision or if-then-else

single-alternative ifs

null case

loop or repetition or iteration or do while

stacking

nesting

priming read or priming input

# SUMMARY

- When you design large, complicated programs, it is easy to write confusing spaghetti code.

- Any program, no matter how complicated, can be constructed using only three sets of flowcharting shapes, or structures.

- With a sequence structure, you perform any number of events in order.

- With a selection or decision structure, you ask a question and, depending on the answer, you take one of two courses of action. Then, no matter which path you follow, you continue on with the next event.

■  With the loop structure, you ask a question. If the answer requires an action, you perform the action and ask the original question again. You exit the structure when the action is no longer required.

■  You can combine structures by stacking or nesting.

■  An initial input step is called a priming input, or priming read.

■  Adhering to the three structures is better programming practice for reasons of clarity, professionalism, efficiency, and modularity.

# E X E R C I S E S

1.  Match the term with the structure diagram. (Since the structures go by more than one name, there are more terms than diagrams.)

    1. sequence           5. decision
    2. selection          6. if-then-else
    3. loop               7. iteration
    4. do while

    a.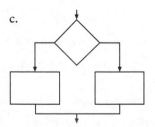

    b.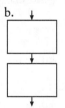

    c.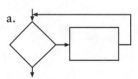

**2.** Match the term with the pseudocode segment. (Since the structures go by more than one name, there are more terms than pseudocode segments.)

1. sequence                    4. decision

2. selection                   5. if-then-else

3. loop                        6. iteration

a. ```
while not EOF
     print ANSWER
```

b. ```
if QUANTITY > 0
     perform FILL-ORDER-ROUTINE
else
     perform BACK-ORDER-ROUTINE
```

c. ```
perform LOCAL-TAX-METHOD
perform STATE-TAX-METHOD
perform FEDERAL-TAX-METHOD
```
```

**After studying Section B, you should be able to:**

■ Recognize structure
■ Describe the case structure
■ Describe the do until structure

# Recognizing Structure and Using Special Structures

## Recognizing Structure

When you are just learning about structured program design, it is difficult to figure out whether a program's logic is structured or not. For example, is the flowchart segment in Figure 2-20 structured?

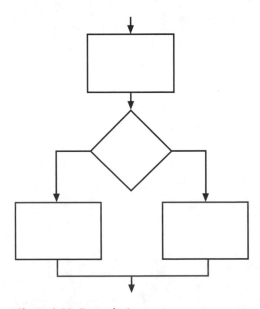

**Figure 2-20:** Example 1

Yes, it is. It has a sequence and a selection structure.
Is the flowchart segment in Figure 2-21 structured?

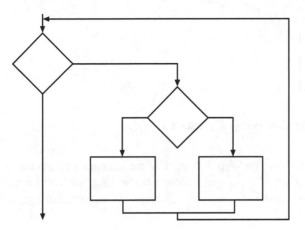

**Figure 2-21:** Example 2

Yes, it is. It has a loop, and within the loop is a selection.
Is the flowchart segment in Figure 2-22 structured?

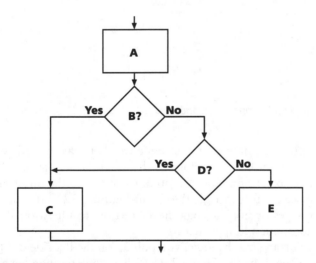

**Figure 2-22:** Example 3

No, it isn't. One way to straighten out a flowchart segment that isn't structured is to use what you can call the "spaghetti bowl" method; that is, imagine the flowchart as a bowl of spaghetti that you must untangle. Imagine you can grab one piece of pasta at the top of the bowl, and start pulling. As you "pull" each symbol out of the tangled mess, you can untangle the separate paths until the entire segment is structured. For example, with the diagram in Figure 2-22, if you start pulling at the top, you encounter a procedure box, labeled Step A. (See Figure 2-23.)

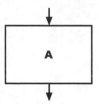

**Figure 2-23:** Untangling Example 3, first step

A single process like Step A is part of an acceptable structure—it constitutes at least the beginning of a sequence structure. So imagine you keep pulling. The next item in the flowchart is a question, Question B, as you can see in Figure 2-24.

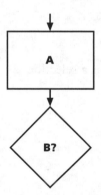

**Figure 2-24:** Untangling Example 3, second step

At this point, you know that the sequence that was started with Step A has ended. Sequences never have decisions in them, so the sequence is finished. Either a selection or a loop is beginning. A loop must return to the question at some later point. You can see from the original logic in Figure 2-22 that whether the answer to Question B is yes or no, the logic never returns to Question B. So B begins a selection structure, not a loop structure.

To continue detangling the logic, you pull up on the left side of Question B. You encounter Step C, as shown in Figure 2-25. When you continue beyond Step C, you reach the end of the flowchart.

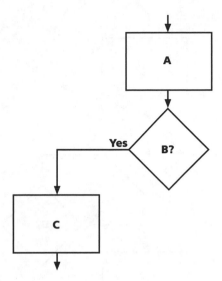

**Figure 2-25:** Untangling Example 3, third step

Now you can turn your attention to the *no* side of Question B. When you pull up on the right side, you encounter Question D. (See Figure 2-26.)

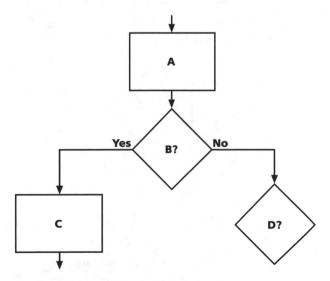

**Figure 2-26:** Untangling Example 3, fourth step

Follow the line on the left side of Question D. If the line is attached somewhere else, as it is (to Step C) in Figure 2-22, just untangle it by repeating the step that is tangled. (In this example you repeat Step C to untangle it from the other usage of C.) Keep pulling after Step C, and you reach the end of the program segment, as shown in Figure 2-27.

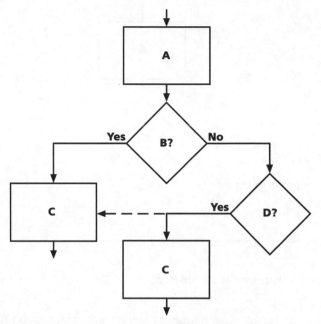

**Figure 2-27:** Untangling Example 3, fifth step

Now pull on the right side of Question D. A process (Step E) pops up, as shown in Figure 2-28; then you reach the end.

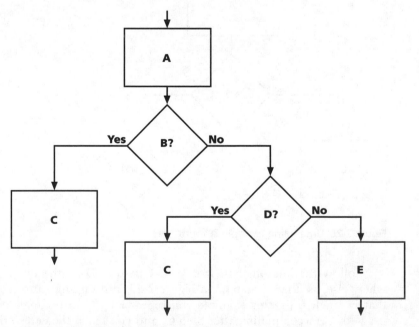

**Figure 2-28:** Untangling Example 3, sixth step

At this point the untangled flowchart has three loose ends. The loose ends of Question D can be brought together to form a selection structure, then the loose ends of Question B can be brought together to form another selection structure. The result is the flowchart shown in Figure 2-29. The entire flowchart segment is structured—it has a sequence (A) followed by a selection inside a selection.

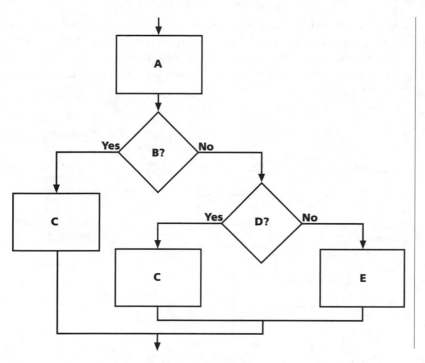

```
do STEP A
if QUESTION B is true
    do STEP C
else
    if QUESTION D is true
        do STEP C
    else
        do STEP E
```

**Figure 2-29:** Flowchart and pseudocode for Untangled Example 3

If you would like to try structuring a very difficult example of an unstructured program, see Appendix A.

## Two Special Structures

You can skip this section for now without any loss in continuity. Your instructor may prefer to discuss the case structure with the Decision chapter and the do until loop with the Looping chapter.

Any logic problem you ever encounter can be solved using only the three structures: sequence, selection, and loop. However, many programming languages allow two more structures: the **case structure** and the **do until loop**. These structures are never *needed* to solve a problem, but sometimes they are convenient. Programmers consider them both to be acceptable, legal structures.

## The Case Structure

You use the **case structure** when there are several distinct possible answers to a question. Suppose you administer a school where tuition is $75, $50, $30, or $10 per credit hour, depending on whether a student is a freshman, sophomore, junior, or senior. The structured flowchart in Figure 2-30 shows a series of decisions that assign the correct tuition to a student.

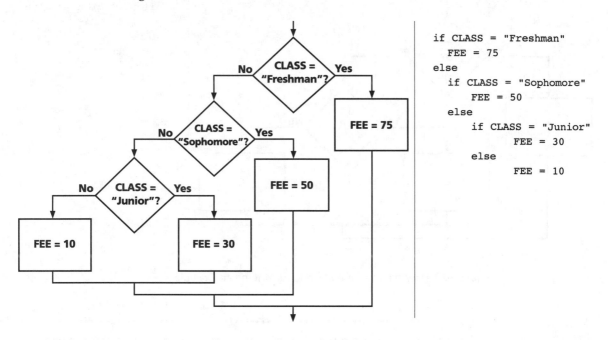

```
if CLASS = "Freshman"
   FEE = 75
else
   if CLASS = "Sophomore"
      FEE = 50
   else
      if CLASS = "Junior"
         FEE = 30
      else
         FEE = 10
```

**Figure 2-30:** Flowchart and pseudocode of tuition decisions

This logic shown in Figure 2-30 is absolutely correct and completely structured. The CLASS="Junior" selection structure is contained within the CLASS="Sophomore" structure, which is contained within the CLASS="Freshman" structure. Note that there is no need to ask if a student is a senior because if a student is not a freshman, sophomore, or junior, it is assumed the student is a senior.

Even though the program segments in Figure 2-30 are correct and structured, many programming languages permit a case structure as shown in Figure 2-31. When you use the case structure, you test a variable against a series of values, taking appropriate action based on the variable's value. To many, these programs seem easier to read, and because you understand that the same results *could* be achieved with a series of structured selections (and thus be structured), the case structure is allowed. That is, if the first one is structured and the second one reflects the first one point by point, then the second one must be structured also.

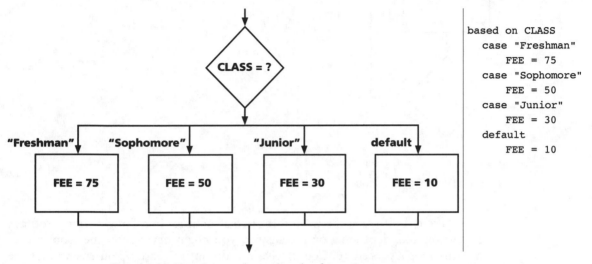

```
based on CLASS
    case "Freshman"
        FEE = 75
    case "Sophomore"
        FEE = 50
    case "Junior"
        FEE = 30
    default
        FEE = 10
```

**Figure 2-31:** Flowchart and pseudocode of case structure

**tip**

The term *default* used in Figure 2-31 means "if none of the other cases were true." Each programming language you learn may use a different syntax for the default case.

## The Do Until Loop

As you will recall, a structured loop (often called a do while) looks like Figure 2-32. A **do until loop** looks like Figure 2-33.

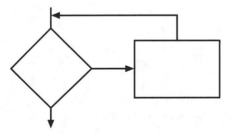

**Figure 2-32:** Do while loop

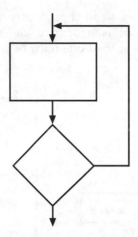

**Figure 2-33:** Do until loop

There is a difference between these two structures. In a do while loop you ask a question and, depending on the answer, you might never enter the loop to execute the loop's procedure. Conversely, in a do until situation you ensure that the procedure executes at least once; then it may or may not execute more times.

You can duplicate the same series of events generated by any do until loop by creating a sequence followed by a do while loop. Consider the flowcharts in Figures 2-34 and 2-35.

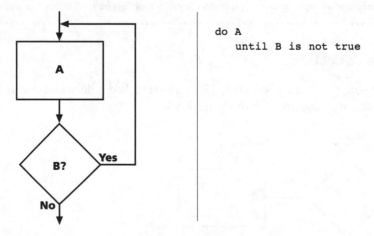

**Figure 2-34:** Flowchart and pseudocode for do until loop

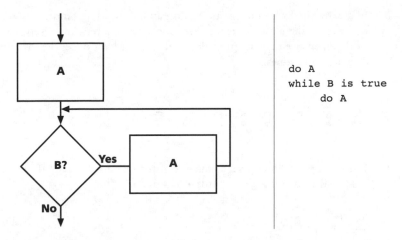

do A
while B is true
        do A

**Figure 2-35:** Flowchart and pseudocode for sequence followed by do while loop

In Figure 2-34, A is done, then B is asked. If B is yes, then A is done and B is asked again. In Figure 2-35, A is done, then B is asked. If B is yes, then A is done and B is asked again. Both flowcharts do exactly the same thing.

Because programmers understand that a do until can be expressed with a sequence followed by a do while, most languages allow the do until. Again, you are never required to use a do until; you can always accomplish the same events with a sequence followed by a do while.

 # TERMS AND CONCEPTS

case structure                              do until loop

 # SUMMARY

- When you are first learning about structured program design, it is difficult to assess whether a program's logic is structured or not.

- One way to straighten a flowchart segment that isn't structured is to imagine the flowchart as a bowl of spaghetti that you must untangle.

- Many programming languages allow two special structures: the case structure and the do until loop.

- You use the case structure when there are several distinct possible answers to a question.

■ In a do while loop you ask a question and, depending on the answer, you might never enter the loop to execute the loop's procedure. Conversely, in a do until situation you ensure that the procedure executes at least once; then it may or may not execute more times.

# E X E R C I S E S

1. Is each of the following segments structured or unstructured? If unstructured, redraw it so it does the same thing but is structured.

a.

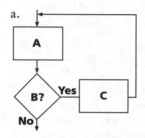

b.

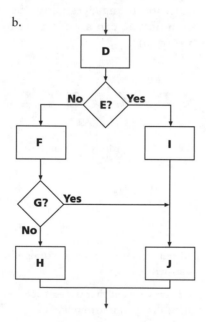

c.

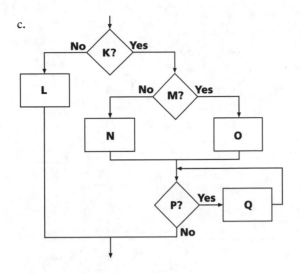

d.

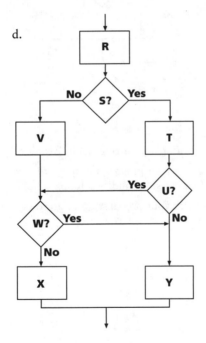

e.

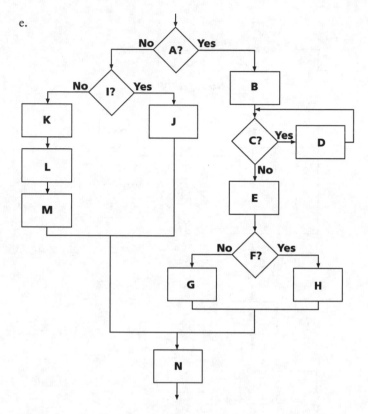

2. Write pseudocode for each example (a through e) in Exercise 1.

3. Draw a structured flowchart of your preparation to go to work or school in the morning. Include at least two decisions and two loops.

4. Write structured pseudocode of your preparation to go to bed at night. Include at least two decisions and two loops.

# Modules, Hierarchy Charts, and Documentation

**case ▶** "I'm amazed that all programming problems can use just three structures," you tell your mentors, Boston Murphy and Lynn Greenbrier, during a coffee break.

"How so?" Boston asks before shoving the last half of a chocolate doughnut in his mouth.

"In a sense, I thought programming was going to be more complicated; yet you tell me all programming problems can use just three structures. That's amazing."

"Using structure well is easy if you modularize your programs," Boston says. "It's something we didn't do much back in the sixties, but with large systems today, it's almost mandatory."

"Not *almost* mandatory," Lynn says pointing with her carrot stick for emphasis. "All the newer languages use modules extensively."

"There seem to be so many details to keep track of," you continue quickly. "Are there any tricks to seeing the big picture in programs?"

"Hierarchy charts," Boston says.

"And good documentation," Lynn adds.

**After studying Section A, you should be able to:**

- Describe the advantages of modularization
- Modularize a program
- Understand how a module can call another module
- Explain the difference between local and global variables
- Create hierarchy charts

# Using Modules

## Modules, Subroutines, Procedures, Functions, or Methods

Programmers seldom write programs as one long series of steps. Instead, they break the programming problem down into reasonable units and tackle one small task at a time. These reasonable units are called **modules**. Programmers also refer to them as **subroutines**, **procedures**, **functions**, or **methods**.

▶ **tip**

> The name that programmers use for their modules usually reflects the programming language they use. COBOL, RPG, and BASIC programmers are most likely to use "subroutine." Pascal and Visual Basic programmers use "procedure" (or "subprocedure"). C and C++ programmers call their modules "functions," while Java programmers are more likely to use the term "method."

You are never required to break a large program into modules, but you want to do so for at least four reasons:

- Modularization provides abstraction.
- Modularization allows multiple programmers to work on a problem.
- Modularization allows you to reuse your work.
- Modularization allows you to identify structures more easily.

### Modularization provides abstraction

One reason modularized programs are easier to understand is that they enable a programmer to see the big picture. **Abstraction** is the process of paying attention to important properties while ignoring nonessential details. Life would be tedious without abstraction. For example, you can create a list of things to accomplish today:

```
Do laundry
Call Aunt Nan
Start term paper
```

Without abstraction, the list of chores would begin:

```
Pick up laundry basket
Put laundry basket in car
Drive to laundromat
Get out of car with basket
Walk into laundromat
Set basket down
Find quarters for washing machine
```

...and so on.

You might list a dozen more steps before you finish the laundry and move on to the second chore on your original list. If you had to become involved with every small, **low-level** detail of every task in your day, you would probably never even make it out of bed in the morning. Using a higher-level, more abstract list makes your day manageable.

Likewise, some level of abstraction occurs in every computer program. Fifty years ago, you had to understand the low-level circuitry instructions your computer used. But now, newer **high-level** programming languages allow you to use English-like vocabulary in which one broad statement corresponds to dozens of machine instructions. No matter which high-level programming language you use, if you display a message on the monitor, you are never required to understand how a monitor works to create each pixel on the screen. You write an instruction like `print MESSAGE` and the details of the hardware operations are handled for you.

Modules or subroutines are another way to achieve abstraction. For example, a payroll program can call a module named COMPUTE-FEDERAL-WITHHOLDING. The mathematical details of the function can be written later, or be written by someone else, or even purchased from an outside source. When you plan your main payroll program, you pay attention only to the fact that somehow a federal withholding tax will have to be calculated; you save the details for later.

## Modularization allows multiple programmers to work on a problem

When you dissect any large task into modules, you gain the ability to divide the task among various people. It is rare that a single programmer writes a program that you buy. Consider any word processing, spreadsheet, or database program you have used. Each program has so many options, and responds in so many possible ways to user selections, that it would take years for a single programmer to write all the instructions needed. Professional software developers are able to come out with new programs in weeks or months instead of years by dividing large programs into modules and assigning each module to an individual programmer or programming team.

## Modularization allows you to reuse your work

If a subroutine or function is useful and well written, you may want to reuse it multiple times within a program or in other programs. For example, a routine that checks the current month to make sure it is valid (not lower than 1 or higher than 12) is useful in many programs written for a business. A program that uses a personnel file that contains each employee's birth date, hire date, last promotion date, and termination date can use the month-validation module four times with each employee record. Other programs in an organization can also use the module; these include programs that ship customer orders, plan employees' birthday parties, and calculate when loan payments should be made. If you write the month-checking instructions so they are entangled with other statements in a program, they are difficult to extract and reuse. On the other hand, if you place the instructions in their own module, the unit becomes easily used and portable to other applications.

There are many real-world examples of **reusability**. When you build a house, you don't invent plumbing and heating systems; you incorporate systems that have already been designed. This certainly reduces the time and effort it takes to build a house. Assuming the plumbing and electrical systems you choose to use are also in service in other houses, it also improves your house's **reliability**. Similarly, software that is reusable saves time and money and is more reliable. If you create the functional components of your programs as stand-alone modules and test them in your current programs, then when you use the modules in future applications, much of the work required will already be done.

## Modularization allows you to identify structures more easily

When you combine several programming tasks into modules, it may be easier for you to identify structures. For example, you learned in Chapter 2 that the selection structure looks like Figure 3-1.

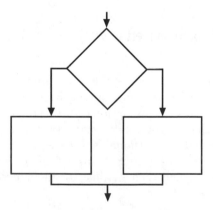

**Figure 3-1:** Selection structure

When you work with a program segment that looks like Figure 3-2, you may question whether it is structured. If you can modularize some of the statements and give them a more abstract group name, as in Figure 3-3, you more easily can "see" that the program involves a major selection and that the program segment is structured.

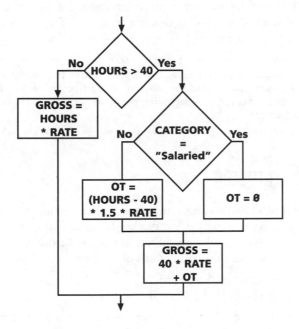

**Figure 3-2:** Section of logic from a payroll program

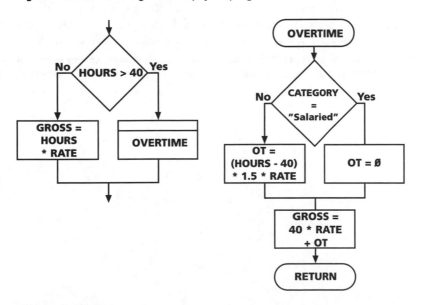

**Figure 3-3:** Modularized logic from a payroll program

The single program segment shown in Figure 3-2 accomplishes the same steps as the two program segments shown together in Figure 3-3, and both programs are structured. The structure may be more obvious in the program segments in Figure 3-3 because you can see two distinct parts—a decision structure calls a subroutine that contains a sequence followed by another decision structure. Neither of the program segments shown in Figures 3-2 and 3-3 is superior to the other in terms of functionality, but you may prefer to modularize to help you identify structures.

As a professional programmer, you never modularize simply to *identify* whether a program is structured—you modularize for reasons of abstraction, ease of dividing the work, and reusability. However, as a beginning programmer, being able to see and identify structure is important.

## Modularizing a program

When you create a module or subroutine, you give the module a name. The rules for naming modules are different in every programming language, but they often are similar to the language's rules for variable names. In this text, module names will follow the same two rules used for variable names:

- Module names must be one word.
- Module names should have some meaning.

When a program uses a module, you can refer to the main program as the **calling program,** because it "calls" the module's name when it wants to use the module. The flowcharting symbol for a subroutine is a rectangle with a bar across the top. You place the name of the module that you are calling inside the rectangle.

Instead of placing only the name of the module you are calling in the flowchart, many programmers insert an appropriate verb such as "perform" or "do" before the module name.

You draw each module separately with its own sentinel symbols. The symbol that is the equivalent of the START symbol in a program contains the name of the module. This name must be identical to the name used in the calling program. The symbol that is the equivalent of the END symbol in a program does not contain "END"; after all, the program is not ending. Instead, the module ends with a "gentler," less final term such as EXIT or RETURN. These words correctly indicate that when the module ends, the logical progression of statements will return to the calling program.

A flowchart and pseudocode for a program that calculates the arithmetic average of two numbers that a user inputs can look like Figure 3-4. Here the **main program**, or calling program, calls three modules.

The logic of the program in Figure 3-4 proceeds as follows:

1. The main program starts.
2. The main program calls the GET-INPUT module.
3. Within the GET-INPUT module, the prompt "Enter a number" displays.
4. Within the GET-INPUT module, the program accepts a value into the FIRST-NUMBER variable.
5. Within the GET-INPUT module, the prompt "Enter another number" displays.
6. Within the GET-INPUT module, the program accepts a value into the SECOND-NUMBER variable.
7. The GET-INPUT module ends, and control returns to the main calling program.
8. The main program calls the CALCULATE-AVERAGE module.
9. Within the CALCULATE-AVERAGE module, a value for the variable AVG is calculated.
10. The CALCULATE-AVERAGE module ends, and control returns to the main calling program.
11. The main program calls the PRINT-RESULT module.
12. Within the PRINT-RESULT module, the value of AVG displays.
13. Within the PRINT-RESULT module, a thank-you message displays.
14. The PRINT-RESULT module ends, and control returns to the main calling program.
15. The main program ends.

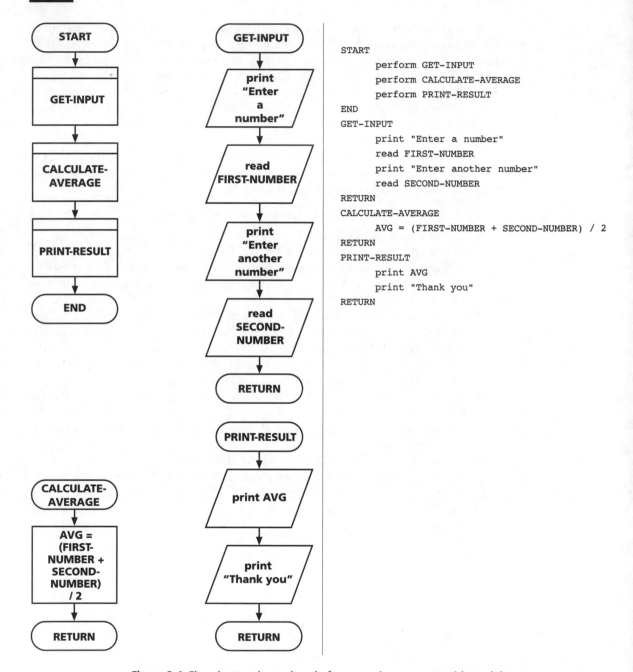

**Figure 3-4:** Flowchart and pseudocode for averaging program with modules

Whenever a main program calls a module, the logic transfers to the module. When the module ends, the logical flow transfers back to the main calling program and begins where it left off.

> **tip**
>
> The computer keeps track of the correct memory address to which it should return after executing a module by recording the memory address in a location known as the *stack*.

## Modules Calling Other Modules

Just as a program can call a module or subroutine, any module can call another module. For example, the program illustrated in Figure 3-4 can be broken down further as shown in Figure 3-5.

After the program in Figure 3-5 begins, the main program calls the GET-INPUT module; the logical flow transfers to that module. From there, the GET-INPUT module calls the GET-FIRST-VALUE module, and the logical flow immediately transfers to the GET-FIRST-VALUE module. When GET-FIRST-VALUE ends, control passes back to GET-INPUT, where GET-SECOND-VALUE is called. Control passes to GET-SECOND-VALUE, and when this module ends, control passes back to GET-INPUT. When GET-INPUT ends, control returns to the main program. Then CALCULATE-AVERAGE and PRINT-RESULT execute as before.

There is an art to deciding whether to break down any particular module further into its own subroutines or submodules. Programmers do follow some guidelines when deciding how far to break down subroutines or how much to put in a subroutine. Some places of business may have arbitrary rules such as "a subroutine should never take more than a page," or "a module should never have more than 30 statements in it," or "never have a method or function with only one statement in it."

Rather than use such arbitrary rules, a better policy is to place together statements that contribute to one specific task. The more the statements contribute to the same job, the higher the **functional cohesion** of the module. A routine that checks the validity of a MONTH variable's value, or one that prompts a user and allows the user to type in a value, would be considered cohesive. A routine that checks date validity, deducts insurance premiums, and computes federal withholding tax for an employee would be said to be less cohesive.

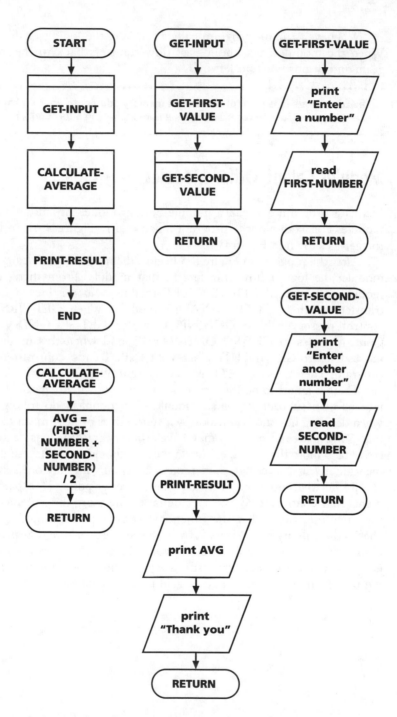

**Figure 3-5:** Flowchart for averaging program with submodules

# Declaring Variables

The primary work of most modules in most programs you write is to manipulate data—for example, to calculate the figures needed for a paycheck, customer bill, or sales report. You store your program data in variables.

Many program languages require you to declare all variables before you use them. **Declaring a variable** involves providing a name for the memory location where the computer will store the variable value, and notifying the computer the type of data to expect. Every programming language requires that you follow specific rules when declaring variables, but all the rules involve identifying at least two attributes for every variable:

- You must declare a data type.
- You must give the variable a name.

You learned in Chapter 1 that different programming languages provide different variable types, but all allow at least the distinction between character and numeric data. You also learned in Chapter 1 that variable names must not contain spaces.

For example, statements such as `char LAST-NAME` and `num SALARY` might declare two variables of different types. There are some programming languages, like BASIC and RPG, in which you are not required to name any variable until the first time you use it. However, languages including COBOL, C, Java, and Pascal require that you declare variables with a name and a type. Some languages require that you declare all variables at the beginning of a program before you write any executable statements; others allow you to declare variables at any point, but require the declaration before you can use the variable. For our purposes, we will follow the convention of declaring all variables at the beginning of a program.

For example, to complete the averaging program shown in Figure 3-5 so that its variables are declared, you can redraw the main program flowchart to look like Figure 3-6. Three input variables are required, FIRST-NUMBER, SECOND-NUMBER, and AVG. The variables are declared as the first step in the program, before you use any of them, and each is correctly identified as numeric. They appear to the side of the "declare variables" step in an **annotation symbol** or **annotation box**, which is simply an attached box containing notes. You can use an annotation symbol any time you have more to write than conveniently fits within a flowchart symbol.

Many programming languages support more specific numeric types with names like int (for integers or whole numbers), float (for floating point or decimal-place values), and double (for double-precision floating point values, which means more memory space is reserved). Many languages distinguish even more precisely. For example, in addition to whole-number integers, C++ and Java allow short integers and long integers, which require less and more memory respectively.

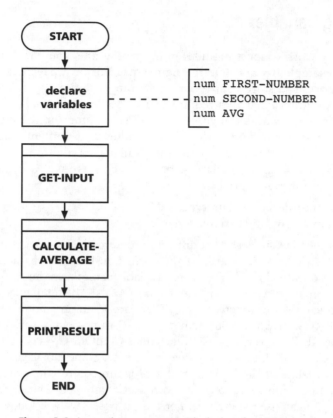

**Figure 3-6:** Averaging program with declared variables

## Creating Hierarchy Charts

When a program has several modules calling other modules, programmers often use a tool besides flowcharts or pseudocode to show the overall picture of how these modules are related to one another. You can use a **hierarchy chart** to illustrate modules' relationships. A hierarchy chart does not tell you what tasks are to be performed within a module; it doesn't tell you *when* or *how* a module executes. It tells you only which routines exist within a program and which routines call which other routines.

The hierarchy chart for the last version of the value-averaging program looks like Figure 3-7. The hierarchy chart shows which modules call which others. You don't know *when* the modules are called or *why* they are called; that information is in the flowchart or pseudocode. A hierarchy chart just tells you which modules *are* called by other modules.

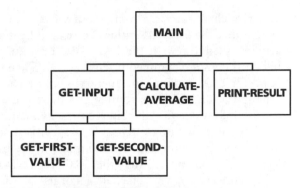

**Figure 3-7:** Hierarchy chart for value-averaging program

You may have seen hierarchy charts for organizations, such as the one in Figure 3-8. The chart shows who reports to whom, not when or how often. Program hierarchy charts operate in an identical manner.

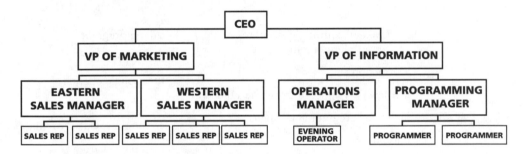

**Figure 3-8:** An organizational hierarchy chart

Figure 3-9 shows an example of a hierarchy chart for the billing program of a mail order company. The hierarchy chart supplies module names only; it provides a general overview of the tasks to be performed without specifying any details.

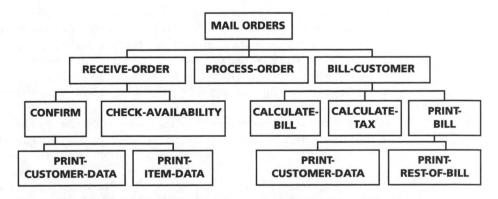

**Figure 3-9:** Billing program hierarchy chart

The hierarchy chart can be a useful tool when a program must be modified months or years after the original writing. For example, if a tax law changes, a programmer may be asked to rewrite the CALCULATE-TAX module in the mail order company billing program diagramed in Figure 3-9. When the programmer changes the CALCULATE-TAX routine, the hierarchy chart shows what other routines depend on the CALCULATE-TAX routine and therefore might be affected. A hierarchy chart is useful for "getting the big picture" in a complex program.

Because program modules are reusable, a specific module may be called from several locations within a program. For example, in the billing program hierarchy chart in Figure 3-9, you can see that the PRINT-CUSTOMER-DATA module is used twice. By convention, you blacken a corner of each box representing the PRINT-CUSTOMER-DATA module. This action alerts anyone reading the chart that any change to this module will have an effect in more than one location.

# TERMS AND CONCEPTS

module (subroutine, procedure,
    function, method)

abstraction

low-level (as opposed to high-level) detail

high-level programming language

reusability

reliability

calling program

main program

functional cohesion

declaring a variable

annotation symbol or annotation box

hierarchy chart

# SUMMARY

- Programmers break programming problems down into reasonable units called modules. Programmers also refer to modules as subroutines, procedures, functions, or methods.
- You break a large program into modules because modularization provides abstraction, allows multiple programmers to work on a problem, allows you to reuse your work, and allows you to identify structures more easily.
- Abstraction is the process of paying attention to important properties while ignoring nonessential details.
- Software that is reusable saves time and money and is more reliable.
- When you create a module or subroutine, you give the module a name. The rules for naming modules are different in every programming language, but they often are similar to the language's rules for variable names.
- When a program uses a module, you can refer to the program as the calling program because it "calls" the module's name when it wants to use the module. The flowcharting symbol for a subroutine, method, or procedure is a rectangle with a bar across the top.

- You draw each module separately with its own sentinel symbols. One terminal symbol contains the name of the module; the other contains EXIT or RETURN.
- Whenever a program calls a module, the logic transfers to the module. When the module ends, the logical flow transfers back to the calling program and begins where it left off.
- Any module can call another module.
- The more the statements contribute to the same job, the higher the functional cohesion of the module.
- Declaring a variable involves providing a name for the memory location where the computer will store the variable value, and notifying the computer the type of data to expect.
- You can use a hierarchy chart to illustrate modules' relationships.

# E X E R C I S E S

1. Redraw the following flowchart so that the compensation calculations are in a module:

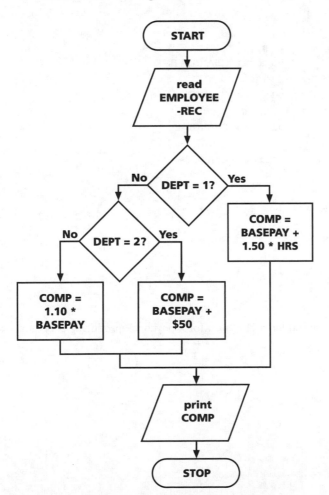

2.  Rewrite the following pseudocode so the discount calculations are in a module.

```
START
    read CUSTOMER-ORDER-RECORD
    if QUANTITY > 100 then
            DISCOUNT = 20
    else
            if QUANTITY > 12 then
                    DISCOUNT = 10
    TOTAL = PRICE-EACH * QUANTITY
    TOTAL = TOTAL - DISCOUNT * TOTAL
    print TOTAL
END
```

3.  What are the final values of variables A, B, and C after this program runs?

```
START
    A = 2
    B = 4
    C = 10
    while C > 6
            perform CHANGE-BC
    if A = 2 then
            perform CHANGE-A
    if C = 10 then
            perform CHANGE-A
    else
            perform CHANGE-BC
END
CHANGE-BC
    B = B + 1
    C = C - 1
RETURN
CHANGE-A
    A = A + 1
    B = B - 1
RETURN
```

4.  Draw a typical hierarchy chart for a paycheck-producing program.

# Documentation

**After studying Section B, you should be able to:**

- Understand the difference between program documentation and user documentation
- Appreciate the need for documentation
- Create printer spacing charts
- Interpret input file descriptions

## Understanding Documentation

**Documentation** refers to all of the supporting material that goes along with a program. There are two broad categories of documentation: that intended for the programmer and that intended for the user. Individuals who use a computer program are called **end users**, or **users** for short. Most likely you have been the end user of an application such as a word processing program or a game. When you purchase software that other programmers have written, you appreciate clearly written instructions on how to install and use the software. These instructions constitute user documentation. In a small organization, programmers may write user documentation, but in most organizations, systems analysts or technical writers produce end-user instructions. End-user instructions may take the form of a printed manual or may be presented online though a web site or on a compact disc.

When programmers begin to plan the logic of a computer program, they require instructions known as **program documentation**. End users never see program documentation; rather, programmers use it in planning or modifying programs.

Program documentation falls into two categories: internal and external. **Internal program documentation** consists of **program comments**, or nonexecuting statements that programmers place within their program code to explain program statements in English. The method for inserting program comments within a program differs in each programming language, but every method provides a means for inserting explanatory comments that do not affect the running of a program. You will learn how to insert comments when you learn a specific programming language.

> In the BASIC programming language, program comments begin with the letters REM (for REMark). In C++ and Java, comments can begin with two forward slashes (//). An RPG program indicates that a line is a comment if there is an asterisk (*) in the sixth typed position in a line.

**External program documentation** includes all the supporting paperwork that programmers develop before they write a program. Since most programs have input, processing, and output, usually there is documentation for all these functions.

## Output Documentation

Output documentation is usually the first to be written. This may seem backwards, but if you're planning a trip, which do you decide first: how to get to your destination or where you're going?

Most requests for programs arise because a user needs particular information to be output, so the planning of program output is usually done in consultation with the person or persons who will be using that output. Only after the desired output is known can the programmer hope to plan the processes needed to produce that output.

Often the programmer does not design the output. Instead, the user who requests the output presents the programmer (or programming team) with an example or sketch of the desired result. The programmer then might work with the user to refine the request, suggest improvements in the design, or clarify the user's needs. If you don't determine precisely what the user wants or needs at this point, you will write a program that the user soon wants redesigned and rewritten.

The most common type of output is a printed report. You can design a printed report on a **printer spacing chart**, which is also referred to as a **print chart** or a **print layout**. Figure 3-10 shows a printer spacing chart. Basically, a printer spacing chart looks like graph paper. The chart has many boxes, and in each box the designer places one character that he or she expects will be printed.

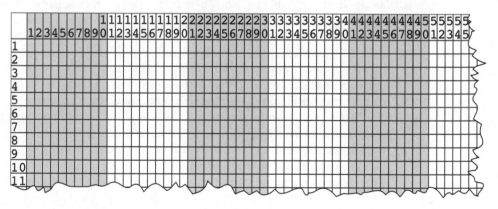

**Figure 3-10:** Printer spacing chart

Besides using handwritten print charts, you can design report layouts on a computer using a word processing program or other design software to lay out the program's output appearance.

For example, if you want to create a printed report with the title INVENTORY REPORT and you decide that the title looks best 11 spaces over from the left of the page and one line down, you would begin to create the printer spacing chart as shown in Figure 3-11.

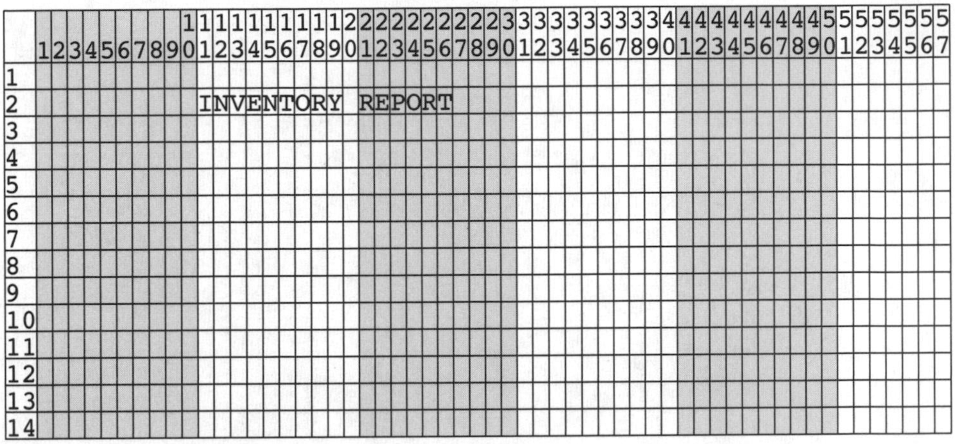

```
                    1111111111222222222233333333334444444444555555 5 5
          1234567890123456789012345678901234567890123456789012345 6 7
 1
 2                  INVENTORY REPORT
 3
 4
 5
 6
 7
 8
 9
10
11
12
13
14
```

**Figure 3-11:** Printer spacing chart with first title

You might want to skip a line and print column headings ITEM NAME, PRICE, and QUANTITY IN STOCK, so the printer spacing chart would evolve into the one in Figure 3-12.

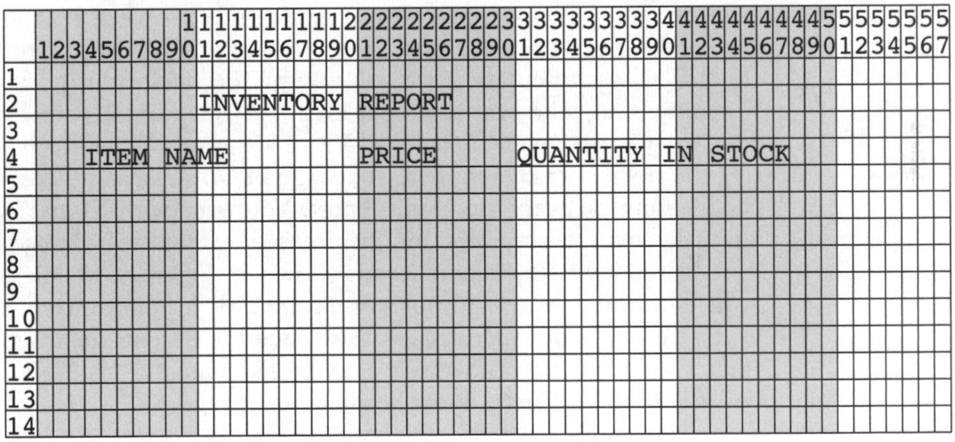

```
                    1111111111222222222233333333334444444444555555 5 5
          1234567890123456789012345678901234567890123456789012345 6 7
 1
 2                  INVENTORY REPORT
 3
 4    ITEM NAME          PRICE      QUANTITY IN STOCK
 5
 6
 7
 8
 9
10
11
12
13
14
```

**Figure 3-12:** Printer spacing chart with title and column headings

The title and column headings will be **constant** on every page of the report, so they are written on the print chart literally.

A print layout typically shows how the data will appear on the report. Of course, the data will probably be different every time the report is run. Thus, instead of writing in actual item names and prices, the users and programmers usually use Xs to represent generic variable character data and 9s to represent generic variable numeric data. (Some programmers use Xs for both character and numeric data.) For example, Figure 3-13 shows how some data will look in the print chart.

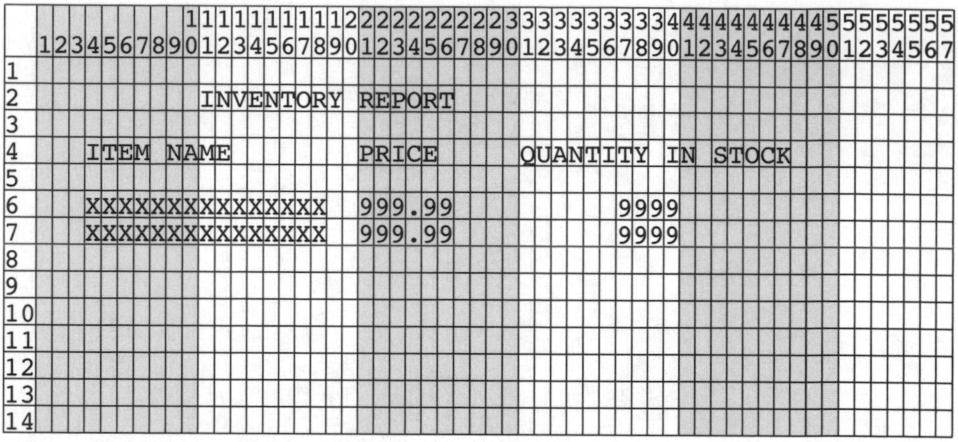

```
                     1111111111222222222233333333334444444444555555555
          1234567890123456789012345678901234567890123456789012345678901234567
 1
 2                   INVENTORY REPORT
 3
 4        ITEM NAME            PRICE        QUANTITY IN STOCK
 5
 6        XXXXXXXXXXXXXXXXX    999.99            9999
 7        XXXXXXXXXXXXXXXXX    999.99            9999
 8
 9
10
11
12
13
14
```

**Figure 3-13:** Print chart with generic data

Each line with its Xs and 9s representing data is a **detail line,** because it contains the data details. Detail lines typically appear many times per page, as opposed to **heading lines,** which usually appear only once per page.

Even though an actual inventory report might eventually go on for hundreds or thousands of detail lines, writing two or three rows of Xs and 9s is sufficient to show how the data will appear. For example, if a report contains employee names and salaries, those data items will occupy the same print positions on output on line after line, whether the output eventually contains 10 employees or 10,000. A few rows of identically positioned Xs and 9s are sufficient to establish the pattern.

In any report layout, then, you write in constant data (like headings) that will be the same on every run of this report. You write with Xs and 9s the variable data (like the items, their prices, and their quantities) that will change from run to run.

In the inventory report layout shown in Figure 3-13, the headings truly are constant, but you should not assume that all headings are completely constant. Let's say that your user decides to include the date in the inventory report heading. The report might now have a layout like Figure 3-14. Notice that now there is variable data, the date, in the heading of the report.

```
            1111111111222222222233333333334444444444555555555
  1234567890123456789012345678901324567890123456789012345 67
1
2            INVENTORY REPORT FOR WEEK OF 99/99/9999
3
4     ITEM NAME          PRICE      QUANTITY IN STOCK
5
6
7
8
9
10
11
12
13
14
```

**Figure 3-14:** Variable data in report heading

If this is going to be a long report that goes to more than one page, perhaps the user will also decide that the headings should appear at the top of every printed page and that page numbers should also be added. Figure 3-15 shows how you might indicate page numbers.

```
            1111111111222222222233333333334444444444555555555
  1234567890123456789012345678901234567890123456789012345 67
1
2            INVENTORY REPORT FOR WEEK OF 99/99/9999 PAGE 99
3
4     ITEM NAME          PRICE     QUANTITY IN STOCK
5
6
7
8
9
10
11
12
13
14
```

**Figure 3-15:** Heading with page numbers

Just as variable data might appear in a heading, constants might appear in the detail lines. For example, if the company sells all of its inventory in dozens, then each number in the QUANTITY IN STOCK column actually represents the number of dozens of that item. The users might choose to see the word DOZEN with each detail line. The print chart in Figure 3-16 indicates that the word DOZEN would literally appear on each line.

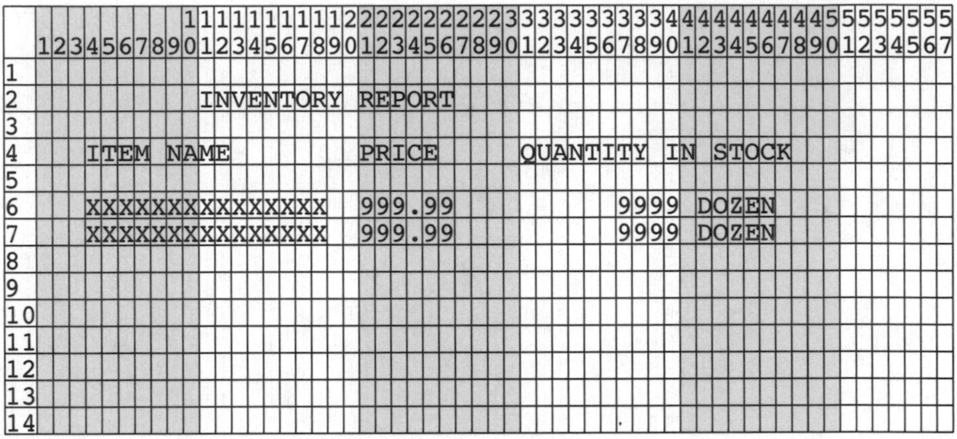

```
              1111111111222222222233333333334444444444555555555
    1234567890123456789012345678901234567890123456789012345678901234567
 1
 2                INVENTORY REPORT
 3
 4      ITEM NAME          PRICE      QUANTITY IN STOCK
 5
 6      XXXXXXXXXXXXXXX     999.99         9999 DOZEN
 7      XXXXXXXXXXXXXXX     999.99         9999 DOZEN
 8
 9
10
11
12
13
14
```

**Figure 3-16:** Print chart with literal in each detail line

Besides header lines and detail lines, reports often include special lines at the end of a report. These may have variable data only, as in Figure 3-17, or constant data only, as in Figure 3-18. Most often, however, reports will have both, as in Figure 3-19.

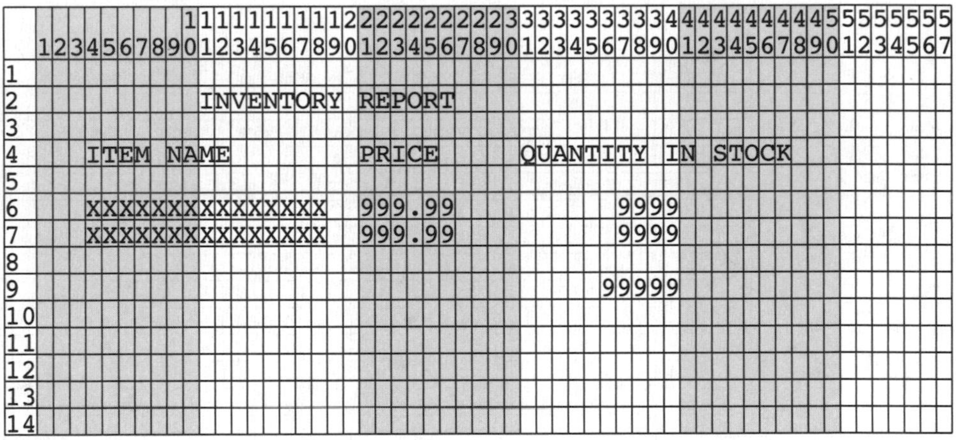

```
              1111111111222222222233333333334444444444555555555
    1234567890123456789012345678901234567890123456789012345678901234567
 1
 2                INVENTORY REPORT
 3
 4      ITEM NAME          PRICE      QUANTITY IN STOCK
 5
 6      XXXXXXXXXXXXXXX     999.99         9999
 7      XXXXXXXXXXXXXXX     999.99         9999
 8
 9                                       99999
10
11
12
13
14
```

**Figure 3-17:** Report with variable data at end

```
         1 1 1 1 1 1 1 1 1 1 2 2 2 2 2 2 2 2 2 2 3 3 3 3 3 3 3 3 3 3 4 4 4 4 4 4 4 4 4 4 5 5 5 5 5 5 5 5
   1 2 3 4 5 6 7 8 9 0 1 2 3 4 5 6 7 8 9 0 1 2 3 4 5 6 7 8 9 0 1 2 3 4 5 6 7 8 9 0 1 2 3 4 5 6 7 8 9 0 1 2 3 4 5 6 7
1
2                 INVENTORY  REPORT
3
4     ITEM NAME             PRICE          QUANTITY IN STOCK
5
6     XXXXXXXXXXXXXXXX      999.99              9999
7     XXXXXXXXXXXXXXXX      999.99              9999
8
9    THANK YOU  FOR  USING  THIS  PROGRAM
10
11
12
13
14
```

**Figure 3-18:** Report with constant data at end

```
         1 1 1 1 1 1 1 1 1 1 2 2 2 2 2 2 2 2 2 2 3 3 3 3 3 3 3 3 3 3 4 4 4 4 4 4 4 4 4 4 5 5 5 5 5 5 5 5
   1 2 3 4 5 6 7 8 9 0 1 2 3 4 5 6 7 8 9 0 1 2 3 4 5 6 7 8 9 0 1 2 3 4 5 6 7 8 9 0 1 2 3 4 5 6 7 8 9 0 1 2 3 4 5 6 7
1
2                 INVENTORY  REPORT
3
4     ITEM NAME             PRICE          QUANTITY IN STOCK
5
6     XXXXXXXXXXXXXXXX      999.99              9999
7     XXXXXXXXXXXXXXXX      999.99              9999
8
9                          GRAND  TOTAL:   999999
10
11
12
13
14
```

**Figure 3-19:** Report with combined constant and variable data at end

Even though lines at the end of a report don't always contain numeric totals, they are usually referred to generically as **total lines**.

## Input Documentation

Once you have planned the design of the output, you need to know what input is available to produce this output. If you are producing a report from stored data, you frequently will be provided with a **file description** that describes the data that are contained in a file. You usually find a file's description as part of an organization's information documentation; physically, the description may be on paper in a binder in the Information Systems Department, or it may be stored on a disk. If the file you will use comes from an outside source, the person requesting the report will have to provide you with a description of the data stored on the file. For example, Figure 3-20 shows an inventory file description.

▶ **tip**

> All programs do not use previously stored input files. Some use interactive input data supplied by a user during the execution of a program.

▶ **tip**

> Some programs produce an output file that is stored directly on a storage device, such as a disk. If your program produces file output instead of printed report output, you will create a file description for your output. Other programs then may use your output file description as an input description for their programs.

---

INVENTORY FILE DESCRIPTION

File name: INVTRY

| FIELD DESCRIPTION | POSITIONS | DATA TYPE | DECIMALS |
|---|---|---|---|
| Name of item | 1—15 | Character | |
| Price of item | 16—20 | Numeric | 2 |
| Quantity in stock | 21—24 | Numeric | 0 |

---

**Figure 3-20:** Inventory file description

The inventory file description in Figure 3-20 shows that each item's name occupies the first 15 characters of each record in the file. Some item names may require all 15 positions, for example "12 by 16 carpet", which contains exactly 15 characters including spaces. Other item names require fewer than the allotted 15 positions, for example, "door mat". In such cases, the remaining allotted positions remain blank. Whether the item name requires all 15 positions or not, the price for each item begins in position 16 of the record.

The price of any item in the inventory file is allowed five positions, 16 through 20. Two of the positions are reserved for decimal places. Typically, decimal points themselves are not stored in data files; they are **implied** or **assumed**. Also typically, numeric data are stored with leading zeros so that all allotted positions are occupied. Thus an item valued at $345.67 is stored as 34567, and an item valued at $1.23 is stored as 00123.

In addition to these field descriptions, the programmer may be given field names to use if such variable names must agree with those being used by other programmers working on the project. In many cases, however, the programmer is allowed to choose his or her own variable names. Therefore you can choose ITEM-NAME, NAME-OF-ITEM, DESCRIPTION, or any other reasonable one-word variable name when you reference the item name within your program.

Recall the data hierarchy relationship introduced in Chapter 1:

- File
- Record
- Field
- Character

The inventory file will contain many records; each record will contain an item name, price, and quantity, which are fields. In turn, for example, the name of an item field may hold up to 15 characters including terms like "12 by 16 carpet", "blue miniblinds", or "diskette holder".

Organizations may use different forms to relay the information about records and fields, but the very least the programmer needs to know is:

- What is the name of the file?
- What data does it contain?
- How much room does the file and each of its fields take up?
- What type of data is each field—character or numeric?

The inventory file description in Figure 3-20 appears to contain all the information the programmer needs to create the output requested in Figure 3-13. The output lists each item's name, price, and quantity, and the input records clearly contain that data. Often, however, a file description more closely resembles the description in Figure 3-21.

---

**INVENTORY FILE DESCRIPTION**

**File name: INVTRY**

| FIELD DESCRIPTION | POSITIONS | DATA TYPE | DECIMALS |
|---|---|---|---|
| Item number | 1–4 | Numeric | 0 |
| Name of item | 5–19 | Character | |
| Size | 20 | Numeric | 0 |
| Manufacturing cost of item | 21–25 | Numeric | 2 |
| Retail price of item | 26–30 | Numeric | 2 |
| Quantity in stock | 31–34 | Numeric | 0 |
| Reorder point | 35–38 | Numeric | 0 |
| Sales rep | 39–48 | Character | |
| Sales last year | 49–54 | Numeric | 0 |

---

**Figure 3-21:** Expanded inventory file description

Now it's harder to see that the information is all there; but it is, and you can still write the program. The input file contains more information than you need for the report you want to print, so you will ignore some of the input fields, such as item number and sales rep. These fields certainly may be used in other reports within the company. Typically, data input files have more data than any one program requires.

However, if the input file description resembles Figure 3-22, then there is not enough data to produce the requested report.

---

INVENTORY FILE DESCRIPTION

**File name: INVTRY**

| FIELD DESCRIPTION | POSITIONS | DATA TYPE | DECIMALS |
|---|---|---|---|
| Item number | 1–4 | Numeric | 0 |
| Name of item | 5–19 | Character | |
| Size | 20 | Numeric | 0 |
| Manufacturing cost of item | 21–25 | Numeric | 2 |
| Retail price of item | 26–30 | Numeric | 2 |
| Reorder point | 35–38 | Numeric | 0 |
| Sales rep | 39–48 | Character | |
| Sales last year | 49–54 | Numeric | 0 |

---

**Figure 3-22:** Insufficient inventory file description

In Figure 3-22, there is no indication that the input file contains a figure for quantity in stock. If the user really needs (or wants) the report as requested, it's out of the programmer's hands until the data can be collected from somewhere.

Assume that a user requests a report in the format shown in Figure 3-23, and that the input file description is the one in Figure 3-22. Now it's more difficult to determine whether you can create the requested report because the input file does not contain a PROFIT field. However, since the input data includes the company's cost and the company's selling price for each item, you can calculate the PROFIT arithmetically within your program and produce the desired output.

```
                  1111111111222222222233333333334444444444555555555
        1234567890123456789012345678901234567890123456789012345 67
 1
 2                  PROFIT REPORT
 3
 4        ITEM NUMBER        PRICE      COST        PROFIT
 5
 6            9999          999.99    999.99      999.99
 7            9999          999.99    999.99      999.99
 8
 9
10
11
12
13
14
```

**Figure 3-23:** Requested profit report

## Completing the Documentation

When you have designed the output and confirmed that it is possible to produce it from the input, then you can plan the logic of the program, code the program, and test the program. The original output design, input description, flowchart or pseudocode, and program code all become part of the program documentation. These pieces of documentation typically are stored together in a binder in the programming department of an organization where they can be studied later when program changes become necessary.

In addition to this program documentation, you typically must create **user documentation**. User documentation includes all the manuals or other instructional materials that nontechnical people use, as well as the operating instructions that computer operators and data-entry personnel may need to refer to in the months to come. It needs to be written clearly, in plain language, with reasonable expectations of the users' expertise. Within a small organization, the programmer may prepare the user documentation. In a large organization, programmers probably will not write the user documentation; either technical writers or systems analysts (who oversee programmers' work and coordinate programmers' efforts) write user documentation. These professionals consult with the programmer to ensure the user documentation is complete and accurate.

The areas addressed in user documentation may include:

- How to prepare input for this program
- To whom the output should be distributed
- How to interpret the normal output
- How to interpret and react to any error message generated by the program
- How frequently the program needs to run

All these issues must be addressed before a program can be said to be fully functional in an organization. When users throughout an organization can supply input data to computer programs and obtain the information they need in order to do their jobs well, then a skilled programmer has provided a complete piece of work.

# TERMS AND CONCEPTS

documentation

user, end user

program documentation

internal and external program
    documentation

program comments

printer spacing chart, print chart, or
    print layout

constant

detail lines, heading lines, and total lines

file description

implied or assumed decimal point

user documentation

# SUMMARY

- Documentation refers to all of the supporting material that goes along with a program.
- There are two broad categories of documentation: that intended for the programmer and that intended for the user.
- Internal program documentation consists of program comments, or nonexecuting statements that programmers place within their program code to explain program statements in English.
- External program documentation includes all the supporting paperwork that programmers develop while they write a program.
- Output documentation is usually the first to be written.
- The most common type of output is a printed report. You design a printed report on a printer spacing chart, which is also referred to as a print chart or a print layout.
- Each print chart line, with its Xs and 9s representing data, is a detail line, because it contains the data details.
- Heading lines usually appear only once per page.
- Lines at the end of a report are usually referred to generically as total lines.
- A file description describes the data that are contained in a file.

- Typically, decimal points themselves are not stored in data files; they are implied or assumed. Also typically, numeric data are stored with leading zeros so that all allotted positions are occupied.
- The original output design, input description, flowchart or pseudocode, and program code all become part of the program documentation. These pieces of documentation typically are stored together in a binder in the programming department of an organization where they can be studied later when program changes become necessary.
- In addition to program documentation, you typically also must create user documentation, which includes all the manuals or other instructional materials that nontechnical people use.

# E X E R C I S E S

1. Design a print chart for a payroll roster that is intended to list for every employee: employee's first name, last name, and salary.

2. Design a print chart for a payroll roster that is intended to list for every employee: employee's first name, last name, hours worked, rate per hour, gross pay, federal withholding tax, state withholding tax, union dues, and net pay.

3. Given the following input file description, determine if there is enough information given to produce each of the requested reports:

**INSURANCE PREMIUM LIST**

**File name: INSPREM**

| FIELD DESCRIPTION | POSITIONS | DATA TYPE | DECIMALS |
|---|---|---|---|
| Name of insured driver | 1–40 | Character | |
| Birth date | 41–46 | Numeric | 0 |
| Gender | 47 | Character | |
| Make of car | 48–57 | Character | |
| Year of car | 58–61 | Numeric | 0 |
| Miles driven per year | 62–67 | Numeric | 0 |
| Number of traffic tickets | 68–69 | Numeric | 0 |

a. A list of the names of all insured drivers

b. A list of very high-risk insured drivers defined as those who are male, under 25 years old, with more than two tickets

    c. A list of low-risk insured drivers defined as those with no tickets in the last three years, over 30 years old

    d. A list of insured drivers to contact about a special premium offer for those with a passenger car who drive under 10,000 miles per year

**4.** Given the INSPREM file description in Exercise 3, design a print chart to satisfy each of the following requests:

    a. A list of every driver's name and make of car

    b. A list of the names of all insured drivers who drive more than 20,000 miles per year

    c. A list of the name, gender, make of car, and year of car for all drivers who have more than two tickets

    d. A report that summarizes the number of tickets held by those who were born before 1930, from 1931–1950, from 1951–1970, and from 1971 on

    e. A report that summarizes the number of tickets held by those in the four birth-date categories listed in Part d, grouped by gender

# Writing a Complete Program

**case** ▶ "Don't tell Boston," Lynn whispers, "but I think you are ready to plan the logic for your first complete program. Boston will think you need years and years of background like he has, but we've given you all the basics."

"Really? Great!" you say.

"Let me go grab a cup of tea, and then we'll get started."

As Lynn disappears down the hall to the right, Boston Murphy emerges from the left. "How's it going?" he asks. "Ready to plan the logic to a complete program?"

"Sure," you say hesitantly. "Do you think I'm ready?"

"Absolutely. Jump right in. Lynn will think you need four years of formal university classes like she has—but I say we've prepared you well. It's time to take the bull by the horns and write a complete program."

After studying Section A, you should be able to:

- Describe the mainline logic of a complete computer program
- Declare variables
- Describe the concept of initialization

# The Structure of Procedural Programs and Initialization Tasks

## The Logical Flow Through a Program

You're ready to plan the logic for your first complete computer program. The output is an inventory report, as shown in Figure 4-1. The report lists inventory items along with the price, cost, and profit of each item.

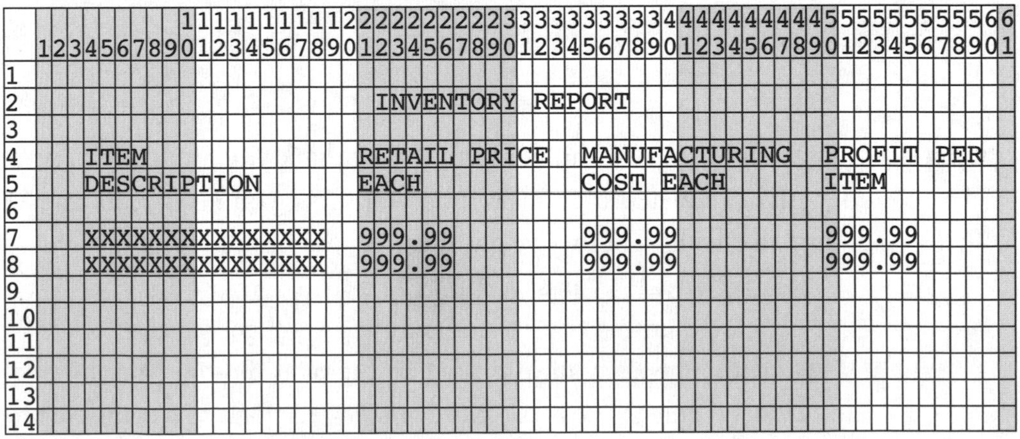

|   | 1 | 2 | 3 | 4 | 5 | 6 | 7 | 8 | 9 | 0 | 1 | 2 | 3 | 4 | 5 | 6 | 7 | 8 | 9 | 0 | 1 | 2 | 3 | 4 | 5 | 6 | 7 | 8 | 9 | 0 | 1 | 2 | 3 | 4 | 5 | 6 | 7 | 8 | 9 | 0 | 1 | 2 | 3 | 4 | 5 | 6 | 7 | 8 | 9 | 0 | 1 | 2 | 3 | 4 | 5 | 6 | 7 | 8 | 9 | 0 | 1 |

```
         1111111111222222222233333333334444444444555555555566
1234567890123456789012345678901234567890123456789012345678901
1
2                      INVENTORY REPORT
3
4    ITEM               RETAIL PRICE    MANUFACTURING      PROFIT PER
5    DESCRIPTION        EACH            COST EACH          ITEM
6
7    XXXXXXXXXXXXXXXX   999.99          999.99             999.99
8    XXXXXXXXXXXXXXXX   999.99          999.99             999.99
9
10
11
12
13
14
```

**Figure 4-1:** Print chart for inventory report

You have been provided with the inventory file description shown in Figure 4-2.

```
INVENTORY FILE DESCRIPTION

File name: INVENTORY

FIELD DESCRIPTION        POSITIONS      DATA TYPE       DECIMALS

Item name                1—15           Character
Price                    16—20          Numeric         2
Cost                     21—25          Numeric         2
Quantity in stock        26—29          Numeric         0
```

**Figure 4-2:** Inventory file description

> In some systems, file names are limited to eight characters, so INVENTORY might be an unacceptable file name.

Examine the print chart and the input file description. Your first task is to determine whether you have all the necessary data to produce the report. The output requires the item name, price, and cost, and you can see that all three are data items on the input file. The output also requires a profit figure for each item; you can determine the profit by subtracting an item's cost from its selling price. The input record contains an additional field, "Quantity in stock". It is common for input records to contain more data than an application needs, so you will ignore this field in your program. You have all the necessary data; you can begin to plan the program.

Where should you begin? It's wise to try to get the big picture first. A program that reads records from an input file and produces a printed report can be written as a **procedural program**—that is, a program in which one procedure follows another from beginning until the end. You write all the instructions for a procedural program, and when the program executes, each instruction takes place in order based on your program's logic. The overall or **mainline logic** of almost every procedural computer program can follow a general structure that consists of three distinct parts.

1. Performing **housekeeping,** or initialization tasks. Housekeeping includes those steps that you must perform at the beginning of a program to get ready for the rest of the program, or to set things up at the beginning.
2. Performing the main loop within the program. The **main loop** contains the steps that are repeated for every record.
3. Performing the end-of-job routine. The end-of-job routine holds the steps you take at the end of the program to finish the application.

> Not all programs are procedural; some are object-oriented. The distinguishing feature of many object-oriented programs is that the user determines timing of events in the main loop of the program by using an input device such as a mouse. As you advance in your knowledge of programming, you will learn more about object-oriented techniques.

You can write any procedural program as one long series of program language statements, but most programmers prefer to break their programs into at least three parts. You can call the three major subroutines, as shown in the flowchart and pseudocode in Figure 4-3. The subroutine names, of course, are entirely up to the programmer.

Figure 4-4 shows the hierarchy chart for this program.

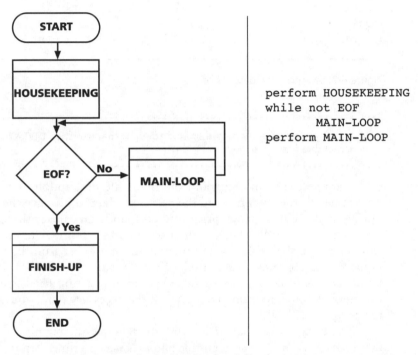

```
perform HOUSEKEEPING
while not EOF
        MAIN-LOOP
perform MAIN-LOOP
```

**Figure 4-3:** Flowchart and pseudocode of mainline logic

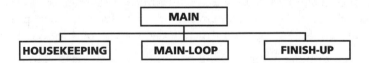

**Figure 4-4:** Hierarchy chart for inventory report program

Breaking down a big program into three basic procedures helps keep the job manageable, allowing you to tackle a large job one step at a time. Dividing the work into routines allows you to assign the three major procedures to three different programmers, if you want. It also helps you keep the program structured.

## Housekeeping Tasks

Housekeeping tasks include all the steps that must take place at the beginning of a program. Very often, this includes four major tasks:

- You declare variables.
- You open files.
- You perform any one-time-only tasks, such as printing headings at the beginning of a report.
- You read the first input record.

### Declaring Variables

Your first task in writing any program is to **declare variables**. When you declare variables, you assign reasonable names to memory locations so that you can store and retrieve data there. Declaring a variable involves selecting a name and a type.

For example, within the inventory report program, you need to supply variable names for the data fields that appear in each input record. You might decide on the variable names and types shown in Figure 4-5.

```
char   INV-ITEM-NAME
num    INV-PRICE
num    INV-COST
num    INV-QUANTITY
```

**Figure 4-5:** Variable declarations for the inventory file

**tip**

Some languages require that you provide a storage size in addition to a type and name for each variable. Other languages provide a predetermined amount of storage based on the variable type; for example, four bytes for an integer or one byte for a character. And most languages require you to provide a length for strings of characters.

You can provide any names you choose for your variables. When you write another program that uses the same input file, you are free to choose completely new variable names. Similarly, other programmers can write programs that use the same file and choose their own variable names. The variable names just represent memory positions; the variable names are internal to your program. The files do not contain the variable names; files contain only data. When you read the characters "Cotton shirt" from an input file, it doesn't matter whether you store those characters at a memory location named INV-ITEM-DESCRIPTION, NAME-OF-ITEM, PRODUCT-NAME, or any other one-word name.

Each of the four individual variable declarations in Figure 4-5 contains a type (character or numeric) and a name. Any one-word names can be chosen for the variables, but a common practice involves beginning similar variables with a common **prefix**, for example, INV. In a large program in which you eventually declare dozens of variables, the INV prefix will help you immediately identify a variable as part of the inventory file.

Creating the inventory report shown in Figure 4-1 involves using the INV-ITEM-NAME, INV-PRICE and INV-COST fields, but you do not need to use the INV-QUANTITY field in this program. However, the information regarding quantity does take room on the input file. If you imagine the surface of a disk as pictured in Figure 4-6, you can envision how the data fields follow one another in the file.

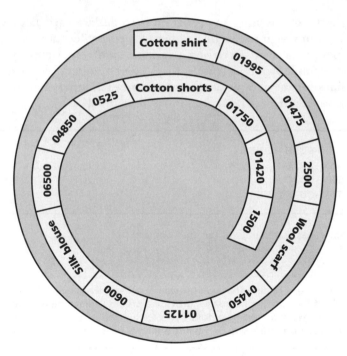

**Figure 4-6:** Representation of typical data for INVENTORY file

When you ask the program to read in an inventory record, four "chunks" of data will be transferred from the input device to the computer's main memory: name, price, cost, and quantity. When you declare the variables that represent the input data, you must provide a memory position for each of the four pieces of data, whether or not they all will be used within this program.

 **tip**

In COBOL you can use the generic name FILLER for all unused data positions. This frees you from the task of creating variable names for items you do not intend to use.

**In some organizations the data file descriptions are already created for you. This makes sense if you consider that dozens of programs within the organization may access the INVENTORY file. The description of variable names and types is stored in one location, and each programmer who uses the file simply imports the data file description into his or her own program. Of course, the programmer must be provided with documentation specifying the chosen names.**

In most programming languages you can give a group of associated variables a **group name**. Just as it is easier to refer to "The Andersons" than it is to list "Nancy, Bud, Jim, Tom, Julie, Jane, Kate, and John", the benefit in using a group name is the ability to reference several variables with one all-encompassing name. For example, writing read INV-RECORD is simpler than writing read INV-ITEM-NAME, INV-PRICE, INV-COST, and INV-QUANTITY. How you assign a group name to several variables differs in each programming language. This book will follow the convention of underlining any group name and indenting the group members beneath, as shown in Figure 4-7.

```
INV-RECORD
      char    INV-ITEM-NAME
      num     INV-PRICE
      num     INV-COST
      num     INV-QUANTITY
```

**Figure 4-7:** Variable declarations for the inventory file including a group name

**A group is often called a *data structure*, or more simply, a *structure*. Some object-oriented languages refer to a group as a *class*.**

In addition to declaring variables, sometimes you want to provide a variable with an initial value. Providing a variable with a value when you create it is known as **initialization,** or defining the variable. For example, for the inventory report shown in Figure 4-1, you might want to create a variable named HEADING and store the value "INVENTORY REPORT". The declaration is char HEADING = "INVENTORY REPORT". This indicates that HEADING is a character variable, and that the character contents are the words "INVENTORY REPORT".

***Declaring*** a variable provides it with a name and type. ***Defining*** a variable provides it with a value.

**tip**

In some programming languages you can declare a variable such as HEADING to be **constant**, or never changing. Even though INV-ITEM-NAME, INV-PRICE, and the others will hold a variety of different values during the execution of a program, the HEADING will never change.

In most programming languages, if you do not provide an initial value when declaring a variable, then the value is unknown, or **garbage**. Some programming languages do provide you with an automatic starting value; for example in BASIC or RPG, all numeric variables automatically begin with the value zero. However, in C++, Java, Pascal, and COBOL, variables do not receive any initial value unless you provide one. No matter which programming language you use, it is always clearest to provide a value for those variables that require them.

When you declare the variable INV-ITEM-NAME, INV-PRICE, INV-COST, and INV-QUANTITY, you do not provide them with any initial value. The values for these variables will be assigned when the first file record is read into memory. It would be *legal* to assign a value to input file record variables—for example, INV-ITEM-NAME = "Cotton shirt", but it would be a waste of time and might mislead others who read your program. The first INV-ITEM-NAME will come from an input device and may or may not be "Cotton shirt".

The report illustrated in Figure 4-1 contains three individual heading lines. The most common practice is to declare one variable or constant for each of these lines. The three declarations are as follows:

```
char HEADING = "INVENTORY REPORT"
char COL-HEAD-1 = "Item          Retail Price  Manufacturing Profit per"
char COL-HEAD-2 = "Description  Each          Cost Each Item"
```

Within the program, when it is time to write these heading lines to an output device, you will code:

```
write HEADING
write COL-HEAD-1
write COL-HEAD-2
```

You do not have to create variables for your headings. Your program can contain the following statements in which you use literal strings of characters instead of variable names. The printed results are the same either way.

```
write "INVENTORY REPORT"
write "Item          Retail Price  Manufacturing Profit per"
write "Description  Each          Cost Each Item"
```

Using variable names, as in write HEADING, is usually more convenient than spelling out the heading's contents, especially if you will use the headings in multiple locations within your program.

**tip**

When you write a program, you will type spaces between the words within column headings so the spacing matches the print chart you created for the program. For convenience, some languages provide you with a tab character. The goal is to provide well-spaced output in readable columns.

Dividing the headings into three lines is not required either, but it is usual practice. In most programming languages you could write all the headings in one statement, using a code that indicates a new line at every necessary line. Alternatively, most programming languages let you produce a character for output without advancing to a new line, so you could write out one character at a time. Storing and writing one complete line at a time is a reasonable compromise.

Every specific programming language provides you with a means to physically advance printer paper to the top of a page when you print the first heading. Similarly, every language provides you with a means for producing double- and triple-spaced lines of text. Because the methods differ from language to language, in this book we will assume that if a print chart shows a heading that prints at the top of the page and then skips a line, then you can add the appropriate language-specific codes when you write the program.

Often you must create dozens of variables when you write a computer program. If you are using a flowchart to diagram the logic, it is impossible physically to fit the variables in one flowchart box. Therefore you often want to use an annotation symbol. Similarly, when writing pseudocode, it is often more convenient to place variable names off to the side. The beginning of a flowchart and corresponding pseudocode for the HOUSEKEEPING module of the inventory report program is shown in Figure 4-8.

**tip**

You learned about the annotation symbol in Chapter 3.

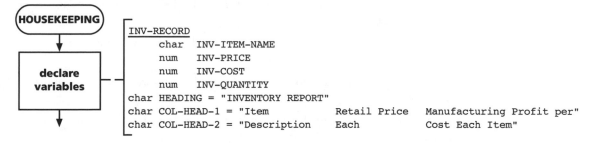

**Figure 4-8:** Beginning of flowchart and pseudocode for inventory report program

# TERMS AND CONCEPTS

| | |
|---|---|
| procedural program | group name |
| mainline logic | main loop |
| housekeeping | initialization |
| declare variables | constant |
| prefix | garbage |

 # SUMMARY

■ A program that reads records from an input file and produces a printed report can be written as a procedural program—that is, a program in which one procedure follows another from beginning until end.

■ The overall or mainline logic of almost every procedural computer program can follow a general structure that consists of three distinct parts: performing housekeeping tasks, performing the main loop within the program, and performing the end-of-job routine.

■ When you declare variables, you assign reasonable names to memory locations so that you can store and retrieve data there. Declaring a variable involves selecting a name and a type.

■ Beginning similar variables with a common prefix is a popular programming practice.

■ In most programming languages, you can give a group of associated variables a group name.

■ Providing a variable with a value when you create it is known as initialization, or defining the variable.

■ When you declare a variable in most programming languages, if you do not provide an initial value, then the value is unknown, or garbage.

■ The most common practice is to declare one variable or constant for each heading line that appears on a report.

■ You use an annotation symbol to list items when they don't fit conveniently in a flowchart symbol.

# E X E R C I S E S

1. A furniture store maintains an inventory file that includes data about every item it sells. The fields include a stock number, description, wholesale price, and retail price. Write a list of variable names you would declare for a program that uses this file.

2. A summer camp keeps a record for every camper including first name, last name, birth date, and scores that range from 1 to 10 in four areas: swimming, tennis, horsemanship, and crafts. The camp wants a printed report listing each camper's data. Design a print chart, then create the variable list you would need to read the file and print the report.

**After studying Section B, you should be able to :**

- Describe typical housekeeping tasks
- Explain the concept of opening files
- Describe writing headings at the beginning of a report
- Explain why you use a priming read in a housekeeping routine
- Write the main loop of a program
- Describe end-of-job functions

# Finishing Housekeeping and Writing the Main-Loop and Finish Routines

## Other Housekeeping Tasks

Declaring variables is an important housekeeping task, but it is not the only one. Usually you also must open files, print headings, and read the first input record.

### Opening Files

If a program will use input files, the computer must be told where the input is coming from—a specific disk drive, for example, or a tape drive. This process is known as **opening a file**. Since a disk may have many files stored on it, the program also needs to know the name of the file being opened for use. In many languages, if no input file is opened, input is accepted from a default or **standard input device**, most often the keyboard.

If a program will have output, you must also open a file for output. Perhaps the output file will be sent to a disk or tape. Although you might not think of a printed report as a file, computers treat a printer as just another output device, and if output will go to a printer, then you must open the printer output device as well. Again, if no file is opened, a default or **standard output device**, usually the monitor, is used.

When you flowchart, you usually write the command to open the files within a parallelogram, because the parallelogram is the input/output symbol and you are opening the input and output devices. You can use an annotation box to list the files that you open, as shown in Figure 4-9.

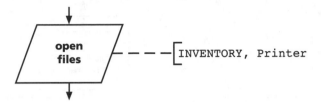

**Figure 4-9:** Specifying files that you open

## Printing Headings

A commonly performed housekeeping task involves printing headings at the top of a report. In the inventory report example, three lines of headings appear at the beginning of the report. In this example, printing the heading lines is straightforward:

```
write HEADING
write COL-HEAD-1
write COL-HEAD-2
```

## Reading the First Input Record

Often, the last task you take care of in a housekeeping routine is to read the first data record into memory. This is appropriate if you recall the mainline logic of the inventory report program from Figure 4-3. When HOUSEKEEPING ends, the next task is to check immediately for EOF. The last HOUSEKEEPING step is to read a record from the input file. If no records exist, the computer will recognize the end-of-file condition, so it makes sense that the next instruction following reading the file should determine whether a record was actually encountered or whether the end of file condition occurred. If EOF is not encountered, there must be a legitimate record to be processed, and the logical flow proceeds to the MAIN-LOOP of the program. However, if EOF is encountered on reading the first record, there is no point in entering the MAIN-LOOP; since there are no records to be processed, the logic flows directly to the FINISH-UP routine.

It is wrong to fail to include reading the first record within the HOUSEKEEPING module. If HOUSEKEEPING does not include a step to read a record from the input file, then you must read a record as the first step in the MAIN-LOOP, as shown in Figure 4-10. The program works well, reading records and printing them until EOF, but then the MAIN-LOOP record processing (computing profit and writing a line) continues without any data to process. Therefore the appropriate place for the priming record read is at the end of the preliminary HOUSEKEEPING steps.

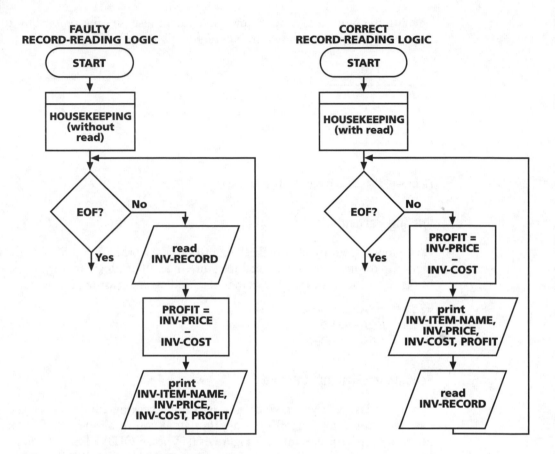

Figure 4-10: Comparing faulty and correct record-reading logic

> **Reading an input record in the HOUSEKEEPING section is an example of a priming read. You learned about the priming read in Chapter 2.**

When you read the four data fields for the inventory file data, you can write `read INV-ITEM-NAME, INV-PRICE, INV-COST, INV-QUANTITY`, but if you have declared a group name such as INV-RECORD, it is simpler to write `read INV-RECORD`. Using the group name is a shortcut to writing each field name.

Figure 4-11 shows completed HOUSEKEEPING routines in flowchart and pseudocode versions.

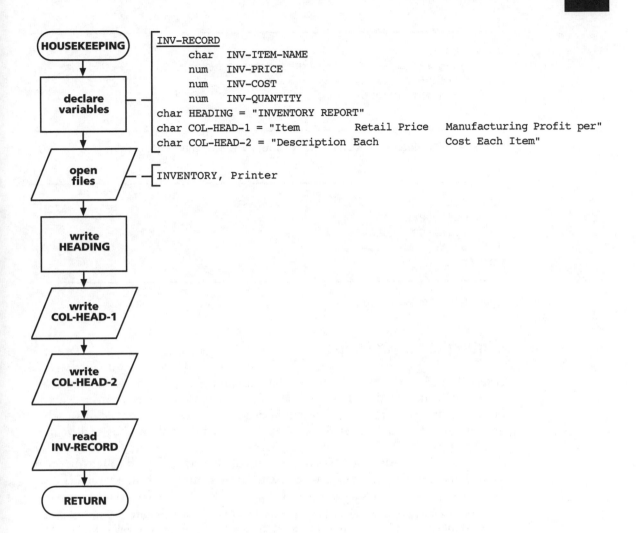

**Figure 4-11:** Flowchart and pseudocode for HOUSEKEEPING routine in inventory report
program

As an alternative, you can place the three heading line statements in their own
subroutine. Therefore the pseudocode for HOUSEKEEPING would be as shown
in Figure 4-12, with the steps in HEADINGS appearing as in Figure 4-13. Either
approach is fine; the logic of the program is the same whether or not the heading
line statements are segregated into their own routine. The programmer can decide
on the program organization that makes the most sense.

```
HOUSEKEEPING
     open files — — — — —[INVENTORY, Printer
     perform HEADINGS             L
     read INV-RECORD
RETURN
```

**Figure 4-12:** Pseudocode for HOUSEKEEPING with HEADINGS subroutine

```
HEADINGS
     write HEADING
     write COL-HEAD-1
     write COL-HEAD-2
RETURN
```

**Figure 4-13:** HEADINGS routine

## Writing the Main Loop

After you declare the variables for a program and perform the housekeeping tasks, the "real work" of the program begins. The inventory report described at the beginning of this chapter and depicted in Figure 4-1 needs just one set of variables and one set of headings, yet there might be hundreds or thousands of inventory items to process. The **main loop** of a program, controlled by the EOF decision, is the program's "workhorse". Each data record will pass once through the main loop, where calculations are performed with the data and the results printed.

If the inventory report contains more records than fit on a page of output, you probably will want to print a new set of headings at the top of each page. You will learn how to do this in Chapter 7.

For the inventory report program, the MAIN-LOOP must include three steps:

1. Calculate the profit for an item.
2. Print the item information on the report.
3. Read the next inventory record.

At the end of HOUSEKEEPING, you read one data record into the computer's memory. As the first step in the MAIN-LOOP, you can calculate an item's profit by subtracting its manufacturing cost from its retail price: PROFIT = INV-PRICE − INV-COST. PROFIT is the programmer-created name for a new spot in computer memory where the value of the profit is stored.

▶ **tip**

Recall that the standard way to express mathematical statements is to assign values from the right side of an equals sign to the left. That is, `PROFIT = INV-PRICE - INV-COST` assigns a value to PROFIT. `INV-PRICE - INV-COST = PROFIT` is an illegal statement.

Because you have a new variable, you must declare PROFIT in the list of declared variables at the beginning of the program. Programmers often work back and forth between the variable list and the logical steps during the creation of a program, listing some of the variables they will need as soon as they start to plan and adding others later as they think of them. Since PROFIT will hold the result of a mathematical calculation, you should declare it as a numeric variable and add it to the list of variables at the beginning of the program. The updated variable list appears in Figure 4-14. Notice that like the headings, PROFIT is not indented. You want to show that PROFIT is not part of the INV-RECORD group; instead, it is a separate variable that you are declaring so that you can store a calculated value.

▶ **tip**

You can declare HEADING, COL-HEAD-1, COL-HEAD-2, and PROFIT in any order. The important point is that none of these four variables are part of the INV-RECORD group.

```
INV-RECORD
      char     INV-ITEM-NAME
      num      INV-PRICE
      num      INV-COST
      num      INV-QUANTITY
char HEADING = "INVENTORY REPORT"
char COL-HEAD-1 = "Item           Retail Price  Manufacturing Profit per"
char COL-HEAD-2 = "Description    Each          Cost Each Item"
num  PROFIT
```

**Figure 4-14:** Variable list for inventory report program, including PROFIT

▶ **tip**

Although you can give any variable any legal name, you probably do not want to begin the variable name for PROFIT with the INV prefix, because PROFIT is not part of the INVENTORY input file.

After you determine an item's profit, you can write a detail line of information on the inventory report: `write INV-ITEM-NAME, INV-PRICE, INV-COST, PROFIT`.

The last step in the MAIN-LOOP of the inventory report program involves reading in the next INV-RECORD. Figure 4-15 shows the flowchart and pseudocode for MAIN-LOOP.

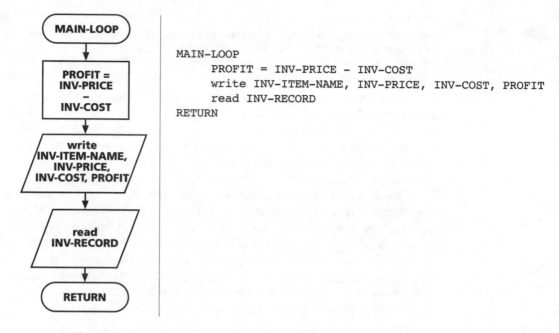

```
MAIN-LOOP
      PROFIT = INV-PRICE - INV-COST
      write INV-ITEM-NAME, INV-PRICE, INV-COST, PROFIT
      read INV-RECORD
RETURN
```

**Figure 4-15:** Flowchart and pseudocode for MAIN-LOOP of inventory report program

Just as headings are printed one full line at a time, detail lines are also printed one line at a time. You can write each field separately, as in the following, but it is most efficient to write one full line at a time.

```
write INV-ITEM-NAME
write INV-PRICE
write INV-COST
write PROFIT
```

In most programming languages you also have the option of calculating the profit and printing it in one statement, as in the following:

```
write INV-ITEM-NAME, INV-PRICE, INV-COST, INV-PRICE - INV-COST
```

If the language you use allows this type of statement in which a calculation takes place within the output statement, it is up to you to decide which format to use. Performing the arithmetic right in the write statement allows you to avoid declaring a PROFIT variable. However, if you need the PROFIT figure for further calculations, then it makes sense to compute the profit and store it in a PROFIT field. Using a separate **work variable** or **work field** such as PROFIT to temporarily hold a calculation is never wrong, and often it's the clearest course of action.

After the detail line has been written, the last step you take before leaving the MAIN-LOOP is to read the next record from the input file into memory. When you exit the MAIN-LOOP, the logic flows back to the EOF question in the main-line logic. If it is not EOF—that is, if an additional data record exists—then you enter the MAIN-LOOP again, compute profit on the second record, print the detail line, and read the third record.

During some execution of the MAIN-LOOP, the program will read a new record and encounter the end of the file. Then when you ask the EOF question in the main line of the program, the answer will be *yes*, and the program will not enter the MAIN-LOOP again. Instead, the program logic will enter the FINISH-UP routine.

## Performing End-Of-Job Tasks

Within any program, the **end-of-job module** holds the steps you must take at the end of the program after all the input records have been processed. Some end-of-job modules print summaries or grand totals at the end of a report. Others may print a message such as "End of Report" so the reader is confident that he or she has received all the information that should be included. Very often, end-of-job modules must close any open files.

The end-of-job module for the inventory report program is very simple. The print chart does not indicate that any special messages such as "Thank you for reading this report" print after the detail lines end. Likewise, there are no required summary or total lines. Nothing special happens. Only one task needs to be performed in the end-of-job routine that this program calls FINISH-UP. In HOUSEKEEPING, you opened files. In FINISH-UP, you close them. The complete FINISH-UP routine, then, is flowcharted and written in pseudocode in Figure 4-16.

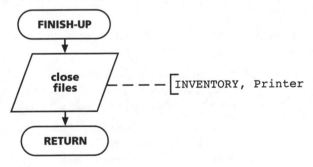

**Figure 4-16:** Flowchart of FINISH–UP routine

Most programmers wouldn't bother with a subroutine for just one statement, but as you create more complicated programs, your end-of-job routines will get bigger, and it will make more sense to see the necessary job-finishing tasks together in a subroutine.

# TERMS AND CONCEPTS

| | |
|---|---|
| opening a file | main loop |
| standard input device | work variable or work field |
| standard output device | end-of-job module |

# SUMMARY

- Housekeeping tasks include all the steps that must take place at the beginning of a program.

- Housekeeping tasks usually include declaring variables, opening files, performing any one-time-only tasks such as printing headings at the beginning of a report, and reading the first input record.

- Opening a file involves identifying the file to be used.

- In many languages, if no input file is opened, input is accepted from a default or standard input device, most often the keyboard. The default or standard output device is usually the monitor.

- Often the last task you take care of in a housekeeping routine is reading the first data record into memory.

- The main loop of a program, controlled by the EOF decision, is the program's "workhorse". Each data record will pass once through the main loop, where calculations are performed with the data and the results are printed.

- Every variable you use in a program must be declared. Programmers often work back and forth during the creation of a program, listing some of the variables they will need as soon as they start to plan and adding others later as they think of them.

- You close any open file with an end-of-job routine.

# E X E R C I S E S

1.  A pet store owner needs a weekly sales report. The output consists of a printed report entitled PET SALES. Fields printed on output are: type of animal and sale price. The input file description is shown below.

    **File name: PETS**

    | FIELD DESCRIPTION | POSITIONS | DATA TYPE | DECIMALS |
    |---|---|---|---|
    | Type of Animal | 1–20 | Character | |
    | Price of Animal | 21–26 | Numeric | 2 |

    a. Design the print chart, draw the hierarchy chart, and draw the flowchart for this program.

    b. Design the print chart, draw the hierarchy chart, and write the pseudocode for this program.

2.  An employer wishes to produce a personnel report. The output consists of a printed report entitled ACTIVE PERSONNEL. Fields printed on output are: last name of employee, first name of employee, and current salary. The input file description is shown below.

    **File name: PERSONNEL**

    | FIELD DESCRIPTION | POSITIONS | DATA TYPE | DECIMALS |
    |---|---|---|---|
    | Last Name | 1–15 | Character | |
    | First Name | 16–30 | Character | |
    | Soc. Sec. Number | 31–39 | Numeric | 0 |
    | Department | 40–41 | Numeric | 0 |
    | Weekly Salary | 42–47 | Numeric | 2 |

    a. Design the print chart, draw the hierarchy chart, and draw the flowchart for this program.

    b. Design the print chart, draw the hierarchy chart, and write the pseudocode for this program.

3.  An employer wishes to produce a personnel report that shows the end result if she gives everyone a 10 percent raise in salary. The output consists of a printed report entitled PROJECTED RAISES. Fields printed on output are: last name of employee, first name of employee, current salary, and projected salary. The input file description is shown below.

    **File name: PERSONNEL**

    | FIELD DESCRIPTION | POSITIONS | DATA TYPE | DECIMALS |
    |---|---|---|---|
    | Last Name | 1–15 | Character | |
    | First Name | 16–30 | Character | |
    | Soc. Sec. Number | 31–39 | Numeric | 0 |
    | Department | 40–41 | Numeric | 0 |
    | Weekly Salary | 42–47 | Numeric | 2 |

    a. Design the print chart, draw the hierarchy chart, and draw the flowchart for this program.

4. An employer needs to determine how much tax to withhold for each employee. Each employee's withholding amount computes as 20 percent of his or her weekly pay. The output consists of a printed report entitled WITHHOLDING FOR EACH EMPLOYEE. Fields printed on output are: last name of employee, first name of employee, hourly pay, weekly pay based on a 40-hour work week, and withholding amount per week. The input file description is shown below.

**File name: EMPLOYEES**

| FIELD DESCRIPTION | POSITIONS | DATA TYPE | DECIMALS |
|---|---|---|---|
| Company ID | 1–5 | Numeric | 0 |
| First Name | 6–17 | Character | |
| Last Name | 18–29 | Character | |
| Hourly Rate | 30–34 | Numeric | 2 |

   a. Design the print chart, draw the hierarchy chart, and draw the flowchart for this program.
   b. Design the print chart, draw the hierarchy chart, and write the pseudocode for this program.

5. A baseball team manager wants a report showing her players' batting statistics. A batting average is computed as hits divided by at-bats and is usually expressed to three decimal positions, for example .235. The output consists of a printed report entitled TEAM STATISTICS. Fields printed on output are: player number, first name, last name, and batting average. The input file description is shown below.

**File name: BASEBALL**

| FIELD DESCRIPTION | POSITIONS | DATA TYPE | DECIMALS |
|---|---|---|---|
| Player Number | 1–2 | Numeric | 0 |
| First Name | 3–18 | Character | |
| Last Name | 19–35 | Character | |
| At-bats | 36–38 | Numeric | 0 |
| Hits | 39–41 | Numeric | 0 |

   a. Design the print chart, draw the hierarchy chart, and draw the flowchart for this program.
   b. Design the print chart, draw the hierarchy chart, and write the pseudocode for this program.

# CHAPTER 5

# Making Decisions

**case** ▶ "We have a lot of work to do this week," says Boston Murphy, one of the expert programmers at Solutions, Inc. "The auditors from the home office are arriving on Friday, and management needs a slew of reports."

"Like what?" you ask.

"They need a list of employees with medical insurance, another list of those with dental insurance, and about ten other lists of employees to compile various attributes."

"You've shown me how to plan and create printed reports," you say, "but the reports we've talked about use every record on an input file. These reports sound like you need to use only some of the records."

"Exactly!" Boston says. "Now you will have to write programs that make decisions."

**After studying Section A, you should be able to:**

- Evaluate Boolean expressions
- Describe the six logical comparison operators
- Understand AND logic
- Write AND decisions for efficiency
- Combine decisions in an AND situation
- Avoid common errors in an AND situation

# Beginning Decisions: Boolean and AND Logic

## Evaluating Boolean Expressions to Make Comparisons

The reason people think computers are smart lies in the computer program's ability to make decisions. A medical diagnosis program that can decide if your symptoms fit various disease profiles seems quite intelligent, as does a program that can offer you different potential vacation routes based on your destination.

The selection structure (sometimes called a decision structure) involved in such programs is not new to you—it's one of the basic structures of structured programming. See Figures 5-1 and 5-2.

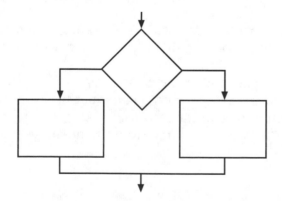

**Figure 5-1:** The dual-alternative selection structure

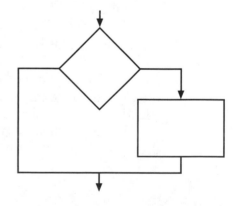

**Figure 5-2:** The single-alternative selection structure

You can refer to the structure in Figure 5-1 as a **dual-alternative** or **binary** selection because there are two possible outcomes: depending on the answer to the question represented by the diamond, the logical flow proceeds either to the left branch of the structure or to the right. The choices are mutually exclusive; that is, the logic can flow only to one of the two alternatives, never both. This selection structure also is called an **if-then-else** structure because it fits the statement:

```
if the ANSWER to the question is yes, then
        do SOMETHING
else
        do SOMETHING ELSE
```

The flowchart segment in Figure 5-2 represents a **single-alternative** or **unary** selection. There is only one outcome of the question for you to take action on. This form of the if-then-else structure is called simply an **if-then,** because no "else" action is necessary.

> **tip**
>
> You can call a single-alternative decision (or selection) a *single-sided decision*. Similarly, a dual-alternative decision is a *double-sided decision* (or selection).

For example, consider Figure 5-3. It shows the flowchart and pseudocode for a typical if-then-else decision in a business program. Many organizations pay employees time-and-a-half (one and a half times their usual hourly rate) for hours in excess of 40 per week. The logic segments in the figure show this decision.

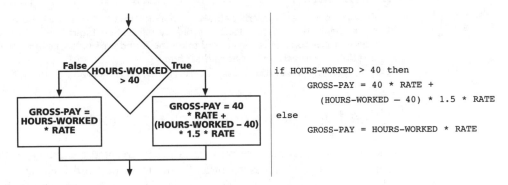

**Figure 5-3:** Flowchart and pseudocode for overtime decision

A typical if-then decision is shown in Figure 5-4. In this decision the employee's paycheck is reduced if the employee participates in the dental plan. No action is taken if the employee is not in the dental plan.

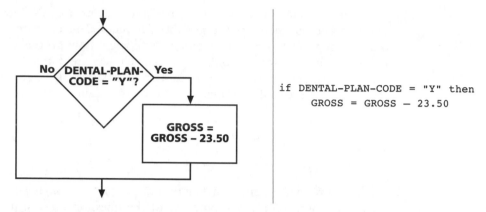

**Figure 5-4:** Flowchart and pseudocode for dental plan decision

The expressions HOURS−WORKED > 40 and DENTAL−PLAN−CODE = "Y" that appear in Figures 5-3 and 5-4 are Boolean expressions. A **Boolean expression** is one that represents only one of two states, usually expressed as true or false. Every decision you make in a computer program involves evaluating a Boolean expression. True/false evaluation is "natural" from a computer's standpoint because computer circuitry consists of two-state, on-off switches, often represented by 1 or 0, so every computer decision yields a true-or-false, yes-or-no, 1-or-0 result.

George Boole was a mathematician who lived from 1815 to 1864. He approached logic more simply than his predecessors did by expressing logical selections with common algebraic symbols. He is considered to be the founder of symbolic logic, and Boolean—or true/false—expressions are named for him.

## Using the Logical Comparison Operators

Usually, you can compare only values that are of the same type; that is, you can compare numeric values to other numeric values and character values to other characters. You can ask every programming question by using only three types of comparisons (Boolean expressions). For any two values that are the same type, you can decide whether:

- The two values are equal.
- The first value is greater than the second value.
- The first value is less than the second value.

**tip**

Usually, character variables are not considered to be equal unless they are identical, even including the spacing and whether or not they appear in upper- or lowercase. For example, "black pen" is *not* equal to "blackpen", "BLACK PEN", or "Black Pen".

**tip**

Some programming languages allow you to compare a character to a number. If this is the case, the character's numeric code value is used in the comparison. For example, most microcomputers use the ASCII coding system in which an uppercase "A" is represented numerically as a 65, an uppercase "B" is 66, and so on.

In any Boolean expression, the two values used can be either variables or constants. For example, the expression TOTAL = 100? compares a variable, TOTAL, to a constant, 100. Depending on TOTAL's value, the expression is true or false. In the expression TOTAL = PREVIOUS-TOTAL?, both values are variables, and the result is also true or false depending on the values stored in each of the two variables. Although it's legal to do this, you would never use the expressions 20 = 20? and 30 = 40?. Such expressions are considered **trivial** because each always results in the same value: true for the first expression and false for the second.

Each programming language supports its own set of **logical comparison operators**, or comparison symbols, that express these Boolean tests. For example, many languages use the equals sign (=) to express testing for equivalency, so BALDUE = 0? compares BALDUE to zero. COBOL programmers can use the equals sign, but they also can spell out the expression as in BALDUE equal to 0?. RPG programmers can write BALDUE EQ 0. C, C++, and Java programmers use two equals signs to test for equivalency, so they write BALDUE == 0? to compare the two values.

**tip**

Some languages use two equals signs for comparisons to avoid confusion with assignment statements like BALDUE = 0. In C or Java this statement only assigns the value 0 to BALDUE; it does not compare BALDUE to zero.

**tip**

Whenever you use a comparison operator, you must provide a value on each side of the operator. Comparison operators are sometimes called *binary operators* because of this requirement.

Most languages allow you to use the algebraic signs for greater than (>) and less than (<) to make the corresponding comparisons. Additionally, COBOL allows you to spell out the comparisons in expressions like DAYS-PAST-DUE is greater than 30 or WEIGHT is less than 200, and RPG allows you to abbreviate greater than and less than in expressions like AGE GT 21 or SIZE LT 6. When you create a flowchart or pseudocode, you can use any form of notation you want. It's simplest to use the symbols > and < if you are comfortable with their meaning.

In addition to the three basic comparisons you can make, most programming languages provide three others. For any two values that are the same type, you can decide whether:

- The first is greater than or equal to the second.
- The first is less than or equal to the second.
- The two are not equal.

Most programming languages allow you to express "greater than or equal to" by typing a greater-than sign immediately followed by an equals sign (>=). When you are drawing a flowchart or writing pseudocode, you may prefer a greater-than sign with a line under it ($\geq$) because mathematicians use that symbol to mean "greater than or equal to." However, when you write a program, you type >= as two separate keys because there is no single key on the keyboard that expresses this concept. Similarly, "less than or equal to " is written with two symbols, < followed by =.

The operators >= and <= are always treated as a single unit; no spaces separate the two parts of the operator.

Although the symbols seem to mean the same thing, no programming language allows => or =< as comparison operators. The equals sign always appears second.

Any logical situation can be expressed using just three types of comparisons: equal, greater than, and less than. You never need the three additional comparisons (greater than or equal, less than or equal, or not equal) but using them often makes decisions more convenient. For example, assume you need to issue a 10 percent discount to any customer whose age is 65 or greater and charge full price to other customers. You can use the greater-than-or-equal-to symbol to write the logic as follows:

```
if AGE >= 65 then
      DISCOUNT = .10
else
      DISCOUNT = 0
```

As an alternative, if you want to use only the three basic comparisons (=, >, and <) you can express the same logic by writing:

```
if AGE < 65 then
      DISCOUNT = 0
else
      DISCOUNT = .10
```

In any decision for which A >= B is true, then A < B is false. Conversely, if A >= B is false, then A < B is true. By rephrasing the question and swapping the actions taken based on the outcome, you can make the same decision in multiple ways. It is often clearest for you to ask a question so the positive or true outcome results in the unusual action. When your company policy is to "provide a discount for those who are 65 and older," the phrase `greater than or equal to` comes to mind, so it is the most natural to use. Conversely, if your policy is to "provide no discount for those under 65," then it is more natural to use the `less than` syntax. Either way, the same individuals receive a discount.

Comparing two amounts to decide if they are *not* equal to each other is the most confusing of all the comparisons. Using "not equal to" in decisions involves thinking in double negatives and makes you prone to including logical errors in your programs. For example, consider the flowchart segment in Figure 5-5.

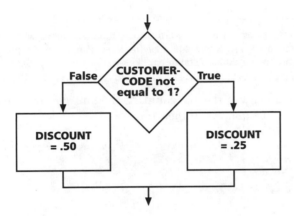

**Figure 5-5:** Using a negative comparison

In Figure 5-5, if the value of CUSTOMER-CODE *is* equal to 1, the logical flow follows the `false` branch of the selection. If the CUSTOMER-CODE not equal to 1 is true, the DISCOUNT is .25; if the CUSTOMER-CODE not equal to 1 is not true, it means the CUSTOMER-CODE *is* 1, and the DISCOUNT is .50. Even using the phrase "CUSTOMER-CODE not equal to 1 is not true" is awkward.

Figure 5-6 shows the same decision, this time asked in the positive. It is much clearer to read `if CUSTOMER-CODE` *is* `1 then DISCOUNT = .25` than it is to try to determine what CUSTOMER-CODE is *not*.

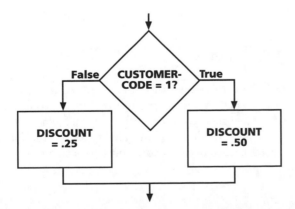

**Figure 5-6:** Using the positive equivalent of the negative comparison in Figure 5-5

Besides being awkward to use, the not equal to comparison operator is the one most likely to be different in the various programming languages you may use. COBOL allows you to write "not equal to"; Pascal uses a less-than sign followed immediately by a greater-than sign (<>); C, C++, and Java use an exclamation point followed by an equals sign (!=). In a flowchart or in pseudocode, you can use the symbol that mathematicians use to mean "not equals," an equals sign with a slash through it (≠). When you program, you will not be able to use this symbol because there is no single key on the keyboard that produces it.

••••••••••••••••••••••••••••••••••••••••••••••••••••••••••••••••••••••••••••

**Although not comparisons can be awkward to use, there are times when your meaning is clearest if you use one. For example, the mainline logic of most of the programs you have worked with in this book includes a statement like** while *not* EOF, perform MAIN-LOOP.

••••••••••••••••••••••••••••••••••••••••••••••••••••••••••••••••••••••••••••

Figure 5-7 summarizes the six comparisons and contrasts trivial (both true and false) and typical examples of their use.

| Comparison | Trivial True Example | Trivial False Example | Typical Example |
|---|---|---|---|
| Equal to | 7 = 7? | 7 = 4? | AMT-ORDERED = 12? |
| Greater than | 12 > 3? | 4 > 9? | HOURS > 40? |
| Less than | 1 < 8? | 13 < 10? | HOURLY-WAGE < 5.65? |
| Greater than or equal to | 5 >= 5? | 3 >= 9? | AGE >= 65? |
| Less than or equal to | 4 <= 4? | 8 <= 2? | OVERDUE <= 60? |
| Not equal to | 16 <> 3? | 18 <> 18? | BALANCE <> 0? |

**Figure 5-7:** Logical comparisons

## Understanding AND Logic

Very often you need more than one selection structure to determine whether an action should take place. For example, suppose that your employer wants a report that lists workers who have registered for both insurance plans offered by the company: the medical plan and the dental plan. This type of situation is known as an **AND** situation because the employee's record must pass two tests—participate in the medical plan *and* participate in the dental plan—before you write that employee's information on the report. An AND situation requires a **nested decision** or a **nested if;** that is, a decision "inside of" another decision. The logic looks like Figure 5-8.

▶ **tip**

You first learned about nesting structures in Chapter 2.

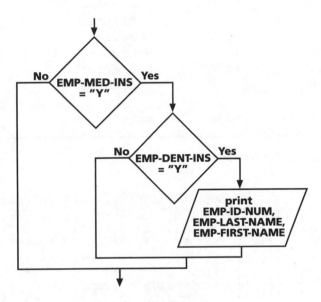

**Figure 5-8:** Flowchart of an AND decision

The AND decision shown in Figure 5-8 is part of a much larger program. To help you develop this program, your employer provides you with the employee data file description shown in Figure 5-9, and you learn that the medical and dental insurance fields contain a single character, "Y" or "N", indicating each employee's participation status. With your employer's approval, you develop the print chart shown in Figure 5-10.

```
EMPLOYEE FILE DESCRIPTION

File Name: Empfile

FIELD DESCRIPTION   POSITIONS   DATA TYPE   DECIMALS   EXAMPLE

ID number           1-4         Numeric     0          1234
Last name           5-20        Character              Kroening
First name          21-35       Character              Ginny
Department          36          Numeric     0          3
Hourly rate         37-40       Numeric     2          17.50
Medical plan        41          Character              Y
Dental plan         42          Character              N
Number of
 dependents         43-44       Numeric     2          0
```

**Figure 5-9:** Employee file description

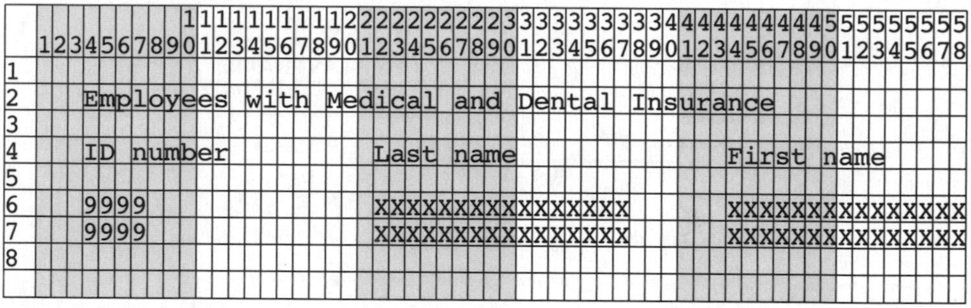

**Figure 5-10:** Print chart for employees participating in both insurance plans

The mainline logic and HOUSEKEEPING routines for this program are diagrammed in Figures 5-11 and 5-12.

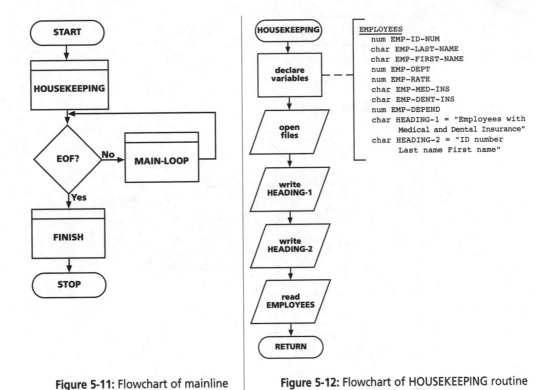

**Figure 5-11:** Flowchart of mainline
logic for medical and
dental participant report

**Figure 5-12:** Flowchart of HOUSEKEEPING routine
for medical and dental
participant report

At the end of the HOUSEKEEPING routine, the first employee record is read into computer memory. Assuming that the EOF condition is not yet met, the logical flow proceeds to the MAIN-LOOP. Within the MAIN-LOOP of this program, you ask the questions that determine whether or not the current employee's record will print; if so, then you print the employee's data. Whether or not the employee meets the medical and dental insurance requirements for printing, the last thing you do in the MAIN-LOOP is read the next input record. Figure 5-13 shows the MAIN-LOOP.

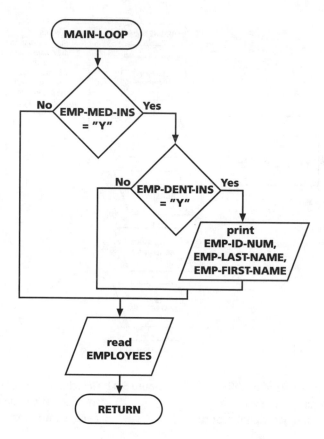

**Figure 5-13:** MAIN-LOOP of program that lists medical and dental participants

The MAIN-LOOP works like this: If the employee has medical insurance, *then* and *only then* test to see if the employee has dental insurance. If so, *then* and *only then* print the employee's data. The dental insurance question is nested entirely within half of the medical insurance question structure. If an employee does not carry medical insurance, there is no need to ask about the dental insurance; the employee is already disqualified from the report. Pseudocode for the entire program is shown in Figure 5-14. Notice how the second (dental insurance) decision within the MAIN-LOOP is indented within the first (medical insurance) decision. This technique shows the second question is asked only when the result of the first comparison is true.

```
START                             EMPLOYEES
    perform HOUSEKEEPING              num EMP-ID-NUM
    while not EOF                     char EMP-LAST-NAME
            perform MAIN-LOOP         char EMP-FIRST-NAME
    perform FINISH                    num EMP-DEPT
END                                   num EMP-RATE
HOUSEKEEPING                          char EMP-MED-INS
    declare variables — — —           char EMP-DENT-INS
    open files                        num EMP-DEPEND
    write HEADING-1                   char HEADING-1 = "Employees with Medical
    write HEADING-2                       and Dental Insurance"
    read EMPLOYEES                    char HEADING-2 = "ID number  Last name
RETURN                                    First name"
MAIN-LOOP
    if EMP-MED-INS = "Y" then
        if EMP-DENT-INS = "Y" then
            print EMP-ID-NUM, EMP-LAST-NAME, EMP-FIRST-NAME
    read EMPLOYEES
RETURN
FINISH
    close files
RETURN
```

**Figure 5-14:** Pseudocode of medical and dental participants report program

# Writing AND Decisions for Efficiency

When you nest decisions because the resulting action requires that two conditions be true, you must decide which of the two decisions to make first. Logically, either selection in an AND situation can come first. However, when there are two selections, you often can improve your program's performance by making an appropriate choice as to which selection to make first.

For example, the nested decision structure in the MAIN-LOOP logic of the program that produces a report of those employees who participate in both the medical and dental insurance plans is written as in Figure 5-15.

```
if EMP-MED-INS = "Y" then
    if EMP-DENT-INS = "Y" then
        print EMP-ID-NUM, EMP-LAST-NAME, EMP-FIRST-NAME
```

**Figure 5-15:** Finding medical and dental plan participants

Alternatively, you can write the decision as in Figure 5-16.

```
if EMP-DENT-INS = "Y" then
    if EMP-MED-INS = "Y" then
        print EMP-ID-NUM, EMP-LAST-NAME, EMP-FIRST-NAME
```

**Figure 5-16:** Finding dental and medical plan participants

Examine the decision statements in the preceding figures. If you want to print employees who participate in the medical AND dental plans, you can ask about the medical plan first, eliminate those employees who do not participate, and ask about the dental plan only for those employees who "pass" the medical insurance test. Or you could ask about the dental plan first, eliminate those who do not participate, and ask about the medical plan only for those employees who "pass" the dental insurance test. Either way, the final list contains only those employees who have both kinds of insurance.

Does it make a difference which question is asked first? As far as the output goes, no. Either way, the same employee names appear on the report—those with both types of insurance. As far as program efficiency goes, however, it *might* make a difference which question is asked first.

Assume you know that out of 1,000 employees in your company, about 90 percent, or 900, participate in the medical insurance plan. Assume you also know that out of 1,000 employees, only about half, or 500, participate in the dental plan.

Using the logic in Figure 5-15, the program asks the first question, EMP-MED-INS = "Y"?, 1,000 times. For approximately 90 percent of the employees, or 900 of the records, the answer is true, thus the EMP-MED-INS field contains the character "Y". So 100 employees are eliminated, and 900 proceed to the next question about dental insurance. Only about half the employees participate in the dental plan, so 450 out of the 900 will appear on the printed report.

Using the alternative logic in Figure 5-16, the program asks the first question, EMP-DENT-INS = "Y"?, 1,000 times. Because only about half of the company's employees participate, only 500 will "pass" this test and proceed to the medical insurance question. Then about 90 percent of the 500, or 450 employees, will appear on the report. Whether you use the logic in Figure 5-15 or 5-16, the same 450 employees who have both kinds of insurance appear on the report.

The difference lies in the fact that using the logic in Figure 5-15, the program must ask 1,900 questions to produce the report—the medical insurance question tests all 1,000 employee records, and 900 continue to the dental insurance question. If you use the logic in Figure 5-16 to produce the report, the program asks only 1,500 questions—all 1,000 records are tested for dental insurance, but only 500 proceed to the medical insurance question. By asking about the dental insurance first, you "save" 400 decisions.

The 400-question difference between the first set of decisions and the second really will not take much time on most computers. But it will take some time, and if there are hundreds of thousands of employees instead of only 1,000, or if many such decisions have to be made within a program, performance time can be significantly improved by asking questions in the proper order.

In many AND situations, the programmer has no idea which of two events is most likely to occur; in that case, you may legitimately ask either question first. Also, even though you know the probability of each of two conditions, the two events may not be mutually exclusive; that is one may depend on the other. For example, if employees with dental insurance are significantly more likely to carry medical insurance than those who don't carry dental insurance, the order in which to ask the question may matter less or not matter at all. However, if you do know the probabilities of the conditions, or can make a reasonable guess, the general rule is: *In an AND situation, ask the question that is* least likely *first*. This eliminates as many records as possible from having to go through the second decision and speeds up processing time.

## Combining Decisions in an AND Situation

Most programming languages allow you to ask two or more questions in a single comparison by using a **logical AND operator.** For example, if you want to select employees who carry both medical and dental insurance, you can use nested ifs, or you can include both decisions in a single statement by writing EMP-DENT-INS = "Y" and EMP-MED-INS = "Y". If the programming language you use allows this construct, you still must realize that the question you place first is the question that will be asked first, and cases that are eliminated based on the first question will not proceed to the second question. The computer can ask only one question at a time; even though you draw the flowchart segment in Figure 5-17, the computer will execute the logic in the flowchart in Figure 5-18.

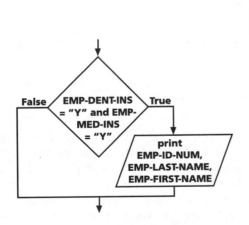

**Figure 5-17:** Flowchart of AND decision using an AND operator

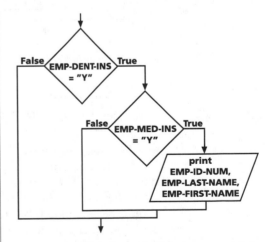

**Figure 5-18:** Computer logic of program containing an AND decision using an AND operator

# Avoiding Common Errors in an AND Situation

When you must satisfy two or more criteria to initiate an event in a program, you must make sure that the second decision is made entirely within the first decision. For example, if a program's objective is to print those employees who carry both medical and dental insurance, then the program segment shown in Figure 5-19 contains three different types of logical errors.

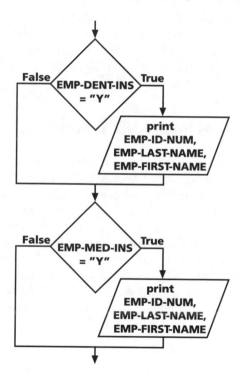

**Figure 5-19**: Incorrect logic to produce report with medical and dental participants

C, C++, and Java use the symbol && to represent the logical AND.

The diagram shows that the program asks the dental insurance question first. However, if an employee participates in the dental program, the employee prints immediately. The employee should not print, because the employee might not have the medical insurance. In addition, an employee with no dental insurance should be eliminated, but the employee's record proceeds to the medical insurance question, where it may print. Additionally, any employee who has both medical and dental insurance will appear twice on this report, having passed each test successfully. The logic shown in Figure 5-19 is *not* correct for this problem.

Beginning programmers often make another type of error when they must make two comparisons on the same field and use a logical AND operator. For example, suppose you want to list employees who make between 10.00 and 11.99 dollars per hour inclusive. You want to select employees whose EMP-RATE is greater than or equal to 10.00 AND whose EMP-RATE is less than 12.00; therefore you need to make two comparisons on the same field. Without the logical AND operator, the comparison is

```
if EMP-RATE >= 10.00 then
     if EMP-RATE < 12.00 then
          print EMP-ID-NUM, EMP-LAST-NAME, EMP-FIRST-NAME
```

**tip**

To check for EMP-RATE values that are 10.00 and greater you can use EMP-RATE > 9.99 as well as EMP-RATE >= 10.00. To check for EMP-RATE values under 12.00, you can write EMP-RATE <= 11.99 as well as EMP-RATE < 12.00.

The correct way to make this comparison with the AND operator is as follows:

```
if EMP-RATE >= 10.00 AND EMP-RATE < 12.00 then
     print EMP-ID-NUM, EMP-LAST-NAME, EMP-FIRST-NAME
```

You substitute the AND operator for the then if. However, some programmers try to make the comparison as follows:

```
if EMP-RATE >= 10.00 AND < 12.00 then
     print EMP-ID-NUM, EMP-LAST-NAME, EMP-FIRST-NAME
```

In most languages, the phrase EMP-RATE >= 10.00 AND < 12.00 is incorrect. When you use a logical AND, you must use a complete Boolean expression on both sides of the AND. The expression to the right of the AND, < 12.00, is not a complete Boolean expression; you must indicate *what* is being compared to 12.00.

**tip**

In COBOL and RPG you can write the equivalent of EMP-RATE >= 10.00 AND < 12.00, and the EMP-RATE variable is implied for both comparisons. Still, it is clearer and preferable to use the two full expressions, EMP-RATE >= 10.00 AND EMP-RATE < 12.00.

# TERMS AND CONCEPTS

dual-alternative decision or selection, binary selection, if-then-else structure

single-alternative decision or selection, unary selection, if-then

Boolean expression

logical comparison operators

AND decision

nested decision, nested if

logical AND operator

# SUMMARY

- A dual-alternative or binary decision or selection has two possible mutually exclusive outcomes. It is also called an if-then-else structure.

- A single-alternative or unary decision or selection is one in which action is taken on only one outcome of the question. This form of the if-then-else structure is called simply an if-then.

- A Boolean expression is one that represents only one of two states—usually expressed as true or false. Every decision you make in a computer program's logic involves a Boolean expression.

- Usually, you can compare only values that are the same type; that is, numeric values compare to other numeric values, and character values compare to other character values.

- You can ask every programming question by using only three types of Boolean comparisons: equal, greater than, and less than.

- Each programming language supports its own set of logical operators, or logical symbols, that express Boolean comparisons.

- In addition to the three basic comparisons you can make, most programming languages provide three others: greater than or equal to, less than or equal to, and not equal.

- An AND situation occurs when two conditions must both be true before any action can be taken; the decisions must be nested.

- For efficiency, in an AND situation ask the question that is least likely first.

- Most programming languages allow you to ask two or more questions in a single comparison by using a logical AND operator. You must use a complete Boolean expression on each side of a logical AND operator.

# EXERCISES

1. Assume the following variables contain the values shown:

    NUMBER-RED = 100    NUMBER-BLUE = 200    NUMBER-GREEN = 300

    DESCRIP-RED = "Wagon"  DESCRIP-BLUE = "Sky"  DESCRIP-GREEN = "Grass"

    For each of the following Boolean expressions, decide whether the statement is true, false, or illegal?
    a. NUMBER-RED = NUMBER-BLUE
    b. NUMBER-BLUE > NUMBER-GREEN
    c. NUMBER-GREEN < NUMBER-RED
    d. NUMBER-BLUE = DESCRIP-BLUE
    e. NUMBER-GREEN = "Green"
    f. DESCRIP-RED = "Red"

    g. DESCRIP-BLUE = "BLUE"

    h. NUMBER-RED <= NUMBER-GREEN

    i. NUMBER-BLUE >= 200

    j. NUMBER-GREEN >= NUMBER-RED + NUMBER-BLUE

2. a. A candy company wants a list of all its best-selling items, including item number and name of candy. Best-selling items are those that sell over 2,000 pounds per month. Input records contain fields for the item number (three digits), the name of the candy (20 characters), the price per pound (four digits, two assumed decimal places), and the quantity in pounds sold last month (four digits, no decimals). Design the print chart, hierarchy chart, and flowchart.

   b. Write the pseudocode for the same problem.

   c. The candy company wants a list of all its high-priced best-selling items. Best-selling items are those that sell over 2,000 pounds per month. High-priced items are those that sell for $10 per pound or more. Design the print chart, hierarchy chart, and flowchart.

   d. Write the pseudocode for the same problem.

3. a. The Literary Honor Society needs a list of English majors who have a grade point average of 3.5 or higher. The student record file includes students' last names and first names (15 characters each), major (10 characters, for example "History" or "English"), and grade point average (two digits, one assumed decimal place). Design the print chart, hierarchy chart, and flowchart for this problem.

   b. Write the pseudocode for the same problem.

4. a. A telephone company charges 10 cents per minute for all calls that are over 20 minutes in length to an area code other than the customer's area code. All other calls are 13 cents per minute. The phone company has a file with one record for every call made in one day. (In other words, a single customer might have many such records on file.) Fields for each call include customer area code (three digits), customer phone number (seven digits), called area code (three digits), called number (seven digits) and call time in minutes (four digits). The company wants a report listing one detail line for each call including the customer area code and number, the called area code and number, the minutes, and the total charge. Design the print chart, hierarchy chart, and flowchart.

   b. Write the pseudocode for the same problem.

5. a. A nursery maintains a file of all plants in stock along with such data as price and characteristics. It is known that only 20 percent of the nursery stock does well in shade and 50 percent of the nursery stock does well in sandy soil. Create the print chart and the hierarchy chart and draw the flowchart that would perform the most efficient search for a plant for a shady, sandy yard.

   b. Write pseudocode for the same problem.

**After studying Section B,**
**you should be able to:**

- Understand OR logic
- Avoid common errors in an OR situation
- Write OR decisions for efficiency
- Combine decisions in an OR situation
- Use selections with ranges
- Avoid common range selection errors
- Use decision tables

# Advanced Selections: OR Logic and Decision Tables

## Understanding OR Logic

Sometimes you want to take action when one *or* the other of two conditions is true. This is called an **OR** situation because either one condition must be met *or* some other condition must be met in order for some event to take place.

For example, suppose your employer wants a list of all employees who participate in either the medical or the dental plan. Assuming you are using the same input file described in Figure 5-9, the mainline logic and HOUSE-KEEPING section for this program are identical to those used in the Figures 5-11 and 5-12. You need only to change the heading on the print chart (Figure 5-10) and change the HEADING-1 variable in Figure 5-12 from `HEADING-1 = "Employees with Medical and Dental Insurance"` to `HEADING-1 = "Employees with Medical or Dental Insurance"`. The substantial changes to the program occur in the MAIN-LOOP.

Figure 5-20 shows the possible logic for the MAIN-LOOP in this OR situation. As each record enters the MAIN-LOOP, you ask the question `EMP-MED-INS = "Y"?`. If the result is true, you print the employee data. Because the employee needs to participate in only one of the two insurance plans to be selected for printing, there is no need for further questioning. If the employee does not participate in the medical insurance plan, then and only then do you need to ask `EMP-DENT-INS = "Y"?`. If the employee does not have medical insurance, but does have dental, you want this employee to print on the report.

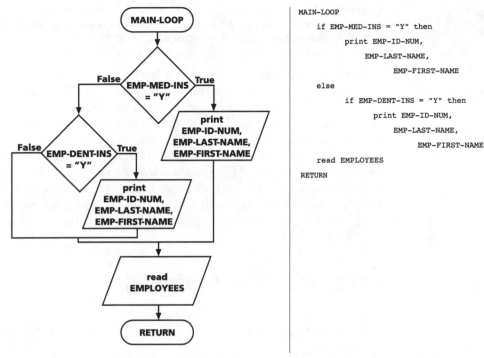

```
MAIN-LOOP
    if EMP-MED-INS = "Y" then
            print EMP-ID-NUM,
                EMP-LAST-NAME,
                    EMP-FIRST-NAME
        else
            if EMP-DENT-INS = "Y" then
                print EMP-ID-NUM,
                    EMP-LAST-NAME,
                        EMP-FIRST-NAME
        read EMPLOYEES
RETURN
```

**Figure 5-20:** Flowchart and pseudocode for MAIN-LOOP that prints employees who have medical or dental insurance

## Avoiding Common Errors in an OR Situation

You might have noticed that the statement `print EMP-ID-NUM, EMP-LAST-NAME, EMP-FIRST-NAME` appears twice in the flowchart and in the pseudocode shown in Figure 5-20. The temptation is to redraw the flowchart in Figure 5-20 to look like Figure 5-21. Logically, the flowchart in Figure 5-21 is correct in that the correct employees print. However, this flowchart is not allowed because it is not structured.

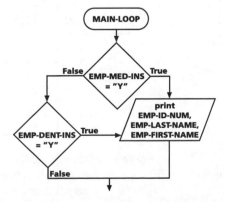

**Figure 5-21:** Incorrect flowchart for MAIN-LOOP

**tip**

If you do not see that Figure 5-21 is not structured, go back and review Chapter 2. In particular, review the example that begins at Figure 2-22.

An additional source of error that is particular to the OR situation stems from a problem with language and the way people use it too casually. When your boss needs a report of all the employees who carry medical or dental insurance, he or she is likely to say, "I need a report of all the people who have medical insurance and all the people who have dental insurance." The request contains the word "and," and the report contains people who have one type of insurance "and" people who have another. However, the records you want to print are those from employees who have medical insurance OR dental insurance OR both. The logical situation is an OR situation. It is up to you as a programmer to clarify what is being asked for and determine that often a request for A and B means a request for A or B or both.

## Writing OR Decisions for Efficiency

You can write a program that creates a report containing all employees who take either the medical or dental insurance by using the MAIN-LOOP in either Figure 5-22 or Figure 5-23.

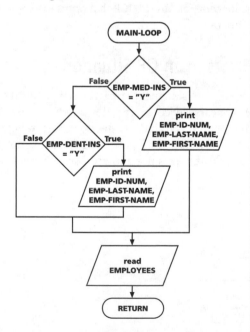

Figure 5-22: MAIN-LOOP to select employees with medical or dental insurance

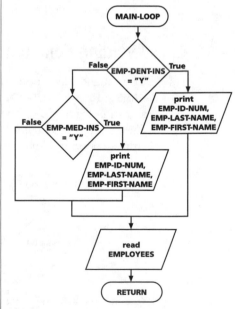

Figure 5-23: Alternate MAIN-LOOP to select employees with medical or dental insurance

You may have guessed that one of these selections is superior to the other if you have some background information about the relative likelihood of each of the conditions you are testing. For example, once again assume you know that out of 1,000 employees in your company, about 90 percent, or 900, participate in the medical insurance plan, and about half, or 500, participate in the dental plan.

When you use the logic shown in Figure 5-22 to select employees who participate in either insurance plan, you ask first about medical insurance. For 900 employees, the answer is `true`; you print these employee records. Only about 100 records continue to the next question about dental insurance, where about half, or 50, fulfill the requirements to print. In the end, you print about 950 employees.

If you use Figure 5-23, you ask `EMP-DENT-INS = "Y"`?. The result is `true` for 50 percent, or 500 employees, whose names then print. Five hundred employee records then progress to the medical insurance question, and the medical insurance question then results in 90 percent of them, or 450, printing.

Using either scenario, 950 employee records appear on the list, but the logic used in Figure 5-22 requires 1,100 decisions, while the logic used in Figure 5-23 requires 1,500 decisions. The general rule is: *In an OR situation ask the question that is most likely first.* Because a record qualifies for printing as soon as it passes one test, asking the most likely question first eliminates as many records as possible from having to go through the second decision. The time it takes to execute the program is decreased.

## Combining Decisions in an OR Situation

When you need to take action when either one or the other of two conditions is met, you can use two separate nested selection structures as in the previous examples. However, most programming languages allow you to ask two or more questions in a single comparison by using a **logical OR operator**—for example, `EMP-DENT-INS = "Y" or EMP-MED-INS = "Y"`. When you use the logical OR operator, only one of the listed conditions must be met for the resulting action to take place. If the programming language you use allows this construct, you still must realize that the question you place first is the question that will be asked first, and cases that you eliminate based on the first question will not proceed to the second question. The computer can ask only one question at a time; even though you draw the flowchart in Figure 5-24, the computer will execute the logic in the flowchart in Figure 5-25.

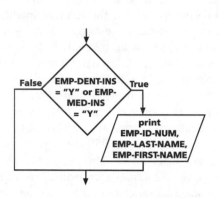

**Figure 5-24:** Flowchart of OR decision using an OR operator

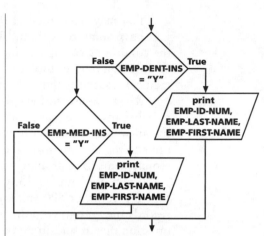

**Figure 5-25:** Computer logic of program containing an OR decision using an OR operator

**tip**

C, C++, and Java use the symbol || to represent the logical OR.

## Using Selections with Ranges

Business programs often need to make selections based on a variable falling within a range of values. For example, suppose you want to print a list of every employee along with his or her supervisor's name. An employee's supervisor is assigned based on the employee's department number as shown in Figure 5-26:

| DEPARTMENT NUMBER | SUPERVISOR |
|---|---|
| 1–3 | Dykeman |
| 4–7 | Erhardt |
| 8–9 | Jackson |

**Figure 5-26:** Supervisors by department

When you write the program that reads each employee's record, you could make nine decisions before printing the supervisor's name, such as EMP–DEPT = 1?, EMP–DEPT = 2?, and so on. However, it is more convenient to find the supervisor by using a range check.

To perform a **range check**, use either the lowest or highest value in each range of values you are using to make your selections. To find each employee's supervisor as listed in Figure 5-26, use either the values 1, 4, and 8, which represent the low ends of each supervisor's department range, or use the values 3, 7, and 9, which represent the high ends.

For example, the pseudocode representing the logic for choosing a supervisor name by using the high-end range values appears in Figure 5-27. You test the EMP-DEPT value for less than or equal to the high end of the lowest range group. If the comparison evaluates as true, you know the SUPERVISOR name. If not, you continue checking.

```
if EMP-DEPT <= 3 then
      SUPERVISOR = "Dykeman"
 else
      if EMP-DEPT <= 7 then
           SUPERVISOR = "Erhardt"
      else
           SUPERVISOR = "Jackson"
```

**Figure 5-27:** Using high-end values for a range check

● ● ● ● ● ● ● ● ● ● ● ● ● ● ● ● ● ● ● ● ● ● ● ● ● ● ● ● ● ● ● ● ● ● ● ● ● ● ● ● ● ● ● ● ● ● ● ● ● ● ● ● ● ● ● ● ● ● ● ● ● ● ● ● ● ● ● ● ● ● ●

**In Figure 5-27, notice how each `else` aligns vertically with its corresponding `if`.**

● ● ● ● ● ● ● ● ● ● ● ● ● ● ● ● ● ● ● ● ● ● ● ● ● ● ● ● ● ● ● ● ● ● ● ● ● ● ● ● ● ● ● ● ● ● ● ● ● ● ● ● ● ● ● ● ● ● ● ● ● ● ● ● ● ● ● ● ● ● ●

The flowchart for choosing a supervisor name using the reverse of this method, by seeking the low-end range values, appears in Figure 5-28. You compare EMP-DEPT to the low end of the highest range first; if the EMP-DEPT falls in the range, the SUPERVISOR is known; otherwise you check the next lower group.

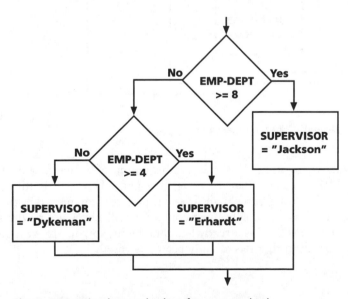

**Figure 5-28:** Using low-end values for a range check

# Common Errors Using Range Checks

Two common errors that occur when programmers perform range checks both involve doing more work than is necessary. Figure 5-29 shows a range check in which the programmer has asked one question too many. If you know that all EMP-DEPT values are positive numbers, then if the EMP-DEPT is not greater than or equal to eight, and it is also not greater than or equal to four, then by default it must be greater than or equal to one. Asking whether EMP-DEPT is greater than or equal to one is a waste of time; no employee record can ever travel the logical path on the far left.

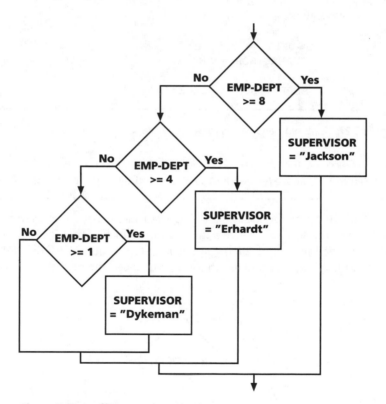

**Figure 5-29:** Inefficient range selection

Similarly, Figure 5-30 shows the beginning of an inefficient range selection. If EMP-DEPT is greater than or equal to eight, "Jackson" is the supervisor. If the EMP-DEPT is not greater than or equal to eight, the next question does not have to check for less than eight. The computer will never get to the second question unless the EMP-DEPT is already less than eight, so you are wasting computer time asking a question that has already been answered.

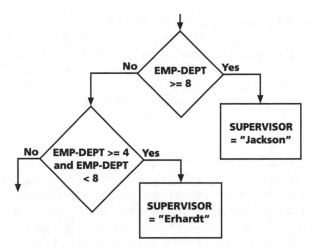

**Figure 5-30:** Partial example of inefficient range selection

## Using Decision Tables

Some programs require multiple decisions to produce the correct output. Managing all the possible outcomes of multiple decisions can be a difficult task, so programmers sometimes use a tool called a decision table to help organize the possible decision outcome combinations.

A **decision table** is a problem-analysis tool that consists of four parts:

- Conditions
- Possible combinations of Boolean values for the conditions
- Possible actions based on the conditions
- The actions that correspond to each Boolean value of each condition

For example, suppose your employer sends you a memo outlining a year-end bonus plan with rules as follows:

```
To: Programming staff

From: The boss

I need a report listing every employee and the
bonus I plan to give him or her. Everybody
gets at least $100. All the employees in
Department 2 get $200 unless they have more
than five dependents. Anybody with more than
five dependents gets $1,000.
```

You can use the mainline logic and HOUSEKEEPING routines from Figures 5-11 and 5-12 as long as you change the print chart so the report heading reads "Bonus Report" and the detail lines include an employee and his or her bonus amount. Before you draw the flowchart or write the pseudocode for the MAIN-LOOP, you can create a decision table to help you manage all the decisions. You can begin to create a decision table by listing all the possible conditions. They are:

- EMP-DEPEND > 5
- EMP-DEPT = 2

Next determine how many possible Boolean value combinations there are for the conditions. In this case, there are four possible combinations, shown in Figure 5-31. An employee can have over five dependents, work in Department 2, both, or neither. Since each condition has two outcomes and there are two conditions, there are 2 * 2, or four possibilities. Three conditions would produce eight possibilities (2 * 2 * 2); four conditions would produce 16 possible outcome combinations (2 * 2 * 2 * 2), and so on.

| Condition | Outcome | | | |
|---|---|---|---|---|
| EMP-DEPEND > 5 | T | T | F | F |
| EMP-DEPT = 2 | T | F | T | F |

**Figure 5-31:** Possible outcomes of bonus conditions

Next list the possible outcome actions. If you declare a numeric variable named BONUS by placing the statement num BONUS in your list of variables at the beginning of the program, then the possible outcomes can be expressed as:

BONUS = 1000
BONUS = 200
BONUS = 100

Finally, choose one required outcome for each possible combination of conditions, as shown in Figure 5-32. Place Xs in the BONUS = 1000 row each time EMP-DEPEND > 5 is true, no matter what other conditions exist, because the memo from the boss said, "Anybody with more than five dependents gets $1000."

| Condition | Outcome | | | |
|---|---|---|---|---|
| EMP-DEPEND > 5 | T | T | F | F |
| EMP-DEPT = 2 | T | F | T | F |
| BONUS = 1000 | X | X | | |
| BONUS = 200 | | | | |
| BONUS = 100 | | | | |

**Figure 5-32:** Decision table for bonuses, part 1 of 3

Next place an X in the BONUS = 200 for every column in which EMP-DEPT = 2 is true, unless the column already has an X. Remember, the memo stated, "All the employees in Department 2 get $200 unless they have more than five dependents." The only column that qualifies is the third column from the left. See Figure 5-33.

| Condition | Outcome | | | |
|---|---|---|---|---|
| EMP-DEPEND > 5 | T | T | F | F |
| EMP-DEPT = 2 | T | F | T | F |
| BONUS = 1000 | X | X | | |
| BONUS = 200 | | | X | |
| BONUS = 100 | | | | |

**Figure 5-33:** Decision table for bonuses, part 2 of 3

Finally place an X in the BONUS = 100 row for any remaining columns (only the last column in this case), because the memo said "Everybody gets at least $100." See Figure 5-34.

| Condition | Outcome | | | |
|---|---|---|---|---|
| EMP-DEPEND > 5 | T | T | F | F |
| EMP-DEPT = 2 | T | F | T | F |
| BONUS = 1000 | X | X | | |
| BONUS = 200 | | | X | |
| BONUS = 100 | | | | X |

**Figure 5-34:** Decision table for bonuses, part 3 of 3

The decision table is complete (count the Xs—there are four possible outcomes). Take a moment and confirm that each bonus is the appropriate value based on the boss's specifications. Now you can start to plan the logic.

If you choose to use a flowchart, you start by drawing the path to the outcome shown in the first column. This result (which occurs when EMP-DEPEND > 5 and EMP-DEPT = 2) is complete. Figure 5-35 illustrates.

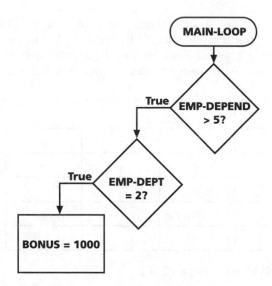

**Figure 5-35:** Flowchart for bonus problem, part 1 of 5

Next add the resulting action shown in the second column of the decision table, which occurs when EMP–DEPEND > 5 is true and EMP–DEPT = 2 is false. See Figure 5-36.

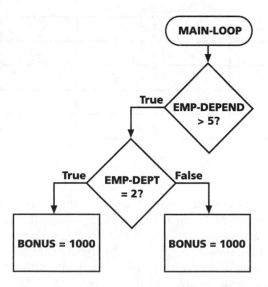

**Figure 5-36:** Flowchart for bonus problem, part 2 of 5

Add the resulting action shown in the third column of the decision table, which occurs when EMP–DEPEND > 5 is false and EMP–DEPT = 2 is true. See Figure 5-37.

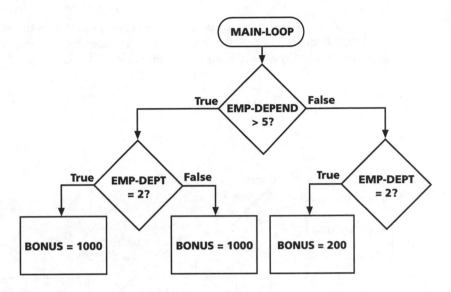

**Figure 5-37:** Flowchart for bonus problem, part 3 of 5

Finally, add the resulting action shown in the fourth column of the decision table, which occurs when both conditions are false, as in Figure 5-38.

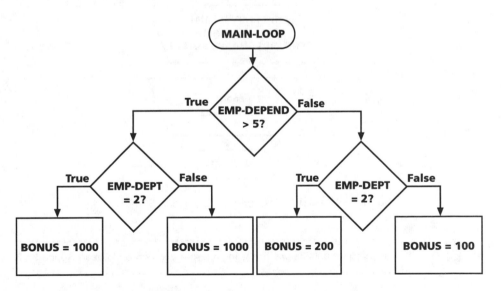

**Figure 5-38:** Flowchart for bonus problem, part 4 of 5

The flowchart segment now is complete and accurately assigns the correct bonus to each employee. Just tie up the ends, print an employee's name with his or her bonus amount, and read the next record. However, if you examine the two leftmost result boxes, you see that the assigned bonus is identical—$1,000 in both cases. Whether the EMP-DEPT equals 2 or not, the BONUS is the same, so there is no point in asking the EMP–DEPT = 2? question. Figure 5-39 simplifies the logic.

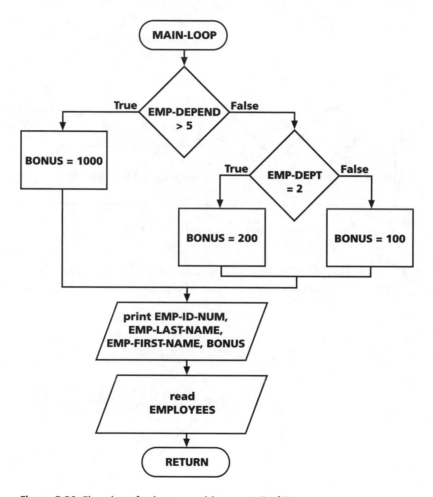

**Figure 5-39:** Flowchart for bonus problem, part 5 of 5

If you would like practice using a larger decision table, read Appendix B.

**TERMS AND CONCEPTS**

| | |
|---|---|
| OR logic | range check |
| logical OR operator | decision table |

 **SUMMARY**

- An OR situation exists when you want to take action when one or the other of two conditions is true.

- Commonly made errors using OR logic include lack of structure and not expressing the logical problem precisely in English.

- In an OR situation, ask the question that is most likely to result in selection first. That is, ask the question that eliminates the most subsequent questions.

- Most programming languages allow you to ask two or more questions in a single comparison by using a logical OR operator.

- Business programs often need to make selections based on a variable falling within a range of values. To perform a range check, use either the lowest or highest value in each range of values you are using to make your selections.

- Two common errors that occur when programmers perform range checks. Both involve including a logical path that no record ever follows, and checking for values that already have been eliminated.

- A decision table is a problem-analysis tool that consists of four parts: conditions, possible combinations of Boolean values for the conditions, possible actions based on the conditions, the actions that correspond to each Boolean value of each condition.

 **EXERCISES**

1.  You have declared variables for an insurance company program as follows:

| FIELD | POSITIONS | EXAMPLE |
|---|---|---|
| num POLICY-NUM | 1-6 | 223356 |
| char LAST-NAME | 7-20 | Falkenburg |
| num AGE | 21-23 | 25 |
| num DUE-MO | 24-25 | 06 |
| num DUE-DAY | 26-27 | 24 |
| num DUE-YEAR | 28-31 | 2004 |
| num ACCIDENTS | 32-34 | 2 |

Draw the selection structures that print the POLICY-NUM and LAST-NAME that satisfy the following requests for lists of policyholders:

a. over 35 years old
b. at least 21 years old
c. no more than 30 years old
d. due no later than March 15 any year
e. due up to and including January 1, 2002
f. due by April 27, 2005
g. due as early as December 1, 2001
h. fewer than 11 accidents
i. no more than 5 accidents
j. no accidents

2. a. Student files contain an ID number (four digits), last and first names (15 characters each), and major field of study (10 characters). Draw the print chart, create the hierarchy chart, and draw the flowchart for a program that lists ID numbers and names for all French or Spanish majors.

b. Write the pseudocode for the same problem.

3. a. A florist wants to send coupons to its best customers so it needs a list of names and addresses for customers who placed orders more than three times last year or spent more than $200 last year. The input file description follows:

File name: FLORIST-CUSTS

| FIELD DESCRIPTION | POSITIONS | TYPE | DECIMALS |
|---|---|---|---|
| Customer ID | 1–3 | Numeric | 0 |
| First name | 4–16 | Character | |
| Last name | 17–30 | Character | |
| Street address | 31–51 | Character | |
| Orders last year | 52–55 | Numeric | 0 |
| Amount spent last year | 56–62 | Numeric | 2 |

(Note: To save room, don't include city or state. Assume all the florist's best customers are in town.) Design the print chart, write the hierarchy chart, and draw the flowchart for this program.

b. Write the pseudocode for the same problem.

4. a. A carpenter needs a program that computes the price of any desk that a customer orders based on the following input fields: desk length in inches and width in inches (three digits each, no decimals), type of wood (20 characters), and number of drawers (two digits). The price is computed as follows:

■ The charge for all desks is a minimum $200.

■ If the surface (length * width) is over 750 square inches, add $50.

■ If the wood is "mahogany" add an additional $150; for "oak" add $125. No charge is added for "pine."

■ An additional $30 is charged for every drawer in the desk.

Design the print chart, write the hierarchy chart, and draw the flowchart for this program.

b. Write the pseudocode for the same problem.

**5.** a. A company is attempting to organize carpools to save energy. Ten percent of the company's employees live in Wonder Lake. Thirty percent of the employees live in Woodstock. Since these towns are both north of the company, the company wants a list of employees who live in either town so it can recommend that these employees drive in together. Flowchart the most efficient process for selecting these employees, assuming there is a field called CITY in each employee's personnel record.

b. Write pseudocode for the same process.

**6.** a. Create a decision table to help plan your next vacation. Possible outcomes for destination are Hawaii, Grandma's house, and nowhere (stay home). If your bank balance is one million dollars or more, you will go to Hawaii. If your bank account is less than one million dollars, you will stay home if your boss says you must work. If your boss says you can go, you will go to Hawaii unless your bank account is below $2,000. In that case, you will go to Grandma's house.

b. Assuming you have declared variables for DESTINATION, BOSS-DECISION, and BANK-BALANCE, flowchart the decision-making process from Exercise 6a.

c. Assuming you have declared variables for DESTINATION, BOSS-DECISION, and BANK-BALANCE, write pseudocode for the decision-making process from Exercise 6a.

**7.** a. A supervisor in a manufacturing company wishes to produce a report showing which employees have increased their production this year over last year so that she can issue them a certificate of commendation. She wishes to have a report with three columns: last name, first name, and either the word "UP" or blanks printed under the column heading PRODUCTION. "UP" gets printed when this year's production is a greater number than last year's production. Input exists as follows:

**PRODUCTION FILE DESCRIPTION**

**File name: PRODUCTN**

| FIELD DESCRIPTION | POSITIONS | DATA TYPE | DECIMALS |
|---|---|---|---|
| Last name | 1–20 | Character | |
| First name | 21–30 | Character | |
| Last year's production | 31–34 | Numeric | 0 |
| This year's production | 35–38 | Numeric | 0 |

Create the decision table for the bonus calculation; then create the print layout chart, hierarchy chart, and flowchart for this program.

b. Write the pseudocode for the same problem.

c. A supervisor in the same manufacturing company wishes to produce a report from the PRODUCTN input file showing bonuses she is planning to give based on this year's production. She wishes to have a report with three columns: last name, first name, and bonus. The bonuses will be distributed as follows:

If this year's production is:

■ 1,000 units or fewer, the bonus is $25

■ 1,001 to 3,000 units, the bonus is $50

■ 3,001 to 6,000 units, the bonus is $100

■ 6,001 units and up, the bonus is $200

Create the print layout chart, hierarchy chart, and either flowchart or pseudocode for this program.

d. Modify Exercise 6c to reflect these new facts, and have the program execute as efficiently as possible:

■ Bonuses will be given only to those whose production this year is higher than last year. This is true for approximately 30 percent of the employees.

■ 75 percent of employees produce over 6,000 units per year, 20 percent produce 3,001 to 6,000, and only 5 percent produce fewer than 1,001.

# Looping

**case** ▶ "What are you working on today?" you ask Lynn Greenbrier, your colleague at Solutions, Inc.

"I'm writing a program that produces ' Handle with care' stickers. The warehouse will stick one on the box of every fragile shipment that goes out," Lynn says.

"But we ship thousands of items a week. That could require a long program."

"Actually," Lynn replies, "it's a very short program. Repetitious actions are efficiently handled by using the power of a loop."

After studying Section A, you
should be able to:

■ Describe the advantages of looping

■ Use a while loop with a loop
control variable

■ Use a counter to control looping

■ Use a loop with a variable
sentinel value

■ Decrement a variable to control
a loop

# Using Loops

## The Advantages of Looping

If making decisions is what makes computers seem intelligent, it's looping that makes computer programming worthwhile. When you use a loop within a computer program, you can write one set of instructions that operates on multiple separate sets of data. Consider the following set of tasks required for each employee in a typical payroll program:

■ Determine regular pay

■ Determine overtime pay, if any

■ Determine federal withholding tax based on gross wages and number of dependents

■ Determine state tax based on gross wages, number of dependents, and state of residence

■ Determine insurance deduction based on insurance code

■ Determine Social Security based on gross

■ Subtract federal tax, state tax, Social Security, and insurance from gross

In reality, this list is too short—companies deduct stock option plans, charitable contributions, union dues, and other items from checks in addition to the items mentioned in this list. Sometimes they also pay bonuses and commissions. Sick days and vacation days are taken into account and handled appropriately. As you can see, payroll programs are complicated.

The advantage of having a computer is that all of the preceding instructions need to be written *only once*. Then the instructions can be repeated over and over again using a **loop,** the structure that repeats actions while some condition continues.

## Using a While Loop with a Loop Control Variable

Recall the loop or do-while structure that you learned about in Chapter 2. (See Figure 6-1). In Chapter 3 you learned that almost every program has a **main loop,** or basic set of instructions that are repeated for every record. The main loop is a typical loop—in it you write one set of instructions that executes repeatedly while records continue to be read from an input file. A few housekeeping tasks are performed at the start of most programs, and a few clean-up tasks are performed at the end. But most of the tasks of a program are located in a main loop; and these tasks repeat over and over for many (sometimes hundreds, thousands, or millions of) records.

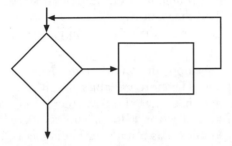

**Figure 6-1:** The while loop

In addition to this main loop, loops also appear within subroutines. They are used any time a task needs to be done several times and you don't want to write identical or similar instructions over and over. Suppose, for example, as part of a much larger program, you want to print a warning message on the computer screen when the user has made a potentially dangerous menu selection (say, "Delete all files"). To get the user's attention, you want to print the message four times. You can write this program segment as shown in Figure 6-2, but using a loop as shown in Figure 6-3 is much more efficient.

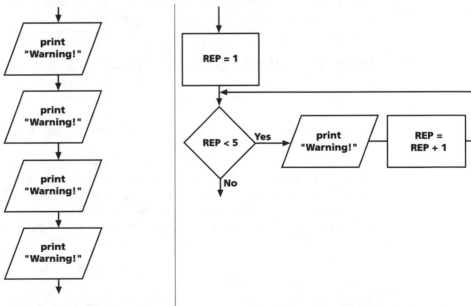

**Figure 6-2:** Printing four warning messages in sequence

**Figure 6-3:** Printing four warning messages in a loop

The flowchart segment in Figure 6-3 shows three steps that must occur in every loop:

1. You must initialize a variable that will control the loop. The variable in this case is named REP.
2. You must compare the variable to some value that stops the loop. In this case you compare REP to the value 5.
3. Within the loop, you must alter the variable. In this case, you alter REP by adding one to it.

On each pass through the loop, the value in the REP variable determines whether the loop will continue. Therefore variables like REP are known as **loop control variables**. Any variable that determines whether or not a loop will continue is a loop control variable. To stop a loop, you compare the loop control value to a **sentinel value** (also known as a limit, or ending value), in this case the value 5. The decision that controls every loop is always based on a Boolean comparison. You can use any of the six comparison operators that you learned about in Chapter 5 to control a loop.

**tip**    Just as with a selection, the Boolean comparison that controls a while loop must compare same-type values: numeric values are compared to other numeric values and character values to other character values.

The statements that execute within a loop are known as the **loop body**. The body of the loop may contain any number of statements, including subroutine calls, decisions, and other loops. Once your program enters the body of a structured loop, the entire loop body must execute. Your program can leave a structured loop only at the comparison that tests the loop control variable.

## Using a Counter to Control Looping

Suppose you own a factory and have decided to place a label on every product you manufacture. The label contains the words "Made for you personally by" followed by the first name of one of your employees. For one week's production, you need 100 personalized labels for each employee.

You already have an existing personnel file that can be used for input. This file has more information than you'll need for this program: an employee last name, first name, Social Security number, address, date hired, and salary. The important feature of the file is that it does contain each employee's name stored in a separate record. The input file description appears in Figure 6-4.

File name: EMPLYEES

| FIELD DESCRIPTION | POSITIONS | DATA TYPE | DECIMALS |
|---|---|---|---|
| Employee last name | 1–20 | Character | |
| Employee first name | 21–35 | Character | |
| Social Security number | 36–44 | Numeric | 0 |
| Address | 45–60 | Character | |
| Date hired | 61–68 | Numeric | 0 |
| Hourly salary | 69–72 | Numeric | 2 |

**Figure 6-4:** Employee data file description

In the mainline of this program, you perform three subroutines: a housekeeping subroutine (HOUSEKEEP), a main loop (MAIN-LOOP), and a finish routine (FINISH-UP). See Figure 6-5.

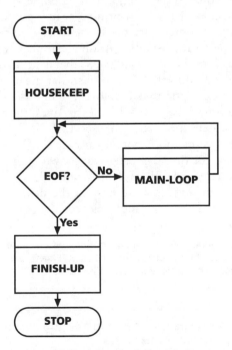

**Figure 6-5:** Mainline logic for label program

The first task for the label program involves naming the fields on the input record so that they can be referred to within the program. As a programmer, you can choose any variable names you like, for example: IN-LAST-NAME, IN-FIRST-NAME, IN-SSN, IN-ADDRESS, IN-DATE, and IN-SALARY.

In Chapter 4 you learned that starting all the field names in the input record with the same prefix such as IN is a common programming technique to help identify these fields in a large program and differentiate them from work areas and output areas that will have other names. Another benefit to using a prefix like IN is that some language compilers also produce a dictionary of variable names for you when you compile your program. These dictionaries show at which lines in the program each data name is referenced. If all your input field names start with the same prefix, they will be together alphabetically in the dictionary and perhaps easier to find and work with.

You also can set up a variable to hold the characters "Made for you personally by" and name it LABEL-LINE. You eventually will print this LABEL-LINE variable followed by the employee's first name (IN-FIRST-NAME).

You will need one more variable: a location called a counter. A **counter** is any numeric variable you use to count something; in this example you need a counter to keep track of how many labels have been printed at any point. Each time you read an employee record, the counter variable is set to zero. Then every time a label is printed, you add one to the counter. Adding one to a variable is called **incrementing** the variable. Before the next employee label is printed, the variable is checked to see if it has reached 100 yet. When it has, that means 100 labels have been printed and the job is done for that employee. While the counter remains below 100, you continue to print labels. As with all variables, the programmer can choose any name for a counter; this program uses LABEL-COUNTER. In this example, LABEL-COUNTER is the loop control variable.

The HOUSEKEEP routine for the label program, shown in Figure 6-6, includes a step to open the files: the employee file and the printer. Unlike a program that produces a report, this program has no headings, so the next and last task performed in HOUSEKEEP is to read the first input record.

Remember, you can give any name you like to subroutines within your programs. This program uses HOUSEKEEP for its first routine, but HOUSEKEEPING, START-UP, PREP, or any other name with the same general meaning could be used.

If you don't know why the first record is read in HOUSEKEEP, go back and review the concept of the priming read presented in Chapter 2.

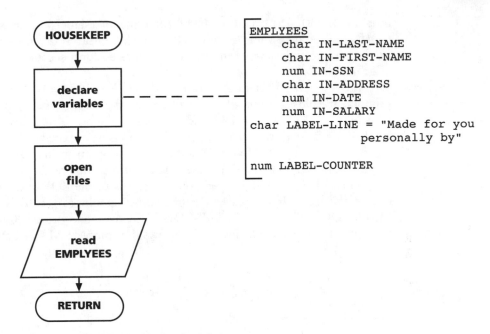

**Figure 6-6:** HOUSEKEEP routine for label program

When HOUSEKEEP is done, the logical flow returns to the EOF question in the mainline. If for some reason you attempt to read the first record at the end of HOUSEKEEP and there is no record, the answer to EOF? is Yes, and the MAIN-LOOP is never entered; instead, the logic of the program flows directly to FINISH-UP.

Usually, however, there are going to be employee records, and the MAIN-LOOP will be entered. When this happens, the first employee record is sitting in memory waiting to be processed. During the execution of MAIN-LOOP, 100 labels will be printed for one employee. The last thing that happens in MAIN-LOOP is that the next employee record is read. Control of the program then returns to the EOF question. If the new read process does not result in the EOF condition, control returns to the MAIN-LOOP where 100 more labels print for a new employee.

The MAIN-LOOP of this label program contains three parts:

- Set the LABEL-COUNTER to 0.
- Compare the LABEL-COUNTER to 100.
- While the LABEL-COUNTER is less than 100, print the LABEL-LINE and the IN-NAME, and add one to the LABEL-COUNTER.

When the first employee record enters MAIN-LOOP, the LABEL-COUNTER is set to zero. Comparing the LABEL-COUNTER to 100 results in a true condition, so the record enters the label-making loop. One label prints for the first employee, the LABEL-COUNTER increases by one, and the logical flow returns to the question LABEL–COUNTER < 100? After the first label is printed, the LABEL-COUNTER holds a value of only 1. It is nowhere near 100 yet, so the value of the Boolean expression is true, and the loop is entered for a second time, thus printing a second label.

After the second printing, LABEL-COUNTER holds a value of 2. After the third printing, it holds a value of 3. Finally, after the 100th label is printed, LABEL-COUNTER has a value of 100, and when the question LABEL–COUNTER < 100? is asked, the answer will finally be no. The loop is now exited.

Before leaving MAIN-LOOP after the program prints 100 labels for an employee, there is one final step: the next input record is read from the EMPLYEES file. When MAIN-LOOP is over, control returns to the EOF question in the main-line of the logic. If it is not EOF (if another employee record is present), enter MAIN-LOOP again, reset LABEL-COUNTER to 0, and print 100 new labels with the next employee's name. Figure 6-7 shows the complete MAIN-LOOP.

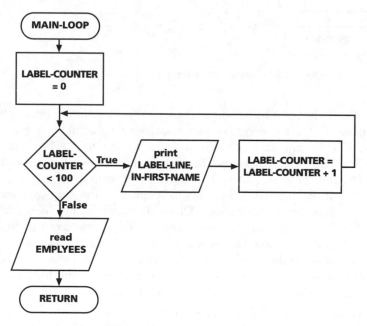

**Figure 6-7:** MAIN-LOOP for label program

At some point when you attempt to read a new record, you encounter the end of the file. Then the MAIN-LOOP is not entered again, and control passes to the FINISH-UP routine. In this program that simply means files will be closed. See Figure 6-8.

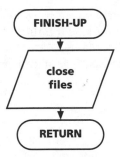

**Figure 6-8:** FINISH-UP routine for label program

## Looping with a Variable Sentinel Value

Sometimes you don't want to be forced to repeat every pass through a loop the same number of times. For example, instead of printing 100 labels for each employee, you might want to vary the number of labels based on how many items a worker actually produces. That way, high-achieving workers won't run out of labels and less productive workers won't have too many. Instead of printing the same number of labels for every employee, a more sophisticated program prints a different number of labels for each employee, depending on that employee's last week's production. For example, you might decide to print enough labels to cover 110 percent of each employee's production rate from the previous week; this ensures that the employee will have enough labels for the week even if his or her production level improves.

For example, assume that employee production data exists on an input file called EMPPROD in the format shown in Figure 6-9.

**File name: EMPPROD**

| FIELD DESCRIPTION | POSITIONS | DATA TYPE | DECIMALS |
|---|---|---|---|
| Last name | 1—20 | Character | |
| First name | 21—35 | Character | |
| Production last week | 36—38 | Numeric | 0 |

**Figure 6-9:** Employee production file description

A real-life production file would undoubtedly have more fields in each record, but these fields supply more than enough information to produce the labels. You need the first name to print on the label, and you need the production last week field in order to calculate the number of labels to print for each employee. The production last week field can contain any number from 0 through 999.

To write this program, you can make some minor modifications to the original label-making program. For example, the input file variables have changed. Notably, you must declare a variable for an IN-LAST-PRODUCTION field.

The major modification to the original label-making program is in the question that controls the label-producing loop. Instead of asking if `LABEL-COUNTER < 100`, you now can ask if `LABEL-COUNTER < IN-LAST-PRODUCTION * 1.1`. The sentinel or limit value can be a variable just as easily as it can be a constant. See Figure 6-10 for the pseudocode.

```
MAIN-LOOP
     LABEL-COUNTER = 0
     while LABEL-COUNTER < IN-LAST-PRODUCTION * 1.1
             print LABEL-LINE, IN-FIRST-NAME
             LABEL-COUNTER = LABEL-COUNTER + 1
     read EMPPROD
RETURN
```

**Figure 6-10:** Pseudocode for label-making MAIN-LOOP

The statement `IN-LAST-PRODUCTION * 1.1` **increases IN-LAST-PRODUCTION by 10 percent. Alternatively, you can perform the calculation as** `IN-LAST-PRODUCTION + .10 * IN-LAST-PRODUCTION`**. The mathematical result is the same.**

## Looping by Decrementing

Rather than increasing a loop control valuable until it passes some sentinel value, sometimes it is more convenient to reduce a loop control variable on every cycle through a loop. For example, assume you want to print enough labels for every worker to just match the IN-LAST-PRODUCTION field. As an alternative to setting a LABEL-COUNTER variable to 0 and increasing it after each label prints, you can simply reduce the IN-LAST-PRODUCTION value every time a label prints, and continue until you have counted down to zero. Decreasing a variable by one is called **decrementing** the variable.

For example, if you write the following, you produce enough labels to equal IN-LAST-PRODUCTION:

```
while IN-LAST-PRODUCTION > 0
        print LABEL-LINE, IN-FIRST-NAME
        IN-LAST-PRODUCTION = IN-LAST-PRODUCTION - 1
```

When you decrement, you can avoid declaring a special variable for the LABEL-COUNTER. You use the IN-LAST-PRODUCTION variable to keep track of the labels; while IN-LAST-PRODUCTION remains above zero, there are more labels to print. However, you can't use this method if you need the value of IN-LAST-PRODUCTION for this record later in the loop. By decrementing the variable, you are changing its value on every cycle through the loop; when you have finished, the original value in IN-LAST-PRODUCTION has been lost.

 **tip**

Do not think the value of IN-LAST-PRODUCTION is gone forever when you decrement it. It still exists in the data file. It is the main memory location called IN-LAST-PRODUCTION that is being reduced.

 # TERMS AND CONCEPTS

| | |
|---|---|
| loop | loop body |
| main loop | counter |
| loop control variable | incrementing |
| sentinel, limit, or ending value | decrementing |

 # SUMMARY

- Looping makes computer programming worthwhile. A loop is a structure that repeats actions as long as some condition continues.

- Most of the tasks of a program are repeated over and over for many records.

- In every loop you must initialize a variable that will control the loop, compare the variable to some value that stops the loop, and alter the variable within the loop.

- Any variable that determines whether or not a loop will continue is a loop control variable.

- To stop a loop, you compare the loop control value to a sentinel, limit, or ending value.

- The decision that controls every loop is always based on a Boolean comparison.

- The statements that execute within a loop are known as the body of the loop.

- Once your program enters the body of a structured loop, the entire loop body must execute.

- A counter is any numeric variable you use to count something, usually by adding one to it on every pass through a loop.

- The sentinel or limit value for a loop can be a variable as well as a constant.
- Two methods of controlling a loop involve incrementing or decrementing a loop control variable.

 # E X E R C I S E S

1. Write pseudocode for the label-making program that is flowcharted in Figures 6-5 through 6-8.

2. Draw a flowchart for the MAIN-LOOP routine for which there is pseudocode in Figure 6-10.

3. a. Design the logic for a program that would print out every number from 1 through 10 along with its square and its cube. Design the print layout chart and create the flowchart for this program.

   b. Write pseudocode for the problem in Exercise 3a.

4. a. Design a program that reads credit card account records and prints payoff schedules for customers. Input records contain an account number, customer name, and balance due. For each customer, print the account number and name; then print the customer's projected balance each month for the next ten months, assuming the customer makes no new purchases and pays off the balance at a rate of 10 percent of the bill per month. Design the print chart, hierarchy chart, and flowchart for this program.

   b. Write pseudocode for the problem in Exercise 4a.

**After studying Section B, you should be able to:**

- Improve loop performance
- Use a for loop
- Use a do until loop
- Nest loops
- Accumulate totals

# More Loop Techniques

## Improving Loop Performance

When you run a computer program that uses the loop in Figure 6-10, hundreds or thousands of employee records may pass through the MAIN-LOOP. If there are 100 employee records, then LABEL-COUNTER is set to zero exactly 100 times; it must be reset to zero once for each employee in order to count correctly each employee's labels.

If the average employee produces 100 items during a week, then the loop within the MAIN-LOOP, the one controlled by the statement `while LABEL-COUNTER < IN-LAST-PRODUCTION * 1.1`, executes 11,000 times—110 times each for 100 employees. Again, this number of repetitions is necessary in order to print the correct number of labels.

The repetition that is *not* necessary is the 11,000 separate multiplication statements that execute. When the statement `while LABEL-COUNTER < IN-LAST-PRODUCTION * 1.1` executes an average of 110 times for each employee, the multiplication of IN-LAST-PRODUCTION by 1.1 occurs 110 separate times for each employee. Performing the same calculation that results in the same mathematical answer 110 times in a row is inefficient. Instead, you can perform the multiplication just once for each employee and use the result 110 times.

Examine the pseudocode in Figure 6-11. The figure shows that you can remove the multiplication from the loop, computing the value that holds the number of labels one time for each employee record. You can use a new variable, such as LABEL-LIMIT, remembering to declare it along with your other variables in the HOUSEKEEP module of the program. Then, for each record, set the LABEL-COUNTER to zero one time and calculate LABEL-LIMIT one time. The while loop now executes while LABEL-COUNTER is less than the already calculated LABEL-LIMIT. You still must recalculate LABEL-LIMIT once for each record, but not once for each label, so you have improved the program's efficiency.

```
MAIN-LOOP
     LABEL-COUNTER = 0
     LABEL-LIMIT = IN-LAST-PRODUCTION * 1.1
     while LABEL-COUNTER < LABEL-LIMIT
              print LABEL-LINE, IN-FIRST-NAME
              LABEL-COUNTER = LABEL-COUNTER + 1
     read EMPPROD
RETURN
```

**Figure 6-11:** Improved MAIN-LOOP for label-making program

The modules illustrated in Figures 6-10 and 6-11 do the same thing: print enough labels for every employee to cover 110 percent of production. As you become more proficient at programming, you will recognize many opportunities to perform the same tasks in alternative, more elegant, and more efficient ways.

## Using a For Loop

The label-making programs discussed in this chapter each contain two loops. For example, Figures 6-12 and 6-13 show the mainline loop and the MAIN-LOOP loop for the program that produces 100 labels for each employee.

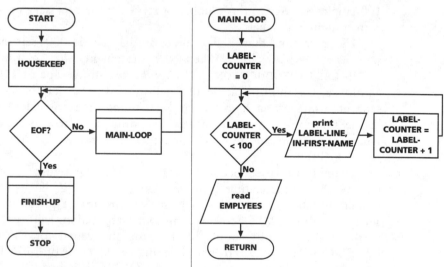

**Figure 6-12:** Mainline logic for label-making program

**Figure 6-13:** MAIN-LOOP logic for label-making program

Entry to the MAIN-LOOP in the mainline logic is controlled by the EOF decision. Within the MAIN-LOOP, label production is controlled by the LABEL-COUNTER. When you execute the mainline loop, you cannot predict how many times the MAIN-LOOP will execute. Depending on the size of the input file, any number of records may be processed; while the program runs you don't know what the total number of records will be. Until you attempt to read a record and encounter the end of the file, you don't know if more records are going to become available. Because you can't determine ahead of time how many records there may be, the mainline loop in the label-making program is called an **indeterminate** or **indefinite loop**.

With some loops, you know exactly how long they will run. If every employee needs 100 printed labels, then the loop within the MAIN-LOOP routine executes exactly 100 times for each employee. This kind of loop, in which you definitely know the repetition factor, is a **definite loop**.

Every high-level computer programming language contains a **while statement** that you can use to code any loop, including indefinite loops (like the mainline loop) and definite loops (like the label-printing loop). You can write the statements like the following:

```
while not EOF perform MAIN-LOOP
```

and

```
while LABEL-COUNTER < 100
      write LABEL-LINE, IN-FIRST-NAME
      add 1 to LABEL-COUNTER
```

In addition to the while statement, most computer languages also support a for statement. You can use the **for statement** or **for loop** with definite loops when you know how many times a loop will repeat. The for statement provides you with three actions in one compact statement. The for statement uses a loop control variable that it automatically:

- initializes
- evaluates
- increments

The for statement usually takes the form:

```
for INITIAL-VALUE to FINAL-VALUE
      do something
```

For example, to print 100 labels, you can write:

```
for LABEL-COUNTER = 0 to 99
      print LABEL-LINE, IN-FIRST-NAME
```

This for statement accomplishes several tasks at once in a compact form:

- The for statement initializes the LABEL-COUNTER to 0.
- The for statement checks the LABEL-COUNTER against the limit value 99 and makes sure that the LABEL-COUNTER is less than or equal to that value.

- If the evaluation is true, the for statement body that prints the label executes.
- After the for statement body executes, the LABEL-COUNTER increases by one, and the comparison to the limit value is made again.

You never are required to use a for statement; the label loop executes correctly using a while statement with LABEL-COUNTER as a loop control varariable. However, when a loop is based on a loop control variable progressing from a known starting value to a known ending value in equal increments, the for loop presents you with a convenient shorthand.

Neither the starting nor the ending value for the loop control variable needs to be known by the programmer; it just must be known by the program. For example, you don't know what a worker's IN-LAST-PRODUCTION value is, but when you tell the program to read a record, the program knows. To do so, you can write a for loop that begins `for LABEL-COUNTER = 1 to IN-LAST-PRODUCTION`.

In several languages, you can provide a for loop with a step value when you want each pass through the loop to change the loop control variable by a value other than one.

## Using the Do Until Loop

When you use either a while or a for loop, the body of the loop may never execute. For example, in the mainline logic in Figure 6-5, the last action in the HOUSEKEEP routine is to read an input record. If the input file contains no records, the result of the EOF decision is true, and the program executes the FINISH-UP routine without ever entering the MAIN-LOOP.

Similarly, when you produce labels while LABEL-COUNTER < IN-LAST-PRODUCTION, the value of IN-LAST-PRODUCTION might be zero, and the label-producing body of the loop might never execute. With a while loop, you evaluate the loop control variable prior to executing the loop body, and the evaluation might indicate that you can't enter the loop.

When you want to ensure that a loop's body executes at least one time, you can use a **do until loop**. In a do until loop, the loop control variable is evaluated after the loop body executes. Therefore, the body always executes at least one time.

You first learned about the do until loop in Chapter 2. Review Chapter 2 to reinforce your understanding of the differences between a while loop and a do until loop.

For example, suppose you want to produce one label for each employee to wear on his or her shirt before you produce enough labels to just cover production. You can write the do until loop that appears in Figure 6-14.

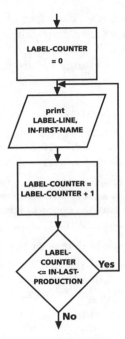

Figure 6-14: Do until loop for producing one extra label

Of course, you could achieve the same results by printing one label, then entering a while loop as in Figure 6-15.

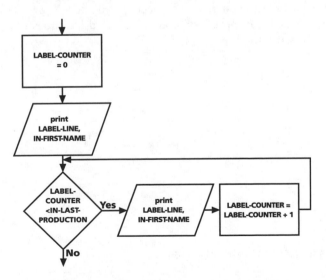

Figure 6-15: Printing one label, then printing enough to cover production

You can see from Figure 6-15 that you never are required to use a do until loop. The same results can always be achieved by performing the loop body steps one time before entering a while loop. If you follow the logic of either of the loops shown in Figures 6-14 and 6-15, you will discover that when an employee has an IN-LAST-PRODUCTION value of 3, then exactly four labels print. Likewise, when an employee has an IN-LAST-PRODUCTION value of 0, then in both cases exactly one label prints. You can accomplish the same results with either type of loop; the do until loop is simply a convenience for those times when you need a loop to execute at least one time.

▶ **tip**

In some languages, the do until loop is called a repeat until loop.

▶ **tip**

If you can express the logic you want to perform by saying "while a is true, keep doing b," you probably want to use a while loop. If what you want to accomplish seems better to fit the statement, "do a until b is true," you probably have the option of using a do until loop.

As you examine Figures 6-14 and 6-15, notice that with the do until loop, the loop controlling question is placed at the *end* of the sequence of the steps that repeat. With the while loop, the loop controlling question is placed at the *beginning* of the steps that repeat. All structured loops share these characteristics:

- The loop controlling question provides either entry to or exit from the repeating structure.
- The loop controlling question provides *the only* entry to or exit from the repeating structure.

You should also notice the difference between *unstructured* loops and the structured do until and while loops. Figure 6-16 diagrams the outline of two unstructured loops. In each case, the decision labeled X breaks out of the loop prematurely. In each case, the loop control, labeled LC, does not provide the only entry to or exit from the loop.

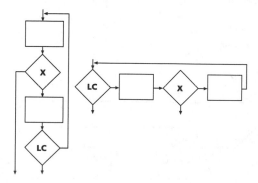

**Figure 6-16:** Examples of unstructured loops

## Nesting Loops

Program logic gets more complicated when you must use loops within loops, or **nesting loops**. For example, suppose your worker records contain average *daily* production figures instead of weekly figures. But suppose you still want to print a week's worth of labels for each worker. If your company operates on a five-day work week, then within the MAIN-LOOP of this program you must produce each worker's daily label count five times. To accomplish this, you need two counters. You have declared a LABEL-COUNTER to count labels, but now you want to produce the daily label count five times. You can declare a variable to count the days and name it DAY-COUNTER. Assuming you declare a variable that holds IN-DAILY-PRODUCTION, the MAIN-LOOP logic looks like Figure 6-17.

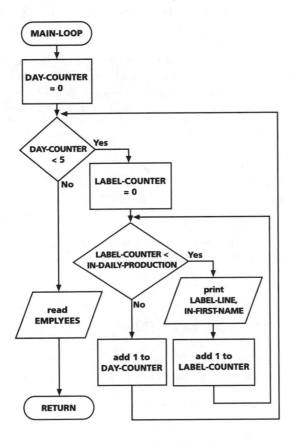

```
MAIN-LOOP
     DAY-COUNTER = 0
     while DAY-COUNTER < 5
          LABEL-COUNTER = 0
          while LABEL-COUNTER < IN-DAILY-PRODUCTION
               print LABEL-LINE, IN-FIRST-NAME
               LABEL-COUNTER = LABEL-COUNTER + 1
          DAY-COUNTER = DAY-COUNTER + 1
     read EMPLYEES
RETURN
```

**Figure 6-17:** Flowchart and pseudocode for five daily production count labels

When you examine Figure 6-17, you see that for each new employee record, the DAY-COUNTER and the LABEL-COUNTER initialize to zero. While the DAY-COUNTER remains under 5, you produce the daily quota of labels. When the daily quota is complete, that is, when LABEL-COUNTER is no longer less than IN-DAILY-PRODUCTION, you have printed one day's worth of labels, so you add one to the DAY-COUNTER and loop back to see if DAY-COUNTER is 5 yet. If not, you enter the loop body and print another day's worth of labels.

In this example, if a worker's daily production is 10, the worker needs 50 labels. Because all the labels are identical, you can achieve the same results by multiplying the worker's daily average figure by 5 and executing a single loop. However, if you want the labels to indicate the day of the week, then you must use nested loops, as in Figure 6-18. Each label prints a day number (0 through 4) along with the LABEL-LINE message and the employee's first name.

```
MAIN-LOOP
    DAY-COUNTER = 0
    while DAY-COUNTER < 5
        LABEL-COUNTER = 0
        while LABEL-COUNTER < IN-DAILY-PRODUCTION
            print "DAY: ", DAY-COUNTER, LABEL-LINE,
                IN-FIRST-NAME
            LABEL-COUNTER = LABEL-COUNTER + 1
        DAY-COUNTER = DAY-COUNTER + 1
    read EMPLYEES
RETURN
```

**Figure 6-18:** Required nested loops for printing labels

**tip**

••••••••••••••••••••••••••••••••••••••••••••••••••••••••••••••••••••••••••••••••

To print day numbers 1 through 5 (instead of 0 through 4), you can print DAY-COUNTER + 1 on each label.

••••••••••••••••••••••••••••••••••••••••••••••••••••••••••••••••••••••••••••••••

When you nest loops you must maintain two individual loop control variables and increment each at the appropriate time.

## Using a Loop to Accumulate Totals

Business reports often include totals. The supervisor who wants a list of employees who participate in the company dental plan often is as interested in *how many* such employees there are as in *who* the individuals are. When you receive your telephone bill at the end of the month, you are usually more interested in the total than in the charges for the individual phone calls. Some business reports list no individual detail records, just totals. Such reports are called **summary reports**.

For example, a real estate broker may maintain a file of company real estate listings. Each record in the file contains the street address and the asking price of a property for sale. The broker wants a listing of all the properties for sale; she also wants a total value for all the company's listings. The print chart appears in Figure 6-19.

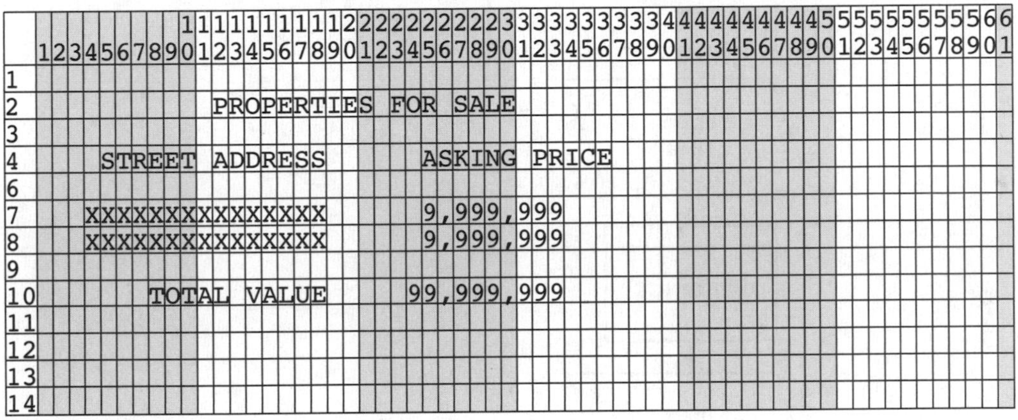

| | 1 2 3 4 5 6 7 8 9 0 | 1 1 1 1 1 1 1 1 1 1 2 2 2 2 2 2 2 2 2 2 3 3 3 3 3 3 3 3 3 3 4 4 4 4 4 4 4 4 4 4 5 5 5 5 5 5 5 5 5 5 6 6 |
|---|---|---|

(Print chart grid showing:)

Row 2: PROPERTIES FOR SALE
Row 4: STREET ADDRESS        ASKING PRICE
Row 7: XXXXXXXXXXXXXXXX        9,999,999
Row 8: XXXXXXXXXXXXXXXX        9,999,999
Row 10: TOTAL VALUE            99,999,999

**Figure 6-19:** Print chart for real estate report

When you read a real estate listing record, besides printing it you must add its value to an accumulator. An **accumulator** is a variable that you use to gather or accumulate values. An accumulator is very similar to a counter. The difference lies in the value that you add to the variable; usually you add just one to a counter, but usually you add some other value to an accumulator. If the real estate broker wants to know how many listings the company holds, you count them. When she wants to know total real estate value, you accumulate it.

In order to accumulate total real estate prices, you declare a numeric variable at the beginning of the program, as shown in Figure 6-20. You must initialize the accumulator, ACCUM-VALUE, to zero. In Chapter 4 you learned that when you use most programming languages, declared variables do not automatically assume any particular value; the unknown value is called garbage. When you read the first real estate record, you will add its value to the accumulator. If the accumulator contains garbage, the addition will not work. Some programming languages issue an error message if you don't initialize a variable you use for accumulating; others let you accumulate, but your results are worthless because you start with garbage.

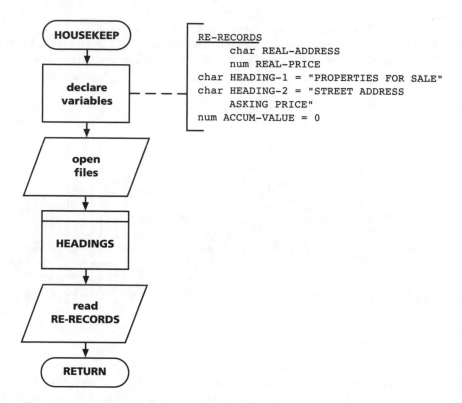

**Figure 6-20:** HOUSEKEEP module for real estate program

If you name the input record fields REAL-ADDRESS and REAL-PRICE, then the MAIN-LOOP of the real estate listing program can be written as shown in Figure 6-21. For each real estate record, you print it, and add its value to the accumulator, ACCUM-VALUE. Then you can read the next record.

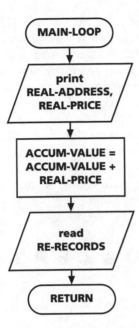

**Figure 6-21:** Flowchart for MAIN-LOOP of real estate listing program

After the program reaches the end of file, the accumulator will hold the grand total of all the real estate values. When you reach the end of the file, the FINISH-UP routine executes, and it is within the FINISH-UP routine that you print the accumulated value. After you print the total, you can close both the input and the output files and return to the mainline where the program ends. See Figure 6-22.

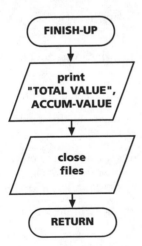

**Figure 6-22:** FINISH-UP routine for real estate program

New programmers often want to reset the ACCUM-VALUE to zero after printing it. Although you *can* take this step, and it won't harm the execution of the program, it does not serve any useful purpose. You cannot set ACCUM-VALUE to zero in anticipation of having it ready for the next program. Program variables exist only for the life of the program, and even if a future program happens to contain a variable named ACCUM-VALUE, the variable will not necessarily occupy the same memory location. Even if you run your program a second time, the variables may occupy physical memory locations different from those they occupied during the first run. At the beginning of the program, it is the programmer's responsibility to initialize all variables that must start with a specific value. There is no benefit to changing a variable's value when it will never be used again during the current execution of the program.

 ## TERMS AND CONCEPTS

indeterminate or indefinite loop        do until loop

definite loop                           nesting loops

while statement or loop                 summary report

for statement or loop                   accumulator

## SUMMARY

- You can improve loop performance by removing mathematical calculations from the comparison expressions you use.

- An indeterminate or indefinite loop is one for which you can't determine the number of repetitions ahead of time.

- A definite loop is one for which you definitely know the repetition factor.

- Every high-level computer programming language contains a while statement that you can use to write indefinite and definite loops.

- Most computer languages also support a for statement that you can use with definite loops when you know how many times a loop will repeat. The for statement usually takes the form: `for INITIAL-VALUE to FINAL-VALUE do something`.

- When you use either a while or a for loop, the body of the loop may never execute.

- When you want to ensure that a loop's body executes at least one time, you can use a do until loop. In a do until loop, the loop control variable is evaluated after the loop body executes.

■ Business reports often include totals. Summary reports are reports that list only totals.

■ An accumulator is a variable that you use to gather or accumulate values. You must initialize an accumulator.

■ Program variables exist only for the life of the program; there is no benefit to changing a variable's value when it will never be used again during the current execution of the program.

# E X E R C I S E S

1. a. Assume you have a bank account that compounds interest on a yearly basis. In other words, if you deposit $100 for two years at 4 percent interest, at the end of one year you will have $104. At the end of two years, you will have the $104 plus 4 percent of that, or $108.16. Draw the logic for a program that would read in a deposit amount, a term, and an interest rate, and print out your running total for each year of the term.

   b. Write pseudocode for the problem in Exercise 1a.

2. a. A school maintains class records in the following format:

   **File name: CLASS**

   | FIELD DESCRIPTION | POSITIONS | DATA TYPE | DECIMALS | EXAMPLE |
   |---|---|---|---|---|
   | Class code | 1–6 | Character | | CIS111 |
   | Section no. | 7–9 | Numeric | 0 | 101 |
   | Teacher | 10–29 | Character | | Gable |
   | Enrollment | 30–31 | Numeric | 0 | 24 |
   | Room | 32–35 | Character | | A213 |

   There is one record for each class section offered in the college. Design the program that would print as many stickers as a class needs to provide one for each enrolled student, plus one for the teacher. Each sticker would leave a blank for the student's (or teacher's) name like this:

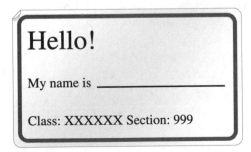

   This border is pre-printed, but you must design the program to print all the text you see on the sticker.

Create the hierarchy chart and flowchart for this problem.

b. Write pseudocode for the problem in Exercise 2a.

3. a. A mail order company often sends multiple packages per order. For each customer order, print the number of labels required based on the number of separate boxes that will be mailed. The mailing labels indicate a box number in the form "Box 9 of 9". For example, an order than requires three boxes produces three labels: "Box 1 of 3", "Box 2 of 3", and "Box 3 of 3". The file description is as follows:

```
SHIPPING FILE DESCRIPTION
File name: ORDERS
```

| FIELD DESCRIPTION | POSITIONS | DATA TYPE | DECIMALS | EXAMPLE |
|---|---|---|---|---|
| Title | 1–3 | Character | | Ms |
| First name | 4–14 | Character | | Kathy |
| Last name | 15–25 | Character | | Lewis |
| Street | 26–40 | Character | | 847 Pine |
| City | 41–51 | Character | | Aurora |
| State | 52–53 | Character | | IL |
| Boxes | 54–55 | Numeric | 0 | 3 |
| Balance due | 56–61 | Numeric | 2 | 129.95 |

Design the print chart for the mailing label, and draw the hierarchy chart and the flowchart for this problem.

b. Write pseudocode for the problem in Exercise 3a.

c. Design a program that creates a report listing each customer in the order file, the number of boxes in the customer's order, and the customer's balance. At the end of the report print a total count of all boxes shipped and the grand total of all balances. Draw the print chart, hierarchy chart, and flowchart for this problem.

d. Write pseudocode for the problem in Exercise 3c.

4. a. A second-hand store is having a seven day sale during which the price of any unsold item drops 10 percent each day. The inventory file includes an item number, description, and original price on day one. For example, an item that costs $10.00 on the first day costs 10 percent less, or $9.00, on the second day. On the third day, the same item is 10 percent less than $9.00, or $8.10. Produce a report that shows the price of the item on each day, one through seven. Draw the print chart, hierarchy chart, and flowchart for this problem.

b. Write pseudocode for the problem in Exercise 4a.

# Control Breaks

**case** ▶ "You look exhausted!" Lynn Greenbrier exclaims as she walks by your desk late one Friday afternoon.

"I've been learning so much here," you reply. "I understand structure and how to use selections and loops. The next thing I'm supposed to learn is how to print different groups of data on different pages and provide subtotals on reports. I love this job! But *any* job gets to be a grind day after day. I feel like every day is the same old thing—get up, go to work, come home, fall asleep—over and over again."

"Once in a while, you need to do something different," Lynn advises. "You need a break in your routine. Take the weekend, do something fun, and come back and pick up where you left off on Monday. Then I'll teach you how to print different groups of data on their own pages, and total groups of data on reports. Those programming techniques represent breaks in the normal routine—exactly the same thing you need in your life right now!"

# Single-Level Control Breaks

## Control Break Logic

A **control break** is a temporary detour in the logic of a program. In particular, programmers refer to a program as a **control break program** when a change in the value of a variable initiates special actions or causes special or unusual processing to occur. In other words, a new value in some variable causes a break in the normal flow of actions in a program. If you have ever read a report that followed a group of listed items with subtotals for that group, then you have read a kind of **control break report**. Some other examples of control break reports produced by control break programs include:

■ All employees listed in order by department number, in which a new page starts for each department

■ All company clients listed in order by state of residence, with a count of clients after each state's client list

■ All books for sale in a bookstore in order by category (such as reference or self-help), with a dollar total for the value of all the books following each category of book

■ All items sold in order by date of sale, switching ink color for each new month

Each of these reports shares two traits:

■ The records used in each report are listed in order by a specific variable: department, state, publisher, or date.

■ When that variable changes, the program takes special action: starts a new page, prints a count or total, or switches ink color.

To write a control break report, you must have placed input records in sorted order based on the field that will cause the breaks. If you are going to write a program that prints employee records on separate pages based on their departments, then the records must be sorted in department-number order before you begin processing. As you grow more proficient in programming logic, you will learn techniques for writing the programs that sort the records; for now, assume input records arrive in your program presorted.

**You will learn techniques for processing unsorted records in Chapter 8.**
······································································

## Single-Level Control Breaks

Suppose you want to print a list of employees, advancing to a new page for each department. Figure 7-1 shows the input file description, from which you can see that the employee department is a two-digit numeric field and that the file has been presorted in employee-department number order. Figure 7-2 shows the desired output—a simple list of employee names.

---

FILE NAME: EMPS-BY-DEPT

Sorted By: Department

| FIELD DESCRIPTION | POSITIONS | DATA TYPE | DECIMALS |
|---|---|---|---|
| Department | 1-2 | Numeric | 0 |
| Last name | 3-14 | Character | |
| First name | 15-26 | Character | |

---

**Figure 7-1:** Employee file description

|   |
|---|
| EMPLOYEES BY DEPARTMENT |
| LAST NAME            FIRST NAME |
| XXXXXXXXXXXXX        XXXXXXXXXXXX |
| XXXXXXXXXXXXX        XXXXXXXXXXXX |
| XXXXXXXXXXXXX        XXXXXXXXXXXX |

**Figure 7-2:** Print chart for employees listed by department

The basic logic of the program works like this: When you read each employee record from the input file, you will determine whether the employee belongs to the same department as the previous employee. If so, you simply print the employee and read another record. If there are 20 employees in a department, these steps are repeated 20 times in a row—read an employee in, and print the employee out. However, eventually you will read in an employee who does not belong to the same department. At that point, before you print the employee who is in the new department, you must print headings on the top of a new page. Then you can proceed to print employees from the new department.

However, there is a slight problem you must solve before you can determine whether a newly input record contains the same department number as the previously input record. When you read a record from an input file, the data that represent department, last name, and first name occupy specific physical locations in computer memory. For each new record, new data need to occupy the same positions, and the first set of data is lost. For example, if you read a record containing data for Alan Andrews in Department 1, when you read the next record for Barbara Bailey in Department 2, "Barbara" replaces Alan, "Bailey" replaces "Andrews" and 2 replaces 1. After you read in a new record, there is no way to look back at the previous record to determine whether that record had a different department number. The previous record's data has been replaced by the new record's data.

The technique you must use to "remember" the old department number is to create a special variable, called a **control break field,** to hold the previous department number. With a control break field, every time you read in a record and print it, you can also save the crucial part of the record that will signal the change or control the program break. In this case, you want to store the department number in this specially created variable. Comparing the new and the old department-number values will determine when the input records have changed and it is time to print headings at the top of a new page.

The mainline logic for the Employees by Department report is the same as the mainline logic for all the other programs you've analyzed so far. It performs a HOUSEKEEPING module, after which an EOF question controls execution of a MAIN-LOOP. At EOF, a FINISH routine executes. See Figure 7-3.

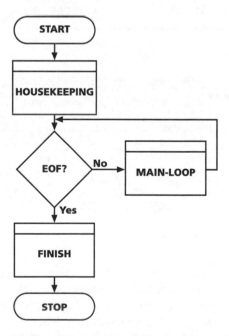

**Figure 7-3:** Mainline logic for Employees by Department report program

The HOUSEKEEPING module begins similarly to others you have seen. You declare variables as shown in Figure 7-4 including those you will use for the input data: EMP-DEPT, EMP-LAST, and EMP-FIRST. You can also declare variables to hold the headings, and an additional variable that is named OLD-DEPT in this example. The purpose of OLD-DEPT is to serve as the control break field. Every time you read a record, you can save its department number in OLD-DEPT before you read the next record.

Note that it would be incorrect to initialize OLD-DEPT to the value of EMP-DEPT when you declare OLD-DEPT. When you declare variables at the beginning of the HOUSEKEEPING module, you have not yet read in the first record; therefore EMP-DEPT does not yet have any usable value. Only after you read the first input record can you use the value of the first EMP-DEPT.

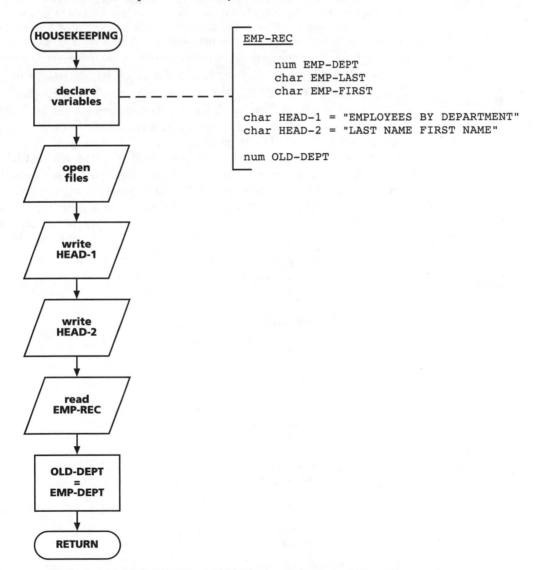

**Figure 7-4:** HOUSEKEEPING module for Employees by Department report program

In the HOUSEKEEPING module you also open the files, print headings, and read the first input record. However, before you leave HOUSEKEEPING, you can

**section A**

set the OLD-DEPT variable equal to the EMP-DEPT value in the first input record. You will write the MAIN-LOOP of the program to check for any change in department number; that's the signal to print headings at the top of a new page. Because you just printed headings and read in the first record, you do not want to print headings again for this record—you want to ensure that the EMP-DEPT and OLD-DEPT are equal within the MAIN-LOOP.

**tip**

As an alternative to the HOUSEKEEPING logic shown here, you can remove printing headings from the HOUSEKEEPING module and set the OLD-DEPT to any impossible value, for example -1. Then in the MAIN-LOOP the first record will force the control break, and the headings will print in the NEW-PAGE control break routine.

The first task within the MAIN-LOOP is to check whether the EMP-DEPT holds the same value as OLD-DEPT. For the first record, on the first pass through the MAIN-LOOP, the values are equal; you set them to be equal in HOUSEKEEPING. Therefore you proceed, printing the employee's record and reading a second record. At the end of the MAIN-LOOP, shown in Figure 7-5, the logical flow returns to the mainline logic shown in Figure 7-3. If it is not EOF, the flow travels back to MAIN-LOOP. There you compare the second record's EMP-DEPT to OLD-DEPT. If the second record holds an employee from the same department, then you simply print that employee's record, and you read a third record into memory. As long as each new record holds the same EMP-DEPT value, you continue reading and printing.

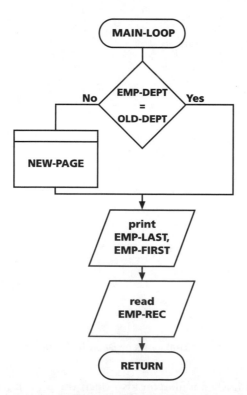

**Figure 7-5:** MAIN-LOOP module for Employees by Department report program

Eventually, you will read in an employee whose EMP-DEPT is not the same as OLD-DEPT. That's when the control break routine, NEW-PAGE, executes. NEW-PAGE must perform two tasks:

■ It must print headings on top of a new page.
■ It must update the control break field.

Figure 7-6 shows the NEW-PAGE module.

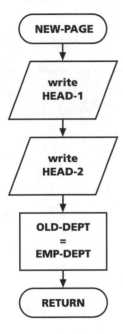

**Figure 7-6:** NEW-PAGE module for Employees by Department report program

In Chapter 4 you learned that specific programming languages provide you with a means to physically advance printer paper to the top of a page. For this book, we adopt the convention that if a print chart shows a heading printing at the top of the page, then you can assume printing the heading causes the paper in the printer to advance to the top of a new page. The appropriate language-specific codes can be added when you code the program in a specific programming language.

When you read an employee whose EMP-DEPT is not the same as OLD-DEPT, you cause a break in the normal flow of the program. The new employee record must "wait" while headings print and the control break field OLD-DEPT acquires a new value. When the control break module ends, the waiting employee record prints on the new page. When you read the *next* employee record, the employee's EMP-DEPT is compared to the updated OLD-DEPT, and if the new employee works in the same department as the one just preceding, then normal control continues with the print-and-read statements.

The NEW-PAGE module performs two tasks required in all control break routines:

- Processes any control break routines for the new group—in this case, writes headings
- Updates the control break field

**As an alternative to updating the control break field within the control break routine, you could set the OLD-DEPT equal to EMP-DEPT just before you read each record. However, if there are 200 employees in Department 55, then you set the OLD-DEPT to the same value 200 times. It's more efficient to set OLD-DEPT to a different value only when there is a change.**

The FINISH routine for the Employees by Department report program requires only that you close the files. See Figure 7-7.

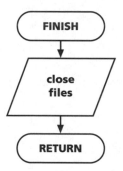

**Figure 7-7:** FINISH module for Employees by Department report program

## Using Control Data Within the Control Break Module

In the Employees by Department report program example, the control break routine printed constant headings at the top of each new page. But sometimes you need to use control data within a control break module. For example, consider the report layout shown in Figure 7-8.

| | 1234567890 | 1111111111 1234567890 | 2222222222 1234567890 | 3333333333 1234567890 | 4444444444 1234567890 | 5555555 1234567 |
|---|---|---|---|---|---|---|
| 1 | | | | | | |
| 2 | EMPLOYEES | FOR DEPARTMENT | 99 | | | |
| 3 | | | | | | |
| 4 | LAST NAME | | FIRST NAME | | | |
| 5 | | | | | | |
| 6 | XXXXXXXXXXXXX | | XXXXXXXXXXXXX | | | |
| 7 | XXXXXXXXXXXXX | | XXXXXXXXXXXXX | | | |
| 8 | XXXXXXXXXXXXX | | XXXXXXXXXXXXX | | | |

**Figure 7-8:** Print chart for employees listed by department identified in heading

The difference between Figure 7-2 and Figure 7-8 lies in the heading. Figure 7-8 shows variable data appearing in the heading—the department number prints at the top of each page of employees. To create this kind of program, the one change you must make in the existing program is to modify the NEW-PAGE routine as shown in Figure 7-9. Instead of printing a fixed heading, you print a heading that contains two parts—a constant beginning ("EMPLOYEES FOR DEPARTMENT") and a variable ending—the department number for the employees who appear on the page. Notice that you use the EMP-DEPT number that belongs to the employee record that is waiting to be printed while this control break module executes. Additionally, you must ensure that the first heading on the report prints correctly. You can modify the HOUSEKEEPING module in Figure 7-4 so that you read the EMP-REC prior to printing the headings.

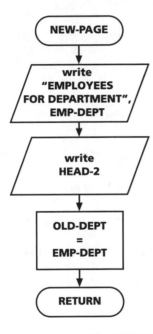

**Figure 7-9:** Modified NEW-PAGE module that prints department number in heading

Figure 7-10 shows a different print chart. For this report, the department number prints *following* the employee list for the department. A message that prints at the end of a page is called a **footer**. Headings usually require information about the *next* record; footers usually require information about the *previous* record.

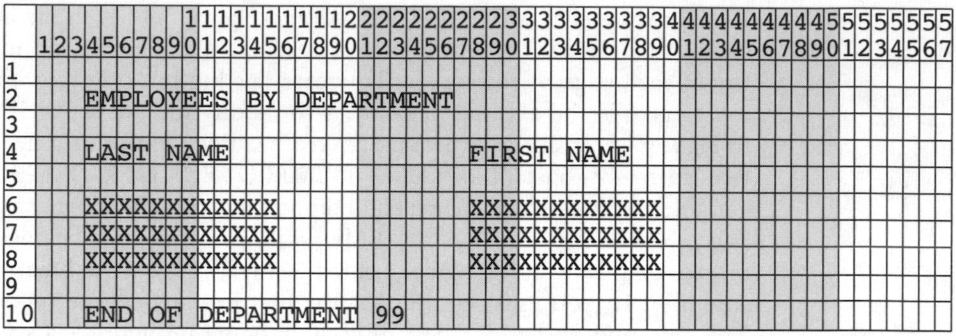

```
         111111111122222222223333333333444444444455555555
123456789012345678901234567890123456789012345678901234567
1
2   EMPLOYEES BY DEPARTMENT
3
4   LAST NAME              FIRST NAME
5
6   XXXXXXXXXXXXX         XXXXXXXXXXXXX
7   XXXXXXXXXXXXX         XXXXXXXXXXXXX
8   XXXXXXXXXXXXX         XXXXXXXXXXXXX
9
10  END OF DEPARTMENT 99
```

**Figure 7-10:** Print chart for employees listed by department identified in footer

Figure 7-11 shows the NEW-PAGE module required to print the department number in an Employees by Department report footer. When you write a program that produces the report shown in Figure 7-10, you continuously read records with EMP-LAST, EMP-FIRST, and EMP-DEPT fields. Each time an EMP-DEPT does not equal the OLD-DEPT, it means that you have reached a department break and that you should perform the NEW-PAGE module. The NEW-PAGE module has three tasks:

■ It must print the footer for the previous department at the bottom of the employee list.
■ It must print headings on top of a new page.
■ It must update the control break field.

When the NEW-PAGE routine prints the footer at the bottom of the old page, you must use the OLD-DEPT number. For example, assume you have printed several employees from Department 12. When you read a record with an employee from Department 13 (or any other department), the first thing you must do is print "END OF DEPARTMENT 12". You print the correct department number by accessing the value of the OLD-DEPT. Then you can print the other headings at the top of a new page and update OLD-DEPT to the current EMP-DEPT, which is 13.

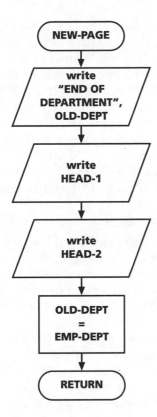

**Figure 7-11:** Modified NEW-PAGE module that prints department number in footer

Now the NEW-PAGE module performs three tasks required in all control break routines:

- It processes any control break routines for the previous group—in this case, writes the footer.
- It processes any control break routines for the new group—in this case, writes headings.
- It updates the control break field.

The FINISH module for the new program containing footers also requires an extra step. Imagine that the last five records on the input file include two employees from Department 78, Amy and Bill, and three employees from Department 85, Carol, Don, and Ellen. The logical flow proceeds as follows:

1. After the first Department 78 employee (Amy) prints, you read in the second Department 78 employee (Bill).
2. At the top of MAIN-LOOP module, Bill's department compares to OLD-DEPT. The departments are the same, so the second Department 78 employee (Bill) is printed. Then you read in the first Department 85 employee (Carol).
3. At the top of the MAIN-LOOP, Carol's EMP-DEPT and the OLD-DEPT are different, so you perform the NEW-PAGE routine, while Carol's record waits in memory.

4. In the NEW-PAGE routine, you print "END OF DEPARTMENT 78". Then you print the headings for the top of the next page. Finally, you set OLD-DEPT to 85. Then you return to the MAIN-LOOP.
5. Back in the MAIN-LOOP you print a line of data for the first Department 85 employee (Carol), whose record waited while NEW-PAGE executed. Then you read the second Department 85 employee (Don).
6. At the top of MAIN-LOOP, you compare Don's department number to OLD-DEPT. The numbers are the same, so you print Don's employee data and read in the last Department 85 employee (Ellen).
7. At the top of MAIN-LOOP, you determine that Ellen has the same department number, so you print Ellen's data and attempt to read from the input file. You encounter EOF.
8. The EOF decision in the mainline logic sends you to the FINISH routine.

You have printed the last Department 85 employee (Ellen), but the department footer for Department 85 has not printed. That's because every time you attempt to read an input record, you don't know whether there will be more records. The mainline logic checks for the EOF condition, but if it determines that it is EOF, the logic does not flow back into the MAIN-LOOP where the NEW-PAGE routine can execute.

To print the footer for the last department, you must print a footer one last time within the FINISH routine. The FINISH module in Figure 7-12 illustrates this. Taking this action is similar to printing the first heading in the HOUSEKEEPING module. The very first heading prints separately from all the others at the beginning; the very last footer must print separately from all the others at the end.

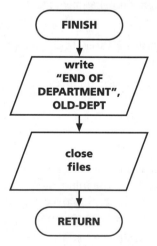

**Figure 7-12:** Modified FINISH module for report program with footer

## Control Breaks with Totals

Suppose you run a bookstore, and one of the files you maintain is called BOOK-FILE and has one record for every book title that you carry. Each record has fields such as TITLE, AUTHOR, CATEGORY-OF-WORK (fiction, reference, self-help, and so on), PUBLISHER, and PRICE, as shown in this file description in Figure 7-13.

---

```
FILE NAME: BOOK-FILE

Sorted by: Category
```

| FIELD DESCRIPTION | POSITIONS | DATA TYPE | DECIMALS |
|---|---|---|---|
| Title | 1—30 | Character | |
| Author | 31—46 | Character | |
| Category | 47—56 | Character | |
| Publisher | 57—72 | Character | |
| Price | 73—77 | Numeric | 2 |

---

**Figure 7-13:** BOOK-FILE file description

To print out a list of all the books that your store carries with the total number of books at the bottom of the list as shown in Figure 7-14, you can use the logic shown in Figure 7-15. In the main loop, named BOOK-LIST, you print a book title, add 1 to the GRAND-TOTAL and read the next record. At the end of the program, in the CLOSE-DOWN routine, you print the GRAND-TOTAL before you close the files.

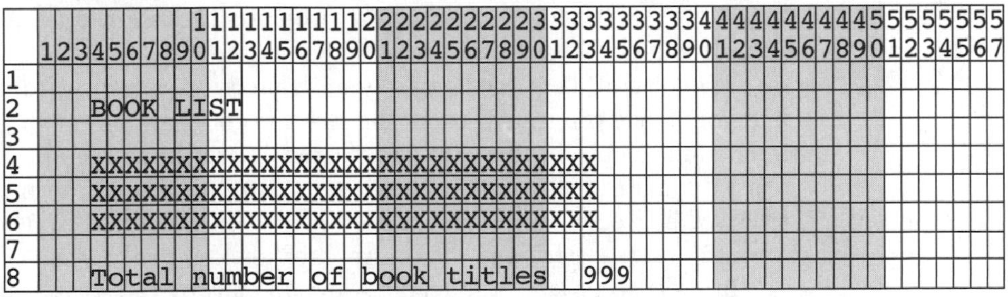

**Figure 7-14:** Print chart for book list

```
START
      perform START-UP
      while not EOF
            perform BOOK-LIST-LOOP
      perform CLOSE-DOWN
END
START-UP
      declare variables — — — — — —┐ BOOK-REC
      open files                    │      char BK-TITLE
      print HEADING                 │      char BK-AUTHOR
      read BOOK-REC                 │      char BK-CATEGORY
RETURN                              │      char BK-PUBLISHER
BOOK-LIST-LOOP                      │      num BK-PRICE
      print BK-TITLE                │ char HEADING = "BOOK LIST"
      add 1 to GRAND-TOTAL          │ num GRAND-TOTAL = 0
      read BOOK-REC                 └
RETURN
CLOSE-DOWN
      print "Total number of book titles", GRAND-TOTAL
      close files
RETURN
```

**Figure 7-15:** Logic for bookstore program

As you can see from the pseudocode in Figure 7-15, the BOOK-LIST-LOOP contains three major tasks:

1. Print a book title.
2. Add 1 to the GRAND-TOTAL.
3. Read in the next book record.

The CLOSE-DOWN module prints the GRAND-TOTAL. You can't print GRAND-TOTAL any earlier in the program because the GRAND-TOTAL isn't complete until the last record has been read.

The logic of the preceding program is pretty straightforward. Suppose, however, that you decide you want a count for each category of book rather than just one grand total. For example, for the categories fiction, reference, and self-help, the output would consist of a list of all fiction books first, followed by a count; then all reference books, followed by a count; and finally all self-help books, followed by a count. The report is a control break report, and the control break field is the BK-CATEGORY.

In order to produce the report with subtotals by category, you must declare two new variables: PREVIOUS-CATEGORY and CATEGORY-TOTAL. Every time you read in a book record, you compare BK-CATEGORY to PREVIOUS-CATEGORY; when there is a category change, you print the count of books for the previous category. CATEGORY-TOTAL holds the count. See Figure 7-16.

```
START
     perform START-UP
     while not EOF
           perform BOOK-LIST-LOOP
     perform CLOSE-DOWN
END
START-UP
     declare variables — — — — — — — — — — —
     open files
     print HEADING
     read BOOK-REC
     PREVIOUS-CATEGORY = BK-CATEGORY
RETURN
BOOK-LIST-LOOP
     if BK-CATEGORY > PREVIOUS-CATEGORY then
           perform CATEGORY-CHANGE
     print BK-TITLE
     add 1 to CATEGORY-TOTAL
     read BOOK-REC
RETURN
CATEGORY-CHANGE
     print "Category Count", CATEGORY-TOTAL
     add CATEGORY-TOTAL to GRAND-TOTAL
     CATEGORY-TOTAL = 0
     PREVIOUS-CATEGORY = BK-CATEGORY
RETURN
CLOSE-DOWN
     perform CATEGORY-CHANGE
     print "Total number of book titles", GRAND-TOTAL
     close files
RETURN
```

```
BOOK-REC
     char BK-TITLE
     char BK-AUTHOR
     char BK-CATEGORY
     char BK-PUBLISHER
     num BK-PRICE
char HEADING = "BOOK LIST"
num GRAND-TOTAL = 0
num CATEGORY-TOTAL = 0
char PREVIOUS-CATEGORY
```

**Figure 7-16:** Logic for bookstore program with subtotals

When you read the first record from the input file, you save the value of BK-CATEGORY in the PREVIOUS-CATEGORY variable. Every time a record enters the BOOK-LIST-LOOP, the program checks to see if this is a new category of work by comparing BK-CATEGORY to the variable called PREVIOUS-CATEGORY. For the first record, the categories match, so the book title prints, the CATEGORY-TOTAL increases by one, and you read the next record. If this record matches the PREVIOUS-CATEGORY, processing continues as usual with the printing of a line and the adding of 1 to the CATEGORY-TOTAL.

At some point the BK-CATEGORY for an input record does not match the PREVIOUS-CATEGORY. At that point, you perform the CATEGORY-CHANGE module. Within the CATEGORY-CHANGE module you print the count of the previous category of books. Then you add the CATEGORY-TOTAL to the GRAND-TOTAL. Adding a total to a higher-level total is called **rolling up the totals.** You could write the BOOK-LIST-LOOP so that as you process each book, you add one to the CATEGORY-TOTAL and add one to the GRAND-TOTAL. Then there would be no need to roll totals up in the CATGORY-CHANGE module. If there are 120 fiction books, you add 1 to CATEGORY-TOTAL 120 times; you also would add 1 to GRAND-TOTAL 120 times. This technique would yield correct results, but you can eliminate 119 addition instructions by waiting until you have accumulated all 120 category counts and adding the total figure to GRAND-TOTAL.

This report break with totals performs four of the five tasks required in all control break routines that include totals:

- It processes any control break routines for the previous group—in this case it writes the CATEGORY-TOTAL.
- It rolls up the current level totals to the next higher level—in this case it adds CATEGORY-TOTAL to GRAND-TOTAL.
- It resets the current level's totals to zero—in this case the CATEGORY-TOTAL is set to zero.
- It processes any control break routines for the new group—in this case there is none.
- It updates the control break field—in this case PREVIOUS-CATEGORY.

The CLOSE-DOWN routine for this type of program is more complicated than it may first appear. It seems as though you should print the GRAND-TOTAL, close the files, and return to the mainline logic. However, when you read the last record, the mainline EOF decision sends the logical flow to the CLOSE-DOWN routine. You have not printed the last CATEGORY-TOTAL, nor have you added the count for the last category into the GRAND-TOTAL. You must take care of both these tasks before printing the GRAND-TOTAL. You can perform these two tasks as separate steps in CLOSE-DOWN, but it is often simplest just to remember to perform the control break routine, CATEGORY-CHANGE, one last time. CATEGORY-CHANGE already executes after every other category completes— that is, every time you encounter a new category during the execution of the program. You also can execute this module after the final category completes, at end of file. Encountering the end of the file is really just another form of break; it signals that the last category has finally completed. The CATEGORY-CHANGE module prints the category total and rolls the totals up to the GRAND-TOTAL level.

**tip**

When you call the CATEGORY-CHANGE module in CLOSE-DOWN, it performs a few tasks you don't need, like setting the value of PREVIOUS-CATEGORY. The convenience of calling the CATEGORY-CHANGE routine and executing a few unneeded statements probably outweighs the machine time that would be saved by rewriting it as another module with only the statements you need.

It is very important to note that this control break program works whether there are three categories of books or 300. Note further that it does not matter what the categories of books are. For example, the program never asks BK-CATEGORY = "fiction"?. Instead, the control of the program breaks when the category field *changes*, and it is in no way dependent on *what* that change is.

**T E R M S   A N D   C O N C E P T S**

control break                           control break field
control break program                   footer
control break report                    rolling up totals

 **S U M M A R Y**

- A control break is a temporary detour in the logic of a program. In particular, programmers refer to a program as a control break program when a change in the value of a variable initiates special processing.

- A report that shows subtotals following each group of listed items is a control break report. Control break reports use records that have been sorted in order by some variable. When that variable changes, the program takes special action.

- Within a control break program, you determine whether each record belongs to the same group as the previous record. When you encounter a new group, you perform a control break routine.

- The technique you must use to "remember" a previous group's value is to create a special variable, called a control break field, to hold it.

- When a record causes a control break, the record waits in memory while the control break module executes. Then the waiting record is processed.

- You can use control data within a control break module. Headings usually require information about the next record; footers usually require information about the previous records.

- When you print footers, you must print a final footer in the end-of-job routine.

- Adding group totals to a higher-level total in a control break program is called rolling up the totals.

- Often, it is simplest to perform a control break routine one last time within the end-of-job routine.

 **E X E R C I S E S**

1. What fields would you want to use as the control break fields to produce a report that lists all inventory items in a grocery store? Design the print chart for the report.

2. What fields would you want to use as the control break fields to produce a report that lists all the people you know? Design the print chart for the report.

3. Write the pseudocode for the employees listed by department program that is flow-charted in this section in Figures 7-3 through 7-7.

4. A used-car dealer keeps track of sales in the following format:

AUTO SALES FILE DESCRIPTION

File name: Auto

Sorted by: Salesperson

| FIELD DESCRIPTION | POSITIONS | DATA TYPE | DECIMALS | EXAMPLE |
|---|---|---|---|---|
| Salesperson | 1—20 | Character | | Miller |
| Make of car | 21—30 | Character | | Ford |
| Vehicle type | 31—40 | Character | | Sedan |
| Sale price | 41—45 | Numeric | 0 | 12500 |

By the end of the week, a salesperson may have sold no cars, one car, or many cars. Create the logic of a program that would print one line for each salesperson with that salesperson's total sales for the week and commission earned, which is 4 percent of the total sales. Create the print chart, hierarchy chart, and either the flowchart or the pseudocode.

5. A community college maintains student records in the following format:

STUDENT FILE DESCRIPTION

File name: STUDENTS

Sorted by: Hour of first class

| FIELD DESCRIPTION | POSITIONS | DATA TYPE | DECIMALS | EXAMPLE |
|---|---|---|---|---|
| Student name | 1—20 | Character | | Danielle Erickson |
| City | 21—30 | Character | | Woodstock |
| Hour of first class | 31—32 | Numeric | 0 | 08 |
| Phone number | 33—42 | Numeric | 0 | 8154379823 |

The records have been sorted by hour of the day. Hour of first class is a two-digit number based on a 24-hour clock (that is, a 1 P.M. first class is recorded as 13).

Create a report that students can use to organize carpools. The report lists the names and phone numbers of students from the city of Huntley. Note that some students come from cities other than Huntley; these students should not be listed on the report.

Start a new page for each hour of the day so that all students starting classes at the same hour are listed on the same page. Include the hour that each page represents in the heading for that page.

# Multiple-Level Control Breaks and Page Breaks

## Multiple-Level Control Breaks

Let's say your bookstore from the last example is so successful that you have a chain of them across the country. Every time a sale is made, you create a record with the fields TITLE, PRICE, CITY, and STATE. You would like a report that prints a summary of books sold in each city and each state similar to the one shown in Figure 7-17. A report such as this one that does not include any information about individual records, but instead includes group totals, is a **summary report.**

This program contains a **multiple-level control break,** that is, the normal flow of control (reading records and counting book sales) breaks away to print totals in response to more than just one change in condition. In this report a control break occurs in response to either one of exactly two conditions—when the contents of the CITY variable changes as well as when the contents of the STATE variable changes.

Just as is in the file you use to create a single-level control break report, the input file you use in a multiple-level control break report must be presorted. The input file that you use for the book sales report must be sorted by CITY *within* STATE. That is, all of one state's records, let's say all records from IA, come first; then all the records from another state, say IL, follow. Within any one state, all of one city's records come first, then all of the next city's records follow. For example, the input file that produces the report shown in Figure 7-17 contains 200 records for book sales in Ames, IA, followed by 814 records for book sales in Des Moines, IA. The basic processing entails reading a book sale record, adding one to a counter, and reading the next book sale record. At the end of any city's records, you print a total for that city; at the end of a state's records, you print a total for that state.

| BOOK SALES BY CITY AND STATE | |
|---|---|
| Ames | 200 |
| Des Moines | 814 |
| Iowa City | 291 |
| Total for IA | 1305 |
| Chicago | 1093 |
| Crystal Lake | 564 |
| McHenry | 213 |
| Springfield | 365 |
| Total for IL | 2235 |
| Springfield | 289 |
| Worcester | 100 |
| Total for MA | 389 |
| Grand Total | 3929 |

**Figure 7-17:** Sample run of Book Sales by City and State report

The HOUSEKEEPING routine of the Book Sales by City and State report program looks similar to the HOUSEKEEPING routine in the last control break program. You declare variables, open files, and read the first record. This time, however, there are multiple fields to save to compare to the old fields. Here you declare two special variables, PREV-CITY and PREV-STATE, as shown·in Figure 7-18. In addition, the Book Sales report shows three kinds of totals, so you declare three special variables, CITY-COUNT, STATE-COUNT, and GRAND-TOTAL, and set all three to zero.

```
HOUSEKEEPING
      declare variables— — —    BOOK-REC
      open files                      char TITLE
      perform HEADINGS                num PRICE
      read BOOK-REC                   char CITY
      PREV-CITY = CITY                char STATE
      PREV-STATE = STATE        char HEAD-1 = "BOOK SALES
RETURN                            BY CITY AND STATE"
                                 char PREV-CITY
                                 char PREV-STATE
                                 num CITY-COUNTER = 0
                                 num STATE-COUNTER = 0
                                 num GRAND-TOTAL = 0
```

**Figure 7-18:** Pseudocode for HOUSEKEEPING module for Book Sales by City and State report program

This program prints both STATE and CITY totals, so you need two control break modules, CITY-BREAK and STATE-BREAK. Every time there is a change in the CITY field, the CITY-BREAK routine performs these standard control break tasks:

- It processes any control break routines for the previous group—prints totals for the previous city.
- It rolls up the current level totals to the next higher level—adds the city count to the state count.
- It resets the current level's totals to zero—sets the city count to zero.
- It processes any control break routines for the new group—in this case there are none.
- It updates the control break field—sets PREV-CITY to CITY.

Within the STATE-BREAK routine, you must perform one new type of task, as well as the control break tasks you are familiar with. The new task is the first task: within a STATE-BREAK, you must first perform a CITY-BREAK automatically (because if there is a change in the state, there must also be a change in the city). The STATE-BREAK routine does the following:

- It processes the lower-level break, in this case CITY-BREAK.
- It processes any control break routines for the previous group—prints totals for the previous state.
- It rolls up the current level totals to the next higher level—adds the state count to the grand total.
- It resets the current level's totals to zero—sets the state count to zero.
- It processes any control break routines for the new group—in this case there are none.
- It updates the control break field—sets PREV-STATE to STATE.

The MAIN-LOOP of a multiple-level control break program checks not only for any change in CITY, but also for any change in STATE. When the CITY changes, a CITY total is printed, and when the STATE changes, a STATE total is printed. As you can see from the sample report in Figure 7-17, all the city totals for each state print before the state total for the same state, so it might seem logical to check for a change in CITY before checking for a change in STATE. However, the opposite is true! For the totals to be correct, you must check for any STATE change first. You check for a STATE change first, because when a CITY changes, the STATE also might be changing, but when the STATE changes, it means the CITY *must* be changing.

Consider these input records shown in Figure 7-19, which are sorted by CITY within STATE:

| TITLE | PRICE | CITY | STATE |
| --- | --- | --- | --- |
| *A Brief History of Time* | 20.00 | Iowa City | IA |
| *The Scarlet Letter* | 15.99 | Chicago | IL |
| *Math Magic* | 4.95 | Chicago | IL |
| *She's Come Undone* | 12.00 | Springfield | IL |
| *The Joy of Cooking* | 2.50 | Springfield | IL |
| *Walden* | 9.95 | Springfield | MA |
| *A Bridge Too Far* | 3.50 | Springfield | MA |

**Figure 7-19:** Sample data for Book Sales by City and State report

When you get to the point in the program where you read the first Illinois record (*The Scarlet Letter*), "Iowa City" is the value stored in the field PREV-CITY and "IA" is the value stored in PREV-STATE. Since the values in the CITY and STATE variables on the new record are both different from the PREV-CITY and PREV-STATE fields, both a city and state total will print. However, consider the problem when you read the first record for Springfield, MA (*Walden*). At this point in the program PREV-STATE is "IL" but PREV-CITY is the same as the current CITY; both contain "Springfield." If you check for a change in CITY, you won't find one at all, and no city total will print even though Springfield, MA, is definitely a different city from Springfield, IL.

Because cities in different states can have the same name, if you write your control break program to check for a change in city first, your program will not recognize that you are working with a new city. Instead, you should always check for the **major-level break** first. If the records are sorted by CITY within STATE, then a change in STATE causes a major break and a change in CITY causes a **minor-level break**. When the STATE value, "MA", is not equal to the PREV-STATE value, "IL", you force a CITY-BREAK, printing a city total for Springfield, IL, before a state total for IL and before continuing with the Springfield, MA, record. You check for a change in STATE first, and if there is one, you perform a CITY-BREAK. In other words, if there is a change in STATE, there is an implied change in CITY, even if the cities happen to have the same name.

**tip**

If you need totals to print by CITY within COUNTY within STATE, we could say we have minor-, intermediate-, and major-level breaks.

Figure 7-20 shows the MAIN-LOOP for the Book Sales by City and State Report program. You check for a change in the STATE value. If there is no change, you check for a change in the CITY value. If there is no change either, you add 1 to the counter for the city and read the next record. When there is a change in the CITY value, you print the city total and add the city total to the state total. When there is a change in the STATE value, you perform the break routine for the last city in the state, and then you print the state total and add it to the grand total.

```
MAIN-LOOP
     if STATE not equal PREV-STATE
          perform STATE-BREAK
     else
          if CITY not equal PREV-CITY
               perform CITY-BREAK
     add 1 to CITY-COUNTER
     read BOOK-REC
RETURN
```

**Figure 7-20:** Pseudocode for MAIN-LOOP for Book Sales by City and State report

Figures 7-21 and 7-22 show the STATE-BREAK and CITY-BREAK modules. The two modules are very similar; the STATE-BREAK routine contains just one extra type of task. When there is a change in STATE, you perform the CITY-BREAK automatically before you perform any of the other necessary steps to change states.

```
STATE-BREAK
     perform CITY-BREAK
     print "Total for", PREV-STATE, STATE-COUNTER
     GRAND-TOTAL = GRAND-TOTAL + STATE-COUNTER
     STATE-COUNTER = 0
     PREV-STATE = STATE
RETURN
```

**Figure 7-21:** Pseudocode for STATE-BREAK module

```
CITY-BREAK
     print PREV-CITY, CITY-COUNTER
     STATE-COUNTER = STATE-COUNTER + CITY-COUNTER
     CITY-COUNTER = 0
     PREV-CITY = CITY
RETURN
```

**Figure 7-22:** Pseudocode for CITY-BREAK module

The sample report for the book sales by city and state shows that you print the grand total for all book sales, so within the CLOSE-DOWN module, you must print the GRAND-TOTAL variable. Before you can do so, however, you must perform both the CITY-BREAK and the STATE-BREAK routines one last time. You can accomplish this by performing STATE-BREAK, because the first step within STATE-BREAK is to perform CITY-BREAK.

Consider the sample data shown in Figure 7-19. While you continue to read records for books sold in Springfield, MA, you continue to add to the CITY-COUNTER for that city. At the moment you attempt to read one more record past the end of the file, you do not know whether or not there will be more records; therefore you have not yet printed either the CITY-COUNTER for Springfield or the STATE-COUNTER for MA. In the CLOSE-DOWN module, you perform STATE-BREAK, which immediately performs CITY-BREAK. Within CITY-BREAK, the count for Springfield prints and rolls up to the STATE-COUNT. Then, when the logic transfers back to the STATE-BREAK module, the total for MA prints and rolls up to the GRAND-TOTAL. Finally, you can print the GRAND-TOTAL, as shown in Figure 7-23.

```
CLOSE-DOWN
     perform STATE-BREAK
     write "Grand Total", GRAND-TOTAL
     close files
RETURN
```

**Figure 7-23:** Pseudocode for CLOSE-DOWN module

Every time you write a program in which you need control break routines, you should check whether you need to perform each of the following tasks within the routines:

- The lower-level break, if any
- Any control break processing for the previous group
- Rolling up the current level totals to the next higher level
- Resetting the current level's totals to zero
- Any control break processing for the new group
- Updating the control break field

## Page Breaks

Many business programs use a control break to start a new page when a printed page fills up with output. In other words, you might want to start a new page based on the number of lines already printed rather than on the contents of an input field such as department number. The logic in these programs involves counting the lines printed, pausing to print headings when the counter reaches some predetermined value, and then going on. This common business task is just another example of providing a break in the usual flow of control.

**tip**

Some programmers may prefer to reserve the term *control break* for situations in which the break is based on the contents of one of the fields in an input record, rather than on the contents of a work field such as a line counter.

Let's say you have a file called CUSTOMER-FILE. It contains 1,000 customers with two character fields that you have decided to call CUST-LAST and CUST-FIRST. You want to print a list of these customers, 60 detail lines to a page. The mainline logic of the program is familiar. The only new feature is a variable called a **line counter**. You will use this variable to keep track of the number of printed lines so that you can break to a new page after printing 60 lines. See Figure 7-24.

```
START
     declare variables — — — —    CUST-REC
     perform GET-READY
     while not EOF                     char CUST-LAST
             perform REPORT            char CUST-FIRST
     perform CLEAN-UP              char HEAD-1 = "CUSTOMER LIST"
                                   char HEAD-2 = "LAST      FIRST"
                                   num LINE-COUNTER = 0
```

**Figure 7-24:** Mainline logic of customer report program

**tip**

When you create a printed report, you need to clarify whether the user wants a specific number of *total* lines per page, including headings, or a specific number of *detail* lines per page following the headings.

Within the GET-READY module (Figure 7-25), you declare the variables, open the files, print the headings, and read the first record. Within the REPORT module (Figure 7-26), you compare the LINE-COUNTER to 60. For the first record, the LINE-COUNTER is zero, so you print the record, add one to the LINE-COUNTER, and read the next record.

```
GET-READY                    REPORT
     open files                   if LINE-COUNTER = 60 then
     write HEAD-1                         perform START-NEW-PAGE
     write HEAD-2                 print CUST-LAST, CUST-FIRST
     read CUST-REC                add 1 to LINE-COUNTER
RETURN                           read CUST-REC
                             RETURN
```

**Figure 7-25:** GET-READY module          **Figure 7-26:** REPORT module for customer report
       for customer report                              program

On every cycle through the REPORT module, you check the line counter to see if it is 60 yet. After the first record is written, LINE-COUNTER is 1. You read the second record and if there is a second record (that is, if it is not EOF), you return to the top of the REPORT module and compare LINE-COUNTER to 60, add 1 to LINE-COUNTER making it equal to 2, and print again.

After 60 records have been read and written, LINE-COUNTER holds a value of 60. When you read the sixty-first record (and if it is not EOF), you enter the REPORT module for the 61st time. The answer to the question `LINE-COUNTER = 60?` is yes, and you break to perform the START-NEW-PAGE module. The START-NEW-PAGE module is a control break routine.

The START-NEW-PAGE module must print the headings that appear at the top of a new page, and it must also set the LINE-COUNTER back to zero. If you neglect to reset the LINE-COUNTER, then its value will increase with each successive record and never be equal to 60 again. When you reset the LINE-COUNTER for a new page, then you will force execution of the START-NEW-PAGE module after 60 more records (120 total) have printed.

---

```
START-NEW-PAGE
     print HEAD-1
     print HEAD-2
     LINE-COUNTER = 0
RETURN
```

---

**Figure 7-27:** START-NEW-PAGE module for customer report

The START-NEW-PAGE module is simpler than many control break modules, because no counters or accumulators are being maintained. In fact, the START-NEW-PAGE module must perform only two of the tasks you have seen required by control break routines.

- It does not perform the lower-level break, because there is none.
- It does not perform any control break processing for the previous group, because there is none.
- It does not roll up the current level totals to the next higher level, because there are no totals.
- It does not reset the current level's totals to zero, because there are no totals.
- It does perform control break processing for the new group by writing headings at the top of the new page.
- It does update the control break field—the line counter.

You may want to remember one little trick that you can use to remove the statements that write the headings from the GET-READY module. If you initialize LINE-COUNTER to 60 when you define the variables at the beginning of the program, on the first pass through MAIN-LOOP you can "fool" the computer into doing the first set of headings automatically. You can take `print HEAD-1` and print HEAD-2 out of the GET-READY module because when you enter the REPORT module the first time, LINE-COUNTER is 60 already, and the START-NEW-PAGE routine prints the headings and resets the LINE-COUNTER to zero.

As within control break report programs that break based on the contents of one of a record's fields, in any program that starts new pages based on a line count, you always must update the line counting variable that causes the unusual action. Using page breaks or control breaks (or both) within reports adds a new degree of organization to your printed output and makes your printed information easier for the user to interpret and use.

##  T E R M S   A N D   C O N C E P T S

summary report                        minor-level break

multiple-level control break          line counter

major-level break

## S U M M A R Y

- A report that does not include any information about individual records, but instead includes group totals, is a summary report.

- In a multiple-level control break, the normal flow of logical control is altered—or breaks—in response to any one of several possible changes in condition.

- Just as it is in a single-level control break report, the input file you use in a multiple-level control break report must be presorted.

- Within a multiple-level control break program, you check for changes in the major-level control break field first. Then you check for changes in the minor-level field.

- In an end-of-job routine, you perform the major-level control break one last time.

- Every time you write a program in which you need control break routines, you should check whether you need to perform any lower-level break or any control break processing for the previous group. Then you roll up the current level totals to the next higher level, reset the current level's totals to zero, and perform any control break processing for the new group. Finally, you update the control break field.

- Many business programs use a control break to start a new page when a printed page fills up with output. The logic in these programs involves counting the lines printed and, when the counter reaches some predetermined value, pausing to print headings before going on.

# EXERCISES

1. If a university is organized into colleges (such as Liberal Arts), divisions (such as Languages), and departments (such as French), what would constitute the major, intermediate, and minor control breaks in a report that prints all classes offered by the university?

2. Write the flowchart for the Book Sales by City and State report program that appears in pseudocode in this section.

3. A zoo keeps track of the expense of feeding the animals it houses. Each record holds one animal's ID number, name, species (elephant, rhinoceros, tiger, lion, and so on), zoo residence (pachyderm house, large cat house, and so on), and weekly food budget. The records take the following form:

---

ANIMAL FEED RECORDS

File name: ANIMFOOD

Sorted by: species within house

| FIELD DESCRIPTION | POSITIONS | DATA TYPE | DECIMALS | EXAMPLE |
|---|---|---|---|---|
| Animal ID | 1—4 | Numeric | 0 | 4116 |
| Animal name | 5—29 | Character | | Elmo |
| Species | 30—45 | Character | | Elephant |
| House | 46—55 | Character | | Pachyderm |
| Weekly food | 56—59 | Numeric | 0 | 75 |
| budget in dollars | | | | |

---

Design a report that lists each animal's ID, name, and budgeted food amount. At the end of each species group, print a total budget for the species. At the end of each house (for example, the species lion, tiger, and leopard are all in the large cat house), print the house total. At the end of the report, print the grand total. Draw the hierarchy chart and create the flowchart or pseudocode for this problem.

4. A soft-drink manufacturer produces several flavors of drink—for example, cola, orange, and lemon. Additionally, each flavor has several versions such as regular, diet, and caffeine-free. The manufacturer operates factories in several states. Assume you have input records that list flavor, version, yearly production in gallons, and state. (For example: REGULAR COLA 2000 KANSAS.) The records have been sorted in alphabetical order by version within flavor within state. Design the report that lists each version and flavor, with minor total production figures for each flavor and major total production figures for each state. Create the hierarchy chart and flowchart or pseudocode for this program.

5. An art shop owner maintains records for each item in the shop, including the artist who made the item, the medium (for example, watercolor, oil, or clay), and the monetary value. The records are sorted by artist within medium. Design a report that lists all the items in the store with a minor total value following each artist's work, and a major total value following each medium. Allow only 40 detail lines per page. Create the hierarchy chart and flowchart or pseudocode for this program.

# CHAPTER

# Arrays

# 8

case ▶ "What are you guys working on?" you ask Lynn Greenbrier and Boston Murphy as you see them hovering over the table in the conference room.

"We're working on a program for the annual charity fundraiser," Lynn says. "Every time an employee makes a contribution, we add it to the department's total."

"I know about control breaks," you reply. "You have sorted the contributions by department, right?"

"No need," says Boston. "We're using an array. An array provides you with multiple memory locations. Each can act as a storage location to accumulate departmental contributions. We can place a contribution in any slot, like the mail carrier in your apartment building can place a letter in any numbered mailbox."

"Are arrays good for anything else?" you ask.

"Are you kidding? An array is like a table," Lynn adds. "Any time you find your program searching through a list of items, you can use an array to help you accomplish your task. Eventually, you'll learn to use an array to sort items in order. For now, let us explain array basics to you."

After studying Section A, you should be able to:

- Describe an array
- Describe how arrays occupy computer memory
- Explain how to use an array to eliminate a series of decisions
- Declare and initialize arrays
- Describe the difference between a run-time and a compile-time array
- Understand how to load array values from a file

# Using Arrays

## Real-Life Arrays

Whenever you require multiple storage locations for objects, you are using a real-life counterpart of a programming array. For example, if you store important papers in a series of file folders, and label each folder with a consecutive letter of the alphabet, then you are using the equivalent of an array. If you store mementos in a series of stacked shoe boxes, each labeled with a year, or if you sort mail into slots, each labeled with a name, then you are also using the equivalent of an array.

When you look down the left side of a tax table to find your income level before looking to the right to find your income tax obligation, you are using an array. Similarly, if you look down the left side of a train schedule to find your station before looking to the right to find the train's arrival time, you are using an array.

Each of these real-life arrays helps you to organize real-life objects. You *could* store all your papers or mementos in one huge cardboard box, or find your tax rate or train's arrival time if both were printed randomly in one large book. However, using an organized storage and display system makes your life easier in each of these cases. Using a programming array will accomplish the same results for your data.

> **Some programmers refer to an array as a *table* or a *matrix*.**

## How Arrays Occupy Computer Memory

An **array** is a series or list of variables in memory, all of which have the same name but are differentiated from one another with special numbers called **subscripts**. Each separate array variable is known as one **element** of the array. Each array element occupies an area in memory next to, or contiguous to, the others, as shown in Figure 8-1. You indicate the number of elements an array will hold—the **size of the array**—when you declare the array along with your other variables.

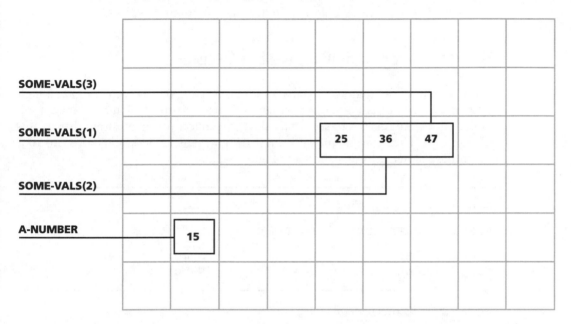

**Figure 8-1:** Appearance of a three-element array in computer memory

Every array element has the same group name, but every element has a unique subscript indicating how far away the individual element is from the first element. Therefore any array's subscripts are always a sequence of integers such as 1 through 5 or 1 through 10. Depending on the syntax rules of the programming language you use, you place the subscript within either parentheses or square brackets following the group name; when writing pseudocode or drawing a flowchart, you can use either form of notation. For example, Figure 8-1 shows how a single variable and an array are stored in computer memory. The single variable, named A-NUMBER, holds the value 15. The array, named SOME-VALS, contains three elements, so the elements are SOME-VALS(1), SOME-VALS(2), and SOME-VALS(3). The value stored in SOME-VALS(1) is 25; different values are stored in SOME-VALS(2) and SOME-VALS(3).

In general, older programming languages such as COBOL and RPG use parentheses to hold their array subscripts. Newer languages such as C++ and Java use square brackets.

In some languages (for example, Java and C) the first array element's subscript is zero; in others (for example, COBOL and RPG) it is one. In Pascal you can identify the starting number as any value you like. In all languages, however, the subscripts must be whole numbers and sequential.

You are never required to use arrays within your programs, but learning to use arrays efficiently can make many programming tasks far more efficient. When you understand how to use arrays, you will be able to provide elegant solutions to problems that otherwise would require tedious programming steps.

## Using an Array to Replace Nested Decisions

Consider a program that keeps statistics for a recycling drive competition at a high school. The school is holding a competition between the freshman, sophomore, junior, and senior classes to see which class can collect the greatest number of aluminum cans. Each time a student brings in some cans, a clerk adds a record to a file in the following format shown in Figure 8-2.

---

File name: STU-RECORDS

| FIELD DESCRIPTION | POSITIONS | DATA TYPE | DECIMALS |
|---|---|---|---|
| Student class | 1 | Numeric | 0 |
| Cans collected | 2—4 | Numeric | 0 |

---

**Figure 8-2:** File description for recycling records

For example, if a junior brings in 25 cans, one record is created with a 3 (for junior) in the class field and a 25 in the cans collected field. If a freshman brings in 10 cans, a record with 1 and 10 is created. If a second junior then brings in 20 more cans, the third record will contain a 3 and a 20.

At the end of the recycling competition, after all the records have been collected, the file may contain hundreds of records, each holding a one-digit number representing a class and up to a three-digit number representing cans. You want to write a program that summarizes the total of the cans brought in by each class. The print chart appears in Figure 8-3.

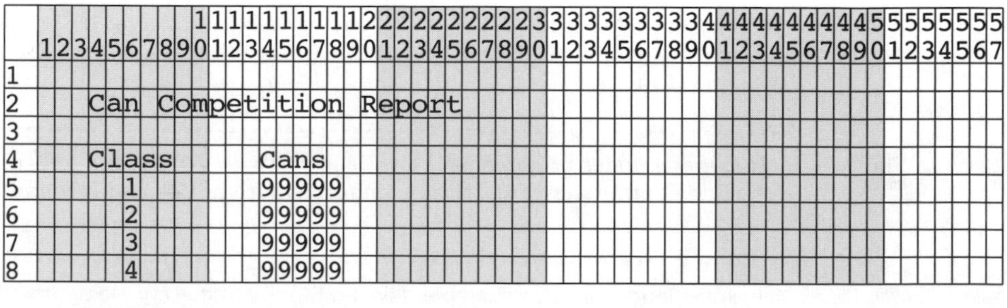

**Figure 8-3:** Print chart for can recycling report

If all the records were sorted in order by the student's class, this report could be a control break report. You would simply read each record for the first (freshman) class, accumulating the number of collected cans in a variable. When you read the first record from a different class, you would print out the total for the previous class, reset the total to zero, and update the control break field before continuing.

**You learned about control break logic in Chapter 7.**

Assume, however, that the records have not been sorted. Could you write the program that would accumulate the four class can-recycling totals? Of course you could! The program would have the same mainline logic as the other programs you have seen, and as flowcharted in Figure 8-4.

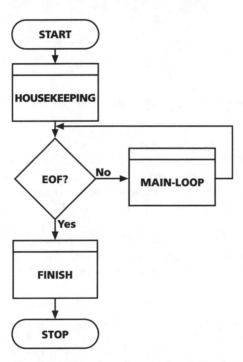

**Figure 8-4:** Flowchart for mainline logic of recycling program

In the HOUSEKEEPING module (Figure 8-5), you declare variables including STU-CLASS and STU-CANS. Then you open the files and read the first record into memory. The headings *could* be printed in HOUSEKEEPING, or, since no other printing will be done in this program until the FINISH routine, you can choose to wait and print the headings there.

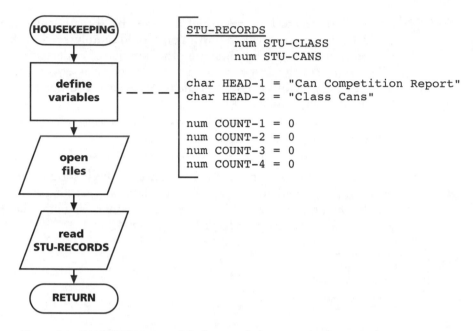

**Figure 8-5:** HOUSEKEEPING module for recycling program

You can use four variables, COUNT-1, COUNT-2, COUNT-3, and COUNT-4, to keep running counts of the collected-can totals for the four different classes. All four of these counter variables need to be initialized to zero. You can tell by looking at the planned output that you need two heading lines, so HEAD-1 will be defined as "Can Competition Report" and HEAD-2 as "Class Cans".

Eventually, four lines will be printed, each with a class number and a count of cans for that class. These lines cannot be printed until the FINISH routine, however, because you won't have a complete count of each class's cans until all input records have been read.

The logic within the MAIN-LOOP of the program is going to require adding a record's STU-CANS value to COUNT-1, COUNT-2, COUNT-3, or COUNT-4, depending on the STU-CLASS. After the STU-CANS have been added to one of the four accumulators, you read the next record, and if it is not EOF, you repeat the decision-making process. When all records have been read, you proceed to the FINISH module where you print the four summary lines with the four class counts. See Figures 8-6 and 8-7.

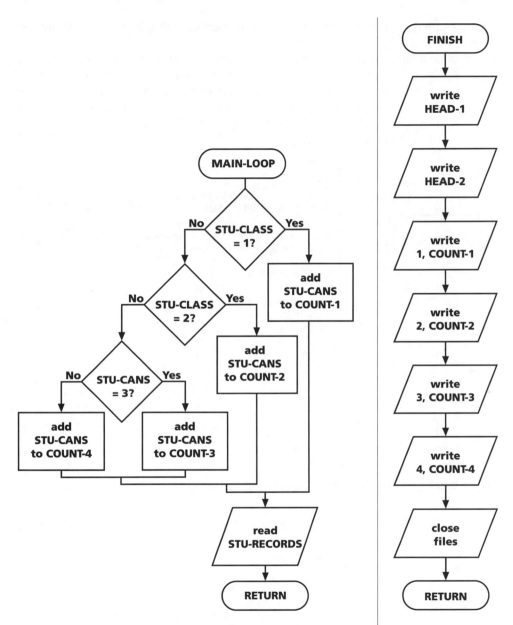

**Figure 8-6:** MAIN-LOOP module for recycling program

**Figure 8-7:** FINISH module for recycling program

The recycling program works just fine, and there is absolutely nothing wrong with it logically. But what if the recycling drive is held at an elementary school with eight classes? Or in a school district with 12 grade levels? Or in a company with 30 departments? With any of these scenarios, the basic logic of the program would remain the same; however, you would need many additional decisions within the

MAIN-LOOP and many additional print statements in FINISH in order to complete the processing.

Using an array provides an alternative approach to this programming problem. When you declare an array, you provide a group name for a number of associated variables in memory. For example, the four can-collection count accumulators can be redefined as a single array named COUNT. The individual elements become COUNT(1), COUNT(2), COUNT(3), and COUNT(4) as shown in the new HOUSEKEEPING module in Figure 8-8.

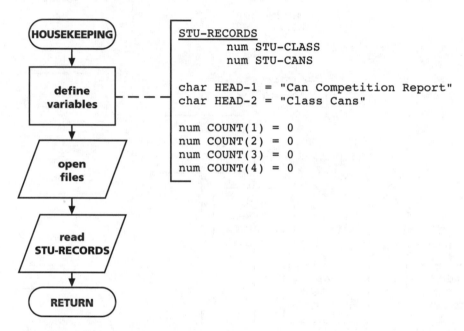

**Figure 8-8:** Modified HOUSEKEEPING declaring COUNT array

With the change to HOUSEKEEPING shown in Figure 8-8, the MAIN-LOOP changes to the version shown in Figure 8-9.

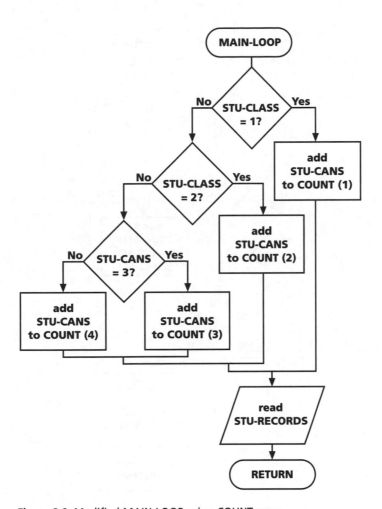

**Figure 8-9:** Modified MAIN-LOOP using COUNT array

Figure 8-9 shows that when the STU-CLASS is 1, the STU-CANS are added to COUNT(1); when the STU-CLASS is 4, the STU-CANS are added to COUNT(4). In other words, the value in STU-CANS is added to one of the elements of a COUNT array instead of to a single variable named COUNT-1, COUNT-2, COUNT-3, or COUNT-4. Big improvement over the original, huh? Of course, it isn't. You still have not taken advantage of the benefits of using the array in this program.

The true benefit of using an array lies in your ability to use a variable as a subscript to the array rather than a constant such as 1 or 4. Notice in the MAIN-LOOP in Figure 8-9 that within each decision, the value you are comparing to STU-CLASS and the constant you are using as a subscript in the resulting "Yes" process are always identical. That is, when the STU-CLASS is 1, the subscript used to add STU-CANS to the COUNT array is 1; when the STU-CLASS is 2, the subscript used for COUNT is 2; and so on. Therefore why not just use STU-CLASS as a subscript? You can rewrite the MAIN-LOOP as shown in Figure 8-10.

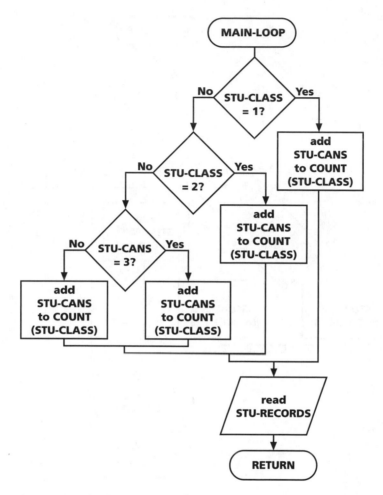

**Figure 8-10:** Modified MAIN-LOOP using variable STU-CANS as a subscript

Of course, this flowchart segment looks no more efficient that the one in Figure 8-9. However, notice that in Figure 8-10 the process box after each decision is exactly the same as every other process box after every other decision. Each box reads add STU-CANS to COUNT(STU-CLASS). If you are always going to take the same action no matter what the answer to a question is, why ask the question? Instead, now you can write the MAIN-LOOP as shown in Figure 8-11.

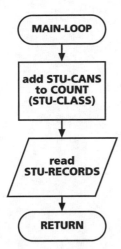

**Figure 8-11:** Modified MAIN-LOOP eliminating decisions

The two steps in Figure 8-11 represent the *whole* MAIN-LOOP! When STU-CLASS is 2, STU-CANS is added to COUNT(2); when STU-CLASS is 4, STU-CANS is added to COUNT(4), and so on. *Now* you have a big improvement to the original MAIN-LOOP from Figure 8-9. What's more, this MAIN-LOOP does not change whether there are 8, 30 or any other number of classes and COUNTs, as long as the classes are numbered sequentially. To use more accumulators, you would declare additional COUNT elements in the HOUSE-KEEPING module, but the MAIN-LOOP logic would remain the same as it is in Figure 8-11.

The FINISH routine also can be improved. Instead of four separate print statements, you can use a variable to control a printing loop, as shown in Figure 8-12. Since you are in the FINISH routine, all input records have been used and STU-CLASS is not currently holding any needed information. In FINISH, you can set STU-CLASS to 1 and then write STU-CLASS and COUNT(STU-CLASS). Then add 1 to STU-CLASS, and use the same set of instructions again. You can use STU-CLASS as a loop control variable to print the four individual COUNT values. The improvement in this FINISH module over the one shown in Figure 8-7 is not as dramatic as the improvement in the MAIN-LOOP; but with more COUNT elements, the only change to FINISH would be in the constant value you use to control the loop. 12 or 30 COUNT values can print as easily as 4 if they are stored in an array.

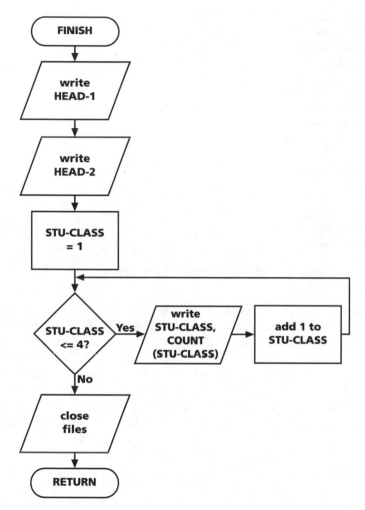

**Figure 8-12:** Modified FINISH module that uses an array

Within FINISH, the STU-CLASS variable is handy to use as a subscript, but any variable could have been used as long as it was:

- A numeric variable with no decimal places
- Initialized to 1
- Incremented by 1 each time the logic passes through the loop

In other words, there is nothing linking STU-CANS to the COUNT array per se; within the FINISH module you simply can use STU-CANS as a variable to be used as a subscript to indicate each successive element within the COUNT array.

The can recycling program *worked* when the MAIN-LOOP contained a long series of decisions, but it is easier to write when you employ arrays. Arrays are never mandatory, but often they can really cut down on your programming time and make a program easier to understand.

## Array Declaration and Initialization

In the can-recycling program, the four COUNTs were declared and initialized to 0s in the HOUSEKEEPING subroutine. The COUNTs needed to start at 0 so that they could be added to during the course of the program. Originally (see Figure 8-8) you provided initialization in the HOUSEKEEPING module as:

```
num COUNT(1) = 0
num COUNT(2) = 0
num COUNT(3) = 0
num COUNT(4) = 0
```

Declaring and initializing each separate COUNT is acceptable only if there are a small number of COUNTs. If the can recycling program were updated to keep track of recycling in a company with 30 departments, you would have to initialize 30 separate fields. It would be too tedious to write 30 separate declaration statements.

Programming languages do not require the programmer to name each of the 30 COUNTs: COUNT(1), COUNT(2), and so on. Instead, you can make a declaration such as one of those in Figure 8-13.

| Declaration | Programming Language |
| --- | --- |
| DIM COUNT(30) | BASIC |
| int count[30]; | C, C++ |
| int count = new int[30]; | Java |
| COUNT OCCURS 30 TIMES PICTURE 9999. | COBOL |
| ARRAY COUNT [1..30] of INTEGER; | Pascal |

Figure 8-13: Declaring a 30-element array named COUNT in several common languages

C, C++, and Java programmers typically use lowercase variable names.

The terms int and INTEGER in the code sample in Figure 8-13 both indicate that the COUNT array will hold whole-number values.

What all the declarations in Figure 8-13 have in common is that they name the array COUNT (or count) and indicate that there will be 30 separate elements. For flowcharting or pseudocode purposes, a statement such as array COUNT(30) will indicate the same thing.

Declaring an array does not necessarily set its individual elements to zero (although it does in BASIC and Java). Most programming languages allow the equivalent of array COUNT(30) all set to 0; you should use a statement like this to initialize an array in your flowcharts or pseudocode.

Alternatively, to start all array elements with the same initial value, you can use an initialization loop in the HOUSEKEEPING section. An **initialization loop** is a loop structure that provides initial values for every element in any array. To create an initialization loop, you must use a numeric field as a subscript. For example, if you declare a field named SUB, and initialize SUB to 1, then you can use a loop like the one shown in the HOUSEKEEPING module in Figure 8-14 to set all the array elements to zero.

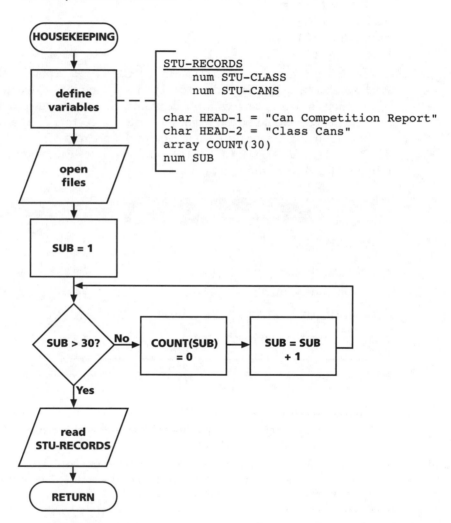

**Figure 8-14:** HOUSEKEEPING module demonstrating one method of initializing array elements

# Run-Time and Compile-Time Arrays

The array that you used to accumulate class counts in the can recycling program is a **run-time array**, or **execution-time array**, because the values that you want to use, the final can counts, are created during an actual run, or execution, of the program. In other words, if the freshman class is going to collect 1,000 cans, you don't know that fact at the beginning of the program. Instead, that value is accumulated during the execution of the program and not known until the end of the program.

Some arrays are not run-time, but rather **compile-time arrays**. Recall from Chapter 1 that compiling is the act of translating a high-level language into machine code (1s and 0s). A compile-time array is one whose final desired values are fixed right at the beginning of the program.

For example, let's say you own an apartment building with five floors and you have records for all your tenants with the information shown in Figure 8-15. The combination of each tenant's floor number and apartment letter provides you with a specific apartment—for example, apartment 3B.

File name: **TENANTS**

| FIELD DESCRIPTION | POSITIONS | DATA TYPE | DECIMALS |
|---|---|---|---|
| Tenant name | 1—40 | Character | |
| Floor number | 41 | Numeric | 0 |
| Apartment letter | 42 | Character | |

**Figure 8-15:** Tenant file description

Every month, you print a rent bill for each tenant. Your rent charges are based on the floor of the building as shown in Figure 8-16.

| Floor | Rent in $ |
|---|---|
| 1 | 350 |
| 2 | 400 |
| 3 | 475 |
| 4 | 600 |
| 5 | 1000 (the penthouse!) |

**Figure 8-16:** Rents by floor

To create a computer program that prints each tenant's name and rent due, you could use five decisions concerning the floor number. However, it is more efficient to use a compile-time array to hold the five rent figures. The array is a compile-time array because you set its values once at the beginning of the program and they never change.

▶ **tip**

> Remember that another name for an array is a *table*. If you can list the rents in a table, that is a clue that using an array may be an appropriate option.

The mainline logic for this program is shown in Figure 8-17. The housekeeping module is named PREP. When you declare variables within PREP, you create an array for the five rent figures and set num RENT(1) = 350, num RENT(2) = 400, and so on. The rent amounts are **hard coded** into the array; that is, they are explicitly assigned to the array elements. The PREP module is shown in Figure 8-18.

```
START
     perform PREP
     while not EOF
             perform FIGURE-RENT
     perform CLEAN-UP
END
```

**Figure 8-17:** Mainline logic for rent program

```
PREP
     declare variables — — — — TENANT-REC
     open files                     char TEN-NAME
     read TENANT-REC                num TEN-FLOOR
RETURN                              char TEN-APT-FLOOR
                               num RENT(1) = 350
                               num RENT(2) = 400
                               num RENT(3) = 475
                               num RENT(4) = 500
                               num RENT(5) = 1000
```

**Figure 8-18:** PREP module for rent program

At the end of PREP, you read a first record into memory. When it enters FIGURE-RENT (the main loop), you can print three items: "Dear", TEN-NAME, and "Here is your monthly rent bill". Then you must print the rent figure. Instead of making a series of selections such as if TEN-FLOOR = 1 then print RENT(1) and if TEN-FLOOR = 2 then print RENT(2), you want to take advantage of the RENT array. The solution is to create a FIGURE-RENT routine that looks like Figure 8-19. You use the TEN-FLOOR as a subscript to access the correct RENT.

When you are deciding what variable to use as a subscript with an array, ask yourself what the subscript value depends on. When you print a RENT, the rent you use depends on the floor on which the tenant lives, so you print the RENT(TEN-FLOOR).

▶ tip

Every programming language will provide you with ways to space your output attractively. For example, a common technique to separate "Dear" from the tenant's name is to include a space after the *r* in *Dear* as in Print "Dear ", TEN-NAME.

```
FIGURE-RENT
     print "Dear ", TEN-NAME, "Here is your monthly rent bill"
     print RENT(TEN-FLOOR)
     read TENANT-REC
RETURN
```

**Figure 8-19:** FIGURE-RENT module of rent program

The CLEAN-UP to this program is very simple—just close the files. See Figure 8-20.

```
CLEAN-UP
     close files
RETURN
```

**Figure 8-20:** CLEAN-UP module for rent program

Without a RENT array, the FIGURE-RENT module would have to contain four decisions and five different resulting actions. With the RENT array, there are no decisions. Each tenant's rent is simply based on the RENT that corresponds to the TEN-FLOOR because the floor number indicates the positional value of the corresponding rent. Arrays can really lighten the load!

## Loading an Array from a File

Writing the rent program from the last section requires that you set values for five RENT array elements in the PREP module. If you write the rent program for a skyscraper, you may have to initialize 100 array elements. Additionally, when the building management changes the rent amounts, you must alter the program to reflect the new values. If the values change frequently, you usually do not want to hard code the values into your program. Instead, you can write your program so that it loads the array from a file.

A file that contains all the rents can be updated by building management as frequently as needed. If you write the rent program so that it accepts this file, you read in the entire RENT-REC file within the PREP module. Figure 8-21 shows how this is done.

```
PREP
      declare variables  — — — — — — ┌ RENT-REC
      open files                     │      num RENT-AMT
      COUNT = 1                      │ TENANT-REC
      read RENT-REC                  │      char TEN-NAME
      while not EOF                  │      num TEN-FLOOR
            RENT(COUNT) = RENT-AMT   │      char TEN-APT-LETTER
            COUNT = COUNT + 1        │ array RENT occurs 5 times
            read RENT-REC            │ num COUNT
      read TENANT-REC                └
RETURN
```

**Figure 8-21:** PREP module for rent program

In the PREP module in Figure 8-21, you set a variable, COUNT, to one. Then you read a record from the RENT-REC file. Each record on the RENT-REC file contains just one field—a rent. The rents in the RENT-REC files are stored in order by floor. When you read in the first RENT-AMT, you store it in the first element of the RENT array. You increase the COUNT to 2, read the second record, and while it's not EOF, you store the second rent in the RENT array. After the RENT-REC file is exhausted, then you begin to read the TENANT-REC file, and the program proceeds as usual. When you use this method, clerical employees can update the RENT-REC file, and your program takes care of loading the rents into the program array.

# TERMS AND CONCEPTS

array

subscripts

element

size of an array

initialization loop

run-time array

execution-time array

compile-time array

hard coded

# S U M M A R Y

- An array is a series or list of variables in memory, all of which have the same name.

- You differentiate array variables, or elements, with a subscript that indicates distance from the first element.

- Each array element occupies an area in memory contiguous to the others. You indicate the number of elements an array will hold, or the size of the array, when you declare it.

- Any array's subscripts are always a sequence of integers such as 1 though 5 or 1 through 10.

- You place a subscript within parentheses or square brackets following the group name.

- Using an array often provides an elegant alternative approach to making multiple decisions in a program.

- The true benefit of using an array lies in your ability to use a variable rather than a constant as a subscript to the array.

- You can declare and initialize array elements separately, or as a group.

- Declaring an array does not necessarily set its individual elements to zero, although it does in some languages. Most programming languages allow you to initialize all array elements to the same value. Alternatively, you can use an initialization loop.

- When you use a run-time or execution-time array, final values are created during an actual run, or execution, of the program.

- Values that are explicitly assigned to variables are hard-coded.

- You can load array values from a file.

# E X E R C I S E S

1. Write pseudocode for the can recycling program that was flowcharted in this chapter.

2. Draw a flowchart for the tenant rent program that was presented in pseudocode in this chapter.

3. The city of Cary is holding a special census. The census takers collect one record for each citizen as follows:

**CENSUS FILE DESCRIPTION**

**File name: CENSUS**

**Not sorted**

| FIELD DESCRIPTION | POSITIONS | DATA TYPE | DECIMALS |
|---|---|---|---|
| Age | 1–3 | Numeric | 0 |
| Gender | 4 | Character | |
| Marital status | 5 | Character | |
| Voting district | 6–7 | Numeric | 0 |

The voting district field contains a number from 1 through 22.

Design the report for, draw the hierarchy chart for, and draw the logic of the program that would produce a count of the number of citizens residing in each of the 22 voting districts.

4. a. The Midville Park District maintains records containing information about players on its soccer teams. Each record contains a player's first name, last name, and team number. The teams are:

| Soccer Teams | |
|---|---|
| Team number | Team name |
| 1 | Goal Getters |
| 2 | The Force |
| 3 | Top Guns |
| 4 | Shooting Stars |
| 5 | Midfield Monsters |

Design the print chart, hierarchy chart, and flowchart or pseudocode for a report that lists each player along with his or her team number and team name.

b. Create the logic for a program that produces a count of the number of players registered for each item listed in Exercise 4a.

**5.** a. A school contains 30 classrooms numbered 1 through 30. Each class may contain any number of students up to 35. Each student takes an achievement test at the end of the school year and receives a possible grade from 0 through 100. One record is created for each student in the school; each record contains a student ID, room number, and grade. Design the print chart, hierarchy chart, and logic for a program that lists the total points scored for each of the 30 classes.

   b. Modify Exercise 5a so that each class average of the test scores prints rather than each class total.

   c. The school in Exercises 5a and 5b maintains a file containing the teacher's name for each classroom. Each record in this file contains a room number 1 through 30, and the last name of the teacher. Modify Exercise 5b so that the correct teacher's name appears on the list with his or her class's average.

# SECTION B

**objectives**

**After studying Section B, you should be able to:**

- Use parallel arrays
- Search an array for an exact match
- Search an array for a range match

# Using Parallel Arrays

## Searching for an Exact Match in an Array

In both the can recycling program and the rent program that you've seen in this chapter, it is convenient that the fields that the arrays depend on hold small whole numbers. The classes in the high school are 1 through 4 and the floors of the building are 1 through 5. Unfortunately, real life doesn't always happen in small whole numbers.

Consider a mail order business in which orders come in with a customer name, address, item number ordered, and quantity ordered as shown in Figure 8-22.

File name: CUST-REC

| FIELD DESCRIPTION | POSITIONS | DATA TYPE | DECIMALS |
|---|---|---|---|
| Customer name | 1–20 | Character | |
| Address | 21–40 | Character | |
| Item number | 41–43 | Numeric | 0 |
| Quantity | 44–45 | Numeric | 0 |

**Figure 8-22:** Mail order customer file description

The item numbers are three-digit numbers, but perhaps they are not consecutive 001 through 999. Instead, over the years, items have been deleted and new items have been added. For example, there may no longer be an 005 or a 129. Sometimes there may be a hundred-number gap or more between items.

Let's say that this season you are down to the items shown in Figure 8-23.

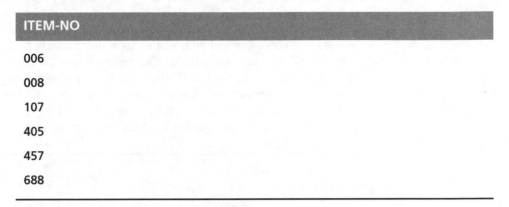

| ITEM-NO |
| --- |
| 006 |
| 008 |
| 107 |
| 405 |
| 457 |
| 688 |

**Figure 8-23:** Available items in mail order company

When a customer orders an item, you want to determine whether the customer has ordered a valid item number. You could use a series of six decisions to determine whether the ordered item is valid, but a superior approach is to create an array that holds the list of valid item numbers. Then you can search through the array for an exact match to the ordered item. If you search through the entire array without finding a match for the item the customer ordered, you can print an error message such as "No such item."

Suppose you create an array with the six elements shown in Figure 8-24. If a customer orders an item 107, you can tell whether it is valid by looking down the list and verifying that 107 is a member of the list. In a similar fashion, you can use a loop to test each TABLE-NO against the ordered item number.

```
TABLE-NO(1) = 006
TABLE-NO(2) = 008
TABLE-NO(3) = 107
TABLE-NO(4) = 405
TABLE-NO(5) = 457
TABLE-NO(6) = 688
```

**Figure 8-24:** Array of valid item numbers

The technique for verifying that an item number exists involves setting a subscript to 1 and setting a flag variable to "N". Then you compare the customer's ordered item number to the first item in the array. If the first item in the array matches the customer ordered item, you can set the flag variable to "Y". If not, you increase the subscript and continue to look down the list. If you check all six valid item numbers and none matches the customer item, then the flag variable is still "N". If the flag variable is "N" after you have looked through the entire list, you can issue an error message. Assuming you declare the customer item as CUST-ITEM-NO, the subscript as X, and the flag as FOUND-IT, then Figure 8-25 shows pseudocode that accomplishes the item verification.

```
X = 1
FOUND-IT = "N"
while X < 7
        if CUST-ITEM-NO = TABLE-NO(X) then
                FOUND-IT = "Y"
        X = X + 1
if FOUND-IT = "N"
        print "No such item"
```

**Figure 8-25:** Pseudocode for finding an exact match for a customer item number

## Using Parallel Arrays

In a mail order company, when you read in a customer's order, you usually want to accomplish more than to simply verify that the item exists. You want to determine the price of the ordered item, multiply that price by quantity ordered, and print out a bill. Prices for six available items are shown in Figure 8-26.

| ITEM-NO | ITEM-PRICE |
|---------|------------|
| 006     | 0.59       |
| 008     | 0.99       |
| 107     | 4.50       |
| 405     | 15.99      |
| 457     | 17.50      |
| 688     | 39.00      |

**Figure 8-26:** Available items in mail order company with prices

You could write a program in which you would read in a customer order record and then use the customer's item number as a subscript to pull a price from an array. To use this method, you would need an array with at least 688 elements. If a customer ordered item 405, the price would then be found at TABLE-PRICE(405), or the 405th element of the array. Such an array would need 688 elements, but because you sell only six items, you would waste 682 of the memory positions. Instead of wasting a large quantity of memory, you can set up this program with two arrays.

Consider the mainline logic in Figure 8-27 and the READY routine in Figure 8-28. Two arrays are set up in READY. One contains six elements named TABLE-NO; all six elements are valid item numbers. The other array also has six elements named TABLE-PRICE, all six elements are prices. Each price in this TABLE-PRICE array is conveniently in the same position as the corresponding item number in the other TABLE-NO array. Two corresponding arrays such as these are **parallel arrays** because each element in one array is associated with the element in the corresponding position in the other array.

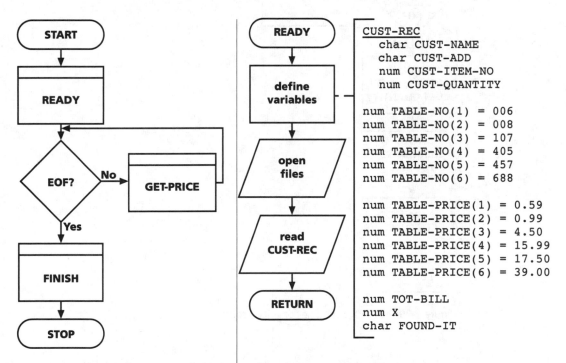

**Figure 8-27:** Mainline logic for price program | **Figure 8-28:** READY module for price program

You can write the GET-PRICE routine as shown in Figure 8-29. The general procedure is to read each item number, look through the TABLE-NO values one at a time, and when a match for the CUST-ITEM-NO on the input record is found, pull the corresponding parallel price out of the list of TABLE-PRICEs.

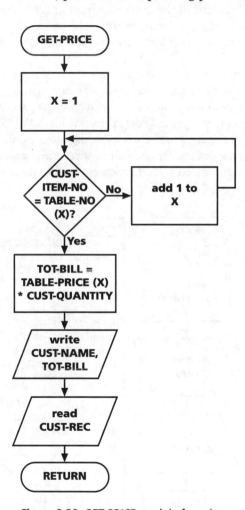

Figure 8-29: GET-PRICE module for price program

You must create a variable to use as a subscript for the arrays. If you name the subscript X, then you can set X equal to 1. Then, if CUST-ITEM-NO is the same as TABLE-NO (X), you can use the corresponding price from the other table, TABLE-PRICE (X), to calculate the customer's bill.

If CUST-ITEM-NO is *not* the same as TABLE-NO (X), then add 1 to X. Because X now holds a value of 2, you next compare TABLE-NO (2) to the order number. X keeps increasing, and eventually a match between CUST-ITEM-NO and TABLE-NO (X) is found.

Once you find a match for the CUST-ITEM-NO in the TABLE-NO array, you know that the price of that item is in the same position in the other table, the TABLE-PRICE array. When TABLE-NO (X) is the correct item, TABLE-PRICE (X) must be the correct price.

Suppose that a customer orders item 457 and walk through the flowchart yourself to see if you come up with the correct price.

The GET-PRICE module in Figure 8-29 is not perfect. You have made one dangerous assumption: that every customer is going to order a valid item number. If a customer is looking at an old catalog and orders item 007, the program is never going to find a match. The value of X will just continue to increase until it reaches a value higher than the number of elements in the array. At that point one of two things will happen. When you use a subscript value that is higher than the number of elements in an array, some programming languages will stop execution of the program and issue an error message. Other programming languages will not issue an error message but will continue to search through computer memory beyond the end of the array. Either way, the program doesn't end "elegantly." Ordering a wrong item number is a frequent error; a good program should be able to handle the mistake.

You can improve the price-finding program by adding a test within the GET-PRICE module; you can check whether the program has searched through the entire table without finding a matching item number. See Figure 8-30.

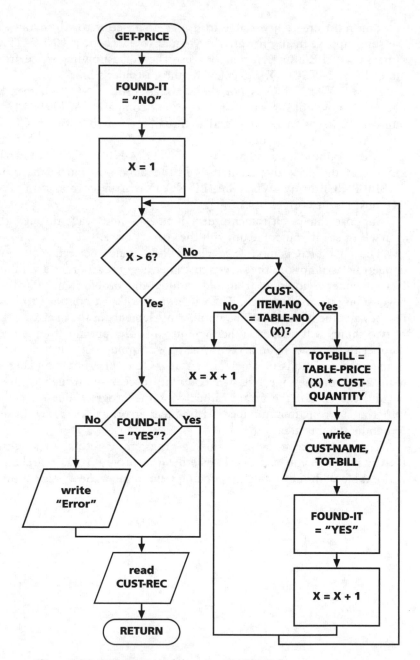

**Figure 8-30:** GET-PRICE module using FOUND-IT flag

In READY, you can set up a variable named FOUND-IT that acts as a flag. A **flag** is a variable that you set to indicate a true or false state. Typically, a variable is called a flag when its only purpose is to tell you whether or not some event has occurred. When you enter the GET-PRICE routine, you can set FOUND-IT equal to "No". Then after setting X to 1, check to see if X is greater than 6 yet. If it is not, compare the CUST-ITEM-NO to TABLE-NO(X). If they are equal, you know the position of the item's price and you can use the price to print the customer's bill and set the FOUND-IT flag to "Yes". If the CUST-ITEM-NO is not equal to TABLE-NO(X), you increase X by 1 and continue to search through the array. When X is 7 (that is, greater than 6), you shouldn't look through the table any more; you've gone through all six legitimate items and you've reached the end. If FOUND-IT doesn't have a "Yes" in it at this point, it means you never found a match for the ordered item number; you never took the Yes path leading from CUST-ITEM-NO = TABLE-NO(X). If FOUND-IT does not have "Yes" stored in it, you should print out an error message; the customer has ordered a nonexistent item.

This program is still a little inefficient. The problem lies in the fact that if lots of customers order item 006 or item 008, their price is found on the first or second pass through the loop. The program continues searching through the item table, however, until X exceeds the value 6. To stop the search once the item has been found and FOUND-IT is set to "Yes", force X to 7 immediately. Then, when the program loops back to check whether or not X is greater than 6 yet, the loop will be exited and the program won't bother checking any of the higher item numbers. Leaving a loop as soon as a match is found is called an **early exit**; it improves the program's efficiency. The larger the array is, the more beneficial it becomes to exit the searching loop as soon as you find what you're looking for.

Figure 8-31, then, shows the final version of the GET-PRICE loop. You search the TABLE-NO array, element by element. If an item number is not matched in a given location, the subscript is increased and the next location is checked. As soon as an item number is located in the table, you print a line, turn on the flag, and force the subscript to a high number (seven) so the program will not check the item number table any further.

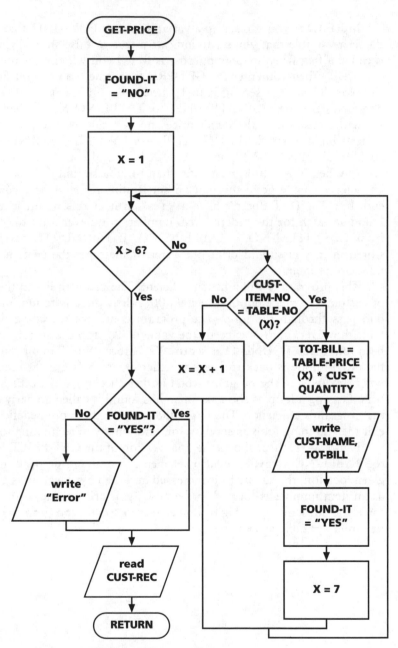

**Figure 8-31:** GET-PRICE module with early exit

# Searching an Array for a Range Match

Customer item numbers need to match numbers in a table exactly in order to determine the correct price of an item. Sometimes, however, programmers want to work with **ranges of values** in arrays.

Recall the customer file description from the last section, shown again in Figure 8-32.

---

**File name: CUST-REC**

| FIELD DESCRIPTION | POSITIONS | DATA TYPE | DECIMALS |
|---|---|---|---|
| Customer name | 1–20 | Character | |
| Address | 21–40 | Character | |
| Item number | 41–43 | Numeric | 0 |
| Quantity | 44–45 | Numeric | 0 |

---

**Figure 8-32:** Customer file description

Suppose the company decides to offer quantity discounts as shown in Figure 8-33.

| Number of items ordered | Discount % |
|---|---|
| 1 – 9 | 0 |
| 10 – 24 | 10 |
| 25 – 48 | 15 |
| 49 or more | 25 |

**Figure 8-33:** Discounts on orders by quantity

You want to be able to read in a record and determine a discount percentage based on the value in the quantity field. One ill-advised approach might be to set up an array with as many elements as any customer might ever order, and store the appropriate discount for each possible number, as shown in Figure 8-34.

```
num DISCOUNT(1) = 0
num DISCOUNT(2) = 0
  .
  .
  .
num DISCOUNT(9) = 0
num DISCOUNT(10) = 10
  .
  .
num DISCOUNT(48) = 15
num DISCOUNT(49) = 25
num DISCOUNT(50) = 25
  .
  .
```

**Figure 8-34:** Usable—but inefficient—DISCOUNT array

This approach has three drawbacks:

- It requires a very large array that uses a lot of memory.
- You must store the same value repeatedly. For example, each of the first nine elements receives the same value, zero.
- Where do you stop adding array elements? Is a customer order quantity of 75 items enough? What if a customer orders 100 items? Or 1,000? No matter how many elements you place in the array, there's a chance that some day a customer will order more.

A better approach is to create just four discount array elements, one for each of the possible discount rates as shown in Figure 8-35.

```
num DISCOUNT(1) = 0
num DISCOUNT(2) = 10
num DISCOUNT(3) = 15
num DISCOUNT(4) = 25
```

**Figure 8-35:** Superior DISCOUNT array

With the new four-element DISCOUNT array, you need a parallel array to search to find the appropriate level for the discount. At first, beginning programmers think they would like to create an array named RANGE and test whether the quantity ordered equals one of the four stored values. For example:

```
num RANGE(1) = 1 through 9
num RANGE(2) = 10 through 24
num RANGE(3) = 25 through 48
num RANGE(4) = 49 and higher
```

However, you cannot create an array like the one above. Each element in any array is simply a single variable. A variable like PAYRATE can hold $6 or $12, but it can't hold every value 6 *through* 12. Similarly, the RANGE(1) variable can hold a 1 or 2 or 9, but it can't hold 1 *through* 9; there is no such numeric value.

One solution is to create an array that holds only the low end value of each range, as Figure 8-36 shows.

```
num RANGE(1) = 1
num RANGE(2) = 10
num RANGE(3) = 25
num RANGE(4) = 49
```

**Figure 8-36:** DISCOUNT array using low end of each discount range

Now the process is to compare each CUST-QUANTITY value with the *last* range limit (RANGE(4)). If the CUST-QUANTITY is at least that value, 49, the customer gets the highest discount rate (DISCOUNT(4)). If the CUST-QUANTITY is not at least RANGE(4), then you check to see if it is at least RANGE(3), or 25. If so, the customer receives DISCOUNT(3), and so on. If you declare a variable named RATE, then Figure 8-37 illustrates the DETERMINE-DISCOUNT process for the program. Assuming the HOUSEKEEPING module correctly declares the variables, this DETERMINE-DISCOUNT module determines the correct discount rate for an order, then calculates and prints a customer bill.

An alternative approach is to store the high end of every range in an array, Then you start with the *lowest* element and check for values *less than* each array element value.

```
DETERMINE-DISCOUNT
    SUB = 4
    while SUB > 0
        if CUST-QUANTITY >= RANGE(SUB)
            RATE = DISCOUNT(SUB)
            SUB = 0
        else
            SUB = SUB - 1
    BILL = CUST-QUANTITY * PRICE-EACH
    BILL = BILL - BILL * RATE
    print CUST-NAME, CUST-ADDRESS, BILL
    read CUST-REC
RETURN
```

**Figure 8-37:** Pseudocode for discount determination

# TERMS AND CONCEPTS

parallel arrays                     early exit

flag                                ranges of values

 # SUMMARY

- Arrays that contain corresponding information are parallel arrays.

- When using parallel arrays, you look through one array for a match, then use the associated value in the other array.

- Often you must create a variable just to use as a subscript for arrays.

- A flag is a variable that tells you whether or not some event has occurred.

- You can use an early exit to improve array-searching efficiency.

- Each array element can hold only a single value.

- You can use an array to search for a range match.

 # EXERCISES

**1.** A fast-food restaurant sells the following products:

| Fast-Food Items | |
| --- | --- |
| Product | Price |
| Cheeseburger | 2.49 |
| Pepsi | 1.00 |
| Chips | .59 |

Create a print chart, hierarchy chart, and flowchart or pseudocode for a program that reads in a record containing a customer number and item name and prints either the correct price or the message "Sorry, we do not carry that" as output.

**2.** Each week, the home office for a fast-food restaurant franchise distributes a file containing new prices for the items it carries. The file contains the item name and current price. Create a print chart, hierarchy chart, and flowchart or pseudocode for a program that loads the current values into arrays. Then the program reads in a customer record containing a customer number and item name, and prints either the correct price or the message "Sorry, we do not carry that" as output.

**3.** The city of Cary is holding a special census. The census takers collect one record for each citizen as follows:

**CENSUS FILE DESCRIPTION**

**File name: CENSUS**

**Not sorted**

| FIELD DESCRIPTION | POSITIONS | DATA TYPE | DECIMALS |
|---|---|---|---|
| Age | 1–3 | Numeric | 0 |
| Gender | 4 | Character | |
| Marital status | 5 | Character | |
| Voting district | 6–7 | Numeric | 0 |

Design the report for, draw the hierarchy chart for, and draw the logic of the program that produces a count of the number of citizens residing in each of the following age groups: under 18, 18 through 30, 31 through 45, 46 through 64, and 65 and older.

**4. a.** A company desires a breakdown of payroll by department. Input records are as follows:

**PAYROLL FILE DESCRIPTION**

**File name: PAY**

| FIELD DESCRIPTION | POSITIONS | DATA TYPE | DECIMALS | EXAMPLE |
|---|---|---|---|---|
| Employee last name | 1–20 | Character | | Dykeman |
| First name | 21–30 | Character | | Ellen |
| Department | 31 | Numeric | 0 | 3 |
| Hourly salary | 32–36 | Numeric | 2 | 12.50 |
| Hours worked | 37–38 | Numeric | 0 | 40 |

Input records come in alphabetical order by employee, *not* in department number order.

The output is a list of the seven departments in the company (numbered 1 through 7) and the total gross payroll (rate times hours) for each department. Create the print layout chart, hierarchy chart, and flowchart or pseudocode for this program.

b. Modify Exercise 4a so that the report lists department names as well as numbers. The names are:

| Department names and numbers | |
| --- | --- |
| Department number | Department name |
| 1 | Personnel |
| 2 | Marketing |
| 3 | Manufacturing |
| 4 | Computer Services |
| 5 | Sales |
| 6 | Accounting |
| 7 | Shipping |

c. Modify the report created in Exercise 4b so that it prints a line of information for each employee containing the employee's name, department number, department name, hourly wage, hours worked, gross pay, and withholding tax.

Withholding taxes are based on the following percentages of gross pay:

| Withholding Taxes | |
| --- | --- |
| Weekly salary | Withholding % |
| 0.00 – 200.00 | 10 |
| 200.01 – 350.00 | 14 |
| 350.01 – 500.00 | 18 |
| 500.01 – up | 22 |

5. The Perfect Party Catering Company keeps records concerning the events it caters as follows:

EVENT RECORDS

File name: PAY

| FIELD DESCRIPTION | POSITIONS | DATA TYPE | DECIMALS | EXAMPLES |
|---|---|---|---|---|
| Event number | 1-5 | Numeric | 0 | 15621 |
| Host name | 6-25 | Character | | Profeta |
| Month | 26-27 | Numeric | | 10 |
| Day | 28-29 | Numeric | | 15 |
| Year | 30-33 | Numeric | | 2002 |
| Meal selection | 34 | Numeric | | 4 |
| Number of guests | 36-40 | Numeric | | 150 |

Additionally, a meal file contains the meal selection codes (such as 4), name of entree (such as "Roast beef"), and current price per guest (such as 19.50).

Design the print chart for a report that lists each event number, host name, date, meal, guests, and gross total price for the party, and price for the party after discount. Print the month *name*—for example, "October" rather than "10". Print the meal selection—for example, a "Roast beef" rather than "4". The gross total price for the party is the price per guest for the meal times the number of guests. The final price includes a discount based on the following table:

| Discounts for Large Parties | |
|---|---|
| Number of guests | Discount in $ |
| 1-25 | 0 |
| 26-50 | $75 |
| 51-100 | $125 |
| 101-250 | $200 |
| 251 and over | $300 |

Create the hierarchy chart and either the flowchart or pseudocode for this problem.

# Advanced Array Manipulation

**case** ▶ "I'm so glad you taught me about arrays," you tell Boston Murphy, one of your mentors at Solutions, Inc. "They seem like a very powerful tool. When I use an array I can eliminate making long strings of decisions in my programs."

"That's for sure," Boston replies, "but you haven't learned everything yet."

"Since an array is a list of items, I'm thinking that I should be able to use arrays to put data items in order," you say. "I've written control break programs in which my program receives sorted data, but how does the data get that way?"

"You *can* use arrays to sort data," Boston says. "Let me show you how."

# Sorts

After studying Section A, you
should be able to:

- Describe the need for sorting data
- Use a bubble sort
- Refine a bubble sort by using a variable for the array size
- Refine a bubble sort by reducing unnecessary comparisons
- Refine a bubble sort by eliminating unnecessary passes through a list

## The Need for Sorting

When you store data records, they exist in some sort of **sequential order**. For example, employee records might be stored in numeric order by Social Security number or department number, or in alphabetic order by last name or department name. Even if the records are stored in a random order—for example, the order in which a data-entry clerk felt like entering them—they still are in *some* order, although probably not the order desired for processing or viewing. When this is the case, the data need to be **sorted**, or placed in order based on the contents of one or more fields. When you sort data, you can sort either in **ascending order**, arranging records from lowest to highest, or **descending order**, arranging records from highest to lowest. Here are some examples:

- A college stores students' records in ascending order by student ID number, but the registrar wants to view the data in descending order by credit hours earned so he can contact those students who are close to graduation.
- A department store maintains customer records in ascending order by customer number, but at the end of a billing period the credit manager wants to extract those records that are 90 or more days overdue. She wants to list these overdue customers in descending order by the amount owed so the customers maintaining the biggest debt can be contacted first.

■ A sales manager keeps records for her salespeople in alphabetical order by last name, but needs to list the annual sales figure for each salesperson so that she can determine the **median** (middle value of a list, *not* the same as the average, or **mean**) annual sale amount.

Sorting is usually reserved for a relatively small number of data items. If thousands of customer records are stored and they frequently need to be accessed in order based on different fields (alphabetical order by customer name one day, zip code order the next), the records would probably not be sorted at all, but would be **indexed**, or **linked**. Indexing and linking are discussed at the end of this chapter.

When computers sort data, they always use numeric values. This is clear when you sort records by fields such as customer number or balance due. However, even alphabetic sorts are numeric because everything that is stored in a computer is stored as a number using a series of 0s and 1s. In every popular computer coding scheme, a "B" is numerically one greater than an "A" and a "y" is numerically one less than a "z". Unfortunately, whether an "A" is represented by a number that is greater or smaller than the number representing an "a" depends on your system. Therefore, to obtain the most useful and accurate list of alphabetically sorted records, you should be consistent in the use of capitalization.

**tip**

Because "A" is always less than "B", alphabetic sorts are always considered ascending sorts.

## Using a Bubble Sort

Many sorting techniques have been developed. One of the simplest to understand is a technique called a **bubble sort**. You can use a bubble sort to arrange records in either ascending or descending order. In a bubble sort, items in a list are compared in pairs, and when an item is out of order, it trades places with the item below it. With an ascending bubble sort, after each adjacent pair of items in a list has been compared once, the largest item in the list will have "bubbled" to the bottom. After many passes through the list, the smallest items rise to the top like bubbles in a carbonated drink.

Assume that five student test scores are stored in a file, and you want to sort them in ascending order for printing. To begin, you can define three subroutines as shown in Figure 9-1: HOUSEKEEPING, SORT-SCORES, and FINISH-UP.

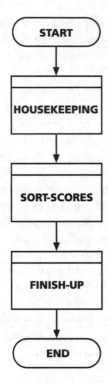

**Figure 9-1:** Mainline logic for score-sorting program

The HOUSEKEEPING routine of this program defines a variable name for each individual score on the input file and sets up an array of five elements in which to store the five scores. The entire file is then read into memory, and one score is stored in each element of the array. See Figure 9-2.

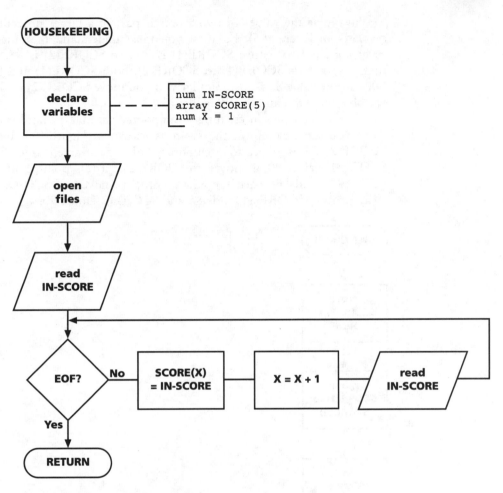

**Figure 9-2:** HOUSEKEEPING module for score-sorting program

When the program logic enters the SORT-SCORES routine, five scores have been placed in the array. For example, assume they are:

```
SCORE(1) = 90
SCORE(2) = 85
SCORE(3) = 65
SCORE(4) = 95
SCORE(5) = 75
```

To begin sorting this list of scores, you compare the first two scores. If they are out of order, you reverse their positions, or **swap their values**. That is, SCORE(1) will assume the value 85 and SCORE(2) will take on the value 90. After this swap, the scores will be in slightly better order than they were originally.

Swapping the values of two scores is part of a larger procedure (as you will see later in Figure 9-5), but first you must understand that there is a trick to reversing any two scores. SCORE(1) is 90 and SCORE(2) is 85. The problem is that if you move SCORE(1) to SCORE(2), both SCORE(1) and SCORE(2) hold 90, and the value 85 is lost. Similarly, if you move SCORE(2) to SCORE(1), both variables hold 85, and the 90 is lost.

The solution lies in creating a temporary variable to hold one of the scores. Then you can accomplish the swap as shown in Figure 9-3. First the value in SCORE(2), 85, is moved to a temporary holding variable, named TEMP. Then the SCORE(1) value, 90, is moved to SCORE(2). At this point, both SCORE(1) and SCORE(2) hold 90. Then the 85 in TEMP is moved to SCORE(1). So after the swap process, SCORE(1) holds 85 and SCORE(2) holds 90.

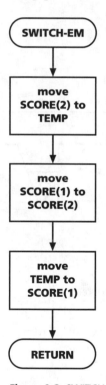

**Figure 9-3:** SWITCH-EM module that swaps the first two values in an array

move SCORE(2) to TEMP **can also be written as** TEMP = SCORE(2).

The SWITCH-EM module in Figure 9-3 is limited in use because it switches only elements 1 and 2 of the SCORE array. The more universal SWITCH-EM shown in Figure 9-4 switches *any* two adjacent elements in an array when the variable X represents the position of the first of the two elements, and the value X + 1 represents the subsequent position.

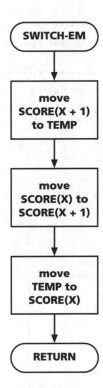

**Figure 9-4:** SWITCH-EM module that swaps any two adjacent values in an array

For an ascending sort, you need to perform the SWITCH-EM modules whenever any given element of the SCORE array (X) has a value greater than the next element (X + 1) of the SCORE array. If the Xth element is not greater than the element at position X + 1, the switch should not take place. See Figure 9-5.

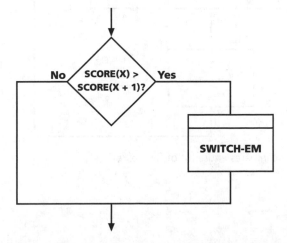

**Figure 9-5:** Decision showing when to call SWITCH-EM module

▶ tip

........................................................................................

**For a descending sort, you would write the decision so that you would perform the switch when SCORE(X) is *less than* SCORE(X + 1).**

........................................................................................

You must execute the decision SCORE(X) > SCORE(X + 1)? four times—when X is 1, 2, 3, and 4. You should not attempt to make the decision when X is 5, because then you would compare SCORE(5) to SCORE(5 + 1), and there is no valid SCORE(6) in the array. Therefore Figure 9-6 shows the correct loop, which continues to make array element swaps while X is less than 5.

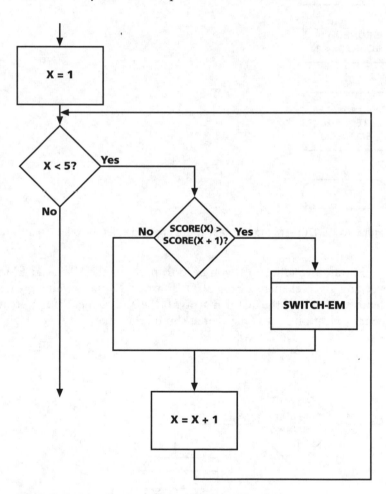

**Figure 9-6:** Loop that compares entire list of five scores

If you have these original scores:

```
SCORE(1) = 90
SCORE(2) = 85
SCORE(3) = 65
SCORE(4) = 95
SCORE(5) = 75
```

then the logic proceeds like this:

1. Set X to 1.
2. X is less than 5, so enter the loop.
3. Compare SCORE(X), 90, to SCORE(X + 1), 85. The two SCOREs are out of order, so they are switched.

   The list is now:

   ```
   SCORE(1) = 85
   SCORE(2) = 90
   SCORE(3) = 65
   SCORE(4) = 95
   SCORE(5) = 75
   ```

4. After the swap, add 1 to X, so X is 2.
5. X is less than 5, so enter the loop a second time.
6. Compare SCORE(X), 90, to SCORE(X + 1), 65. These two values are out of order, so swap them.

   Now the result is:

   ```
   SCORE(1) = 85
   SCORE(2) = 65
   SCORE(3) = 90
   SCORE(4) = 95
   SCORE(5) = 75
   ```

7. Add 1 to X, so X is now 3.
8. X is less than 5, so enter the loop.
9. Compare SCORE(X), 90, to SCORE(X + 1), 95. These values are in order, so no switch is made.
10. Add 1 to X, making it 4.
11. X is less than 5, so enter the loop.
12. SCORE(X), 95, is larger than SCORE(X + 1), 75, so switch them.

Now the list is as follows:

```
SCORE(1) = 85
SCORE(2) = 65
SCORE(3) = 90
SCORE(4) = 75
SCORE(5) = 95
```

13. Add 1 to X.
14. X is 5, so do not enter the loop again.

When X reaches 5, every element in the list has been compared with the one adjacent to it. The highest score, a 95, has "sunk" to the bottom of the list. However, the scores still are not in order. They are in slightly better ascending order than they were to begin with, because the largest value is at the bottom of the list, but they are still out of order. You need to repeat the entire procedure illustrated in Figure 9-6 so that 85 and 65 (the current SCORE(1) and SCORE(2) values) can switch places, and 90 and 75 (the current SCORE(3) and SCORE(4) values), can switch places. Then the scores will be 65, 85, 75, 90, 95. You will have to perform the procedure yet again to swap the 85 and 75.

As a matter of fact, if the scores had started out in the worst possible order (95, 90, 85, 75, 65), the process shown in Figure 9-6 would have to take place four times. In other words, you would have to pass through the list of values four times making appropriate swaps before the numbers would appear in perfect ascending order. You need to place the loop in Figure 9-6 within another loop that executes four times.

Figure 9-7 shows the complete logic for the SORT-SCORES module. The SORT-SCORES module uses a loop control variable named Y to cycle though the list of scores four times. With an array of five elements, it takes four comparisons to get through the array once, and it takes four sets of those comparisons to get the entire array in sorted order.

When you sort the elements in an array, the general rule is that whatever the number of elements in the array, the greatest number of pair comparisons you need to make during each loop is *one fewer* than the number of elements in the array. Additionally you need to process the loop *one fewer* number of times than the number of elements in the array. For example, if you want to sort a ten-element array, you make nine pair comparisons on each of nine rotations through the loop, executing a total of 81 score comparison statements.

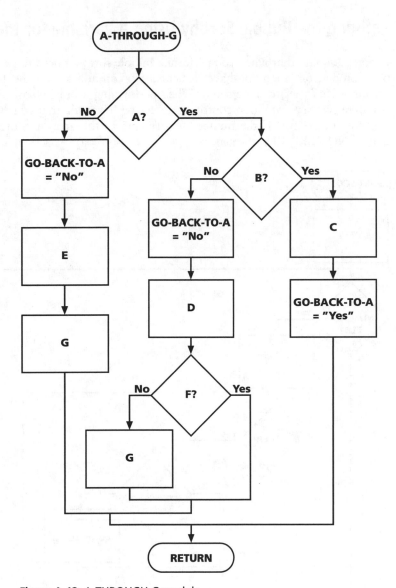

**Figure A-13:** A-THROUGH-G module

# Refining the Bubble Sort by Using a Variable for the Array Size

Keeping in mind that when you perform a bubble sort you need to perform one fewer pair comparisons than you have elements, you can add a refinement that makes the sorting logic easier to understand. When performing a bubble sort on an array, you compare two separate loop control variables with a value that equals the number of elements in the list. If the number of elements in the array is stored in a variable named NUMBER-ELS, the general logic for a bubble sort is shown in Figure 9-8.

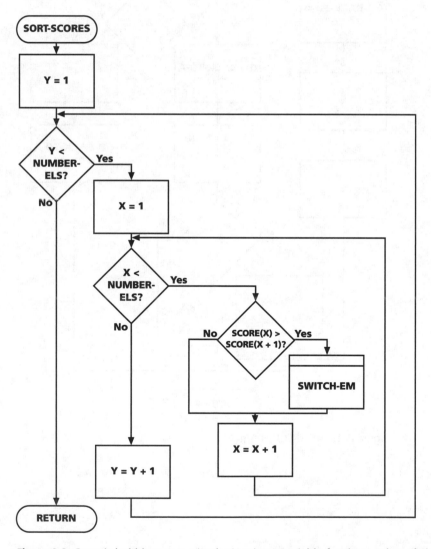

**Figure 9-8:** Generic bubble sort routine logic using a variable for the number of elements

To use the logic shown in Figure 9-8, you must declare NUMBER-ELS along with the other variables in the HOUSEKEEPING module. You can set the value of NUMBER-ELS to 5 there, because you know there are five elements in the array to be sorted. The NUMBER-ELS variable will also be useful in a module that prints the scores, sums them, or performs any other activity with the list, as well as for sorting loops. For example, the FINISH-UP module in Figure 9-9 uses the NUMBER-ELS variable to control the print loop. The advantage to using a NUMBER-ELS variable instead of a constant such as 5 in your program is that if you modify the program array so that it accommodates more or fewer scores in the future, you can simply change the value in NUMBER-ELS. Then you do not need to alter every instance of the constant throughout the program; the NUMBER-ELS variable automatically holds the correct value.

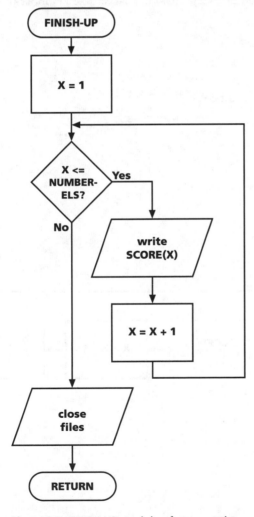

**Figure 9-9:** FINISH-UP module of score-sorting program

Sometimes you don't want to initialize the NUMBER-ELS variable at the start of the program. You might not know how many array elements there are—for example, sometimes there are only three or four scores to sort. In other words, what if the size of the list to be sorted varies? Rather than initializing NUMBER-ELS to a final value, you can count the input scores, then give NUMBER-ELS its value after you know how many scores exist.

When you read each IN-SCORE during HOUSEKEEPING, X increases by one. After one IN-SCORE, X is two; after two IN-SCOREs, X is three, and so on. After you reach EOF, X indicates one more than the number of elements in the array, so you can set NUMBER-ELS to X – 1. Figure 9-10 shows the new HOUSEKEEPING module. With this approach, it doesn't matter if there are not enough IN-SCOREs to fill the array. You simply make one fewer pair comparisons than the number of the value held in NUMBER-ELS instead of always making a larger fixed number of pair comparisons.

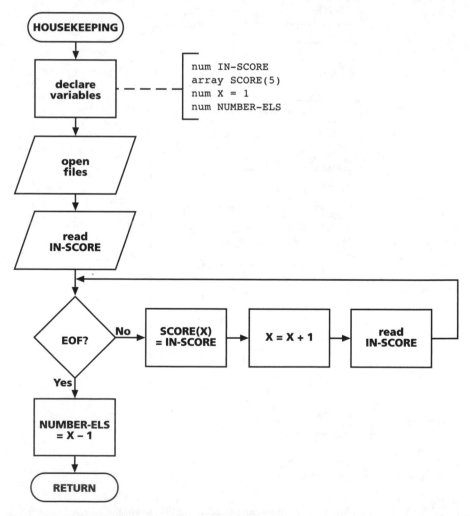

Figure 9-10: HOUSEKEEPING module for variable size array

**tip**

If you choose to initialize X to zero rather than one, then you can set NUMBER-ELS to the value of X rather than X – 1.

When you count the input records and use the NUMBER-ELS variable, it does not matter if there are not enough scores to fill the array. However, it does matter if there are more scores than the array can hold. Every array must have a finite size, and it is an error to try to store data past the end of the array. When you don't know how many elements will be stored in an array, you must overestimate the number of elements you declare. If the number of scores in the SCORE array can be five or fewer, then you can declare the SCORE array to have a size of 5, and you can use five elements or fewer. Figure 9-11 shows the pseudocode that provides one possibility for an additional improvement to the HOUSEKEEPING module in Figure 9-10. If you use the logic in Figure 9-11, you read IN-SCORES until EOF, but if the array subscript X exceeds 5, you display a warning message and do not attempt to store any additional IN-SCOREs in the SCORE array.

```
HOUSEKEEPING                                        ┌ num IN-SCORE
    declare variables  — — — — — — — — — │ array SCORE(5)
    open files                                       │ num X = 1
    read IN-SCORE                                     │ num Y
    while not EOF                                     └ num NUMBER-ELS
            if X > 5 then
                print "Warning! Too many scores"
            else
                SCORE(X) = IN-SCORE
            X = X + 1
            read IN-SCORE
        NUMBER-ELS = X — 1
    RETURN
```

**Figure 9-11:** Pseudocode for HOUSEKEEPING that prevents overextending the array

## Refining the Bubble Sort by Reducing Unnecessary Comparisons

You can make additional improvements to the bubble sort created in the last sections and illustrated in Figure 9-8. When you perform a bubble sort, you pass through a list, making comparisons and swapping values if two values are out of order. If you are performing an ascending sort, then after you have made one pass through the list, the largest value is guaranteed to be in its correct final position at the bottom of the list. Similarly, the second-largest element is guaranteed to be in its correct second-to-last position after the second pass through the list, and so on. If you continue to compare every element pair in the list on every pass through the list, you are comparing elements that are already guaranteed to be in their final correct position.

On each pass through the array, you can afford to stop your pair comparisons one element sooner. In other words, after the first pass through the list, there is no longer a need to check the bottom element; after the second pass, there is no need to check the two bottom elements. You can accomplish this by setting a new variable, PAIRS-TO-COMPARE, to the value of NUMBER-ELS − 1. On the first pass through the list, every pair of elements is compared, so PAIRS-TO-COMPARE *should* equal NUMBER-ELS − 1. But for each subsequent pass, PAIRS-TO-COMPARE should be reduced by 1, because after the first pass there's no need to check the bottom element any more. See Figure 9-12.

```
SORT-SCORES
    PAIRS-TO-COMPARE = NUMBER-ELS − 1
    Y = 1
    while Y < NUMBER-ELS
        X = 1
        while X <= PAIRS-TO-COMPARE
            if SCORE(X) > SCORE(X + 1) then
                perform SWITCH-EM
            X = X + 1
        Y = Y + 1
        PAIRS-TO-COMPARE = PAIRS-TO-COMPARE − 1
RETURN
```

**Figure 9-12:** Pseudocode for SORT-SCORES module using PAIRS-TO-COMPARE variable

## Refining the Bubble Sort by Eliminating Unnecessary Passes through the List

A final improvement that could be made to the bubble sort in Figure 9-12 is one that reduces the number of passes through the array. If array elements are so badly out of order that they are in reverse order, then it takes as many passes through the list as the value in NUMBER-ELS to complete all the comparisons and swaps needed to get the list in order. However, when the array elements are nearly in order to start, all the elements may be correctly arranged after only a few passes through the list. All subsequent passes result in no swaps. For example, assume the original scores are as follows:

```
SCORE(1) = 65
SCORE(2) = 75
SCORE(3) = 85
SCORE(4) = 90
SCORE(5) = 95
```

The bubble sort module in Figure 9-12 would pass through the array four times, making four sets of pair comparisons. It would always find that SCORE(X)

is *not* greater than SCORE(X + 1), so no switches would ever be made. The scores would end up in the proper order, but they *were* in the proper order in the first place! A lot of time has been wasted.

A possible remedy is to add a flag that you set on any pass through the list when all elements are already in the correct order. For example, you can create a variable named SWITCH-OCCURRED and set it to "No" at the start of each pass through the list. You can change its value to "Yes" each time the SWITCH-EM subroutine is performed (that is, each time a switch is necessary).

If you ever "make it through" the entire list of pairs without making a switch, the SWITCH-OCCURRED flag will *not* have been set to "Yes", meaning that no switch has occurred and that the array elements must already be in the correct order. This *might* be on the first or second pass through. If the array elements are already in the correct order at that point, there is no need to make more passes through the list. But when a list starts out in the worst possible order, a switch needs to be made *every time through the list*. You can stop making passes through the list when SWITCH-OCCURRED is "No" after a complete trip through the array.

Figure 9-13 illustrates a sort that uses a SWITCH-OCCURRED flag. At the beginning of SORT-SCORES, initialize SWITCH-OCCURRED to "Yes" before entering the comparison loop the first time. Then immediately set SWITCH-OCCURRED to "No". When a switch occurs—that is, when the SWITCH-EM module executes—set SWITCH-OCCURRED to "Yes".

```
SORT-SCORES
    PAIRS-TO-COMPARE = NUMBER-ELS - 1
    SWITCH-OCCURRED = "YES"
    while SWITCH-OCCURRED = "YES"
        X = 1
        SWITCH-OCCURRED = "NO"
        while X <= PAIRS-TO-COMPARE
            if SCORE(X) > SCORE(X + 1) then
                perform SWITCH-EM
                SWITCH-OCCURRED = "YES"
            X = X + 1
        PAIRS-TO-COMPARE = PAIRS-TO-COMPARE - 1
RETURN
```

**Figure 9-13:** Bubble sort with SWITCH-OCCURRED flag

With the addition of the flag in Figure 9-13, you no longer need the variable Y, which was keeping track of the number of passes through the list. Instead, you just keep going through the list until you can make a complete pass without any switches. For a list that starts out in perfect order, you go through the loop only once. For a list that starts out in the *worst* possible order, you will make a switch with every pair every time through the loop until PAIRS-TO-COMPARE has been reduced to 0. In this case, on the last pass through the loop, X is set to 1, SWITCH-OCCURRED is set to "No", X is no longer less than or equal to PAIRS-TO-COMPARE, and the loop is exited.

# TERMS AND CONCEPTS

| | |
|---|---|
| sequential order | mean |
| sorted | indexed |
| ascending order | linked |
| descending order | bubble sort |
| median | swap their values |

# SUMMARY

- When you store data records, they exist in some sort of sequential order.

- When you need to view data records in some order other than their stored order, you need to sort the data records or place them in order based on the contents of one or more fields.

- When you sort data, you can sort either in ascending order, arranging records from lowest to highest, or in descending order, arranging them from highest to lowest.

- Sorting is usually reserved for a relatively small number of data items.

- When computers sort data, they always use numeric values. Even alphabetic sorts are really numeric.

- You can use a bubble sort to arrange records in either ascending or descending order. In a bubble sort, items in a list are compared in pairs, and when an item is out of order, it trades places with the item below it.

- You swap values by using a temporary holding variable.

- Using a bubble sort, the greatest number of pair comparisons during each pass through the array is one fewer than the number of elements in the array. Additionally, you must pass through the comparison loop one fewer number of times than there are elements in the array.

- If you use a variable to hold the number of array elements in a sort, you can easily modify the sort routine to accommodate an array with more or fewer elements.

- For flexibility, rather than initialize a variable to the number of array elements to be sorted, you can count input records.

- When you don't know how many elements will be stored in an array, you must over-estimate the number of elements you declare.

- You can afford to stop your pair comparisons one element sooner on each pass through the array while performing a bubble sort.

- When doing a bubble sort, you can add a flag that you set on any pass through the list when all elements are already in the correct order.

# E X E R C I S E S

1. Write pseudocode that reflects the logic of the score-sorting program that is flow-charted in Figures 9-1 through 9-9.

2. Professor Zak allows students to drop the two lowest scores on the ten 100-point quizzes she gives during the semester. Develop the logic for a program that reads in student records that contain ID number, last name, first name, and ten quiz scores. The output lists student ID, name and total points on the eight highest quizzes.

3. The Hinner College Foundation holds an annual fundraiser for which they maintain records that each contain a donor name and contribution amount. Assume that there are never more than 300 donors. Develop the logic for the program that sorts the donation amounts in descending order. Output lists the highest five donation amounts.

4. A greeting-card store maintains customer records with data fields for first name, last name, address, and annual purchases in dollars. At the end of the year they invite the 100 customers with the highest annual purchases to an exclusive sale event. Develop the flowchart or pseudocode for this problem.

5. a. The village of Ringwood has taken a special census. Every census record contains a household ID number, size, and income. Ringwood has exactly 75 households. Village statisticians are interested in the median household size and the median household income. Develop the logic for the program that determines these figures.

   b. The village of Marengo has also taken a special census and collected records similar to those of Ringwood. The exact number of household records has not yet been determined, but you know that there are fewer than 1,000 households in Marengo. Determine the same statistics as in Exercise 5a.

**After studying Section B, you should be able to:**

■ Use an insertion sort

■ Use a selection sort

■ Describe indexed files

■ Describe linked lists

■ Use multidimensional arrays

# Other Sorts

## Using an Insertion Sort

The bubble sort works well and is relatively easy for novice array users to understand and manipulate, but even with all the improvements you added to the original bubble sort in the last lesson, it is actually one of the least efficient sorting methods available. An **insertion sort** provides an alternative method for sorting data, and it usually requires fewer comparison operations.

As with the bubble sort, when you use an insertion sort you also look at each pair of elements in an array. When you find an element that is smaller than the one before it, this element is considered to be "out of order." As soon as you locate such an element, you search the array backward from that point to see where an element smaller than the out-of-order element is located. At that point, you insert the out of order element into position by moving each subsequent element down one.

For example, consider these scores:

```
SCORE(1) = 65
SCORE(2) = 80
SCORE(3) = 95
SCORE(4) = 75
SCORE(5) = 90
```

Using an insertion sort, you compare SCORE(1), 65, and SCORE(2), 80, and determine that they are in order and leave them alone. Then you compare SCORE(2), 80, and SCORE(3), 95, and leave them alone. When you compare SCORE(3), 95, and SCORE(4), 75, you determine that the 75 is "out of order."

Next you look backward from the SCORE(4) of 75. SCORE(3) is not smaller, nor is SCORE(2); but since SCORE(1) is smaller than SCORE(4), SCORE(4) should follow SCORE(1). So you store SCORE(4) in a temporary variable, then move SCORE (2), (3), and (4) "down" the list. You move SCORE(3), 95, to SCORE(4)'s position. Then move SCORE(2), 80, to SCORE(3)'s position. Finally, assign the value of the temporary variable, 75, to the SCORE(2) position. The results:

```
SCORE(1)  =  65
SCORE(2)  =  75
SCORE(3)  =  80
SCORE(4)  =  95
SCORE(5)  =  90
```

You then continue on down the list, comparing each pair of variables. A complete insertion sort module is shown in Figure 9-14.

```
INSERTION-SORT
            Y = 1
            while Y < NUMBERS-ELS
                X = 1
                while X < NUMBER-ELS
                    if SCORE(X + 1) < SCORE(X) then
                        TEMP = SCORE(X + 1)
                        POS = X
                        while SCORE(POS) > TEMP and POS > 0
                          SCORE(POS + 1) = SCORE(POS)
                          POS = POS - 1
                        SCORE(POS + 1) = TEMP
                    X = X + 1
                Y = Y + 1
RETURN
```

**Figure 9-14:** Sample insertion sort module

The logic for the insertion sort is slightly more complicated than that for the bubble sort, but the insertion sort is more efficient because for the average out-of-order list, fewer "switches" are needed to put the list in order.

## Selection Sort

A **selection sort** provides another sorting option. In a selection sort, the first element in the array is assumed to be the smallest. Its value is stored in a variable—for example, SMALLEST—and its position in the array (1) is stored in another variable—for example, POSITION. Then every subsequent element in the array is tested. If one with a smaller value than SMALLEST is found, SMALLEST is set to the new value, and POSITION is set to that element's position. After the entire array has been searched, SMALLEST will hold the smallest value, and POSITION will hold its position.

The element originally in POSITION (1) is then switched with the SMALLEST value, so at the end of the first pass through the array, the lowest value ends up in the first position, and the value that was in the first position is where the smallest value used to be.

For example, given:

```
SCORE(1) = 95
SCORE(2) = 80
SCORE(3) = 75
SCORE(4) = 65
SCORE(5) = 90
```

First you place 95 in SMALLEST. Then check SCORE(2); it's less than 95, so place 2 in POSITION and 80 in SMALLEST. Then test SCORE(3). It's smaller than SMALLEST, so place 3 in POSITION and 75 in SMALLEST. Then test SCORE(4). Since it is smaller than SMALLEST, place 4 in POSITION and 65 in SMALLEST. Finally, check SCORE(5); it *isn't* smaller than SMALLEST.

So at the end of the first pass through the list, POSITION is 4 and SMALLEST is 65. You move the value 95 to SCORE(POSITION), or SCORE(4) and the value of SMALLEST, 65, to SCORE(1). The list becomes:

```
SCORE(1) = 65
SCORE(2) = 80
SCORE(3) = 75
SCORE(4) = 95
SCORE(5) = 90
```

Now that the smallest value is in the first position, you repeat the whole procedure, starting with POSITION (2). After you have passed through the list NUMBER-ELS − 1 times, all elements will be in the correct order. Walk through the logic shown in Figure 9-15.

---

```
SELECTION-SORT
     POSITION = 1
     while POSITION < NUMBER-ELS
          X = POSITION
          SMALLEST = SCORE(X)
          Y = X + 1
          while Y <= NUMBER-ELS
                    if SCORE(Y) < SMALLEST then
                          X = Y
                          SMALLEST = SCORE(Y)
                    Y = Y + 1
          SCORE(X) = SCORE(POSITION)
          SCORE(POSITION) = SMALLEST
          POSITION = POSITION + 1
RETURN
```

---

**Figure 9-15:** Sample selection sort module

Like the insertion sort, the selection sort almost always requires fewer switches than the bubble sort, but the variables may be a little harder to keep track of because the logic is a little more complex. Thoroughly understanding at least one of these sort techniques provides you with a valuable tool for arranging data and increases your understanding of the capabilities of arrays.

## Using Indexed Files

Sorting a list of five scores does not require significant computer resources. However, many data files contain thousands of records, and each record might contain dozens of data fields. Sorting large numbers of data records requires considerable time and computer memory. When a large data file needs to be processed in ascending or descending order based on some field, it is usually more efficient to store and access records based on their logical order rather than sort them and access them in their physical order.

When records are stored, they are stored in some **physical order**. For example, if you write the name of each of ten friends on an index card, the stack of cards has some physical order. You can arrange the cards alphabetically by the friends' last names, chronologically by age of the friendship, or randomly by throwing the cards in the air and picking them up as you find them. Whichever way you do it, the records still follow each other in *some* order. In addition to their current physical order, you may think of the cards as having a **logical order** based on any criteria you choose—from the tallest friend to the shortest, from the one who lives farthest away to the closest, and so on. Sorting the cards in order takes time; using the cards in their logical order without physically rearranging them is often more efficient.

A common method of accessing records in logical order is to use an index. Using an index involves identifying a key field for each record. A record's **key field** is the field whose contents make the record unique from all other records in a file. For example, multiple employees can have the same last name, first name, salary, or street address, but each employee possesses a unique Social Security number, so a Social Security number field makes a good key field for a personnel file. Similarly, a product number makes a good key field on an inventory file.

When you **index** records, you store a list of key fields paired with the storage address for the corresponding data record. When you use an index, you can store records on a **random-access storage device**, such as a disk. Each record can be placed in any physical location on the disk, and you can use the index as you would use the index in the back of a book. If you pick up a 600-page American history text because you need some facts about Betsy Ross, you do not want to start on page one and work your way through the text. Instead, you turn to the index, discover Betsy Ross is located on page 418, and go directly to that page.

As pages in a book have numbers, computer locations have **addresses**. In Chapter 1 you learned that every variable has a numeric address in computer memory; likewise, every data record on a disk has a numeric address at which it is stored. You can store records in any physical order on the disk, but the index can find the records in order based on their addresses. For example, you might store employees on a disk in the order in which they are hired. However, you often need to process the employees in Social Security number order. As each new employee is added to such a file, the employee can physically be placed anywhere there is room available on the disk. Her Social Security number is inserted in proper order in the index, along with the physical address at which her record is located.

> You do not need to determine a record's exact physical address in order to use it. A computer's operating system takes care of the job of locating available storage for your records.

You can picture an index based on Social Security numbers by looking at Figure 9-16.

| Social Security Number | Location |
| --- | --- |
| 111-22-3456 | 6400 |
| 222-44-7654 | 4800 |
| 333-55-1234 | 2400 |
| 444-88-9812 | 5200 |

**Figure 9-16:** Sample index

When you want to access the data for employee 333-55-1234, you tell your computer to look through the index, then proceed to the memory location specified. Similarly, when you want to process records in order based on Social Security number, you tell your system to retrieve records at the locations in the index in sequence. Thus, even though employee 111-22-3456 may have been hired last, and the record is stored at the highest physical address on the disk, if the employee record has the lowest Social Security number, it will be accessed first during any ordered processing.

When a record is removed from an indexed file, it does not have to be physically removed. It can simply be deleted from the index and thus will not be part of any further processing.

## Linked Lists

Another way to access records in a desired order, even though they may not be physically stored in that order, is to create a **linked list**. In its simplest form, creating a linked list involves creating one extra field in every record of stored data. This extra field holds the physical address of the next logical record. For example, a record that holds a customer's ID, name, and phone number might contain the fields:

CUST-ID
CUST-NAME
CUST-PHONE-NUM
CUST-NEXT-CUST

Every time you use a record, you access the next record based on the address held in the CUST-NEXT-CUST field.

Every time you add a new record to a linked list, you look through the list searching for the correct logical location for the new record. For example, assume that customer records are stored at the addresses shown in Figure 9-17, and that they are linked in customer number order.

| Address of Record | CUST-ID | CUST-NAME | CUST-PHONE | CUST-NEXT-CUST |
|---|---|---|---|---|
| 0000 | 111 | Baker | 234-5676 | 7200 |
| 7200 | 222 | Vincent | 456-2345 | 4400 |
| 4400 | 333 | Silvers | 543-0912 | 6000 |
| 6000 | 444 | Donovan | 329-8744 | EOF |

**Figure 9-17:** Linked customer list

You can see from Figure 9-17 that each customer's record contains a CUST-NEXT-CUST field that stores the address of the customer who follows in customer ID number order. The next customer's address may be physically distant, and the addresses are not in sequential order, but each customer is linked to the customer who follows him or her by ID value.

If a new customer with number 245 and the name Newberg is acquired, the computer operating system would find an available storage location for her, perhaps 8400. Then the procedure would be:

1. Compare the new customer's ID, 245, with the first record's ID, 111. The value 245 is higher, so you save the current address 0000 in a variable you can name SAVE-ADDRESS. Examine the next customer record that physically exists at the CUST-NEXT-CUST address, 7200.
2. Compare 245 with 222. The value 245 is higher, so save the current address, 7200, in SAVE-ADDRESS and examine the next customer record at address 4400.
3. Compare 245 with 333. The value 245 is lower, so that means customer 245 should logically precede customer 333. Set the CUST-NEXT-CUST field in Newburg's record (customer 245) to 4400, which is the address of customer 333. Also set the CUST-NEXT-CUST field of the record located at SAVE-ADDRESS (7200, Vincent, customer 222) to the new address, 8400. The updated list appears in Figure 9-18.

| Address of Record | CUST-ID | CUST-NAME | CUST-PHONE | CUST-NEXT-CUST |
| --- | --- | --- | --- | --- |
| 0000 | 111 | Baker | 234-5676 | 7200 |
| 7200 | 222 | Vincent | 456-2345 | 8400 |
| 8400 | 245 | Newberg | 222-9876 | 4400 |
| 4400 | 333 | Silvers | 543-0912 | 6000 |
| 6000 | 444 | Donovan | 329-8744 | EOF |

**Figure 9-18:** Updated customer list

As with indexing, when records are removed from a linked list, they do not need to be physically deleted. If you need to remove customer 333 from the preceding list, all you need to do is change Newberg's CUST-NEXT-CUST field to Donovan's address: 6000. Silvers' record would then be bypassed during any further processing.

More sophisticated linked lists store *two* additional fields with each record. One field stores the address of the next record and the other field stores the address of the *previous* record so that the list may be accessed either forward or backward.

## Using Multidimensional Arrays

An array that represents a single list of values is called a **single-dimensional array** or **one-dimensional array**. For example, an array that holds five rent figures that apply to five floors of a building can be displayed in a single column as in Figure 9-19.

```
RENT(1)  =      350
RENT(2)  =      400
RENT(3)  =      475
RENT(4)  =      600
RENT(5)  =     1000
```

**Figure 9-19:** A single-dimensional RENT array

You used the single-dimensional RENT array in Chapter 8.

The location of any RENT value in Figure 9-19 depends on only a single variable—the floor of the building. Sometimes, however, locating a value in an array depends on more than one variable. If you must represent values in a table or grid that contains rows and columns instead of a single list, then you might want to use a **multidimensional array**, specifically, a **two-dimensional array**.

Assume that the floor is not the only factor determining rent in your building, but that another variable, NUMBER-OF-BDRMS, also needs to be taken into account. The rent schedule might be the one shown in Figure 9-20.

| Floor | 1-bedroom apartment | 2-bedroom apartment | 3-bedroom apartment |
|-------|---------------------|---------------------|---------------------|
| 1 | 350 | 390 | 435 |
| 2 | 400 | 440 | 480 |
| 3 | 475 | 530 | 575 |
| 4 | 600 | 650 | 700 |
| 5 | 1000 | 1075 | 1150 |

**Figure 9-20:** Rent schedule based on floor and number of bedrooms

Each element in a two-dimensional array requires two subscripts to reference it—one subscript to determine the row and a second to determine the column. Thus the fifteen separate RENT values for a two-dimensional array based on the rent table in Figure 9-20 would be those shown in Figure 9-21.

```
RENT(1,1) =   350
RENT(1,2) =   390
RENT(1,3) =   435
RENT(2,1) =   400
RENT(2,2) =   440
RENT(2,3) =   480
  .
  .
  .
RENT(5,3) = 1150
```

**Figure 9-21:** RENT array values based on floor and bedrooms

If you store tenant records that contain two fields named FLOOR and NUMBER-OF-BDRMS, then the appropriate rent can be printed out with the statement: write RENT(FLOOR, NUMBER-OF-BDRMS). The first subscript represents the two-dimensional RENT array row; the second subscript represents the RENT array column.

• • • • • • • • • • • • • • • • • • • • • • • • • • • • • • • • • • • • • • • • • • • • • • •

Some languages access two-dimensional array elements with separate subscript notation. In C++ and Java, for example, the second-floor, three-bedroom rate might be written rent[2][3]. The convention in C++ and Java is to make variable names lowercase and to use square brackets for array subscripts.

• • • • • • • • • • • • • • • • • • • • • • • • • • • • • • • • • • • • • • • • • • • • • • •

Two-dimensional arrays are never actually *required*. The same 15 categories of rent information could be stored in three separate single-dimensional arrays of five elements each as shown in Figure 9-22.

| | | |
|---|---|---|
| RENT-ONE(1)  =  350 | RENT-TWO(1)  =  390 | RENT-THREE(1)  =  435 |
| RENT-ONE(2)  =  400 | RENT-TWO(2)  =  440 | RENT-THREE(2)  =  480 |
| RENT-ONE(3)  =  475 | RENT-TWO(3)  =  530 | RENT-THREE(3)  =  575 |
| RENT-ONE(4)  =  600 | RENT-TWO(4)  =  650 | RENT-THREE(4)  =  700 |
| RENT-ONE(5)  = 1000 | RENT-TWO(5)  = 1075 | RENT-THREE(5)  = 1150 |

**Figure 9-22:** Three separate one-dimensional arrays

If you use the three separate arrays in Figure 9-22, then you can determine rent with the logic in Figure 9-23.

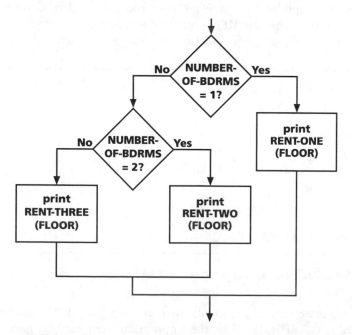

**Figure 9-23:** Determining rent with three one-dimensional arrays

Of course, don't forget that arrays are never *required*. You could also make 15 separate decisions to determine the rent. See Figure 9-24.

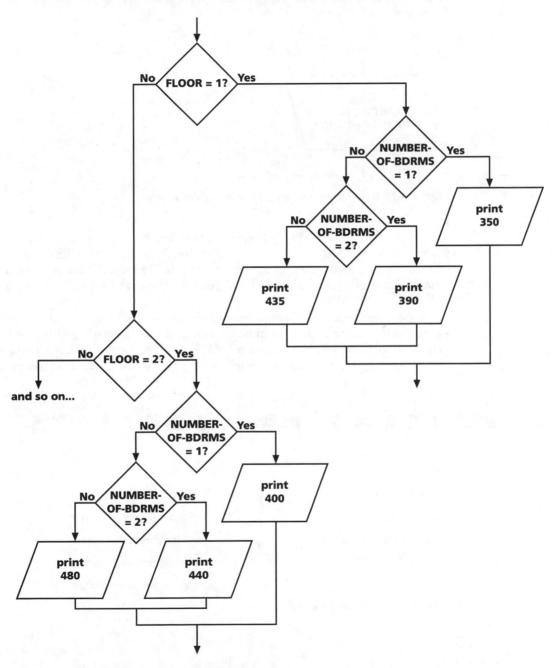

**Figure 9-24:** Determining rent with no array

Using three single-dimensional arrays as in Figure 9-23 makes the rent-determining process easier than using no array, as in Figure 9-24. However, if you use a two-dimensional array, as in Figure 9-25, the rent-determining process is as simple as it can be.

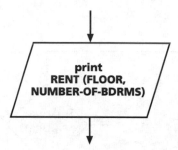

**print
RENT (FLOOR,
NUMBER-OF-BDRMS)**

**Figure 9-25:** Determining rent with a two-dimensional array

Some languages allow **three-dimensional arrays.** For example, rent might not only be determined by the two factors, FLOOR and NUMBER-OF-BDRMS. There might also be twelve different buildings. The third dimension of a three-dimensional array to hold all these different rents would be a variable such as BUILDING-NUMBER.

Some languages allow even more dimensions. It's usually hard for people to keep track of more than three dimensions, but if rent is determined by five variable factors—for example, floor number, number of bedrooms, building number, city number, and state number—you might want to try to use a five-dimensional array.

# TERMS AND CONCEPTS

insertion sort

selection sort

physical order

logical order

key field

index

random-access storage device

addresses

linked list

single- or one-dimensional array

multidimensional array

two-dimensional array

three-dimensional array

# SUMMARY

- An insertion sort provides a method for sorting data that usually requires fewer comparison operations than a bubble sort.

- When you use a selection sort, you search for the smallest value in a list, then swap it with the first position value. Then you search for the second-lowest value and swap it with the second position value, and so on.

- When a large data file needs to be processed in ascending or descending order based on some field, it is usually more efficient to store and access records based on their logical order than to sort them and access them in their physical order.

- A common method of accessing records in logical order involves using an index that is organized by a key field. When you index records, you store a list of key fields paired with the storage address for the corresponding data record.

- When you use a random-access storage device such as a disk, each record can be placed in any physical location on the disk and accessed in any order.

- Addresses represent computer storage locations.

- You can store records in any physical order on the disk, but the index can find the records in order based on their addresses.

- When a record is removed from an indexed file, it does not have to be physically removed; it can simply be deleted from the index.

- Creating a linked list involves creating one extra field in every record; this extra field holds the physical address of the next logical record.

- When a record is removed from a linked list, it does not need to be physically deleted. Instead, you can update the link of the previous record.

- An array that represents a single list of values is called a single-dimensional array or one-dimensional array.

- If you must represent values in a table or grid that contains rows and columns instead of a single list, then you might want to use a multidimensional array—specifically, a two-dimensional array.

- Each element in a two-dimensional array requires two subscripts to reference it—one subscript to determine the row and a second to determine the column.

# EXERCISES

1. Develop the flowchart that corresponds to the pseudocode for the insertion sort shown in Figure 9-14.

2. Develop the flowchart that corresponds to the pseudocode for the selection sort shown in Figure 9-15.

3. Create the flowchart or pseudocode that reads in a file of 10 employee salaries and prints them out lowest to highest. Use an insertion sort.

4. Create the flowchart or pseudocode that reads in a file of 10 employee salaries and prints them out highest to lowest. Use a selection sort.

5. The MidAmerica Bus Company charges passengers fares based on the number of travel zones they cross. Additionally, discounts are provided for multiple passengers traveling together. Ticket fares are shown in the following table.

| | ZONES CROSSED | | | |
|---|---|---|---|---|
| PASSENGERS | 1 | 2 | 3 | 4 |
| 1 | 7.50 | 10.00 | 12.00 | 12.75 |
| 2 | 14.00 | 18.50 | 22.00 | 23.00 |
| 3 | 20.00 | 21.00 | 32.00 | 33.00 |
| 4 | 25.00 | 27.50 | 36.00 | 37.00 |

Develop the logic for a program that reads in records containing number of passengers and zones crossed. The output is the ticket charge.

6. a. In golf, par is a number that represents a standard number of strokes a player will need to complete a hole. Instead of using an absolute score, players can compare their scores on a hole to the par figure and determine whether they are above or below par. Families can play nine holes of miniature golf at the Family Fun Miniature Golf Park. So that family members can compete fairly, the course provides a different par for each hole based on the player's age. The par figures are shown in the following table.

| | HOLES | | | | | | | | |
|---|---|---|---|---|---|---|---|---|---|
| AGE | 1 | 2 | 3 | 4 | 5 | 6 | 7 | 8 | 9 |
| 4 and under | 8 | 8 | 9 | 7 | 5 | 7 | 8 | 5 | 8 |
| 5 – 7 | 7 | 7 | 8 | 6 | 5 | 6 | 7 | 5 | 6 |
| 8 – 11 | 6 | 5 | 6 | 5 | 4 | 5 | 5 | 4 | 5 |
| 12 – 15 | 5 | 4 | 4 | 4 | 3 | 4 | 3 | 3 | 4 |
| 16 and over | 4 | 3 | 3 | 3 | 2 | 3 | 2 | 3 | 3 |

Develop the logic for a program that reads in records containing a player's name, age, and nine hole scores. For each player, print a page that contains the player's name and score on each of the nine holes with one of the phrases "Over par", "Par", or "Under par" next to each score.

b. Modify the program in exercise 6a so that at the end of the report the golfer's total displays. Include the figure indicating how many strokes over or under par the player is for the entire course.

# Using Menus and Validating Input

**case ▶** "Ready for lunch?" asks Lynn Greenbrier, one of your mentors at Solutions, Inc., as she passes by your desk. "We're going down to Tony's—they have a fantastic sprout and tofu stew."

"And their barbeque beef with fries is pretty good too," adds Boston Murphy, your other mentor.

"Gee, that sounds like quite a menu," you say. "It's nice that you can have so many choices."

"Your programs will be better, too, when you provide the user with choices interactively," Boston observes. "We'll show you how it's done—but not until after lunch!"

**After studying Section A, you should be able to:**

- Describe the difference between interactive and batch programs
- Use a single-level menu
- Describe the concept of the black box
- Make improvements to menu-driven programs
- Use the case structure to manage a menu

# Using Menus

## Using Interactive Programs

You can divide computer programs into two broad categories on the basis of how they get their data. Programs for which all the data is gathered prior to running use **batch processing**. Programs that depend on user input while they are running use **interactive processing**.

Many computer programs use batch processing with sequential files of data records that have been collected for processing. All standard billing, inventory, payroll, and similar programs work this way, and all the program logic you have developed while working through this text works this way. Records are gathered over a period of time—hours, days, or even months. Programs that use batch processing typically read an input record, process it according to coded instructions, output the result, and read another record. Batch processing gets its name because the data records are not processed at the time they are created; instead, they are "saved" and processed in a batch. For example, you do not receive a credit-card bill immediately after every purchase, when the record is created. All your purchases during a one-month period are gathered and processed at the end of that billing period.

Many computer programs cannot be run in batches. They must be run interactively—that is, they must interact with a user while they are running. Airline and theater ticket reservation programs must select tickets for you while you are interacting with them, not at the end of the month. A computerized library catalog system must respond to library patrons' requests immediately, not at the end of every week. Interactive computer programs are often called **real-time applications**, because they run while a transaction is taking place, not at some later time. Interactive processing also is called **online processing**, because the user's data or requests are gathered during the execution of the program. A batch processing system can be **off-line**; that is, data such as time cards or purchase information can be collected well ahead of the actual computer processing of the paychecks or bills.

A **menu** program is a common type of interactive program in which the user sees a number of options on the screen and can select any one of them. For example, an educational program that drills you on elementary arithmetic skills might display three options as shown in Figure 10-1.

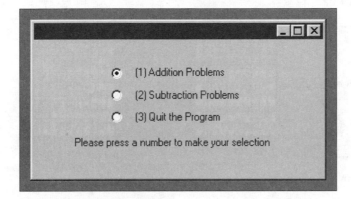

**Figure 10-1:** Arithmetic drill menu

The final option, Quit the Program, is a very important one; without it there would be no elegant way for the program to terminate. A menu that does not contain a *Quit* option is very frustrating to the user.

Some menu programs require the user to enter a number to choose a menu option. For example, the user enters a 2 to perform a subtraction drill from the menu shown in Figure 10-1. Other menu programs require the user to enter a letter of the alphabet—for example, S for a subtraction drill. Still other programs allow the user to use a pointing device such as a mouse to point to a choice on the screen. The most sophisticated programs allow the user to employ whichever of those selection methods is most convenient at the time.

## Using a Single-Level Menu

Suppose you want to write a program that displays a menu like the one shown in Figure 10-1. The program drills a student's arithmetic skills—if the student chooses the first option, five addition problems display, and if the student chooses the second option, five subtraction problems display. This program uses a **single-level menu**. That is, the user makes a selection from only one menu before using the program for its ultimate purpose—arithmetic practice. With more complicated programs, a user's choice from an initial menu often leads to other menus; the user must make several selections before reaching the desired destination.

You can start by writing a program that requires the user to enter a digit to make a menu choice. The mainline logic for an interactive menu program is not substantially different from any of the other sequential file programs you've seen so far in this book. There is a START-UP subroutine, a LOOPING subroutine, and a CLEAN-UP subroutine, as shown in Figure 10-2.

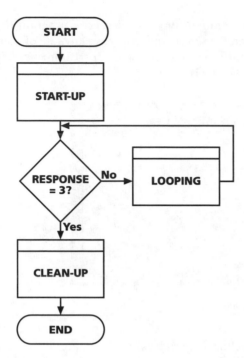

**Figure 10-2:** Mainline logic for arithmetic drill menu program

The only difference between the mainline logic in Figure 10-2 and that of other programs you have worked with lies in the main loop control question. When a program's input data comes from a data file, asking whether the input file is at the end-of-file (EOF) condition is appropriate. An interactive, menu-driven program is not controlled by an end-of-file condition; rather it is controlled by a user's menu response. The mainline logic, then, is more appropriately controlled by the question RESPONSE = 3? as shown in Figure 10-2.

The START-UP routine in the arithmetic drill program defines variables and opens files. One of the variables is named RESPONSE; this is the numeric variable that will hold the user's menu choice. START-UP also displays the menu for the first time so that the user can make a choice. See Figure 10-3.

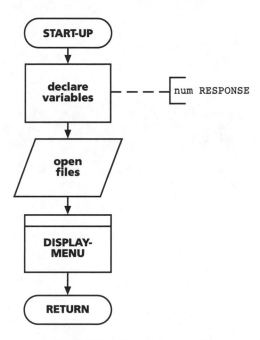

**Figure 10-3:** START-UP module for arithmetic drill program

You can include all the instructions that display the user menu directly in the START-UP routine, or you can place the instructions in their own module, DISPLAY-MENU, as shown in Figure 10-4. The DISPLAY-MENU module writes the four menu lines on the screen, and then the `read` RESPONSE statement reads in the user's numeric choice from the keyboard.

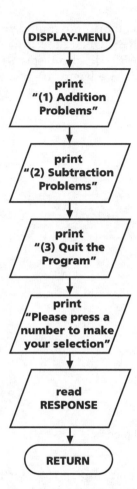

**Figure 10-4:** DISPLAY-MENU module of arithmetic drill program

When the logic of the program leaves START-UP, the user has entered a value for RESPONSE. In the mainline logic (Figure 10-2), if the RESPONSE is not a 3 (for the *Quit the Program* option), then the program enters the LOOPING routine. The LOOPING routine performs one of two subroutines, ADDITION or SUB-TRACTION, based on the decision made about the user's input. Whichever type of arithmetic drill is performed, the DISPLAY-MENU routine is called again, and the user has the opportunity to select the same arithmetic drill, a different one, or the *Quit the Program* option. See Figure 10-5.

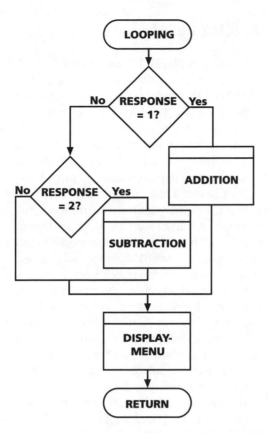

**Figure 10-5:** LOOPING module for arithmetic drill program

When the LOOPING routine ends, control is passed to the main program. If the user has entered the value 3 to select the *Quit the Program* option during the DISPLAY-MENU routine, the question RESPONSE = 3? sends the program to the CLEAN-UP routine. That routine simply closes the files, as shown in Figure 10-6.

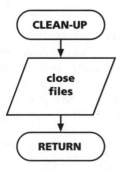

**Figure 10-6:** CLEAN-UP module for arithmetic drill program

## Coding Modules as Black Boxes

Any steps can occur within the ADDITION and SUBTRACTION modules. The contents of these modules do not affect the main structure of the program in any way. You can write an ADDITION module that requires the user to solve very simple single-digit addition problems like 3 + 4, or you can write an ADDITION module that requires the user to solve more difficult multidigit addition problems like 9267 + 3488. As you will recall from Chapter 2, part of the advantage of modular, structured programs lies in your ability to break programs into routines that can be assigned to any number of programmers and then be pieced back together at each routine's single entry or exit point. Thus any number of different ADDITION or SUBTRACTION modules can be used within the arithmetic drill program.

Programmers often refer to modules such as ADDITION and SUBTRACTION as existing within a **black box**. This means that the module statements are "invisible" to the rest of the program. You probably own many real-life objects that are black boxes to you—a television or a stereo for example. You might not know how these devices work internally, and if someone substitutes new internal mechanisms in your devices, you might not know or care so long as the devices continue to work properly. Similarly, many different ADDITION or SUBTRACTION modules can function within the arithmetic drill menu program.

Because many versions of a module can substitute for one another, programmers frequently don't bother with module details at all when they first develop a program. They concentrate on the mainline logic and on understanding what the called modules will do, not how they will do it. When programmers develop systems containing many modules, they often code "empty" black box procedures, called **stubs**. Later they can code the details in the stub routines.

Figure 10-7 shows a possible ADDITION module. The module displays five problems, one at a time, waits for the user's response, and displays a message indicating whether the user is correct.

••••••••••••••••••••••••••••••••••••••••••••••••••••••••••••••••••••••••••••••••••••

**You can write a SUBTRACTION module using a format that is almost identical to the ADDITION module. The only necessary change is the computation operation used in the actual problems.**

••••••••••••••••••••••••••••••••••••••••••••••••••••••••••••••••••••••••••••••••••••

The ADDITION module shown in Figure 10-7 is repetitious; a basic set of statements repeats five times changing only the actual problem values that the user should add. A more elegant solution involves storing the problem values in arrays and using a loop. For example, if you declare two arrays as shown in Figure 10-8, then the loop in Figure 10-9 displays and checks five problems. The power of using an array allows you to alter a subscript in order to display five separate addition problems.

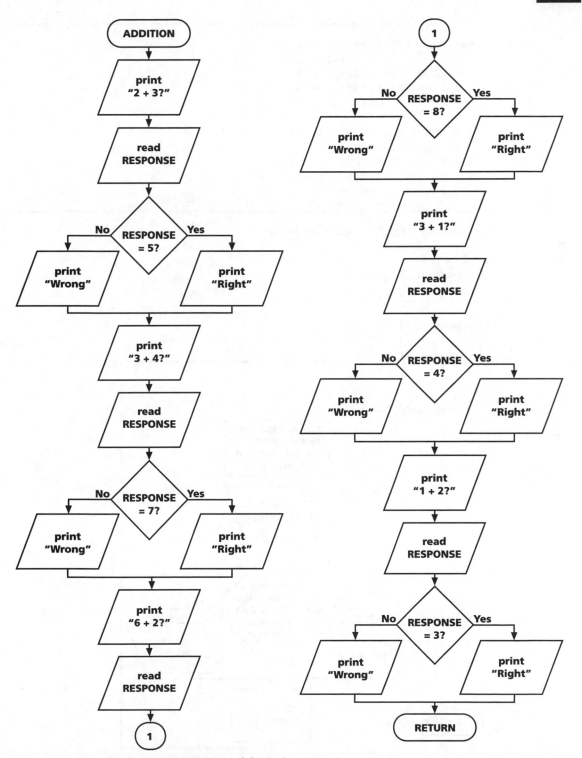

**Figure 10-7:** ADDITION module version 1

```
num PROB-VAL-FIRST(1)  =  2
num PROB-VAL-FIRST(2)  =  3
num PROB-VAL-FIRST(3)  =  6
num PROB-VAL-FIRST(4)  =  3
num PROB-VAL-FIRST(5)  =  1

num PROB-VAL-SECOND(1)  =  3
num PROB-VAL-SECOND(2)  =  4
num PROB-VAL-SECOND(3)  =  2
num PROB-VAL-SECOND(4)  =  1
num PROB-VAL-SECOND(5)  =  2
```

**Figure 10-8:** Arrays for addition problems

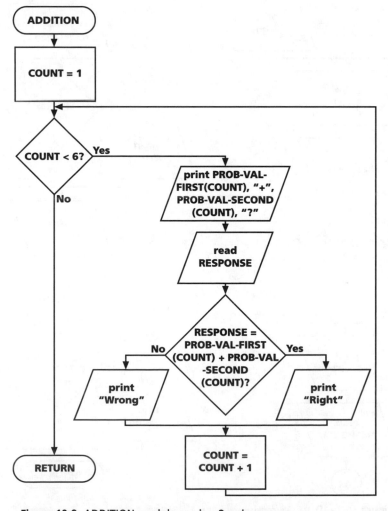

**Figure 10-9:** ADDITION module version 2, using arrays

**To use the ADDITION module shown in Figure 10-9, you have to declare the numeric variable COUNT.**

The ADDITION module in Figure 10-9 is more compact and efficient than the module shown in Figure 10-7. However, a student will not want to use the ADDITION module more than two or three times. Every time a user executes the program, the same five addition problems display. Once the student has solved all the addition problems, he or she probably will be able to provide memorized answers without practicing arithmetic skills at all. Fortunately, most programming languages provide you with built-in modules or **functions**, which are subroutines that automatically provide a mathematical value such as a square root, absolute value, or random number. The random number generating functions usually take a form similar to RANDOM(X), where X is a value you provide for the maximum random number you want. Different computer systems use different formulas for generating a random number; for example, many use part of the current clock time when the random number function is called. However, a programming language's built-in functions can operate as black boxes just as your program modules do, so you need not know exactly how the functions do their jobs. You can use the random number generating function without knowing how it determines the specific random number. Figure 10-10 shows an ADDITION module in which two random numbers, each 10 or less, are generated for each of five arithmetic problems. Using this technique, you do not have to store values in an array, and the user encounters different addition problems every time he or she uses the program.

Popular spreadsheet programs also contain functions. As in programming, they are built-in modules that return requested values such as square root or absolute value. Most spreadsheets also contain dozens of specialized functions to support financial applications such as computing future value of an investment.

To use the logic shown in Figure 10-10 you also must remember to declare FIRST and SECOND as numeric variables.

You can make many additional improvements to any of the ADDITION modules shown in Figures 10-7, 10-9, and 10-10. For example, you might want to give the user several chances to calculate the correct answer, or you might want to vary the messages displayed. However you change the ADDITION or SUBTRACTION modules in the future, the main structure of the menu program does not have to change; modularization has made your program easily modifiable to meet changing needs.

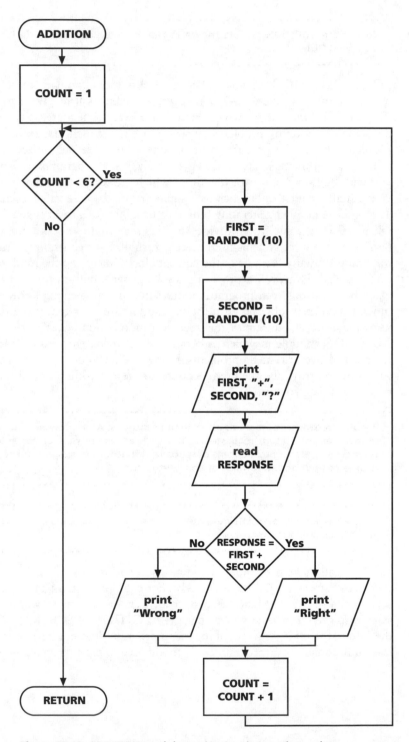

**Figure 10-10:** ADDITION module version 3, using random values

# Making Improvements to a Menu Program

When the menu displays at the end of the LOOPING module of the arithmetic drill program, if the user selects anything *other than 3*, the LOOPING module is entered again. Note that if the user chooses 4 or 9 or any other invalid menu item, the menu is simply displayed again. Unfortunately, the user may be confused by the repeated display of the menu. Perhaps the user is familiar with another program in which option 9 has always meant Quit. When using the arithmetic drill program, the user who does not read the menu carefully may press 9, get the menu back, press 9, and get the menu back again. The programmer can assist the user by displaying a message when the selected RESPONSE is not one of the allowable menu options, as shown in Figure 10-11.

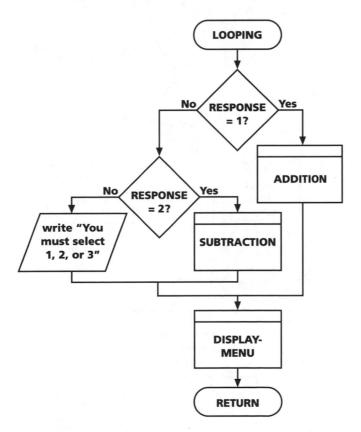

**Figure 10-11:** Adding error message to LOOPING module for arithmetic drill program

There is a saying in programming that no program is ever really completed. You always can continue to make improvements. For example, the LOOPING module in Figure 10-11 shows that a helpful message ("You must select 1, 2, or 3") displays when the user selects an inappropriate option. However, if the user does not understand the message, or simply does not stop to read the message, he or she might keep entering invalid data. As a user-friendly improvement to your program, you can add a counter that keeps track of a user's invalid responses. You can decide that after, say, three invalid entries, you will issue a stronger message, such as "Please see the system administrator for help." Figure 10-12 shows this logic. Of course, you must remember to declare ERROR-COUNT in your variable list in the START-UP module, and initialize it to zero. Then each time the user chooses as invalid response and you display the message "You must select 1, 2, or 3", you can add 1 to the ERROR-COUNT. When the ERROR-COUNT exceeds 2, you display the stronger message.

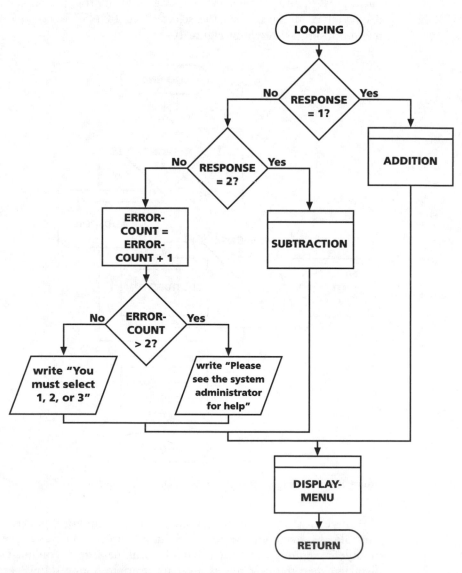

**Figure 10-12:** LOOPING module with stronger error message

You can make an additional improvement to the LOOPING module in Figure 10-12. Suppose the user starts the program and enters a 5. RESPONSE is not 1 or 2 or 3, so you add 1 to ERROR-COUNT, display the message "You must select 1, 2, or 3", and display the menu. Suppose the user enters a 5 again. Once again the response is not 1 or 2 or 3, so you add 1 to ERROR-COUNT, which is now 2, display the message "You must select 1, 2, or 3", and display the menu. If the user enters a 5 again, the ERROR-COUNT exceeds 2 and the user gets the message "Please see the system administrator for help." Assume the user gets help and figures out that he or she must type 1, 2, or 3. The next time the user makes a selection error, the ERROR-COUNT will increase to 4 and the stronger "system administrator" message will appear immediately. If you want to give the user three more chances before the stronger message displays again, then you should reset the ERROR-COUNT to zero every time the user makes a valid choice. This technique will allow the user to make three bad selections after any good selection before the stronger message appears. See Figure 10-13.

## Using the CASE Structure to Manage a Menu

The arithmetic drill program contains just three valid user options: numeric entries that represent Addition, Subtraction, or Quit. Many menus include more than three options, but the main logic of such programs is not substantially different from that in programs with only three. You just include more decisions that lead to additional subroutines. For example, Figure 10-14 shows the main logic for a menu program with four optional arithmetic drills.

In Chapter 2 you learned about the case structure. You can use the case structure to make decisions when you need to test a single variable against several possible values. The case structure is particularly convenient to use in menu-driven programs, because you decide from among several courses of action based on the value in the user's response variable. The case structure often is a more convenient way to express a series of individual decisions.

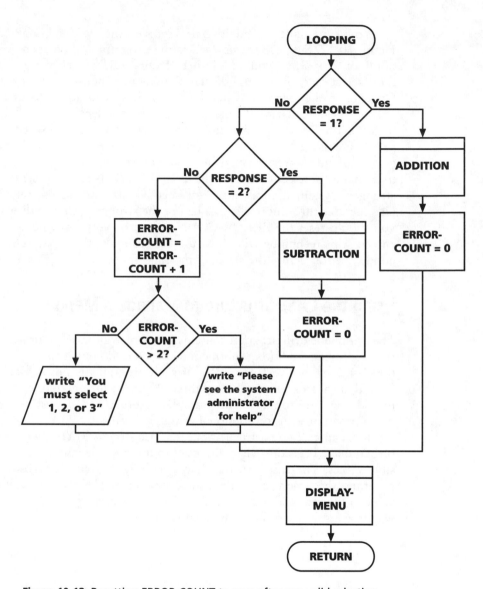

**Figure 10-13:** Resetting ERROR-COUNT to zero after any valid selection

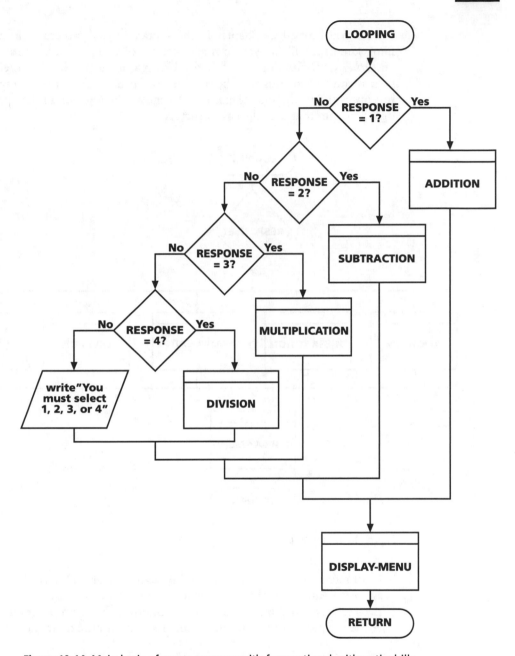

**Figure 10-14:** Main logic of menu program with four optional arithmetic drills

As you learned in Chapter 2, the syntax of case structures in most programming languages allows you to make a series of comparisons, and if none are true, an *Other* or *Default* option executes. Using a default option is a great convenience in a menu-driven program, because a user usually can enter many more invalid responses than valid ones. Figure 10-15 shows the logic of a four-option arithmetic drill program that uses the case structure.

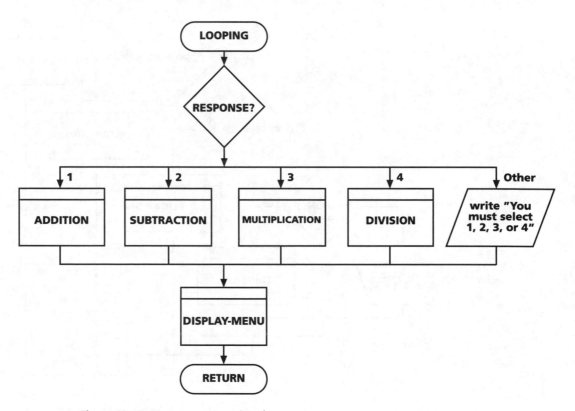

**Figure 10-15:** Menu program using the case structure

All menu-driven programs should be **user friendly**. That is, they should make it easy for the user to make desired choices. Instead of requiring a user to type numbers to select an arithmetic drill, you can improve the menu program by allowing the user the additional option of typing the first letter of the desired option, for example

*A* for addition. To enable the menu program to accept alphabetic characters as a variable named RESPONSE, you must make sure you declare RESPONSE as a character variable in the START-UP module. Numeric variables can hold only numbers, but character variables can hold alphabetic characters such as *A* as well as numbers.

Programmers often overlook the fact that computers recognize uppercase letters as being different from their lowercase counterparts. Thus a response of *A* is different from a response of *a*. A good menu-driven program probably would allow any of three responses for the first option of *(1) Addition*—*1*, *A*, or *a*. Figure 10-16 shows the case structure that performs the menu option selection when the user can enter a variety of responses for each menu choice.

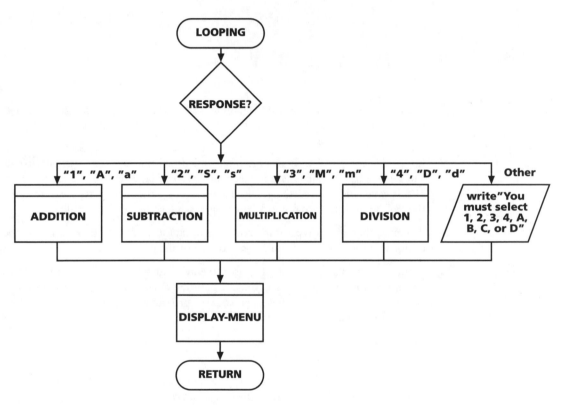

**Figure 10-16:** Menu program using the case structure with multiple allowed responses

# TERMS AND CONCEPTS

batch processing                single-level menu

interactive processing          black box

real-time applications          stubs

online processing               functions

off-line processing             user friendly

menu

 # SUMMARY

■ Programs for which all the data is gathered prior to running the program use batch processing; programs that depend on user input while the program is running use interactive processing.

■ Interactive computer programs are often called real-time applications, because they run while a transaction is taking place, not at some later time. Interactive processing also is called online processing, because the user's data or requests are gathered during the execution of the program. A batch processing system can be off-line.

■ A menu program is a type of interactive program in which the user sees a number of options on the screen and can select any one of them.

■ Menu programs might require the user to enter a number or a letter of the alphabet. Other programs allow the user to use a pointing device such as a mouse to point to a choice on the screen. The most sophisticated programs allow the user to employ whichever of those selection methods is most convenient at the time.

■ With a single-level menu, the user makes a selection from only one menu before using the program for its ultimate purpose.

■ An interactive, menu-driven program is not controlled by an end-of-file condition; rather, it is controlled by a user's menu response.

■ Part of the advantage of writing modular, structured programs lies in your ability to break programs into routines that can be assigned to any number of programmers and then be pieced back together at each routine's single entry or exit point.

■ Programmers often refer to modules as existing within a black box when the module statements are "invisible" to the rest of the program.

- Most programming languages provide you with built-in modules or functions, which are subroutines that automatically provide you with a mathematical value such as a random number.

- The programmer can assist the user by displaying helpful, customized error messages.

- You can use the case structure to make decisions when you need to test a single variable against several possible values. The case structure is particularly convenient to use in menu-driven programs.

- All menu-driven programs should be user friendly.

- Programmers often overlook the fact that computers recognize uppercase letters as different from their lowercase counterparts.

# E X E R C I S E S

1. a. Draw the logic for the flowchart or write the pseudocode for a program that gives you the following options for a trivia quiz:

> (1) Movies
> (2) Television
> (3) Sports
> (4) Quit

When the user selects an option, display a question that falls under the category. After the user responds, display whether the answer was correct.

 b. Modify the program in Exercise 1a so that when the user selects a trivia quiz topic option, you display five questions in the category instead of just one.

2. Draw the logic for the flowchart or write the pseudocode for the program that presents you with the following options for a banking machine:

> (1) Deposit
> (2) Withdrawal
> (3) Quit

After you select an option, the program asks you for the amount of money to deposit or withdraw, then displays your balance and allows you to make another selection. When the user selects Quit, display the final balance.

3.  Draw the logic for the flowchart or write the pseudocode for a program that gives you the following options:

| | |
|---|---|
| (1) Hot dog | 1.50 |
| (2) Fries | 1.00 |
| (3) Lemonade | .75 |
| (4) End order | |

You should be allowed to keep ordering from the menu until you press *4* for *End order*, at which point you should see a total amount due for your entire order.

4.  Draw the logic for the flowchart or write the pseudocode for a program that gives you the following options for registering for college classes:

| | |
|---|---|
| (1) English 101 | 3 |
| (2) Math 260 | 5 |
| (3) History 100 | 3 |
| (4) Sociology 151 | 4 |
| (5) Quit | |

You should be allowed to select as many classes as you want before you choose the Quit option, but you should *not* be allowed to register for the same class twice. The program accumulates the hours for which you have registered, and displays your tuition bill at $50 per credit hour.

# Multilevel Menus and Validating Input

## Using Multilevel Menus

Sometimes a program requires more options than can easily fit in one menu. When you need to present the user with a large number of options, you invite several potential problems:

- Not all the options will appear on the screen, and the user might not realize that additional options are available.
- If you try to force all the options to fit on the screen, the screen is too crowded to be visually pleasing.
- If you present the user with too many choices, the user is confused and frustrated.

When you have many menu options to present, using a **multilevel menu** may be more effective than using a single-level menu. With a multilevel menu, the selection of a menu option leads to another menu where the user can make further, more refined selections.

For example, an arithmetic drill program might contain three difficulty levels for each type of problem. After the user sees a menu like the one shown in Figure 10-17, he or she can choose to quit the program. A menu that controls whether or not the program will continue is often called the **main menu** of a program. Alternatively, the user can choose to continue the program, selecting an Addition, Subtraction, Multiplication, or Division arithmetic drill. No matter which drill choice the user makes, you can display a second menu like the one shown in Figure 10-18. A second-level menu can be called a **submenu**.

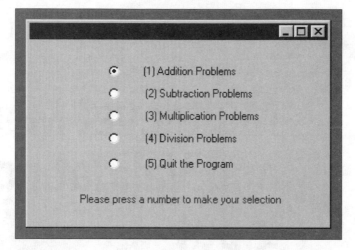

**Figure 10-17:** First or main menu for arithmetic drill program

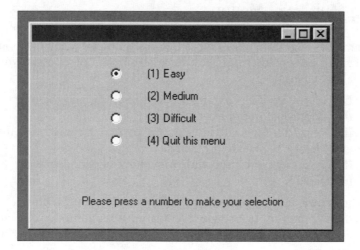

**Figure 10-18:** Second or submenu for arithmetic drill program

The mainline logic of this multilevel menu program calls a START-UP module in which the user sees the first menu that presents options for the four types of arithmetic problems—*Addition*, *Subtraction*, *Multiplication*, and *Division*. When the user makes a selection—for example, *Addition*—the mainline logic determines that RESPONSE is not 5, so the LOOPING module executes. Figures 10-19, 10-20, and 10-21 show pseudocode for the mainline logic, START-UP module, and DISPLAY-MENU module, respectively.

```
START
    perform START-UP
    while RESPONSE not equal to 5
            perform LOOPING
    perform CLEAN-UP
END
```

**Figure 10-19:** Pseudocode for mainline logic for multilevel menu program

```
START-UP
    declare variables— — — — ┌ num RESPONSE
    open files                └ num DIFFICULTY-RESPONSE
    perform DISPLAY-MENU
RETURN
```

**Figure 10-20:** Pseudocode for START-UP module for multilevel menu program

```
DISPLAY-MENU
    print "(1) Addition"
    print "(2) Subtraction"
    print "(3) Multiplication"
    print "(4) Division"
    print "(5) Quit"
    print "Please press a number to make your selection."
    read RESPONSE
RETURN
```

**Figure 10-21:** Pseudocode for DISPLAY-MENU module for multilevel menu program

Unless the user chooses to quit by entering a 5 for RESPONSE in the START-UP module, the LOOPING module executes. The LOOPING module uses a case structure to select one of five actions. Either the user has entered the correct REPSONSE to select addition, subtraction, multiplication, or division problems, or else the user has selected an invalid option. If the user selects an invalid option, an error message ("Sorry. Invalid entry.") displays. Whether or not the user selects an entry that results in performance of one of the four arithmetic drill modules, the final step in the LOOPING module involves displaying the drill choice menu again and waiting for the next RESPONSE. Back in the mainline logic, the new RESPONSE value is tested, and if the user has entered anything other than *5*, the LOOPING routine will execute again. Figure 10-22 shows the pseudocode for LOOPING.

```
LOOPING
    based on RESPONSE
            case 1
                   perform ADDITION
            case 2
                   perform SUBTRACTION
            case 3
                   perform MULTIPLICATION
            case 4
                   perform DIVISION
            default
                   print "Sorry. Invalid entry."
    perform DISPLAY-MENU
RETURN
```

**Figure 10-22:** Pseudocode for LOOPING module for multilevel menu program

If the user selects a valid option in the LOOPING routine, then one of the four arithmetic drill modules executes. For example, if the user selects *1* for *Addition Problems*, then the ADDITION module executes. Within the ADDITION module, the first task is to allow the user to select a problem difficulty level from a submenu like the one shown in Figure 10-18. Figure 10-23 shows the pseudocode for the ADDITION module. Within the ADDITION module, you call another module to display the difficulty level. Shown in Figure 10-24, this module allows the user to choose easy, medium, or difficult addition problems. If the user selects to quit this menu by entering a *4*, then the user will leave the addition module and return to the main menu where he or she can choose a different type of arithmetic problem, choose addition again, or quit. If the user makes a selection other than *4*, then the case structure determines one of four actions: either one of three addition problem modules executes, or the user is informed that he or she has made an invalid choice. In any case, the last action of the ADDITION module is to display the difficulty level menu again. While the user continues to choose not to quit, the user can continue to select addition problem drills at any of the three difficulty levels.

```
ADDITION
     perform DISPLAY-DIFFICULTY-MENU
     while DIFFICULTY-RESPONSE is not equal to 4
          based on DIFFICULTY-RESPONSE
               case 1
                    perform EASY-ADD-PROBLEMS
               case 2
                    perform MEDIUM-ADD-PROBLEMS
               case 3
                    perform DIFFICULT-ADD-PROBLEMS
               default
                    print "Sorry. Invalid selection."
          perform DISPLAY-DIFFICULTY-MENU
RETURN
```

**Figure 10-23:** Pseudocode for ADDITION module for multilevel menu program

```
DISPLAY-DIFFICULTY-MENU
     print "(1) Easy"
     print "(2) Medium"
     print "(3) Difficult"
     print "(4) Quit this menu"
     print "Please press a number to make your selection."
     read DIFFICULTY-RESPONSE
RETURN
```

**Figure 10-24:** Pseudocode for DISPLAY-DIFFICULTY-MENU module for multilevel menu program

The SUBTRACTION, MULTIPLICATION, and DIVISION modules can contain code similar to that in the ADDITION module. That is, each module can cause a submenu of difficulty levels to display. The actual arithmetic problems do not execute until the user reaches the EASY-ADD-PROBLEMS module or one of its counterparts.

Many programs have multiple menu levels. For example, you might want the EASY-ADD-PROBLEMS module to display a new menu asking the user for the number of problems to attempt. Figure 10-25 shows a possible menu.

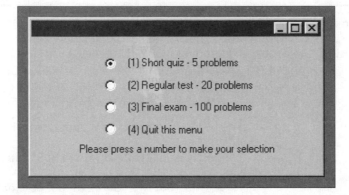

**Figure 10-25:** Third menu for arithmetic drill program

You would not need to learn any new techniques to create as many levels of menus as the application warrants. Each new module can display a menu, accept a response, and while the user does not select the *quit* option, you perform another module based on the selection (or inform the user of an error) and display the menu and accept a response again.

## Validating Input

Menu programs rely on a user's input to select one of several paths of action to take. Other types of programs also require user data entry. Whether they are using a menu or supplying information to a program, you cannot count on users to enter valid data. Users will make incorrect choices because they don't understand the valid choices or simply because they make typographical errors. Therefore the programs you write will be better if you employ **defensive programming**. Programming defensively means that you try to prepare for all possible errors before they occur. Incorrect user entries are by far the most common source of computer errors.

••••••••••••••••••••••••••••••••••••••••••••••••••••••••••••••••••••••••••••••••
Validating data is also called *editing* data.
••••••••••••••••••••••••••••••••••••••••••••••••••••••••••••••••••••••••••••••••

You can circumvent potential problems caused by a user's invalid data entries by validating the user's input. **Validating input** involves checking the user's responses to ensure they fall within acceptable bounds. Validating input does not eliminate all program errors. For example, if a user can choose option *1* or option *2* from a menu, validating the input means you check to make sure the user response is *1* or *2*. If the user enters a *3*, you can issue an error message. However, if the user enters a *2* when she really wants a *1*, there is no way you can validate the response. Similarly, if a user must enter his birth date, you can validate that the month falls between 1 and 12; you cannot usually verify that the user has typed his true birth date.

Programmers employ the acronym GIGO to mean "garbage in, garbage out." It means
that if your input is incorrect, your output is worthless.

The action you take when you find invalid data depends on the application.
Within an interactive program, you may require the user to reenter the data. If your
program uses a data file, you may print a message so someone can correct the
invalid data. Alternatively, you can force the invalid data to a default value. For
example, you may decide that if a month value does not fall between 1 and 12, you
will force the field to 0 or 99. This will indicate to those who use the data that no
valid value exists.

New programmers often make two kinds of mistakes when validating data:

- When there is more than one possible correct entry, they use incorrect logic
  to check for valid responses.
- They fail to account for the user making multiple invalid entries.

For example, assume a user is required to respond Y or N to a yes-or-no
question. The pseudocode in Figure 10-26 appears to check for valid responses.

```
print "Do you want to continue? Enter Y or N."
read USER-ANSWER
if USER-ANSWER not equal to "Y" or USER-ANSWER not equal to "N" then
      print "Invalid response. Please type Y or N"
      read USER-ANSWER
```

**Figure 10-26:** Invalid method for validating user response

The logic shown in Figure 10-26 is intended to ensure that the user enters a Y or
an N. However, if you use the logic shown in Figure 10-26, every user will see the
"Invalid response" error message, no matter what the user types. Remember that
when you use OR logic that only one of the two expressions used in each half of the
OR expression must be true for the whole expression to be true. For example, if the
user types a B, then the USER-ANSWER is not equal to Y. Therefore USER-
ANSWER not equal to "Y" is true, and the "Invalid response" message displays.
However, if the user types an N, the USER-ANSWER also is not equal to Y. Again,
the condition in the if statement is true and the "Invalid response" message prints
even though the response actually is valid. Similarly, if the user types a Y, USER-
ANSWER not equal to "Y" is false, but USER-ANSWER not equal to "N"
is true, so again "Invalid response" prints. Every character that exists is either not Y
or not N, even Y and N. The correct logic prints the "Invalid response" message
when the USER-ANSWER is not Y *and it is also not* N. See Figure 10-27.

You first learned about OR decision logic in Chapter 5.

```
print "Do you want to continue? Enter Y or N."
read USER-ANSWER
if USER-ANSWER not equal to "Y" and USER-ANSWER not equal to "N" then
     print "Invalid response. Please type Y or N"
     read USER-ANSWER
```

**Figure 10-27:** Improved method for validating user response

If you use the logic shown in Figure 10-27, you will correctly display the error message and get a new USER-ANSWER when the user types an invalid response. However, you have not made allowance for the user typing an invalid response a second time. Instead of using a decision statement to check for a valid response, you can use a loop to continue to issue error messages and get new input so long as the user continues to make invalid selections. Figure 10-28 shows the logic for the best method through which to validate user input.

```
print "Do you want to continue? Enter Y or N."
read USER-ANSWER
while USER-ANSWER not equal to "Y" and USER-ANSWER not equal to "N"
        print "Invalid response. Please type Y or N"
        read USER-ANSWER
```

**Figure 10-28:** Best method for validating user response

## Types of Data Validation

The data you use within computer programs is varied. It stands to reason that data requires a variety of data validation methods. You learned to check for an exact match of Y or N in the last section. In addition, some of the techniques you want to master include validating:

- data type
- range
- reasonableness and consistency of data
- presence of data

### Validating a Data Type

Some programming languages allow you to check data to make sure it is the correct type. Although this technique varies from language to language, you can often make a statement like the one shown in Figure 10-29. In this program segment the phrase not numeric is used to check whether the entered data falls within the category of numeric data.

```
print "Enter salary."
read EMPLOYEE-SALARY
while EMPLOYEE-SALARY not numeric
        print "Invalid salary. Please reenter."
        read EMPLOYEE-SALARY
```

**Figure 10-29:** Method for checking data for correct type

**tip**

Some languages require you to check data against the actual machine codes (such as ASCII or EBCDIC) used to store the data to determine if the data is the appropriate type.

## Validating a Data Range

Sometimes a user response or other data must fall within a range of values. For example, when the user enters a month, you typically require it to fall between 1 and 12 inclusive. The method you use to check for a valid range is similar to one you use to check for an exact match; you continue to prompt for and receive responses while the user's response is out of range. See Figure 10-30.

```
print "Enter month."
read USER-ANSWER
while USER-ANSWER < 1 OR USER-ANSWER > 12
        print "Invalid response. Please enter month."
        read USER-ANSWER
```

**Figure 10-30:** Method for validating user response within range

## Validating Reasonableness and Consistency of Data

Data items can be the correct type and within range, but still not be correct. You have experienced this phenomenon in your own day-to-day life if anyone has ever spelled your name incorrectly or billed you for too much. The data may have been the correct type—that is, alphabetic letters were used in your name—but the name itself was incorrect. There are many data items than you cannot check for reasonableness; it is just as reasonable that your name is Catherine as it is that your name is Katherine or Kathryn.

There are, however, many data items that you can check for reasonableness. If you make a purchase on May 3, 2002, then the payment cannot possibly be due prior to that date. Within your organization, if you work in Department 12, you cannot possibly make more than $20.00 per hour. If your ZIP code is 90201, your state of residence cannot be New York. If your pet's breed is stored as

"Great Dane," then its species cannot be "bird." Each of these examples involves comparing two data fields for reasonableness and consistency. You should consider making as many such comparisons as possible when you write your own programs.

## Validating Presence of Data

Sometimes data is missing from a file, either on purpose or by accident. A job applicant might fail to submit an entry for the LAST-SALARY field or a client has no entry for the EMAIL-ADDRESS field. A data-entry clerk may accidentally skip a field when typing in records. Many programming languages allow you to check for missing data with a statement similar to `if EMAIL-ADDRESS is blank perform NO-EMAIL-MODULE`. You can place any instructions you like within the NO-EMAIL-MODULE, including forcing the field to a default value or issuing a message.

Good defensive programs are those in which you try to foresee all possible inconsistencies and errors. The more accurate your data, the more useful information you will produce as output from your programs.

 **T E R M S   A N D   C O N C E P T S**

| | |
|---|---|
| multilevel menu | defensive programming |
| main menu | validating input |
| submenu | |

**S U M M A R Y**

- When a program requires more options than can easily fit in one menu, you can use a multilevel menu. With a multilevel menu, the selection of a menu option leads to another menu where the user can make further, more refined selections.

- A menu that controls whether or not the program will continue is often called the main menu of a program. A second-level menu can be called a submenu.

- Each module in a multilevel menu program can display a menu, accept a response, and while the user does not select the *Quit* option, perform another module based on the selection (or inform the user of an error) and display the menu and accept a response again.

- Whether they are using a menu or supplying information to a program, you cannot count on users to enter valid data; you should employ defensive programming.

- You can circumvent potential problems caused by a user's invalid data entries by validating the user's input or checking the user's responses to ensure they fall within acceptable bounds.

- New programmers often make two kinds of mistakes when validating data: they use incorrect logic to check for valid responses, and they fail to account for the user making multiple invalid entries.

- You can validate data by checking for an exact match, a type, a range, reasonableness and consistency, and presence.

 # E X E R C I S E S

1. Suggest two subsequent levels of menus for each of the first two options in this main menu:

   > (1) Print records from file
   > (2) Delete records from file
   > (3) Quit

2. Draw the flowchart or write the pseudocode for a program that displays the rules for a sport or a game. The user can select from a menu like the following:

   > (1) Sports
   > (2) Games
   > (3) Quit

   If the user chooses *1* for *Sports*, display options for four different sports of your choice (for example, soccer, or basketball).

   If the user chooses 2 for Games, display options for:

   > (1) Card games
   > (2) Board games
   > (3) Quit

   Display options for at least two card games (for example, Hearts) and two board games (for example, Monopoly) of your choice. Then display a one- or two-sentence summary of the game rules.

3.  Draw the menus, then draw the flowchart or write the pseudocode for a program that displays United States travel and tourism facts. The main menu should allow the user to choose a region of the country. The next level should allow the user to select a state in that region. The final level should allow the user to select a city, at which point the user can view facts such as the city's population and average temperature. Write the complete module for only one region, one state, and one city.

4.  Design the menus, and then draw the flowchart or write the pseudocode for an interactive program for a florist. The first screen asks the user to choose indoor plants, outdoor plants, nonplant items, or quit. When the user chooses indoor or outdoor plants, list at least three appropriate plants of your choice. When the user chooses a plant, display its correct price. If the user chooses the nonplant option, offer a choice of gardening tools, gift items, or quit. Depending on the user selection, display at least three gardening tools or gift items. When the user chooses one, display its price.

5.  Design the menus, then draw the flowchart or write the pseudocode for an interactive program for a company's customer database. Store the customers' ID numbers in a 20-element array; store their balances due in a parallel 20-element array. The menu options include add customers to the database, find a customer in the database, print the database, and quit. If the user chooses to add customers, allow the user to enter up to 20 customer IDs and balances; if the user chooses to print, then print all the IDs and balances. If the user chooses to find a customer, provide a second menu with three options—find by number, find by balance, or quit.

6.  Design the logic for a program that creates job applicant records. The program asks a user for his or her first name, middle initial, last name, birth date (month, day, and year), current age, date of application (month, day, and year), job title applying for, and expected salary. Perform as many validation checks as you can think of to ensure that complete and accurate records are created.

# Sequential File Merging, Matching, and Updating

**case** ▶ "I see you're looking at all those index cards I gave you," Lynn Greenbrier says.

"Yes, thanks so much," you reply. "Putting all these programming tips on cards has been a great help to me. I've got a set of cards from you and a set of cards from Boston. Each pile is in alphabetical order. Now I want to create one combined stack and maintain the alphabetical order."

"We do that with files all the time," Lynn replies. "It's called merging. Let's talk about how you can accomplish a merge of two computer files."

**After studying Section A, you should be able to:**

■ Describe the organization of sequential data files you can use in a merge program

■ Create the mainline and house-keeping logic for a merge program

■ Create the MAIN-LOOP and FINISH-UP module logic for a merge program

# Sequential File Merging

## Examining Sequential Data Files to Use in a Merge Program

A **sequential file** is a file whose records are stored one after another in some order. You can store records in a sequential file in the order in which the records are created. For example, if you maintain records of your friends, you might store them in the order in which you met these friends—your best friend from kindergarten is record 1 and the friend you just made last week is record 30.

Often, however, the order of the records in a sequential file is based on the contents of one or more of the fields in each record. Perhaps it is most useful for you to store your friends sequentially in alphabetical order by last name, or maybe in order by birthday.

Other examples of sequential files include:

■ A file of employees stored in order by Social Security number
■ A file of parts for a manufacturing company stored in order by part number
■ A file of customers for a business stored in alphabetical order by last name

**tip**

Recall from Chapter 9 that the field on which you sort records is often called the key field.

Businesses often need to merge two or more sequential files. **Merging files** involves combining two or more files while maintaining the sequential order. For example:

- You have a file of current employees in Social Security number order and a file of newly hired employees also in Social Security number order. You need to merge these two files into one combined file before running this week's payroll program.
- You have a file of parts manufactured in the Northside factory in part number order and a file of parts manufactured in the Southside factory also in part number order. You need to merge these two files into one combined file to create a master list of available parts.
- You have a list of last year's customers in alphabetical order and a list of this year's customers in alphabetical order. You want to create a mailing list of all customers in order by last name.

For you to be able to merge files, it is important that two closely related conditions are met:

- Each file used in the merge must be sorted in order based on some field.
- Each file used in the merge must be sorted in the same order (ascending or descending) on the same field as the others.

Suppose your business has two locations, one on the East Coast and one on the West Coast, and each location maintains a customer file in alphabetical order by customer name. Each file contains fields for name and customer balance. You can call the fields in the East Coast file EAST-NAME and EAST-BALANCE and the fields in the West Coast file WEST-NAME and WEST-BALANCE. You want to merge the two files to create one master file containing records for all customers. Figure 11-1 shows some sample data for the files; you want to create a merged file like the one shown in Figure 11-2.

| East Coast File | | West Coast File | |
|---|---|---|---|
| EAST-NAME | EAST-BALANCE | WEST-NAME | WEST-BALANCE |
| Able | 100.00 | Chen | 200.00 |
| Brown | 50.00 | Edgar | 125.00 |
| Dougherty | 25.00 | Fell | 75.00 |
| Hanson | 300.00 | Grand | 100.00 |
| Ingram | 400.00 | | |
| Johns | 30.00 | | |

**Figure 11-1:** Sample data for two customer files

| MERGED-NAME | MERGED-BALANCE |
|---|---|
| Able | 100.00 |
| Brown | 50.00 |
| Chen | 200.00 |
| Dougherty | 25.00 |
| Edgar | 125.00 |
| Fell | 75.00 |
| Grand | 100.00 |
| Hanson | 300.00 |
| Ingram | 400.00 |
| Johns | 30.00 |

**Figure 11-2:** Merged customer file

## Creating the Mainline and HOUSEKEEPING Logic for a Merge Program

The mainline logic for a program that merges two files is the same main logic you've used before in other programs: a HOUSEKEEPING module, a MAIN-LOOP module that repeats until the end of the program, and a FINISH-UP module. Most programs you have written repeat the MAIN-LOOP until the EOF condition occurs. In this program there are two input files, so checking for EOF on one of them is insufficient. Instead, the mainline logic will check a flag variable such as BOTH-AT-EOF. You will set the BOTH-AT-EOF flag to "Y" after you have encountered EOF on both input files. Figure 11-3 shows the mainline logic.

**tip**

................................................................
You first used flag variables in Chapter 8.
................................................................

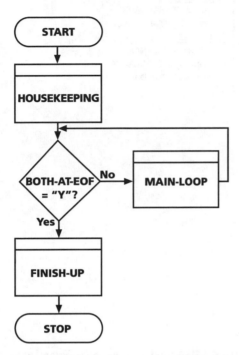

**Figure 11-3:** Flowchart for mainline logic of merge program

When you declare variables within HOUSEKEEPING, you must declare the BOTH-AT-EOF flag and initialize it to any value other than "Y". In addition, you need to define two input files, one for the file from the East Coast office, and one for the file from the West Coast. Figure 11-4 shows that the files are called EAST-FILE and WEST-FILE. Their variable fields are EAST-NAME, EAST-BALANCE, WEST-NAME, and WEST-BALANCE, respectively.

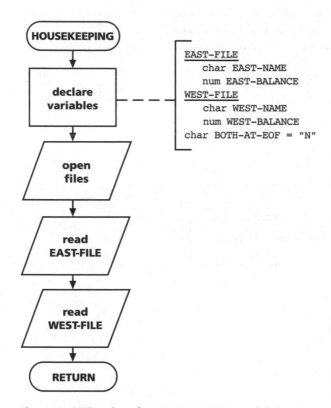

**Figure 11-4:** Flowchart for HOUSEKEEPING module in merge program, version 1

The output from this program is a merged file containing all the records from the two input files. Logically, writing to a file and writing a printed report are very similar—each involves sending data to an output device. The major difference is that when you write a data file, typically you do not include headings or other formatting for people to read like you do when you create a printed report. A **data file** contains data for only another computer program to read.

In many organizations, both data files and printed report files are sent to disk storage devices when they are created. Later, as time becomes available on the organization's busy printers, the report disk files are transferred to paper.

Typically, you read the first file input record into memory at the end of a HOUSEKEEPING module. In this file merging program with two input files, you will read one record from *each* input file into memory at the end of the HOUSE-KEEPING module.

You will modify this HOUSEKEEPING module later in this chapter after you learn about handling the EOF condition in this program.

## Creating the MAIN-LOOP and FINISH-UP for a Merge Program

When you begin the MAIN-LOOP, two records—one from EAST-FILE and one from WEST-FILE—are sitting in the memory of the computer. One of these records needs to be written to the new output file first. Which one? If you want the list in alphabetical order, write the one that has the lower alphabetical value in the name field first. So MAIN-LOOP begins like Figure 11-5.

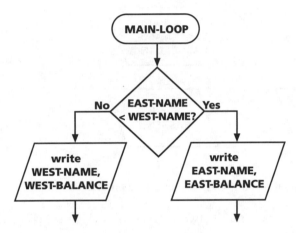

**Figure 11-5:** Beginning of MAIN-LOOP

Using the sample data from Figure 11-1, you can see that the record containing "Able" should be written to the output file while Chen's record waits in memory because the EAST-NAME, "Able," is alphabetically lower than the WEST-NAME, "Chen".

Should Chen's record be written to the output file next? Not necessarily. It depends on the next EAST-NAME following Able's record on the EAST-FILE. You need to read that EAST-FILE record into memory and compare it to "Chen". Since in this case the next record on the EAST-FILE contains the name "Brown," this EAST-FILE record is written.

Is it Chen's turn to be written now? You really don't know until you read another record from the EAST-FILE and compare. Since this one contains the name "Dougherty", it is indeed time to write Chen's record. After Chen's record is written to output, should you now write Dougherty's record? You don't know until you read the next record from the WEST-FILE whether that record should be placed before or after Dougherty's record.

So the MAIN-LOOP proceeds like this: compare two records; write the record with the lower alphabetical name, and read another record from the *same* input file. See Figure 11-6.

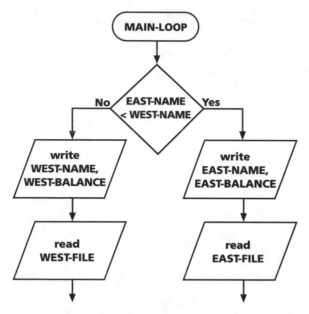

**Figure 11-6:** Continuation of MAIN-LOOP for merge program

Recall the names from the two original files (Figure 11-7) and walk through the processing steps.

1. Compare "Able" and "Chen". Write Able's record. Read Brown's record.
2. Compare "Brown" and "Chen". Write Brown's record. Read Dougherty's record.
3. Compare "Dougherty" and "Chen". Write Chen's record. Read Edgar's record.
4. Compare "Dougherty" and "Edgar". Write Dougherty's record. Read Hanson's record.
5. Compare "Hanson" and "Edgar". Write Edgar's record. Read Fell's record.
6. Compare "Hanson" and "Fell". Write Fell's record. Read Grand's record.
7. Compare "Hanson" and "Grand". Write Grand's record. Read from the WEST-FILE, encountering EOF.

| EAST-NAME | WEST-NAME |
| --- | --- |
| Able | Chen |
| Brown | Edgar |
| Dougherty | Fell |
| Hanson | Grand |
| Ingram | |
| Johns | |

**Figure 11-7:** Names from two files to merge

What happens now? Is the program over? It shouldn't be, because records for Hanson, Ingram, and Johns all need to be included on the new output file and none of them has been written yet. You need to find a way to write the Hanson record as well as read and write all the remaining EAST-FILE records. And you can't just write statements to read and write from the EAST-FILE; sometimes when you run this program, records on the EAST-FILE will finish first alphabetically, and in that case you need to continue reading from the WEST-FILE.

An elegant solution to this problem involves setting the field on which the merge is based to a "high" value when the end of the file is encountered. A **high value** is one that is greater than any possible value in a field. Programmers often use all 9s in a numeric field and all Zs in a character field to indicate a high value. Every time you read from the WEST-FILE, you can check for EOF, and when it occurs, set the WEST-NAME to "ZZZZZ". Similarly, when reading the EAST-FILE, set EAST-NAME to "ZZZZZ" when EOF occurs. When both EAST-NAME and WEST-NAME are "ZZZZZ", then you set the BOTH-AT-EOF variable to "Y". Figure 11-8 shows the complete MAIN-LOOP logic.

**tip**

You might choose to completely fill the EAST-NAME and WEST-NAME fields with Zs instead of using only five. Although it is unlikely that a person will have the last name ZZZZZ, you should be careful to ensure that the value you choose for a high value is actually a higher value than any legitimate value.

Using the sample data in Figure 11-7, when WEST-FILE is read and EOF is encountered, WEST-NAME gets set to "ZZZZZ". Now when you enter the MAIN-LOOP again, EAST-NAME and WEST-NAME are compared and EAST-NAME is still "Hanson". EAST-NAME (Hanson) is therefore lower than WEST-NAME (ZZZZZ). The data for EAST-NAME's record is written to the output, and another EAST-FILE record (Ingram) is read.

**tip**

Several programming languages contain a name you can use for a value that is even higher than all Zs or all 9s. It is the value that occurs when every bit in a byte is an "on" bit. For example, in COBOL this value is called HIGH-VALUES and in RPG it is called HIVAL.

The complete run of the file merging program now executes the first six steps as listed previously and then proceeds as follows:

7. Compare "Hanson" and "Grand". Write Grand's record. Read from the WEST-FILE, encountering EOF and setting WEST-NAME to "ZZZZZ".
8. Compare "Hanson" and "ZZZZZ". Write Hanson's record. Read Ingram's record.
9. Compare "Ingram" and "ZZZZZ". Write Ingram's record. Read Johns's record.

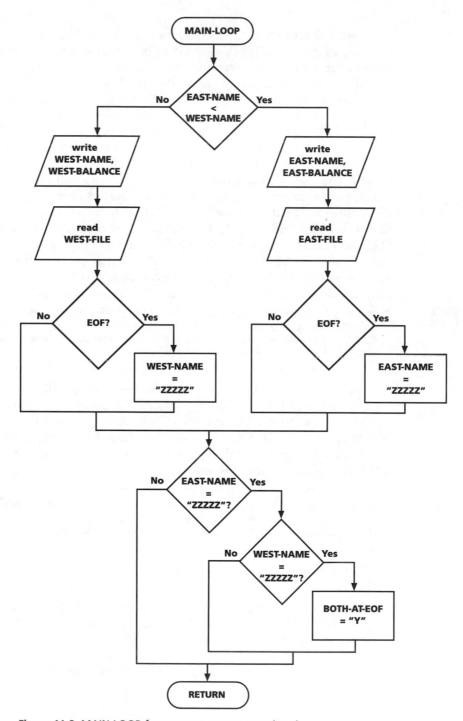

**Figure 11-8:** MAIN-LOOP for merge program completed

10. Compare "Johns" and "ZZZZZ". Write Johns's record. Read from the EAST-FILE, encountering EOF and setting EAST-NAME to "ZZZZZ".

11. Now that both names are "ZZZZZ", set the flag BOTH-AT-EOF equal to "Y".

When the BOTH-AT-EOF flag variable equals "Y", then the mainline logic proceeds to the FINISH-UP module. Figure 11-9 shows FINISH-UP.

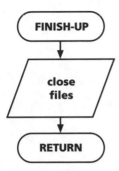

**Figure 11-9:** FINISH-UP module for merge program

**tip**

Notice that if two names are equal during the merge process, for example, there is a "Hanson" record in each file, then both Hansons will be included in the final file. When the EAST-NAME and WEST-NAME match, the EAST-NAME is not lower than the WEST-NAME, so you write the WEST-FILE "Hanson" record. After you read the next WEST-FILE record, EAST-NAME will be lower than the next WEST-NAME, and the EAST-FILE "Hanson" record will be output.

## Modifying the HOUSEKEEPING Module to Check for EOF

Recall that in the HOUSEKEEPING module for this merge program, you read one record from each of the two input files. Although it is unlikely that you will reach the end of file after attempting to read the first record on a file, it is good practice to check for EOF every time you read. So in HOUSEKEEPING, you read from one of the input files. Whether you encounter EOF or not, you then read from the other input file, but if both files are at EOF—that is, if both key fields already have been set to "ZZZZZ"—you can set the BOTH-AT-EOF flag to "Y". Then, if BOTH-AT-EOF is "Y", meaning that there are no records to merge, the mainline logic will send the program to the FINISH-UP module immediately. Figure 11-10 shows the modified HOUSEKEEPING module.

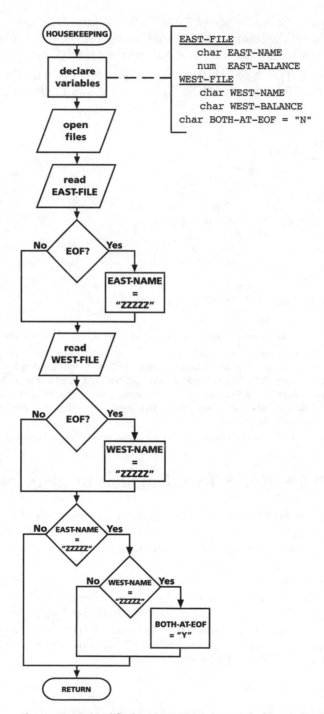

EAST-FILE
    char EAST-NAME
    num  EAST-BALANCE
WEST-FILE
    char WEST-NAME
    char WEST-BALANCE
char BOTH-AT-EOF = "N"

**Figure 11-10:** Modified HOUSEKEEPING module for merge program

**T E R M S   A N D   C O N C E P T S**

sequential file                          data file

merging files                           high value

 **S U M M A R Y**

- A sequential file is a file whose records are stored one after another in some order.

- The order of the records in a sequential file often is based on the contents of one or more of the fields in each record.

- For you to be able to merge files, each file used in the merge must be sorted in order based on some field, and each file used in the merge must be sorted in the same order (ascending or descending) on the same field as the others.

- The mainline logic for a program with two input files can check a flag variable to control the main loop.

- A data file contains data for only another computer program to read; a printed report contains headings and other formatting.

- In a file merging program with two input files, you will read one record from *each* input file into memory at the end of the HOUSEKEEPING module.

- In the main loop of a file merging program you compare two records; write the record with the lower key field, and read another record from the *same* input file.

- A high value is one that is greater than any possible value in a field. You set a key field to a high value at end of file in a file merge program.

- It is good practice to check for EOF every time you read, so you can add checks for EOF for both files in the housekeeping module of a program with two input files.

# E X E R C I S E S

1.  The Springwater Township School District has two high schools—Jefferson and Audubon. Each school maintains a student file with fields containing student ID, last name, first name, and address. Each file is in student ID number order. Write the flowchart or pseudocode for the program that merges the two files into a file containing a list of all students in the district, maintaining student ID number order.

2.  a. The Redgranite Library keeps a file of all books borrowed every month. Each file is in Library of Congress number order and contains additional fields for author and title. Write the flowchart or pseudocode for the program that merges the files for January and February to create a list of all books borrowed in the two-month period.

    b. Modify the program from Exercise 2a so that if there is more than one record for a book number, you print the book information only once.

    c. Modify the program from Exercise 2b so that if there is more than one record for a book number, you not only print the book information only once, but also print a count of the total number of times the book was borrowed.

3.  a. Hearthside Realtors keeps a file for each salesperson in the office. Each file contains the salesperson's transactions for the year in descending sale price order. Two salespeople, Diane and Mark, have formed a partnership. Write the flowchart or pseudocode that produces a merged list of their transactions.

    b. Modify the program in Exercise 3a so that the appropriate salesperson's name appears following each transaction.

4.  Dartmoor Medical Associates maintains two patient files—one for the Lakewood office and one for the Hanover office. Each record contains the name, address, city, state, and zip code of a patient, and the file is maintained in zip code order. Merge the two files to produce one master name and address file that Dartmoor can use for addressing its monthly *Healthy Lifestyles* newsletter mailing in zip code order.

After studying Section B, you should be able to:

- Describe the difference between master and transaction files
- Match records from a transaction file to update a field within a master record
- Allow multiple transactions for a single master file record
- Update files by adding, deleting, or changing records

# File Matching and Updating

## Master and Transaction File Processing

When two related sequential files seem "equal" in that they hold the same *type* of information—for example, when one holds customers from the East Coast and one holds customers from the West Coast—you often need to merge the files to use as a single unit. Some related sequential files, however, are unequal, and you do not want to merge them. For example, you might have a file containing records for all your customers sorted on a key field that holds a customer ID number and contains additional customer data such as name, address, and balance due. You might have another file that contains data for every purchase a customer makes. Such a file would also be sorted by customer number and contain purchase information such as a dollar amount. Although both files contain a customer ID number, the file with the customer names and addresses is an example of a **master file**. You use a master file to hold relatively permanent data about your customers. The file with the customer purchases is a **transaction file**. You use a transaction file to hold more temporary data. You may maintain certain customers' names and addresses for years, but the transaction file will contain new data daily, weekly, or monthly depending on your organization's billing cycle. Often, you periodically use a transaction file to find a **matching record** in a master file so you can **update the master file** by making changes to the values in its fields. For example, the file containing transaction purchase data might be used to update each master file record's balance due field. At other times you might match a transaction file's records to its master file counterpart to create a new entity that draws information from both files—an invoice, for example.

Here are a few other examples of files that have a master-transaction relationship:

- A library maintains a master file of all patrons and a transaction file with information about each book or other item checked out.
- A college maintains a master file of all students and a transaction file for each course registration.

- A telephone company maintains a master file for every telephone line (number) and a transaction file with information about every call.

When you update a master file, you can take two approaches:

- You can actually change the information on the master file. When you use this approach, the information that existed on the master file prior to the transaction processing is lost.
- You can create a new copy of the master file, making the changes on the new version. Then you can store the previous version of the master file for a period of time in case there are questions or discrepancies regarding the update process. The saved version of a master file is often called the **parent file**; the updated version is the **child file**.

........................................................................................

**tip**

When a child file is updated, it becomes a parent, and its parent becomes a grandparent. Individual organizations create policy concerning the number of generations of backup files they will save before discarding them.

........................................................................................

## Matching Files to Update Fields in Master File Records

The logic you use to perform a match between master and transaction file records is similar to the logic you use to perform a merge. As with a merge, you must begin with both files sorted in the same order on the same field.

Assume you have a master file with fields as shown in Figure 11-11.

---

```
File name: CUST-REC
```

| FIELD DESCRIPTION | POSITIONS | DATA TYPE | DECIMALS |
|---|---|---|---|
| CUST-NUMBER | 1–3 | numeric | 0 |
| CUST-NAME | 4–23 | character | |
| CUST-ADDRESS | 24–43 | character | |
| CUST-PHONE | 44–53 | numeric | 0 |
| CUST-SALES-VOLUME | 54–60 | numeric | 2 |

---

**Figure 11-11:** Master customer file description

At the end of each week, you want to update the CUST-SALES-VOLUME field with any new sale transaction that occurred during the week. Assume a transaction file contains one record for every transaction that has occurred. The fields in the transaction file are shown in Figure 11-12.

```
File name: TRANS-REC

FIELD DESCRIPTION        POSITIONS    DATA TYPE     DECIMALS

TRANS-NUMBER             1—3          numeric       0
TRANS-DATE              4—11          numeric       0
TRANS-AMOUNT           12—17          numeric       2
```

**Figure 11-12:** Transaction file description

You want to create a new master file on which almost all the information is the same as on the original file, but the CUST-SALES-VOLUME field has been increased to reflect the most recent transaction. The process involves going through the old master file one record at a time and determining whether there is a new sale for that customer. If there is no transaction for a customer, the new customer record will contain exactly the same information as the old customer record. If, however, there is a transaction for a customer, the TRANS-AMOUNT should be added to the CUST-SALES-VOLUME field before writing the updated master file record to output.

The mainline logic (Figure 11-13) and HOUSEKEEPING (Figure 11-14) modules for this matching program look similar to their counterparts in a file merging program. Two records are read, one from the master file and one from the transaction file. When you encounter EOF for either file, store a high value (999) in the customer number field. Using the READ-CUST and READ-TRANS modules moves the reading of files and checking for EOF off into their individual modules, as shown in Figure 11-15.

```
START
      perform HOUSEKEEPING
      while BOTH-AT-EOF = "N"
            perform MAIN-LOOP
      perform FINISH-UP
END
```

**Figure 11-13:** Mainline logic for file matching program

```
HOUSEKEEPING
      declare variables — — — — — —   CUST-REC
      open files                             num CUST-NUMBER
      perform READ-CUST                      char CUST-NAME
      perform READ-TRANS                     char CUST-ADDRESS
      if CUST-NUMBER = 999                   num CUST-PHONE
            if TRANS-NUMBER = 999            num CUST-SALES-VOLUME
                  BOTH-AT-EOF = "Y"     TRANS-REC
RETURN                                       num TRANS-NUMBER
                                             num TRANS-DATE
                                             num TRANS-AMOUNT
                                         BOTH-AT-EOF = "N"
```

**Figure 11-14:** HOUSEKEEPING module for file match program

> In the file merging program, you placed "ZZZZZ" in the customer name field at end of file because character fields were being compared. Because in this example numeric fields (customer numbers) are being used, at end of file you can store 999, the highest numeric value for a three-digit number, in the customer number field.

```
READ-TRANS                           READ-CUST
    read TRANS-REC                       read CUST-REC
    if EOF                               if EOF
        TRANS-NUMBER = 999                   CUST-NUMBER = 999
RETURN                               RETURN
```

**Figure 11-15:** READ-TRANS and READ-CUST modules for match program

In the file merging program, your first action in the MAIN-LOOP was to determine which file held the record with the lower value; then you wrote that file to output. In a matching program you need to determine more than whether one file's key field is larger than another's; it's also important to know if they are *equal*. You want to update a master file record's CUST-SALES-VOLUME field only if the transaction contains an exact match for the customer number. So now, in the MAIN-LOOP module, you compare the CUST-NUMBER and the TRANS-NUMBER. There are three possibilities:

- The TRANS-NUMBER equals the CUST-NUMBER.
- The TRANS-NUMBER is higher than the CUST-NUMBER.
- The TRANS-NUMBER is lower than the CUST-NUMBER.

If the CUST-NUMBER and the TRANS-NUMBER are equal, you add the TRANS-AMOUNT to the CUST-SALES-VOLUME, and then write the updated master record to the output file and read in both a new master record and a new transaction record.

**The logic used here assumes there can be only one transaction per customer. Later in this chapter you will develop the logic for a program in which the customer can have multiple transactions.**

If the TRANS-NUMBER is higher than the CUST-NUMBER, that means there wasn't a sale for that customer. That's all right; every customer does not make a transaction every period. In such cases, you just write the original customer record to output exactly the same way it came in on input; then get the next customer record to see if this is the customer to whom the transaction pertains.

Finally, if the TRANS-NUMBER is lower than the CUST-NUMBER on the master file, you are trying to record a transaction for which no master record exists. That means there must be an error, for a transaction should always have a master record. You can handle this error in a variety of ways; here you will write an error message to an output device before reading the next transaction record. A human operator can then read the message and take appropriate action.

Whether the TRANS-NUMBER was higher than, lower than, or equal to the CUST-NUMBER, at the bottom of the MAIN-LOOP you check whether both CUST-NUMBER and TRANS-NUMBER are 999; when they are, you set the BOTH-AT-EOF flag to "Y".

Figure 11-16 shows some sample data you can use to walk through the logic for this program.

| Master File | | Transaction File | |
|---|---|---|---|
| CUST-NUMBER | CUST-SALES-VOLUME | TRANS-NUMBER | TRANS-AMOUNT |
| 100 | 1000.00 | 100 | 400.00 |
| 102 | 50.00 | 105 | 700.00 |
| 103 | 500.00 | 108 | 100.00 |
| 105 | 75.00 | 110 | 400.00 |
| 106 | 5000.00 | | |
| 109 | 4000.00 | | |
| 110 | 500.00 | | |

**Figure 11-16:** Sample data for matching program

The program proceeds as follows:

1. Read customer 100 from the master file and customer 100 from the transaction file. Customer numbers are equal, so 400.00 is added to 1000.00 and a new master file record is written out with a 1400.00 sales volume figure. Then read a new record from each file.

2. The customer number on the master file is 102 and the customer number on the transaction file is 105, so there are no transactions today for customer 102. Write out the master record just the way it came in, and read a new master record.

3. Now the master customer number is 103 and the transaction customer number is still 105. This means customer 103 has no transactions, so you write out the master record as is and read a new one.

4. Now the master customer number is 105 and the transaction number is 105. The new sales volume figure is 775.00, and a new master record is written out. Read one record from each file.

5. Now the master number is 106 and the transaction number is 108. Write out customer record 106 as is, and read another master.

6. Now the master number is 109 and the transaction number is 108. An error has occurred. The transaction record indicates that you made a sale to customer 108, but there is no master record for customer number 108. Either there is an error in the transaction customer number, or the transaction is correct but you have failed to create a master record. Either way, write an error message so that a clerk is notified and can handle the problem. Then get a new transaction record.

7. Now the master number is 109 and the transaction number is 110. Write out master record 109 with no changes and read a new one.

8. Now the master number is 110 and the transaction number is 110. Add the 400.00 transaction to the previous 500.00 figure and write out a new record with a 900.00 figure in it. Read one record from each file.

9. Since both files are done, end the job.

Figure 11-17 shows the pseudocode for the logic just described. The final result is a new master file in which some records contain exactly the same data they contained going in, but others (for which a transaction has occurred) that have been updated with a new sales volume figure.

```
MAIN-LOOP
    if CUST-NUMBER = TRANS-NUMBER then
            CUST-SALES-VOLUME = CUST-SALES-VOLUME + TRANS-AMOUNT
            write CUST-REC
            perform READ-CUST
            perform READ-TRANS
    else
            if TRANS-NUMBER > CUST-NUMBER then
                    write CUST-REC
                    perform READ-CUST
            else
                    write "An Error has occurred in transaction", TRANS-NUMBER
                    perform READ-TRANS
    if CUST-NUMBER = 999
            if TRANS-NUMBER = 999
                    BOTH-AT-EOF = "Y"
RETURN
```

**Figure 11-17:** Pseudocode for MAIN-LOOP logic for file matching program

## Allowing Multiple Transactions for a Single Master File Record

You would use very similar logic if you wanted to allow multiple transactions for a single customer. Figure 11-18 shows the new logic. There is a small but important difference between logic that allows multiple transactions per master file record and logic that allows only a single transaction per master file record. If a customer can have multiple transactions, whenever a transaction matches a customer you add the transaction amount to the master sales volume figure. But *then* you read only from the transaction file. The next transaction might also pertain to the same master customer. Only when a transaction number is greater than a master file customer number, do you write the customer master record.

```
MAIN-LOOP
    if CUST-NUMBER = TRANS-NUMBER then
            CUST-SALES-VOLUME = CUST-SALES-VOLUME + TRANS-AMOUNT
            perform READ-TRANS
    else
            if TRANS-NUMBER > CUST-NUMBER then
                    write CUST-REC
                    perform READ-CUST
            else
                    write "An Error has occurred in transaction ", TRANS-NUMBER
                    perform READ-TRANS
    if CUST-NUMBER = 999
            if TRANS-NUMBER = 999
                    BOTH-AT-EOF = "Y"
RETURN
```

**Figure 11-18:** MAIN-LOOP logic allowing multiple transactions for each master file record

# Updating Records in Sequential Files

In the example in the last section, you needed to update a field in some of the records in a master file with new data. A more sophisticated kind of update program allows you to make changes to data in a record and update a master file by adding new records or eliminating records you no longer want.

Assume you have a master employee file as shown on the left side of Figure 11-19. Sometimes a new employee is hired and must be added to this file, or an employee quits and must be removed from the file. Sometimes you need to change an employee record by recording a raise in salary, for example, or a change of department.

For this kind of program, it's common to have a transaction file in which each record contains all the same fields as the master file, with one exception. The transaction file has one extra field to indicate whether this transaction is meant to be an addition, a deletion, or a change—for example, a one-letter code of "A", "D", or "C". Figure 11-19 shows the master and transaction file layouts.

| File name: CUST-REC | | File name: TRANS-REC | |
|---|---|---|---|
| FIELD DESCRIPTION | POSITIONS | FIELD DESCRIPTION | POSITIONS |
| EMP-NUM | 1—3 | TRANS-NUM | 1—3 |
| EMP-NAME | 4—23 | TRANS-NAME | 4—23 |
| EMP-SALARY | 24—28 | TRANS-SALARY | 24—28 |
| EMP-DEPT | 29—30 | TRANS-DEPT | 29—30 |
| | | TRANS-CODE | 31 |

**Figure 11-19:** Master and transaction files for update program

A typical **addition record** on the transaction file would contain data in the fields TRANS-NUM, TRANS-NAME, TRANS-SALARY, TRANS-DEPT; this is a new employee, and data for all the fields must be entered for the first time. In addition, such a record contains an "A" in the TRANS-CODE field.

A typical **deletion record** really needs only the "D" code and the TRANS-NUM. If the TRANS-NUM matches an EMP-NUM on a master record, that's the record you want to delete. There is no need for data indicating the salary, department, or anything else for a record you are deleting.

A typical **change record** contains the "C" code and needs data only in the fields that are going to be changed. In other words, if an employee's salary is staying the same, the TRANS-SALARY field will be blank; but if the employee is transferring to Department 28, then the department field of the transaction record would hold a 28.

The mainline logic for an update program is the same as that for the merging and matching programs as shown in Figure 11-13. Within the HOUSEKEEPING module you declare the variables, open the files, and read the first record from each file. You can use the READ-EMP and READ-TRANS modules to set the key fields EMP-NUM and TRANS-NUM to very high values at EOF. See Figures 11-20 and 11-21.

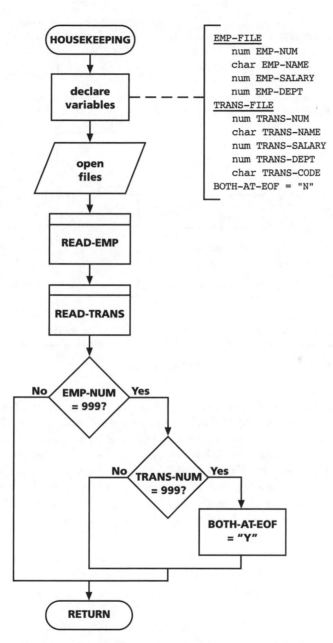

**Figure 11-20:** HOUSEKEEPING module for update program

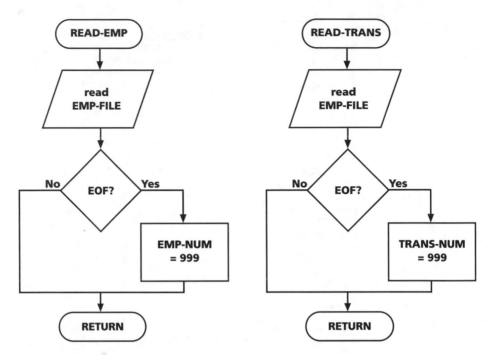

**Figure 11-21:** READ-EMP and READ-TRANS modules

The MAIN-LOOP of this program begins like the matching program. You need to know whether the EMP-NUM on the master file and the TRANS-NUM on the transaction file are equal or if one or the other is higher. To keep the MAIN-LOOP simple, you can create modules for each of these three scenarios: THEY-ARE-EQUAL, EMP-IS-LARGER-THAN-TRANS, and TRANS-IS-LARGER-THAN-EMP. (Of course, you might choose shorter module names.) At the end of the MAIN-LOOP module, you can set the BOTH-AT-EOF flag to "Y" if both files have completed. Figure 11-22 shows the MAIN-LOOP module.

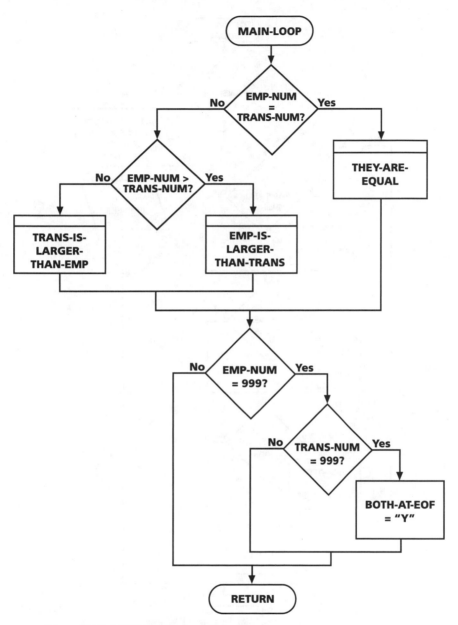

**Figure 11-22:** MAIN-LOOP of update program

You perform the THEY-ARE-EQUAL module only if a record on the master file and a record on the transaction file have the same employee number. This should be the situation when a change such as a new salary is being made to a record, or when a record is to be deleted. If the master file and the transaction file records are equal, but the TRANS-CODE on the transaction record is an "A", then an error situation has occurred. You should not be attempting to add a full employee record when the employee already exists in the master file.

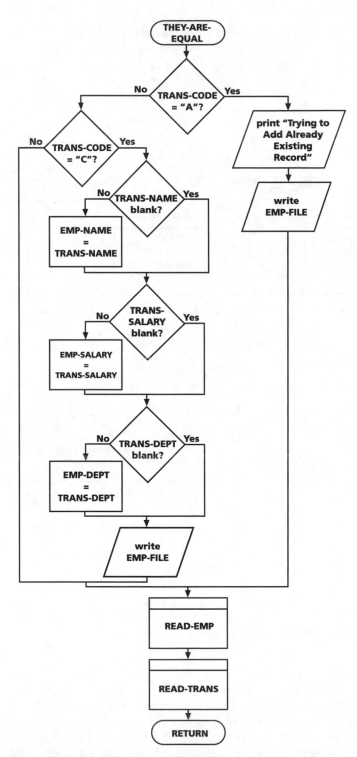

**Figure 11-23:** THEY-ARE-EQUAL module for update program

As shown in Figure 11-23, within the THEY-ARE-EQUAL module you check the TRANS-CODE and perform one of three actions:

- If the code is an "A", print an error message. But what is the error? (Is the code wrong? Was this meant to be a change or a delete of an existing employee? Is the employee number wrong—was this meant to be the addition of some new employee?) Since you're not really sure, you can only print out an error message to let an employee know that an error situation has occurred; then the employee can handle the error. You should also write the existing master record to output exactly the same way it came in without making any changes.
- If the code is a "C", you need to make changes. You must check each field on the transaction record. If any field is blank, the data on the new master record should come from the old master record. If, however, a field on the transaction record contains data, this data is intended to be a change. The corresponding field on the new master record should come from the transaction record. For all changed fields, then, you replace the contents of the old field on the master file with the new value in the corresponding field on the transaction file. Then write the master file record.
- If the code is not an "A" or a "C", it must be a "D" and the record should be deleted. How do you delete a record from a new master file? Just don't write it out to the new master file!

**Checking a field to determine if it is blank is done differently in various programming languages. In some languages, you compare the TRANS-NAME to a space character, as in TRANS-NAME = " ". In other languages you can use a pre-defined language-specific constant like blank, as in TRANS-NAME = blank.**

**To keep the illustration simple here, you can assume that all the transaction records have been checked by a previous program and all TRANS-CODEs are "A", "C", or "D". If this were not the case, you could simply add one more decision to the THEY-ARE-EQUAL module. If the TRANS-CODE is not "C", ask if it is "D". If so, delete the record; if not, it must not be "A", "C", or "D", so write an error message.**

Finally, at the end of the THEY-ARE-EQUAL module, after the master file record and the transaction file record have matched and been dealt with, you read one new record from each of the two input files.

Suppose, in the MAIN-LOOP, the master file record and the transaction file record do *not* match. If the master file record has a higher number than the transaction file record, then you execute the EMP-IS-LARGER-THAN-TRANS module as shown in Figure 11-24. This means you have read a transaction record for which there is no master record.

If the transaction record contains code "A", that's fine because an addition transaction shouldn't have a master record. The transaction record data simply becomes the new master record and each of its fields is written to the new output file.

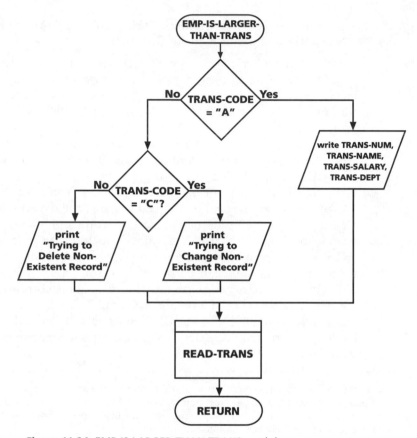

**Figure 11-24:** EMP-IS-LARGER-THAN-TRANS module

However, if the transaction code is "C" or "D", an error has occurred. You are attempting to make a change to a nonexistent record, or you are attempting to delete a nonexistent record. Either way, a mistake has been made. You must print an error message.

At the end of the EMP-IS-LARGER-THAN-TRANS routine, you should not read another master file record. After all, there could be several more transactions that represent new additions to the master file. You want to keep reading transactions until a transaction matches or is greater than a master record. Therefore only a transaction record should be read.

The last possibility in the MAIN-LOOP module is that a master file record is smaller than the transaction file record in memory. If there is no transaction for a given master file record, then the TRANS-IS-LARGER-THAN-EMP subroutine is entered. This just means that the master file record has no changes or deletions, so you simply write the new master record out exactly like the old master record, and read another master record. See Figure 11-25.

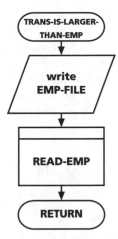

**Figure 11-25:** TRANS-IS-LARGER-THAN-EMP module

At some point, one of the files will reach EOF. If the transaction file reaches the end first, TRANS-NUM is set to 999 in the READ-TRANS routine. Each time MAIN-LOOP is entered after TRANS-NUM is set to 999, EMP-NUM will be lower than TRANS-NUM. The TRANS-IS-LARGER-THAN-EMP routine will be performed. That's the routine that writes out records from the master file without alteration. This is exactly what you want to have happen. There obviously were no transactions for these final records on the master file, because all the records in the transaction file have been dealt with.

But if the master file reaches the end first, EMP-NUM is set to 999 in the READ-EMP routine. Now each time MAIN-LOOP is entered, the TRANS-NUM will be lower than the EMP-NUM for all remaining records. The EMP-IS-LARGER-THAN-TRANS routine is the one that will be performed. The transactions that are left over at the end of the transaction file will be checked. If they are additions, they will be written to the new master as new records. However, if they are changes or deletions, a mistake has been made because there are no corresponding master file records.

Whichever file reaches the end first, the other continues to be read from and processed. When that file reaches EOF, the BOTH-AT-EOF flag will finally be set to "Y". Then you can perform the FINISH-UP module, as shown in Figure 11-26.

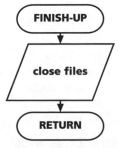

**Figure 11-26:** FINISH-UP module for update program

Merging files, matching files, and updating a master file from a transaction file are processes that require a significant number of steps because as you read each new input record, you must account for many possible scenarios. Planning the logic for programs like these takes a fair amount of time, but if you plan the logic carefully, you will end up creating programs that perform a lot of valuable work for years to come. Separating the various outcomes into manageable modules keeps the program organized and allows you to develop the logic one step at a time.

# TERMS AND CONCEPTS

| | |
|---|---|
| master file | child file |
| transaction file | addition record |
| matching record | deletion record |
| update the master file | change record |
| parent file | |

# SUMMARY

- When two related sequential files seem "equal," that is, they hold the same *type* of information, you often need to merge the files to use as a single unit. Some related sequential files, however, are "unequal"; these files often are master and transaction files.

- A master file holds relatively permanent data; a transaction file holds more temporary data.

- In many organizations you periodically use a transaction file to find a match in a master file so you can update or make changes to a master file.

- When you update a master file, you can take two approaches: you can actually change the information on the master file, or you can create a new copy of the master file, making the changes on the new version. The saved version of a master file is often called the parent file; the updated version is the child file.

- To perform a master-transaction match, you must begin with both files sorted in the same order on the same field.

- Updating a master file from a transaction file involves going through the old master file one record at a time and determining whether there is a corresponding transaction. If there are no transactions for a master record, the new master record will contain exactly the same information as the old master record. If there is a transaction, you make a change to one or more fields in the master file.

- In a matching program, you must determine whether a transaction's key field is equal to, greater than, or less than a master file record's key field.

- To allow multiple transactions, when a transaction matches a master file record, you process the transaction and then read only from the transaction file. Only when a transaction key field is greater than a master file record key field do you write the master record.

- Some update programs allow you to make changes to data in a record and update a master file by adding new records or eliminating records you no longer want.

- A transaction file can contain an extra field to indicate whether this transaction is meant to be an addition, a deletion, or a change.

- Besides the appropriate code, a typical addition record on the transaction file contains data in every field, a typical deletion record needs only a key field, and a typical change record needs data only in the fields that are going to be changed.

- Merging files, matching files, and updating a master file from a transaction file are processes that require a significant number of steps; separating the various outcomes into manageable modules keeps the program organized and allows you to develop the logic one step at a time.

# E X E R C I S E S

1. a. The Timely Talent Temporary Help Agency maintains an employee master file that contains employee ID number, last name, first name, address, and hourly rate for each of the temporary employees it sends out on assignments. The file has been sorted in employee ID number order.

    Each week, a transaction file is created with a job number, address, customer name, employee ID, and hours worked for every job filled by Timely Talent workers. The transaction file is also sorted in employee ID order.

    Write the program that matches the master and transaction file records and print one line for each transaction indicating job number, employee ID number, hours worked, hourly rate, and gross pay. Assume each temporary worker works at most one job per week; print one line for each worker who has worked that week.

    b. Modify Exercise 1a so that any individual temporary worker can work any number of separate jobs in a week. Print one line for each job that week.

    c. Modify Exercise 1b so that although any worker can work any number of jobs in a week, you accumulate the worker's total pay for all jobs and print one line per worker.

2. You run a talent agency that books bands for social functions. You maintain a master file in the following format:

TALENT FILE DESCRIPTION

File name: BANDS

| FIELD DESCRIPTION | POSITIONS | DATA TYPE | DECIMALS | EXAMPLE |
|---|---|---|---|---|
| Band code | 1–3 | numeric | 0 | 176 |
| Band name | 4–33 | character | | The Polka Pals |
| Contact person | 34–53 | character | | Jay Sakowicz |
| Phone | 54–63 | numeric | 0 | 8154556012 |
| Musical style | 64–71 | character | | Polka |
| Hourly rate | 72–76 | numeric | 2 | 07500 |

Once a month you make changes to the file using transaction records with the same format as the master records, plus one additional field that holds a transaction code. The transaction code is "A" if you are adding a new band to the file, "C" if you are changing some of the data in an existing record, and "D" if you are deleting a band from the file.

An addition transaction record contains a band code, an "A" in the transaction code field, and the new band's data. During processing, an error can occur if you attempt to add a band code that already exists on the file. This is not allowed, and an error message is printed.

A change transaction record contains a band code, a "C" in the transaction code field, and data for only those fields that are changing. For example, a band that is raising its hourly rate from $75 to $100 per hour would contain empty fields for the band name, contact person information, and style of music, but the hourly rate field would contain the new rate. During processing, an error can occur if you attempt to change data for a band number that doesn't exist on the master file; print an error message.

A deletion transaction record contains a band code, a "D" in the transaction code field, and no other data. During processing, an error can occur if you attempt to delete a band number that doesn't exist on the master file; print an error message.

Two forms of output are created. One is the new updated master file with all changes, additions, and deletions. The other is a printed report of errors that occurred during processing. Rather than just a list of error messages, each line of the printed output should list the appropriate band code along with the corresponding message.

Design the print chart for the error report, and the hierarchy chart and flowchart or pseudocode for the program.

# Advanced Modularization Techniques and Object-Oriented Programming

**case▶** "What's in the box?" you ask Boston Murphy, as he enters your office with a small carton. Reading the side, you add, "TeleMaster?"

"It's for your computer," he says. "It's a modem. I'll plug it into your system unit and into the wall connection over there, and voila! Your computer's ready to communicate with the outside world!"

"I wish I understood how those work," you say. "You just plug it in, but I have no idea what's going on inside."

"That's the beauty of it," says Boston. "Most useful objects are like black boxes—you don't have to understand their inner working in order to benefit from their capabilities. To most of us, devices like modems demonstrate the principles of abstraction and encapsulation. Those are principles you should be applying in your programs, too."

**After studying Section A, you should be able to:**

- Describe the concepts of modularization and abstraction in procedural programs
- Pass a variable to a module
- Return a value from a module
- Use an IPO chart
- Describe the advantages of encapsulation

# Advanced Modularization Techniques

## Principles of Modularization and Abstraction in Procedural Programs

Throughout most of computer programming history, which now totals about 50 years, the majority of programs were written procedurally. A **procedural program** consists of a series of steps or procedures that take place one after the other. The programmer determines the exact conditions under which a procedure takes place, how often it takes place, and when the program stops. The logic for every program you have developed so far using this book has been procedural.

**tip**   You first learned the term *procedural* program in Chapter 4.

It is possible to write procedural programs as one long series of steps. However, by now you should appreciate the benefits of **modularization,** or breaking programs into reasonable units called modules, subroutines, functions, or methods:

- Modularization provides **abstraction**; in other words, it allows you to see the "big picture" more easily.
- Modularization allows multiple programmers to work on a problem, each contributing one or more modules that later can be combined into a whole program.
- Modularization allows you to reuse your work; you can call the same module from multiple locations within a program.
- Modularization allows you to identify structures more easily.

You first learned the term *modular* in Chapter 2; you learned about *abstraction* in Chapter 3.

As beneficial as using modules is, the modules and subroutines you have used throughout this book also have two major drawbacks:

- Although the modules you have used allow multiple programmers to work on a problem, each programmer must know the *names* of *all* the variables used in the other modules within the program.
- Although the modules you have used enable you to reuse your work by allowing you to call them from multiple locations within a program, you can't use the modules in different programs unless the new programs use the *same variable names*.

These two limitations stem from the same fact: the variables you have used throughout this book have been global variables. A **global variable** is one that is available to every module in a program. That is, every module has access to the variable, can use its value, and can change its value. When you declare a variable named TOTAL in a program's HOUSEKEEPING module, add to it in a MAIN-LOOP module, and print it in a FINISH module, then TOTAL is a global variable within that program.

With many older computer programming languages, all variables are global variables. Newer, more modularized languages allow you to use local variables as well. A **local variable** is one whose name and value are known only to its own module. A local variable is declared within a module and ceases to exist when the module ends.

Languages that use only global variables are most likely to call their modules subroutines. Languages that allow local variables and the passing of values are more likely to call their modules procedures, methods, or functions.

Many languages refer to a local variable *going out of scope* at the end of its module. In other words, the program "loses sight of" the variable.

When you declare local variables within modules, you do so in a declare variables step. Usually, this is the first step within a module, but some languages allow you to declare variables at any point within a module. Sometimes you declare a local variable because the value is needed only within one module. For example, consider a very simple program that asks a student just one arithmetic question. For simplicity, this example won't loop; it provides a single user with a single question. A program such as this one could be contained in a single main module, but you can divide it into three separate modules as shown in Figure 12-1. The program contains three steps: HOUSEKEEPING, ASK-QUESTION, and FINISH.

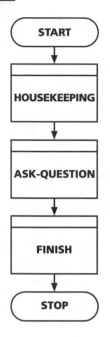

**Figure 12-1:** Mainline logic for a program
that uses local variables

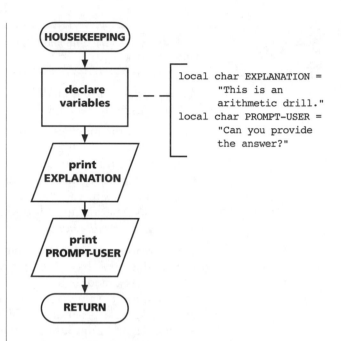

**Figure 12-2:** HOUSEKEEPING module for program
that uses local variables

Figure 12-2 shows the HOUSEKEEPING module in which directions display on the screen. Within HOUSEKEEPING you can declare variables named EXPLANATION and PROMPT-USER to hold the directions. EXPLANATION and PROMPT-USER can be local to HOUSEKEEPING because ASK-QUESTION and FINISH never need access to these variables—these modules do not need to use the variables or alter them in any way.

**tip**

Programming languages that use local variables do not require you to modify the variable declaration with the term *local* as shown in Figure 12-2. The term *local* is used in Figure 12-2 just for emphasis.

Within the ASK-QUESTION module, you display an arithmetic problem, accept an answer, determine whether the answer is correct, and write a message. The ASK-QUESTION does not need to know about the EXPLANATION and PROMPT-USER variables, but ASK-QUESTION needs a USER-ANSWER variable in which to store the user's answer to the arithmetic problem. Within the ASK-QUESTION module, you declare the USER-ANSWER variable, use it to hold the user's answer, and then use it to determine whether the user's answer is correct. By the time you reach the end of the ASK-QUESTION module, the USER-ANSWER variable has served its purpose; there is no reason for either the HOUSEKEEPING module or the FINISH module to have access to the USER-ANSWER variable. Figure 12-3 shows the USER-ANSWER variable being declared locally within the ASK-QUESTION module.

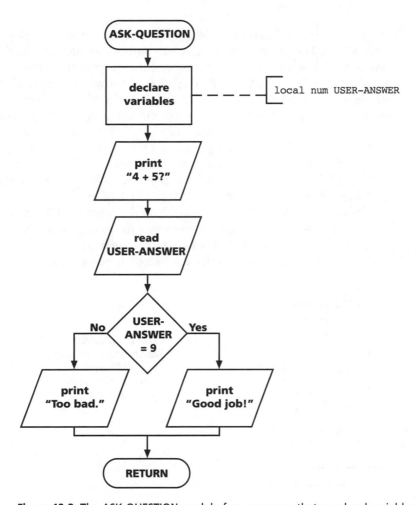

**Figure 12-3:** The ASK-QUESTION module for a program that uses local variables

This arithmetic drill program employs a principle known as **encapsulation**, also known as **information hiding** or **data hiding**. These terms all mean the same thing—that the data or variables you use are completely contained within and accessible only to the module in which they are declared. In other words, the data and variables are "hidden from" the other program modules. Using encapsulation provides you with two advantages:

- Because each module needs to use only the variable names declared within the module, multiple programmers can create the individual modules without knowing the data names used by the others.
- Because the variable names in each module are hidden from all other modules, programmers can even use the same variable names as those used in other modules and no conflict will arise.

Consider the HOUSEKEEPING module for the arithmetic drill program shown in Figure 12-2. The programmer who works on this module can give the local variables any name he or she wants. For example, the programmer *could* decide to call the PROMPT-USER variable USER-ANSWER as shown in Figure 12-4. In a program that employs local variables, giving the HOUSEKEEPING module's variable this name would have no effect on the usefulness of the identically named variable defined in the ASK-QUESTION module. The two USER-ANSWER variables are completely separate variables with unique memory addresses. One holds the character prompt "Can you provide the answer?" and the other holds a numeric user answer. Changing the value of USER-ANSWER in one module, which is what happens when the user enters an arithmetic problem answer in the ASK-QUESTION module, has no effect whatsoever on the separate USER-ANSWER variable in the other module. As programs grow in size and complexity, it is a great convenience for a programmer who is working on a module not to have to worry about conflicting with all the other variable names used in the dozens of other modules that are part of the same large program.

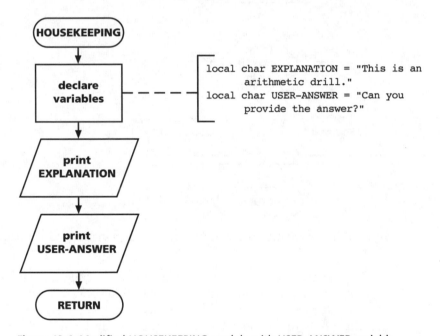

Figure 12-4: Modified HOUSEKEEPING module with USER-ANSWER variable

## Passing Variables to Modules

It may be convenient for a programmer to use local variables without worrying about naming conflicts, but, by definition, a local variable is accessible to one module only. The problem is that sometimes more than one module needs access to the same variable value. Consider the arithmetic drill program. Instead of a single arithmetic problem, it is more reasonable to expect such a program to ask the user a series of problems and keep score. Figure 12-5 shows a revised ASK-QUESTION module that accesses an array to provide a series of five questions for the arithmetic drill. The module compares the user's answer to the correct answer that is stored in the corresponding position in a parallel array and adds 1 to a CORRECT-COUNT variable when the answer is correct.

Suppose you want to print the count of correct answers, the percentage of correct answers, and one of five messages, based on the user's performance. There are enough steps involved in the process of displaying the final statistics that you want to place these steps in their own module, named FINAL-STATISTICS. But if you want to modularize the process that prints the final statistics, then you must access the CORRECT-COUNT value from within the FINAL-STATISTICS module. If CORRECT-COUNT is declared locally to ASK-QUESTION, the FINAL-STATISTICS module does not have access to it. If CORRECT-COUNT is declared locally in the FINAL-STATISTICS module, then ASK-QUESTION cannot add to it. If you attempt to solve the dilemma by declaring a local CORRECT-COUNT variable in *each* module, they are not the same variable, and adding to the CORRECT-COUNT variable in one module does not alter the value of the unique CORRECT-COUNT variable in the other module. If you decide not to use local variables, but declare CORRECT-COUNT as a global variable, your program will work, but you will have avoided using the principle of encapsulation and will have lost the advantages it provides.

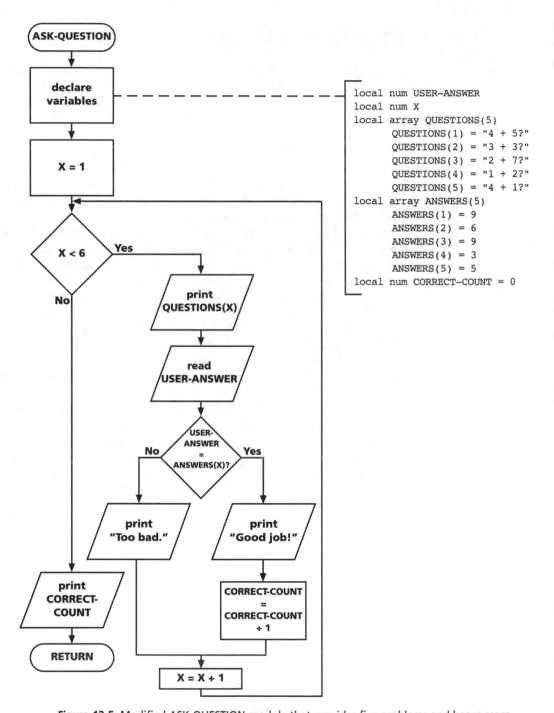

```
local num USER-ANSWER
local num X
local array QUESTIONS(5)
        QUESTIONS(1) = "4 + 5?"
        QUESTIONS(2) = "3 + 3?"
        QUESTIONS(3) = "2 + 7?"
        QUESTIONS(4) = "1 + 2?"
        QUESTIONS(5) = "4 + 1?"
local array ANSWERS(5)
        ANSWERS(1) = 9
        ANSWERS(2) = 6
        ANSWERS(3) = 9
        ANSWERS(4) = 3
        ANSWERS(5) = 5
local num CORRECT-COUNT = 0
```

**Figure 12-5:** Modified ASK-QUESTION module that provides five problems and keeps score

The solution to using a locally declared variable within another module lies in passing the local variable from one module to the other. **Passing a variable** means that a you are sending a copy of data in one module of a program to another module for use. Exactly how this is accomplished differs slightly among languages, but it usually involves including the variable name within parentheses in the call to the module that needs to receive a copy of the value. Figure 12-6 shows how you can modify the ASK-QUESTION module to pass a copy of the CORRECT-COUNT value to FINAL-STATISTICS. Then, in the FINAL-STATISTICS module, you declare a name for the passed value within parentheses in the **module header** or introductory title statement; Figure 12-7 shows how FINAL-STATISTICS receives the value as part of its module's header. The passed variable named within the module header often is called a **parameter** or an **argument**.

A module call that includes a parameter looks like an array name with a variable subscript. For example, is FINAL–STATISTICS(CORRECT–COUNT) a call to the FINAL-STATISTICS module using a parameter, or is it a reference to the CORRECT-COUNT element of an array named FINAL-STATISTICS? To avoid confusion, many languages use square brackets to indicate array subscripts and reserve parentheses for passing variables.

In Figure 12-7, the FINAL-STATISTICS module declares a numeric variable named NUM-RIGHT in its header statement. This indicates that this variable is not a regular variable that is declared locally within the module, but is a special variable that receives its value from the outside. In Figure 12-7, NUM-RIGHT receives its value because ASK-QUESTION calls FINAL-STATISTICS and passes CORRECT-COUNT to it, as shown in Figure 12-6. Within the FINAL-STATISTICS module, NUM-RIGHT takes on the value of CORRECT-COUNT, and the percentage of correct answers is calculated using NUM-RIGHT.

Passing a copy of a value to a module sometimes is called *passing by value*. Some languages allow you to pass the actual memory address of a variable to a module; this is called *passing by reference*. When you pass by reference, you lose some of the advantages of information hiding because the module has access to the address of the passed variable, not just a copy of the value of the passed variable. However, program performance improves because the computer doesn't have to make a copy of the value, thereby saving time.

Within the FINAL-STATISTICS module, you *could* choose to name the passed local value CORRECT-COUNT instead of NUM-RIGHT. Whether the variable name that holds the count in FINAL-STATISTICS is the same as or different from the corresponding value in the ASK-QUESTION module is irrelevant. CORRECT-COUNT and NUM-RIGHT represent two unique memory locations, no matter what name you decide to give to the variable within the FINAL-STATISTICS module that holds the count of right answers.

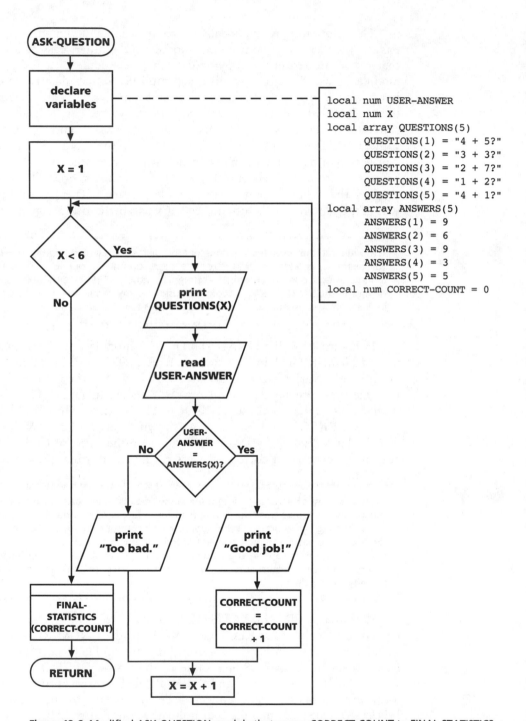

```
local num USER-ANSWER
local num X
local array QUESTIONS(5)
       QUESTIONS(1) = "4 + 5?"
       QUESTIONS(2) = "3 + 3?"
       QUESTIONS(3) = "2 + 7?"
       QUESTIONS(4) = "1 + 2?"
       QUESTIONS(5) = "4 + 1?"
local array ANSWERS(5)
       ANSWERS(1) = 9
       ANSWERS(2) = 6
       ANSWERS(3) = 9
       ANSWERS(4) = 3
       ANSWERS(5) = 5
local num CORRECT-COUNT = 0
```

**Figure 12-6:** Modified ASK-QUESTION module that passes CORRECT-COUNT to FINAL-STATISTICS

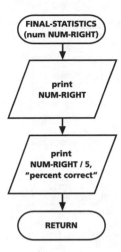

**Figure 12-7:** FINAL-STATISTICS module that receives CORRECT-COUNT value and calls it NUM-RIGHT

## Returning a Value from a Module

Suppose you decide to organize the arithmetic drill program so that the FINAL-STATISTICS module computes the user's correct percentage, but the ASK-QUESTION module handles the printing of the final statistics. In this case, you pass CORRECT-COUNT to the FINAL-STATISTICS module as before, but the FINAL-STATISTICS module must **return the value** of the calculated correct percentage back to ASK-QUESTION. Just as you can pass a value into a module, you can pass back, or return a value to a calling module. Usually, this is accomplished within the return statement of the called module as shown in Figure 12-8.

Notice that within the ASK-QUESTION module, you call the FINAL-STATISTICS module, and pass in the CORRECT-COUNT value. Then you assign the return value of the FINAL-STATISTICS module to CORRECT-PERCENT. CORRECT-PERCENT is a variable that is declared locally in the ASK-QUESTION module. This step indicates that the value returned by the FINAL-STATISTICS module will be the value assigned to the CORRECT-PERCENT variable. Then you can use the CORRECT-PERCENT variable within the remainder of the ASK-QUESTION module.

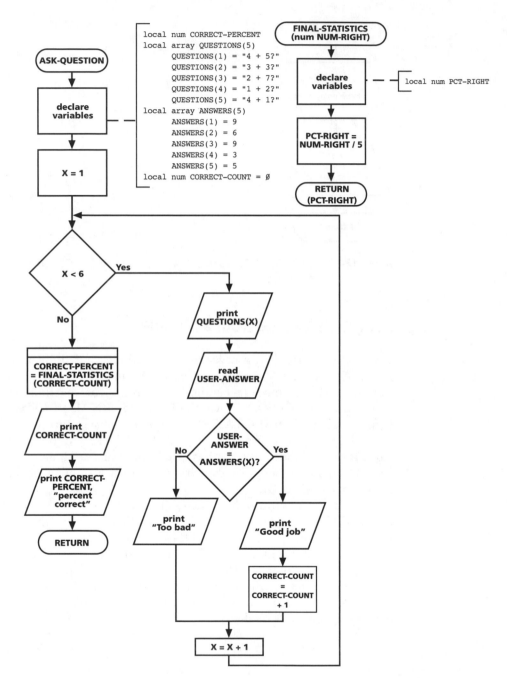

**Figure 12-8:** ASK-QUESTION and FINAL-STATISTICS with a value passed into and out of FINAL-STATISTICS

## Using an IPO Chart

When designing modules to use within larger programs, some programmers find it helpful to use an **IPO chart**, which identifies and categorizes each item needed within the module as pertaining to input, processing, or output. For example, when you design the FINAL-STATISTICS module in the arithmetic drill program, you can start by placing each of the module's components in one of the three processing categories, as shown in Figure 12-9.

| Input | Processing | Output |
| --- | --- | --- |
| correct count | divide correct count by total number of problems producing percentage correct | percentage correct |

**Figure 12-9:** IPO chart for FINAL-STATISTICS module

The IPO chart in Figure 12-9 provides you with an overview of the processing steps involved in the FINAL-STATISTICS module. Like a flowchart or pseudocode, an IPO chart is just another tool to help you plan the logic of your programs.

## The Advantages of Encapsulation

When you write a module that receives a variable, you can name the variable any name you like. This feature is especially beneficial if you consider that a well-written module may be used in dozens of programs, each supporting its own unique variable names. To beginning programmers, using only global variables seems like a far simpler option than declaring local variables and being required to pass them from one module to another. If a variable holds a CORRECT-COUNT, why not call it CORRECT-COUNT and let every module in the program have access to the data stored there?

As an example of why this is a limiting idea, consider this: The FINAL-STATISTICS module of the arithmetic drill program may be useful in other programs within the organization—maybe the company creates drills in subjects other than arithmetic; but all drills require final statistics. If the variables that FINAL-STATISTICS uses are not declared to be local, then every programmer working on every application within the organization will have to know the names of those variables to avoid conflict. If it is well written, the FINAL-STATISTICS module may be used by other programs in the company for years to come. If its variables are global, then all the programmers working on all those programs must be aware of the name and the purpose of the CORRECT-COUNT variable.

What if the FINAL-STATISTICS module is so useful that you sell it to other companies? Now, if CORRECT-COUNT is global, all programmers in the *world* will need to know its name and will have to avoid using it for any other purpose in their programs. Multiply those limitations by all the variable names used in all the programs that exist anywhere, and you can see that using global variable names correctly will soon become an impossible task.

Passing values to a module helps facilitate encapsulation. A programmer can write a program (or module) and use procedures developed by others without knowing the details of those procedures. For example, you do not need to understand how a telephone connects you to the person you want; you need only to understand the **interface,** or outside connection, to the procedure; that is, you need to know only what number to enter into a telephone to get a specific result. Using a procedure requires only that you know what information to send to the procedure. You don't need to know—maybe you don't even care—how the procedure uses the data you send, so long as the results are what you want.

When procedures use local variables, the procedures become miniprograms that are relatively autonomous. Routines that contain their own sets of instructions and their own variables are not dependent on the program that calls them. The details within a routine are hidden and contained or encapsulated, which helps to make the routine reusable.

There are many real-world examples of encapsulation. When you build a house, you don't invent plumbing and heating systems. You incorporate systems that have already been designed. You don't need to know all the fine details of how the systems work; they are self-contained units you attach to your house. This certainly reduces the time and effort it takes to build a house. Assuming the plumbing and electrical systems you choose to use are already in use in other houses, choosing existing systems also improves your house's **reliability**. Not only is it unnecessary to know how your furnace works, but if you replace one model with another, you don't care if its internal operations are different. Whether heat is created from electricity, natural gas, or a hamster on a wheel, only the result—a warm house—is important to you.

Similarly, software that is reusable saves time and money and is more reliable. If the FINAL-STATISTICS routine has been tested before, you can be confident that it will work correctly when you use it within a different program. If another programmer creates a new and improved FINAL-STATISTICS module, you don't care how it works so long as it correctly calculates and prints with the data you send to it.

The concept of passing variables to modules allows programmers to create variable names locally in a module without changing the value of similarly named variables in other modules. The ability to pass values to modules makes programming much more flexible because independently-created modules can exchange information efficiently. However, there are limitations to the ways procedural programs use modules. Any program that uses a module must not reuse its name for any other module within the same program. You also must know exactly what type of data to pass to a module, and if you have use for a similar module that works on a different type of data or a different number of data items, you must create a new module with a different name. These limitations are eliminated in programs that are object-oriented.

# TERMS AND CONCEPTS

| | |
|---|---|
| procedural programs | module header |
| modularization | parameter or argument |
| abstraction | returning a value |
| global variable | IPO chart |
| local variable | interface or outside connection |
| encapsulation (information hiding, data hiding) | reliability |
| passing variables | |

# SUMMARY

■ Procedural programs consist of a series of steps or procedures that take place one after the other.

■ Modularization involves breaking programs into reasonable units called modules, subroutines, functions, or methods. Modularization provides abstraction, allows multiple programmers to work on a problem, and allows you to reuse your work.

■ A global variable is one that is available to every module in a program.

■ A local variable is one whose name and value are known only to its own module. A local variable is declared within a module and ceases to exist when the module ends.

■ Encapsulation (also known as information hiding or data hiding) means that the data or variables are completely contained within and accessible only to the module in which they are declared.

■ Using encapsulation provides you with two advantages: multiple programmers can create the individual modules without knowing the data names used by the others, and programmers can even use the same variable names as those used in other modules and no conflict will arise.

- Being able to pass a variable means that a copy of data in one module of a program can be sent to another module for use. You declare a name for the passed value within parentheses in the module header (the introductory title statement).

- Just as you can pass a value into a module, you can pass back or return a value to a calling module. Usually, this is accomplished within the return statement of the called module.

- When designing modules to use within larger programs, some programmers find it helpful to use an IPO chart, which identifies and categorizes each entity needed within the module as pertaining to input, processing, or output.

- When you write a module that receives a variable, you can name the variable any name you like without regard to other modules' variable names.

- Passing values to a module helps facilitate encapsulation. You need only to understand the interface, or outside connection, to the procedure.

- Software that is reusable saves time and money and is more reliable.

- There are limitations to procedural programming with modules in that any program that uses a module must not reuse its name for any other module within the same program. In addition, if you have use for a similar module that works on a different type of data, you must create a new module with a different name.

# E X E R C I S E S

1. Create an IPO chart for each of the following modules:
   a. the module that produces your paycheck
   b. the module that calculates your semester tuition bill
   c. the module that calculates your monthly car payment

2. a. Plan the logic for a program that contains two modules. The first module asks for your employee ID number. Pass the ID number to a second module that prints a message indicating whether the ID number is valid or invalid. A valid employee ID number falls between 100 and 799 inclusive.

   b. Plan the logic for a program that contains two modules. The first module asks for your employee ID number. Pass the ID number to a second module that returns a code to the first module that indicates whether the ID number is valid or invalid. A valid employee ID number falls between 100 and 799 inclusive. The first module prints an appropriate message.

**3.**    a. Plan the logic for an insurance company's premium-determining program that contains three modules. The first module prompts the user for the type of policy needed—health or auto. Pass the user's response to the second module where the premium is set—$250 for a health policy or $175 for auto. Pass the premium amount to the last module for printing.

     b. Modify Exercise 3a so that the second module calls one of two additional modules— one that determines the health premium or one that determines the auto premium. The health insurance module asks the user whether he or she smokes; the premium is $250 for smokers and $190 for nonsmokers. The auto insurance module asks the user to enter the number of traffic tickets he or she has received in the last three years. The premium is $175 for those with three or more tickets, $140 for those with one or two tickets, and $95 for those with no tickets. Each of these two modules returns the premium amount to the second module, which sends the premium amount to the printing module.

## SECTION B
### overview

After studying Section B, you should be able to:

■ Describe object-oriented programming

■ Define a class

■ Instantiate and use objects

■ Describe the concept of inheritance

■ Describe the concept of polymorphism

■ Appreciate the benefits of object-oriented programming

# Object-Oriented Programming

## An Overview of Object-Oriented Programming

**Object-oriented programming** is a style of programming that focuses on an application's data and the methods you need to manipulate that data. Object-oriented programming uses all of the concepts you are familiar with from modular procedural programming, such as variables, modules, and passing values to modules. Modules in object-oriented programs continue to use sequence, selection, and looping structures. They make use of arrays. However, object-oriented programming adds several new concepts to programming and involves a different way of thinking. There's even a considerable amount of new vocabulary involved. First you will read about object-oriented programming concepts in general; then you will learn the specific terminology.

................................................................................

**tip**    Most object-oriented programming languages use the term *method* in place of module, subroutine, or procedure.

................................................................................

With object-oriented programming:

■ You analyze the objects you are working with and the tasks that need to be performed with and on those objects.

■ You pass messages to objects, requesting the objects to take action.

■ The same message works differently (and appropriately) when applied to different objects.

■ A module or procedure can work appropriately with different types of data it receives, without the need to write separate modules.

■ Objects can share or inherit traits of objects that have already been created, reducing the time it takes to create new objects.

■ Encapsulation and information hiding are more complete than with the modules used in procedural programs.

But what, first of all, is an object? The real world is full of objects. Consider a door. A door needs to be opened and closed. You open a door by using an easy-to-use interface known as a doorknob. Object-oriented programmers would say you are "passing a message" to the door when you "tell" it to open by turning its knob. The same message (turning a knob) has a different result when applied to your radio than when applied to a door. The procedure you use to open something—call it the "open" procedure—works differently on a door to a room than it does on a desk drawer, a bank account, a computer file, or your eyes, but you can call all those procedures "open."

With object-oriented programming you focus on the objects that will be manipulated by the program—for example, a customer invoice, a loan application, or a menu from which the user will select an option. You define the methods each of the objects will use; you also define the information that must be passed to those methods.

With object-oriented programming, you can create multiple methods with the same name, and they will act differently and appropriately when they are used with different types of objects. For example, you can use a method named PRINT to print a customer invoice, loan application, or envelope. Because you use the same method name, PRINT, to describe the different actions needed to print these diverse objects, you can see that object-oriented programming languages let you use the same method name.

Another important concept in object oriented programming is **inheritance**, the process of acquiring the traits of one's predecessors. In the real world, a new door with a stained-glass window inherits most of its traits from a standard door. It has the same purpose, it opens and closes in the same way, and it has the same knob and hinges. The door with the stained-glass window simply has one additional trait—its window. Even if you have never seen a door with a stained-glass window, when you encounter one you know what it is and how to use it because you understand the characteristics of all doors. With object-oriented programming, once you have created an object, you can develop new objects that possess all the traits of the original object plus any new traits you desire. If you develop a CUSTOMER-BILL object, there is no need to develop an OVERDUE-CUSTOMER-BILL object from scratch. You can create the new object to contain all the characteristics of the already developed object and simply add necessary new characteristics. This not only reduces the work involved in creating new objects, but also makes new objects easier to understand because they possess most of the characteristics of already developed objects.

Real-world objects often employ encapsulation or information hiding. When you use a door, you usually are unconcerned with the latch or hinge construction features, and you don't have access to the interior workings of the knob or what may be written on the inside of the door panel. You care only about the functionality and the interface. Similarly, the detailed workings of objects you create within object-oriented programs can be hidden to outside programs and modules if you want them to be. When the details are hidden, programmers can focus on the functionality and the interface, as people do with real-life objects.

In summary, in order to understand object-oriented programming, you must consider four concepts that are integral components of all object-oriented programming languages:

- classes
- objects
- inheritance
- polymorphism

## Defining Classes

A **class** is a category of things. An **object** is a specific item that belongs to a class; an object is an **instance** of a class. A class defines the characteristics of its objects and the methods that can be applied to its objects.

For example, Dish is a class. When you know an object is a Dish you know you can hold it in your hand, and you know you can eat from it. myDilbertMugWithTheChipInTheHandle is an object, and it is an instance of the Dish class. This is an **is-a relationship**, because you can say, "My coffee mug **is a** Dish." Each button on the toolbar of a word processing program is an instance of a Button class. In a program used to manage a hotel, PENTHOUSE and BRIDAL-SUITE are instances of HotclRoom.

•••••••••••••••••••••••••••••••••••••••••••••••••••••••••••••••••••••••••••••••••••

In object-oriented languages like C++ and Java, most class names are written with the initial letter and each new word in uppercase, such as *Dish* or *HotelRoom*. Specific objects' names usually are written in lowercase or a combination of uppercase and lowercase—for example, *pentHouse* or *bridalSuite*. Even though you have seen variable names in all uppercase letters throughout this book, we will follow the more usual object-oriented style of mixing cases here.

•••••••••••••••••••••••••••••••••••••••••••••••••••••••••••••••••••••••••••••••••••

A class contains three parts:

- Every class has a name.
- Although not required, most classes contain data.
- Although not required, most classes contain methods.

For example, you can create a class named Employee. Data members of the Employee class include fields like idNumber, lastName, hourlyWage, and weeklySalary. You have worked with very similar constructs throughout this book; the name and data of a class constitute what procedural programming languages call a record.

The methods of a class include all the actions you want to perform with the class; these are what you call modules or subroutines in procedural programming. Appropriate methods for the Employee class include setEmployeeData, calculateWeeklyPay, and showEmployeeData. The job of setEmployeeData is to give values to an Employee's data fields, the purpose of calculateWeeklyPay is to multiply the Employee's hourlyWage by 40, and the purpose of showEmployeeData is to print the values in the Employee's data fields. In other words, the Employee class methods are simply what you would have created as modules in a procedural program that uses employee records. The major difference is that with object-oriented languages, you think of the class name, data, and methods as a single encapsulated unit, as shown in Figure 12-10.

| class Employee |
| --- |

num idNum

char lastName

num hourlyWage

num weeklySalary

---

setEmployeeData(num id, char last, num rate)

   idNum = id

   lastName = last

   if rate <= 25.00 then

      hourlyWage = rate

   else hourlyWage = 25.00

RETURN

calculateWeeklyPay

   weeklySalary = hourlyWage * 40

RETURN

showEmployeeData

   print idNum, lastName, weeklySalary

RETURN

---

**Figure 12-10:** Employee class

Notice that the header for the setEmployeeData method indicates that this method will require three arguments—a numeric ID number, a character name, and a numeric pay rate. These values that are passed in from the outside are then assigned to the field names within the Employee class. This is the commonly used method of assigning values to class fields. Usually you do not want any outside programs or methods to alter your class's data fields unless you have control over the process by forcing the other programs and methods to use a procedure such as setEmployeeData. Object-oriented programmers usually specify to their data fields **private** access—that is, the data cannot be accessed by any method that is not part of the class. For example, this setEmployeeData method does not allow any Employee's hourly wage to be set higher than 25.00. The methods themselves, like setEmployeeData, support **public access**—that is, other methods may use these methods that control access to the private data.

## Instantiating and Using Objects

When you write an object-oriented program, you create objects that are members of a class in the same way you create variables in procedural programs. Instead of declaring a numeric variable named MONEY with a statement such as num `MONEY`, you **instantiate**, or create, a class object with a statement such as `Employee mySecretary`. When you declare MONEY as a numeric variable, you automatically gain many capabilities—for example, you can perform math with the value in the MONEY variable and you can compare its value to other numeric variables. Similarly, when you declare mySecretary as an Employee type object, you also automatically gain many capabilities. You can use any of an Employee's methods (setEmployeeData, calculateWeeklyPay, and showEmployeeData) with the mySecretary object. The usual syntax is to provide an object name, a dot (period), and a method name. For example, you can write a program such as the one shown in pseudocode in Figure 12-11.

```
START
    declare variables — — — — —⌐ Employee mySecretary
    mySecretary.setEmployeeData(123, "Tyler", 10.00)
    mySecretary.calculateWeeklyPay
    mySecretary.showEmployeeData
END
```

**Figure 12-11:** Program that uses an Employee object

In the program in Figure 12-11, the focus is on the object—the Employee named mySecretary—and the methods you can use with that object. This is the essence of object-oriented programming.

## Inheritance

The concept of class is useful because of its reusability; you can create new classes that are descendents of existing classes. The **descendent classes** (or **child classes**) can inherit all of the attributes of the **original class** (or **parent class**), or the descendent class can override those attributes that are inappropriate. In geometry, a Cube is a descendent of a Square. A Cube has all the attributes of a Square, plus one more: depth. A Cube, however, has a different method of calculating total area (or volume) than a Square has. In programming, if you already have created a

Square class and you need a Cube class, it makes sense to inherit existing features from the Square class, adding only the new feature (depth) that a Cube requires and modifying the method that calculates volume.

**tip**

**Some programmers call a parent class a *base class* or *superclass*. You can refer to a child class as a *derived class* or *subclass*.**

As another example, to accommodate part-time workers in your personnel programs, you might want to create a child class from the Employee class. Part-time workers need an ID, name, and hourly wage just as regular employees do, but the regular Employee pay calculation assumes a 40-hour work week. You might want to create a PartTimeEmployee class that inherits all the data fields contained in an Employee, but adds a new one—hoursWorked. In addition, you want to create a new, modified setEmployeeData method that includes hoursWorked, and a new calculateWeeklySalary method that operates correctly for PartTimeEmployees. This new method multiplies hourlyWage by hoursWorked instead of by 40. The showEmployeeData module that exists within the Employee class works appropriately for both the Employee and the PartTimeEmployee class, so there is no need to include a new version of this module within the PartTimeEmployee class. PartTimeEmployee objects can simply use their parent's existing method. The complete PartTimeEmployee class appears in Figure 12-12.

| class PartTimeEmployee descends from Employee |
| --- |
| num hoursWorked |

setEmployeeData(num id, char last, num rate, num hours)

    Employee's setEmployeeData (id, last, rate)

    hoursWorked = hours

RETURN

calculateWeeklyPay

    weeklySalary = hourlyWage * hours

RETURN

**Figure 12-12:** PartTimeEmployee class

The PartTimeEmployee class shown in Figure 12-12 contains five data fields—all the fields that an Employee contains, plus one new one, hoursWorked. The PartTimeEmployee class also contains three methods. The methods setEmployeeData and calculateWeeklyPay have been rewritten for the child PartTimeEmployee class. These methods **override** (take precedence over) the parent class method when a

PartTimeEmployee object uses them. Notice that the setEmployeeData method in the PartTimeEmployee class requires an extra argument that the Employee class version does not. The PartTimeEmployee class uses three of the four arguments it receives to pass on to its parent where the idNum, lastName, and hourlyWage fields can be set.

The PartTimeEmployee class also contains the showEmployeeData class, which it inherits unchanged from its parent. When you write a program such as the one shown in Figure 12-13, different setEmployeeData and calculateWeeklyPay methods containing different statements are called for the two objects, but the same showEmployeeData method is called in each case.

```
START
    declare variables — — — —┐Employee mySecretary
                             └PartTimeEmployee myDriver
    mySecretary.setEmployeeData(123, "Tyler", 10.00)
    myDriver.setEmployeeData(345, "Greene", 8.50, 15)
    mySecretary.calculateWeeklyPay
    myDriver.calculateWeeklyPay
    mySecretary.showEmployeeData
    myDriver.showEmployeeData
END
```

**Figure 12-13:** Program that uses Employee and PartTimeEmployee objects

● ● ● ● ● ● ● ● ● ● ● ● ● ● ● ● ● ● ● ● ● ● ● ● ● ● ● ● ● ● ● ● ● ● ● ● ● ● ● ● ● ● ● ● ● ● ● ● ● ● ● ● ● ● ● ● ● ● ● ● ● ●

**A good way to determine if a class is a parent or a child is to use the "is-a" test. A child "is an" example of its parent. For example, a PartTimeEmployee "is an" Employee. However, it is not necessarily true that an Employee "is a" PartTimeEmployee.**

● ● ● ● ● ● ● ● ● ● ● ● ● ● ● ● ● ● ● ● ● ● ● ● ● ● ● ● ● ● ● ● ● ● ● ● ● ● ● ● ● ● ● ● ● ● ● ● ● ● ● ● ● ● ● ● ● ● ● ● ● ●

## Polymorphism

Methods or functions need to operate differently depending on the context. Object-oriented programs use the feature **polymorphism** to allow the same operation to be carried out differently depending on the context; this is never allowed in nonobject-oriented languages.

Suppose you need two methods—one that multiplies two values and another that multiplies three values. Without polymorphism, you must write a different module with a unique name for each method, because two methods with the same name—one that requires two arguments and one that requires three—cannot coexist in a program. Just as your blender can produce juice whether two or three vegetables are inserted, with polymorphism, the multiplication function will produce a product whether it receives two or three numbers. Similarly, a calculateWeeklyPay method can operate differently depending on whether an Employee or a PartTimeEmployee uses it. Similarly, you may want a computeGradePointAverage method to operate differently for a Pass-Fail course than it does for a graded one, or you want a word processing program to produce different results when you press Delete with one word in a document highlighted than when you press Delete with a file name highlighted.

When you write a polymorphic method in an object-oriented programming language, you must write each version of the method, and that can entail a lot of work. The benefit to polymorphism does not seem obvious while you are writing the methods, but the benefits are realized when you can use the methods in all sorts of applications. When you can use a single, simple, easy-to-understand method name such as showData with all sorts of objects such as Employees, PartTimeEmployees, InventoryItems, and Transactions, then your objects behave more like their real-world counterparts and your programs are easier to understand.

Figure 12-14 shows an Inventory class that contains several versions of a changeData method. When an Inventory item uses the changeData method, the computer will determine which of the three available methods to call based on the arguments used with the method.

---

**class Inventory**

num stockNum

char itemDescription

num price

---

setInvData(num id, char desc, num pr)

   stockNum = id

   itemDescription = desc

   price = pr

RETURN

changeData(char desc)

   itemDescription = desc

RETURN

changeData(num pr)

   price = pr

RETURN

---

**Figure 12-14:** Inventory class

| class Inventory |
|---|

```
changeData(char desc, num pr)
    itemDescription = desc
    price = pr
RETURN
showInvData
    print stockNum, itemDescription, price
RETURN
```

**Figure 12-14:** Inventory class (continued)

When you execute the program shown in Figure 12-15, each of the three changeData methods will be called one time, depending on the argument used. When you read the program, it should seem clear in each instance whether the programmer intends to change the price or the description or both. The method name changeData is clear, appropriate, and easy to remember, no matter which type of data needs the change.

```
START
    declare variables _ _ _ _ _ _ _ _ _ Inventory wheelCover
    wheelCover.setInvData(3772, "Chrome cover", 49.95)
    wheelCover.changeData(39.95)
    wheelCover.changeData("Deluxe chrome cover")
    wheelCover.changeData(29.95, "Super deluxe chrome cover")
    wheelCover.showInvData
```

**Figure 12-15:** Program that uses all three versions of changeData

# The Advantages of Object-Oriented Programming

Using the features of object-oriented programming languages provides you with many benefits as you develop your programs. When you use objects in your programs, you save development time because each object automatically includes appropriate, reliable methods. When you use inheritance, you can develop new classes more quickly by extending classes that already exist and work; you need to concentrate only on the new features your new class adds. When you use preexisting objects, you need to concentrate only on the interface to those objects, not on the internal instructions that make them work. By using methods that are polymorphic, you can use reasonable, easy-to-remember names for methods and concentrate on the purpose of the methods rather than on memorizing different method names.

# TERMS AND CONCEPTS

object-oriented programming

inheritance

class

object

instance

is-a relationship

private access

public access

instantiate an object

descendent or child class

original or parent class

overrride

polymorphism

# SUMMARY

- Object-oriented programming is a style of programming that focuses on an application's data and the methods you need to manipulate that data.

- Object-oriented programming uses all of the concepts in modular, procedural programming, plus it requires you to analyze the objects you are working with and the tasks that need to be performed with and on those objects.

- With object-oriented programming you pass messages to objects, requesting the objects to take action, and the same message works differently (and appropriately) when applied to different objects.

- With object-oriented programming a module can work appropriately with different types of data it receives without the need to write separate modules, and modules can inherit the traits of objects that have already been created.

- Four integral components of all object-oriented languages are: classes, objects, inheritance, and polymorphism.

- A class is a category of things; an object is a specific instance of a class. A class defines the characteristics of its objects and the methods that can be applied to its objects.

- A class contains three parts: a name, data, and methods.

- Usually you do not want any outside programs or methods to alter your class's data fields unless you have control over the process. Data usually is private, while methods usually support public access.

■ Creating a class object is known as instantiating an object.

■ You can create new classes that are descendents of existing classes. The descendent classes (or child classes) can inherit all of the attributes of the original class (or parent class), or the descendent class can override those attributes that are inappropriate.

■ You can create child class methods that override parent class methods with the same name.

■ Object-oriented programs use the feature of polymorphism to allow the same operation to be carried out differently depending on the context.

■ When you write a polymorphic method in an object-oriented programming language, you must write each version of the method; the benefits of polymorphism are realized when you can use the methods in all sorts of applications.

■ Using the features of object-oriented programming languages provides you with many benefits. You save development time because each object automatically includes appropriate, reliable methods. You can develop new classes more quickly by extending classes that already exist and work, and you need to concentrate only on the new features your new class adds. You can use reasonable, easy-to-remember polymorphic names for methods.

 **E X E R C I S E S**

1. Design a class named CustomerRecord that holds a customer number, name, and address. Include methods to set the values for each data field, and print the values for each data field.

2. a. Design a class named Book that holds a stock number, author, title, price, and number of pages for a book. Include methods to set the values for each data field and print the values for each data field.
   b. Design a class named TextBook that is a child class of Book. Include a new data field for the grade level for the book. Override the Book class methods that set and print the data so that you accommodate the new grade level field.

3. a. Design a class named Player that holds a player number and name for a sports team participant. Include methods to set the values for each data field and print the values for each data field.
   b. Design two classes named BaseballPlayer and BasketballPlayer that are child classes of Player. Include a new data field in each class for the player's position. Include an additional field in the BaseballPlayer class for batting average. Include a new field in the BasketballPlayer class for free-throw percentage. Override the Player class methods that set and print the data so that you accommodate the new fields.

# Programming Graphical User Interfaces

**case ▶** "That's 87 games of Free Cell in a row that I've won!" you hear Boston Murphy hoot from his cubical at Solutions Inc.

"What's the fascination with that game?" you ask.

"Part of it is that it's fun using the graphical environment to point and click," he says.

"Some of my programs might be more interesting if I could include graphical objects to use with the mouse," you muse.

"Let's talk about it," Boston says. "After just one more game."

After studying Section A, you should be able to:

- Describe the principles of event-driven programming
- Describe typical user-initiated actions and GUI components
- Understand the principles of good GUI design
- List typical GUI component attributes that you can alter

# Event-Driven Programming Using Components of Graphical User Interfaces

## Event-Driven Programming

From the 1950s, when people began to use computers to help them perform various jobs, right through the 1960s and 1970s, almost all interaction between humans and computers was based on the command line. The **command line** is the line on your computer screen at which you type entries to communicate with the computer's operating system. An **operating system** is the software that you use to run a computer and manage its resources. Interacting with a computer operating system was difficult because the user had to know the exact syntax (that is, the correct sequence of words and symbols that form the operating system's command set) to use when typing commands, and had to spell and type those commands accurately.

Fortunately for today's computer users, operating system software is now available that allows them to use a mouse or other pointing device to select pictures or **icons** on the screen. This type of environment is a **graphical user interface**, or **GUI**. Computer users can expect to see a standard interface in the GUI programs they use. Rather than memorizing difficult commands that must be typed at a command line, GUI users can select options from menus and click on buttons to make their preferences known to a program. Users can select objects that look like their real-world counterparts and get the expected results. For example, users may select an icon that looks like a pencil when they want to write something, or they may click an icon shaped like a recycling bin when they want to delete files.

GUI programs are called **event-based** or **event-driven** because actions occur based on user-initiated events such as clicking a mouse button. When you program with event-driven languages, the emphasis is on the objects that the user can manipulate, such as buttons and menus, and on the events that the user can initiate with those objects, such as clicking or double-clicking. The programmer writes instructions that correspond to each type of event.

Event-driven programs require unique considerations for the programmer. The program logic you have developed so far in this book is procedural; each step occurs in the order the programmer determines. In a procedural program, if you issue a prompt and a statement to read the user's response, you have no control over how much time the user takes to enter a response, but you do control the fact that processing goes no further until the input is completed. In contrast, with event-driven programs, the user might initiate any number of events in any order. For example, if you use a word processing program, you have dozens of choices at your disposal at any moment. You can type words, select text with the mouse, click a button to change text to bold or to italics, chose a menu item, and so on. With each word processing document you create, you choose options in any order that seems appropriate at the time. The word processing program must be ready to respond to any event you initiate.

Within an event-driven program, a component from which an event is generated is the **source** of the event. A button that a user can click is an example of a source; a text field that one can use to enter text is another source. An object that is "interested in" an event that you want to respond to is sometimes called a **listener**. It "listens for" events so it knows when to respond. Not all objects can receive all events—you probably have used programs in which clicking on many areas of the screen has no effect at all. If you want an object, such as a button, to be a listener for an event, such as a mouse click, you must write the appropriate program statements.

Although event-based programming is relatively new, the instructions that programmers write to correspond to events are still simply sequences, selections, and loops. Event-driven programs still declare variables, use arrays, and contain all the attributes of their procedural-program ancestors. An event-based program may contain components with labels like "Sort Records," "Merge Files," or "Total Transactions." The programming logic you use when writing code for each of these processes is the same logic you have been learning about throughout this text. Writing event-driven programs simply involves thinking in terms of possible events as the modules that constitute the program.

**tip**

In object-oriented languages, the procedural modules that depend on user-initiated events are often called *scripts*.

## User-Initiated Actions and GUI Components

To understand GUI programming, you need to have a clear picture of the possible events a user can initiate. These include the events listed in Figure 13-1.

| Event | Description |
| --- | --- |
| key press | pressing a key on the keyboard |
| mouse point | placing the mouse pointer over an area on the screen |
| mouse click or left mouse click | pressing the left mouse button |
| right mouse click | pressing the right mouse button |
| mouse double click | pressing the left mouse button two times in rapid sequence |
| mouse drag | holding the left mouse button down while moving the mouse over the desk surface |

**Figure 13-1:** Common user-initiated events

You also need to be able to picture common GUI components. These include those listed in Figure 13-2. Figure 13-3 shows a screen that contains several common GUI components.

| GUI components | Description |
| --- | --- |
| Label | A rectangular area that displays text |
| Text field | A rectangular area into which the user can type a line of text |
| Button | A rectangular object you can click; usually it appears to press inward like a push button |
| Check box | A label positioned beside a square; you can click the square to display or remove a check mark—allows the user to turn an option on or off |
| Check box group | A group of check box objects in which the options are mutually exclusive; when the user selects any one check box, the others are turned off—often round rather than square and called a set of radio buttons or option buttons |

**Figure 13-2:** Common GUI components (to be continued on following page)

| GUI components | Description |
| --- | --- |
| List box or choice | Displays a drop-down menu that contains other options; when the user selects an option from the drop-down list, the selected item replaces the original item in the display—all other items are unselected |
| List | Similar to a list box, but the user may make multiple selections |
| Toolbar | A strip of icons that activate menu items |

**Figure 13-2:** Common GUI components (continued)

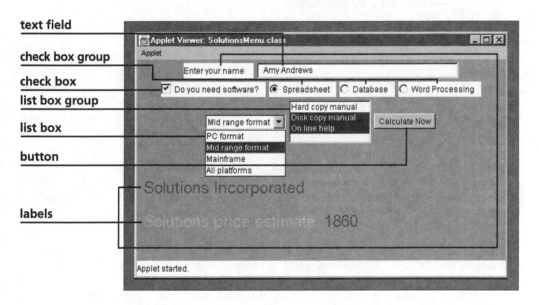

**Figure 13-3:** Illustration of common GUI components

When you program in a language that supports event-driven logic, you do not create the GUI components you need from scratch. Instead, you call prewritten routines that draw the GUI components on the screen for you. In some programming languages you write statements that call the routines that create the GUI objects; in others you can drag GUI objects onto your screen from a toolbar. Either way, you do not worry about the details of constructing the components. Instead, you concentrate on the actions that you want to take place when a user initiates an event from one of the components. Thus GUI components are excellent examples of the best principles of object-oriented programming—they represent modules that operate like black boxes, making them easy for you to use.

GUI components are often referred to as *widgets*, which is short for *windows gadgets*.

## Designing Graphical User Interfaces

There are several general design principles you should consider when you create a program that will use a GUI. Among them are:

- The interface should be natural and predictable.
- The interface should be attractive, easy to read, and nondistracting.
- To some extent, it's helpful if your applications can be customized by the user.
- The program should be forgiving.
- The GUI is only an interface.

### The Interface Should Be Natural and Predictable

The GUI program interface should represent objects like their real-world counterparts. In other words, it makes sense to use an icon that looks like a recycling bin when you want to allow a user to delete files. Using a recycling bin icon is "natural" in that people use one in real life when they want to discard real-life items. Using a recycling bin is also predictable, because a number of other programs employ the recycling bin icon. Some icons may be natural, but if they are not predictable as well, then they are not as effective. An icon that depicts a recycling truck is just as "natural" as far as corresponding to the real world, but because other programs do not use a truck icon for this purpose, it is not as predictable.

Graphical user interfaces should also be predictable in their layout. For example, with most GUI programs you use a menu bar at the top of the screen, and the first menu item is almost always *File*. If you design a program interface in which the menu runs vertically down the right side of the screen, or in which *File* is the last menu option instead of the first, you will confuse the people who use your program. Either they will make mistakes when using it, or they may give up using it entirely. It doesn't matter if you can prove that your layout plan is more efficient than the standard one—if you do not use a predictable layout, your program will meet rejection from users in the marketplace.

### The Interface Should Be Attractive, Easy to Read, and Nondistracting

If your interface is attractive, people are more likely to use it. If it is easy to read, they are less likely to make mistakes and more likely to want to use it. And if the interface is easy to read, it will more likely be considered attractive. When it comes to GUI design, fancy fonts and weird color combinations are the signs of amateur designers. In addition, you should make sure that unavailable screen options are either sufficiently dimmed or removed, so the user does not waste time clicking on components that aren't functional.

**Dimming a component is also called *graying* the component.**

Screen designs should not be distracting. When there are too many components on a screen, users can't find what they're looking for. When a text field or button is no longer needed, it should be removed from the interface. You also want to avoid distracting users with overly creative design elements. When the user presses a button to open a file, he or she may be amused the first time a file name dances across the screen or the speakers play a tune. But after one or two experiences with your creative additions, users will find that intruding design elements simply hamper the actual work of the program.

**GUI programmers sometimes refer to screen space as *real estate*. Just as a plot of real estate becomes unattractive when it supports no open space, your screen becomes unattractive when you fill the limited space with too many components.**

### To Some Extent, It's Helpful If Your Applications Can Be Customized By the User

Every user works in his or her own way. If you are designing an application that will use numerous menus and toolbars, it's helpful if users can position the components in the order that's easiest for them to work with. Users appreciate being able to change features like color schemes. Allowing a user to change the background color in your application may seem frivolous to you, but to users who are color blind, it might make the difference in whether they use your application at all.

### The Program Should Be Forgiving

Perhaps you have experienced the inconvenience of accessing a voice mail system in which you selected several sequential options only to find yourself at a dead end with no recourse but to hang up and redial the number. Good program design avoids the corresponding user situation. You should always provide an escape route to accommodate users who have made bad choices or changed their minds. By providing a Back button or functional Escape key, you will provide more functionality to your users.

### The GUI Is Only an Interface

The most important principle of GUI design is to remember always that any GUI is only an interface. Using a mouse to click on items and drag them around is not the point of any business programs except those that train people how to use a mouse. Instead, the point of a graphical interface is to help people be more productive. To that end, the design should help the user see what options are available, allow the user to use the components in the ordinary way, and not force the user to concentrate on how to interact with your application. The real work of any GUI program is done after the user presses a button or makes a list box selection. Then actual program tasks take place.

## Attributes of GUI Components

When you design a program with premade or preprogrammed graphical components, you will want to change their appearance to customize them for the current application. Each programming language provides its own means of changing components appearances. Some commonly used methods that you will want to consider using include:

- setting the size of the component
- setting the color of the component
- setting the screen location of the component
- setting the font for any text contained in or on the component
- setting the component to be visible or invisible
- setting the component to be dimmed or undimmed, sometimes called enabled or disabled

You must learn the exact names of the methods to use in each individual programming language you learn, but all languages that support creating event-driven applications have some means of allowing you to set components' attributes.

 **TERMS AND CONCEPTS**

command line                      event-based or event-driven programs

operating system                  event source

icon                              event listener

graphical user interface (GUI)

## SUMMARY

- Interacting with a computer by typing entries at a command line is a difficult and error-prone process.

- A graphical user interface, or GUI, lets you interact with a computer using icons that appear on the screen.

■ GUI programs are event-based or event-driven, because actions occur based on user-initiated events such as clicking a mouse button.

■ When you program with event-driven languages, the emphasis is on the objects that the user can manipulate and on the events that can occur with those objects.

■ Event-driven programs require unique considerations for the programmer. With event-driven programs, the user might initiate any number of events in any order.

■ Within an event-driven program, a component on which an event is generated is the source of the event. An object that is interested in an event is sometimes called a listener.

■ Although event-based programming is relatively new, the instructions that programmers write to correspond to events are still simply sequences, selections, and loops.

■ Common user-initiated events include pressing keys on the keyboard and pointing, clicking, double-clicking, and dragging with a mouse.

■ Common GUI components include labels, text fields, buttons, check boxes, check box groups, list boxes, and toolbars.

■ When you program in a language that supports event-driven logic, you do not create the GUI components you need from scratch. Instead, you call prewritten routines that draw the GUI components on the screen for you.

■ There are several general design principles you should consider when you create a program that will use a GUI. The interface should be natural, predictable, attractive, easy to read, and nondistracting. It is helpful if the interface can be customized and is forgiving. The GUI should not overwhelm the program; it is just an interface.

■ Some commonly used methods to consider for changing the appearance of components include setting the size, color, location, font, visibility, and brightness of the component.

# E X E R C I S E S

1. Take a critical look at three GUI applications with which you are familiar—for example, a spreadsheet, a word processing program, and a game. Describe how well each conforms to the GUI design guidelines listed in this chapter.

2. Select one element of poor GUI design in a program with which you are familiar. Describe how you would improve the design.

3. Select a GUI program that you have never used before. Describe how it conforms to the GUI design guidelines listed in this chapter.

After studying Section B, you
should be able to:

■ Describe the steps involved in
developing an event-driven
application

■ Analyze an event-driven application
problem

■ Create a storyboard

■ Define objects in an object
dictionary

■ Define the connections between
GUI application screens

■ Plan the logic for an event-driven
program

■ Describe and use object-oriented
exception handling techniques

# Developing an Event-Driven Application and Handling Exceptions

## The Steps to Developing an Event-Driven Application

In Chapter 1, you first learned the steps to developing a computer program. They are:

1. Understand the problem.
2. Plan the logic.
3. Code the program.
4. Translate the program into machine language.
5. Test the program.
6. Put the program into production.

Developing an event-driven application is more complicated than developing a standard procedural program. You can include three new steps between understanding the problem and developing the logic. The complete list of development steps for an event-driven application is as follows:

1. Understand the problem.
2. Create storyboards.
3. Define the objects.
4. Define the connections between the screens the user will see.

5. Plan the logic.
6. Code the program.
7. Translate the program into machine language.
8. Test the program.
9. Put the program into production.

The three new steps involve elements of object-oriented, GUI design—creating storyboards, defining objects, and defining the connections between the user screens. As with procedural programming, you cannot proceed to write an event-driven program unless you first understand the problem.

## Understanding the Problem

Suppose you want to create a simple interactive premium-determining program to be used by prospective insurance customers. The users should be able to use a graphical interface to select a policy type—health or auto. Next the users answer pertinent questions, such as how old they are, whether they smoke, and what their driving records are like. Although most insurance premium amounts would be based on more characteristics than these, let's assume policy rates are determined as shown in Figure 13-4. The final output of the program is a second screen that shows the semiannual premium amount for the chosen policy.

| Health policy premiums | Auto policy premiums |
| --- | --- |
| base rate: $500 | base rate: $750 |
| add $100 if over age 50 | add $400 if more than 2 tickets |
| add $250 if smoker | subtract $200 if over age 50 |

Figure 13-4: Insurance premiums based on customer characteristics

## Creating Storyboards

A **storyboard** represents a picture or sketch of a screen the user will see when running a program. Filmmakers have long used storyboards to illustrate key moments in the development of a plot they are planning; similarly GUI storyboards represent "snapshot" views of the screens the user will encounter during the run of a program. If the user could view at most four screens during execution of the insurance premium program, then you would draw four storyboard cells or frames.

Figure 13-5 shows two storyboard sketches for the insurance program. They represent the introductory screen at which the user selects a premium type and answers questions, and the final screen that displays the semi-annual premium.

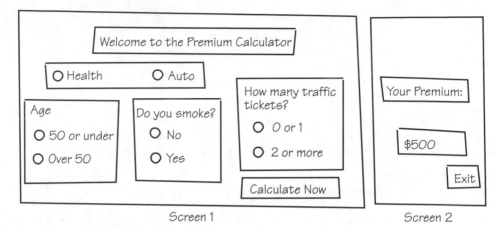

**Figure 13-5:** Storyboard for insurance program

## Defining the Objects in an Object Dictionary

An event-driven program may contain dozens, or even hundreds, of objects. To keep track of them, programmers often use an object dictionary. An **object dictionary** is a list of the objects used in a program, including which screens they are used on and whether any code, or script, is associated with them.

Figure 13-6 shows an object dictionary for the insurance premium program. The type and name of each object to be placed on a screen is listed in the left column. The second column shows the screen number on which the object appears. The next column names any variables that are affected by an action on the object. The right column indicates whether any code or script is associated with the object. For example, the label named welcomeLabel appears on the first screen. It has no actions associated with it—it does not call any methods nor does it change any variables; it is just a label. The calculateButton however, does cause execution of a method named calcRoutine. This is the method that calculates the semiannual premium amount and stores it in the premiumAmount variable. Depending on the programming language you use, you might need to name calcRoutine something similar to "calculateButton.click" to indicate that it is the module that executes when the user clicks the calculateButton.

> Some organizations also include the disk location where an object is stored as part of the object dictionary.

| Object name | Screen number | Variables affected | Script? |
|---|---|---|---|
| label welcomeLabel | 1 | none | none |
| choice healthOrAuto | 1 | policyType | none |
| choice age | 1 | ageOfInsured | none |
| choice smoker | 1 | insuredIsSmoker | none |
| choice tickets | 1 | numTickets | none |
| button calculateButton | 1 | premiumAmount | calcRoutine |
| label yourPremium | 2 | none | none |
| text field premAmtField | 2 | none | none |
| button exitButton | 2 | none | exitRoutine |

**Figure 13-6:** Object dictionary for insurance premium program

## Defining the Connections Between the User Screens

The insurance premium program is a small program, but with larger programs you may need to draw the connections between the screens to show how they interact. Figure 13-7 shows an **interactivity diagram** for the screens used in the insurance premium program. The figure shows that the first screen calls the second screen and the program ends.

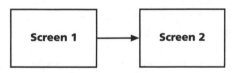

**Figure 13-7:** Diagram of interaction for insurance premium program

Figure 13-8 shows how a diagram might look for a more complicated program in which the user has several options available at screens 1, 2, and 3. Notice how each screen may lead to different screens depending on the options the user selects at any one screen.

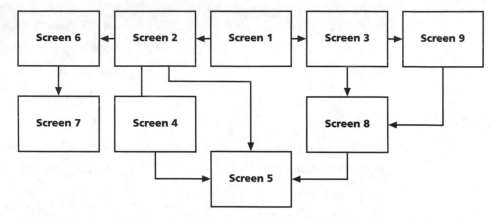

**Figure 13-8:** Diagram of interaction for a hypothetical complicated program

## Planning the Logic

In an event-driven program, you design the screens, define the objects, and define how the screens will connect. Then you can plan the logic for each of the modules (or methods or scripts) that the program will use. For example, based on the program requirements shown in Figure 13-4, you can write the pseudocode for the calcRoutine for the insurance premium program as shown in Figure 13-9. The calcRoutine does not execute until the user presses the calculateButton. At that point, the user's choices are used to calculate the premium amount.

```
calcRoutine
        if policyType = "H" then
                premiumAmount = 500
                if ageOfInsured > 50 then
                        premiumAmount = premiumAmount + 100
                if insuredIsSmoker = "Y" then
                        premiumAmount = premiumAmount + 250
        else
                premiumAmount = 750
                if numTickets > 2 then
                        premiumAmount = premiumAmount + 400
                if ageOfInsured > 50 then
                        premiumAmount = premiumAmount - 200
RETURN
```

**Figure 13-9:** Pseudocode for calcRoutine

The pseudocode in Figure 13-9 should look very familiar to you—it uses decision-making logic you have used since the early chapters of this book. The basic structures of sequence, selection, and looping will continue to serve you well whether you are programming in a procedural or event-driven environment.

# Object-Oriented Error Handling: Throwing Exceptions

A great deal of the effort that goes into writing programs involves checking data items to make sure they are valid and reasonable. A great advantage to using GUI data-entry objects is that you can control much of what a user enters by limiting the user's options. For example, if the only two insurance policy type options a user can select are *Health* or *Auto*, then you can eliminate checking for a valid policy type within your interactive program. However, there are many occasions on which you must allow the user to enter data. Data-entry operators who create the files used in business computer applications spend their entire working day entering facts and figures that your applications use; they can and do make typing errors. When programs depend on the data that average nontypist users enter interactively, the chance of error is even more likely. In Chapter 10, you learned some useful techniques to check for valid and reasonable input data. Object-oriented, event-driven programs employ a more specific group of methods for checking and handling errors. As a group, these methods are called **exception handling** methods. The generic name used for errors in object-oriented languages is **exceptions**, because, presumably, errors are not usual occurrences; they are the "exceptions" to the rule.

Programmers had to deal with error conditions long before object-oriented methods were conceived. Probably the most often used error-handling method was to terminate the program, or at least the module in which the offending statement occurred. For example, Figure 13-10 shows a segment of pseudocode that causes the insurance premium calcRoutine module to end if the policyType is invalid. Not only is this method of handling an error unforgiving; it isn't even structured.

```
calcRoutine
        if policyType not = "H" and policyType not = "A" then
            RETURN
        else if policyType = "H" then
            premiumAmount = 500
            if ageOfInsured > 50 then
                premiumAmount = premiumAmount + 100
            if insuredIsSmoker = "Y" then
                premiumAmount = premiumAmount + 250
        else
            premiumAmount = 750
            if numTickets > 2 then
                premiumAmount = premiumAmount + 400
            if ageOfInsured > 50 then
                premiumAmount = premiumAmount - 200
RETURN
```

**Figure 13-10:** Unforgiving, unstructured method of error handling

In the example in Figure 13-10, if the policyType is an invalid value, the module in which the code appears is terminated. If the program in which this module is contained is a spreadsheet or a game, the user may be annoyed that the program has stopped working and that an early exit has been made. If the program that contains this module is one that determines whether an emergency room patient is covered for a surgical procedure, the results may be far more serious.

Rather than ending a program prematurely just because it encounters a piece of invalid data, a more elegant solution involves looping until the data item becomes valid, as shown in the example in Figure 13-11. The flag variable errorFlag is set to one at the beginning of the module, so that the while loop statements will execute at least once. You set the errorFlag to zero, and then check the policyType so you can perform the correct policy calculations. If the policyType is neither "H" nor "A", you prompt the user to reenter the policy type, and then set the errorFlag to zero so that the loop repeats.

 **tip**

You first used a loop to ensure valid data in Chapter 10.

```
calcRoutine
        errorFlag = 1
        while errorFlag = 1
                errorFlag = 0
                if policyType = "H" then
                        premiumAmount = 500
                        if ageOfInsured > 50 then
                                premiumAmount = premiumAmount + 100
                        if insuredIsSmoker = "Y" then
                                premiumAmount = premiumAmount + 250
                else if policyType = "A" then
                        premiumAmount = 750
                        if numTickets > 2 then
                                premiumAmount = premiumAmount + 400
                        if ageOfInsured > 50 then
                                premiumAmount = premiumAmount - 200
                else
                        print "Invalid policy type. Please reenter"
                        read policyType
                        errorFlag = 1
RETURN
```

**Figure 13-11:** Using a loop to handle interactive errors

There are at least two drawbacks to using the error-handling logic shown in Figure 13-11. First, one of the principles of modular and object-oriented programming is reusability. The purpose of the calcRoutine module is to calculate premiums based on user data. The program you are working on now may allow the user to reenter the policy data any number of times, but other programs in the insurance system may need to limit the number of chances the user gets to enter correct data or may allow no second chance at all. A flexible calcRoutine will simply calculate the premium amount without deciding what to do about data errors. The calcRoutine will be most flexible if it can detect an error and then notify the main program that an error has occurred. Each main program that uses the module can then determine how to handle the offending data.

The other drawback with forcing the user to reenter data is that the technique works only with interactive programs. Program errors can occur as a result of many factors other than invalid data entry by a user sitting at a terminal—for example, a disk drive might not be ready, a file might not exist on the disk, or stored data items might be invalid. You cannot continue to reprompt a disk file for valid data; if stored data is invalid, it remains invalid. Object-oriented exception handling techniques overcome the limitations of simply repeating a request.

In object-oriented terminology, an exception is an object that you **throw**, or pass, from the module where a problem occurs to another module that will **catch** the exception and handle the problem. This object can be any data type—a numeric or character data item or a programmer-created object such as a record complete with its own data fields and methods. For example, Figure 13-12 shows a calcRoutine module that throws an errorFlag only if the policyType is neither "H" nor "A". If the policyType is "H" or "A", the premium is calculated and the module ends naturally.

```
calcRoutine
        errorFlag = 1
        if policyType = "H" then
                premiumAmount = 500
                if ageOfInsured > 50 then
                        premiumAmount = premiumAmount + 100
                if insuredIsSmoker = "Y" then
                        premiumAmount = premiumAmount + 250
        else if policyType = "A" then
                premiumAmount = 750
                if numTickets > 2 then
                        premiumAmount = premiumAmount + 400
                if ageOfInsured > 50 then
                        premiumAmount = premiumAmount - 200
        else
                throw errorFlag
RETURN
```

**Figure 13-12:** Throwing an exception

The module in Figure 13-12 can be used within the program segment shown in Figure 13-13. In this program segment a variable named thrownCode is set to one. This ensures the while loop will execute at least once. Then the calcRoutine (Figure 13-12) executes. If the calcRoutine throws the errorFlag that has a value of 1, then the program segment in Figure 13-13 will bypass all statements following the method call (`perform calcRoutine`) and proceed directly to the catch statement. Here the program will catch the thrown value and store it in the thrownCode variable. The two statements `print "Reenter the policy type."` and `read  policyType` constitute the **catch block**, or group of statements that execute when a value is caught. The catch block statements execute if and only if a value has been caught in the thrownCode variable. Then, because thrownCode is one, the while loop executes again and the calcRoutine is attempted again. If the calcRoutine is successful (that is, if the policyType is a valid one), then nothing is thrown from the calcRoutine and the catch block in Figure 13-13 never executes. If the calcRoutine is successful, it does not throw anything, so the logic proceeds to the statement following `perform calcRoutine`, which is the statement that sets thrownCode to zero, stopping the loop from executing again.

```
thrownCode = 1
while thrownCode = 1
        perform calcRoutine
        thrownCode = 0
        catch thrownCode
                print "Reenter the policy type."
                read policyType
```

**Figure 13-13:** Program segment using calcRoutine

The program segment in Figure 13-13 is difficult to follow if you are new to exception handling techniques. You can see how flexible using thrown exceptions is when you consider the program segment in Figure 13-14. This program segment also uses the calcRoutine, but does not allow the user to reenter the policyType. This program simply assumes the premium amount is zero for invalid policy types. If the calcRoutine throws a value, the block of code following the `catch` in Figure 13-14 executes. Notice that the program doesn't have to use the value that is thrown; the fact that a value *is* thrown is all that is required to cause the catch block to execute.

```
perform calcRoutine
catch thrownCode
        premiumAmount = 0
```

**Figure 13-14:** Another program segment using calcRoutine

The general principle of exception handling in object-oriented programming is that a module that uses data should be able to detect errors, but not be required to handle them. The handling should be left to the application that uses the object, so that each application can use each module in the way that is most appropriate for that application.

 # TERMS AND CONCEPTS

| | |
|---|---|
| storyboard | exceptions |
| object dictionary | throw exception |
| interactivity diagram | catch exception |
| exception handling | catch block |

# SUMMARY

- The complete list of development steps for an event-driven application include understanding the problem, creating storyboards, defining objects, defining the connections between the screens the user will see, planning the logic, coding the program, translating the program into machine language, testing the program, and putting the program into production.

- A storyboard represents a picture or sketch of a screen the user will see when running a program.

- An object dictionary is a list of the objects used in a program, including which screens they are used on and whether any code, or script, is associated with them.

- With large programs you may need to draw an interactivity diagram defining the connections between the screens to show how they interact.

- In an event-driven program, you design the screens, define the objects, and define how the screens will connect. Then you can plan the logic for each of the modules (or methods or scripts) that the program will use. The basic structures of sequence, selection, and looping will continue to serve you well whether you are programming in a procedural or event-driven environment.

- Exception handling methods are the group of methods that object-oriented, event-driven programs use to handle errors.

- The generic name used for errors in object-oriented languages is exceptions, because, presumably, errors are not usual occurrences; they are the "exceptions" to the rule.

- There are at least two drawbacks to using the traditional error-handling logic of looping until valid data are entered. It does not support reusability, and it is not flexible.

- In object-oriented terminology, an exception is an object that you throw, or pass, from the module where a problem occurs to another module that will catch the exception and handle the problem. This object can be any data type—a numeric or character data item, or a programmer-created object such as a record complete with its own data fields and methods.

- A catch block is a group of statements that execute when an exception is caught.

- The general principle of exception handling in object-oriented programming is that a module that uses data should be able to detect errors, but not be required to handle them. The handling should be left to the application that uses the object, so that each application can use each module in the way that is most appropriate for that application.

# E X E R C I S E S

1.  Design the storyboards, interactivity diagram, object dictionary, and any necessary scripts for an interactive program for customers of Sunflower Floral Designs. Allow customers the option of choosing a floral arrangement ($25 base price), cut flowers ($15 base price), or a corsage ($10 base price). Let the customer choose roses, daisies, chrysanthemums, or irises as the dominant flower. If the customer chooses roses, add $5 to the base price. After the customer clicks an "Order Now" button, display the price of the order.

2.  Design the storyboards, interactivity diagram, object dictionary, and any necessary scripts for an interactive program for customers of Toby's Travels. Allow customers the option of at least five trip destination options and four means of transportation, each with a unique price. After the customer clicks the "Plan Trip Now" button, display the price of the trip.

3.  a. Design a method that calculates the cost of a painting job for College Student Painters. Variables include whether the job is location "I" for interior, which carries a base price of $100, or "E" for exterior, which carries a base price of $200. College Student Painters charges an additional $5 per square foot over the base price. The method should throw an exception if the location code is invalid.
    b. Write a module that calls the module designed in exercise 3a. If the module throws an exception, force the price of the job to zero.
    c. Write a module that calls the module designed in exercise 3a. If the module throws an exception, require the user to reenter the location code.
    d. Write a module that calls the module designed in exercise 3a. If the module throws an exception, force the location code to "E" and the base price to $200.

# CHAPTER 14

# Program Design

**case ▶** "You're so organized!" you marvel at Lynn Greenbrier's desk at Solutions, Inc. "Your file folders are even color coded! Boston's cubicle is *nothing* like yours!"

"I heard that!" Boston bellows as he comes around the corner. "Don't worry," he adds as he sees you blush, "I'm well aware that my office is a mess. But my programs aren't."

"That's true," says Lynn. "An organized program is more important than an organized desk. Let us show you a few tricks of the trade to use in organizing your programs so they look and operate efficiently and professionally."

After studying Section A, you should be able to:

- Describe the need for good program design
- Understand the advantages of storing program components in separate files
- Select useful and appropriate variable and module names

# Program Design Issues

## The Need for Good Design

As your programs become larger and more complicated, the need for good planning and design increases. Think of an application you use, such as a word processor or a spreadsheet. The number and variety of user options is staggering. Not only would it be impossible for a single programmer to write such an application, but without thorough planning and design, the components would never work together properly. Ideally, each program module you design needs to work well as a stand-alone module and as an element of larger systems. Just as a house with poor plumbing or a car with bad brakes is fatally flawed, a computer-based application can be great only if each component is designed well.

## Storing Program Components in Separate Files

When you start to work on professional programs, you will see that many of them are quite lengthy. Some contain hundreds of variables and thousands of lines of code. Often programs contain dozens of decisions and loops. Throughout this book you have learned to manage lengthy procedural programs by breaking them into modules. If you write object-oriented programs, you organize program components as a series of object classes. However, whether a program consists of a single long series of instructions, or multiple methods and classes, it is still difficult to manage all the program components.

Most modern programming languages allow you to store program components in separate files. If you write a module and then store it in the same file as the program that uses it, your program files become large and hard to work with on a screen or on multiple printed pages. In addition, when you define a useful module or object class, you will want to use it in many programs. You can copy class and module definitions from one file to another, of course, but this method is time consuming as well as prone to error. A better solution (if you are using a language that allows it) is to store your modules in individual files and include them in any program that uses them. The statement you use to accomplish accessing modules from separate files varies from language to language, but it usually involves using a verb such as *include*, *import*, or *copy* followed by the name of the file that contains the module.

For example, suppose your company has a standard employee record definition, part of which is shown in Figure 14-1. Files with the same format are used in many applications within the organization—personnel reports, production reports, payroll, and so on. It would be a tremendous waste of resources if every programmer rewrote this file definition in every application. Instead, once a programmer writes the statements that constitute the file definition, those statements should be imported in their entirety into any program that uses a record with the same structure. For example, Figure 14-2 shows how the data fields in Figure 14-1 would be defined in the C programming language. If the statements in Figure 14-2 are saved in a file named Employees, then any C program can include the statement `#include Employees`, and all the data fields are automatically defined.

 **tip**

> The pound sign (#) is used with the include statement in C to notify the compiler that it is part of a special type of statement called a *pre-processor directive*.

---

EMPLOYEE FILE DESCRIPTION

FILE NAME: EMPLOYEES

| FIELD DESCRIPTION | POSITIONS | DATA TYPE | DECIMALS |
|---|---|---|---|
| Employee ID | 1–4 | numeric | 0 |
| Last name | 5–19 | character | |
| First name | 20–34 | character | |
| Hire date | 35–42 | numeric | 0 |
| Hourly wage | 43–47 | numeric | 2 |
| Birth date | 48–55 | numeric | 0 |

… and so on

---

**Figure 14-1:** Partial Employee file description

---

```
struct Employee
{
        int employeeID;
        char lastName[15];
        char firstName[15];
        long hireDate;
        double hourlyWage;
        long birthDate;
};
```

---

**Figure 14-2:** Data fields in Figure 14-1 defined in the C language

- - - - - - - - - - - - - - - - - - - - - - - - - - - - - - - - - - - - - - - - - - - - - - - - -

Don't be concerned with the syntax used in the file description in Figure 14-2. The words *struct, int, char, long* and *double* are all part of the C programming language, and are not important to you now. Simply concentrate on how the variable names reflect the field descriptions in Figure 14-1.

- - - - - - - - - - - - - - - - - - - - - - - - - - - - - - - - - - - - - - - - - - - - - - - - -

Now suppose you write a useful module that checks dates to ensure that they are valid. For example, the two digits that represent a month can be neither less than 01 nor greater than 12. Any program that uses the employee file description shown in Figure 14-1 might want to call the date-validating module several times in order to validate any employee's hire date, birth date, and other dates. Not only do you want to call this module from several locations within any one program, you also want to call it from many programs. If the module is useful and well written, you may even want to market it to other companies. By storing the module in its own file, you enable its use to be flexible. When you write a program of any length, you should consider storing each of its components in its own file.

Storing components in separate files can provide an advantage beyond ease of reuse. When you let others use your programs or modules, you often provide them with only the compiled (that is, machine-language) version of your code, not the **source code**, which is composed of readable statements. Storing your program statements in a separate, nonreadable, compiled file is an example of **implementation hiding**, or hiding the details of how the program or module works. The manner in which your code functions is hidden from the programmers who use your code. A programmer who cannot see your well-thought-out modules is more likely to use them simply as they were intended and to refrain from making adjustments in your code, thereby introducing error. Of course, in order to work with your modules or data definitions, a programmer who uses them must know the names and types of data you are using. Typically, you provide programmers who use your definitions with written documentation of the data names and purposes.

- - - - - - - - - - - - - - - - - - - - - - - - - - - - - - - - - - - - - - - - - - - - - - - - -

Recall from Chapter 1 that when you write a program in a programming language, you must compile or interpret it into machine language before the computer can actually carry out your instructions.

- - - - - - - - - - - - - - - - - - - - - - - - - - - - - - - - - - - - - - - - - - - - - - - - -

## Selecting Variable and Module Names

An often-overlooked element in program design is the selection of good data and module names. In Chapter 1 you learned that every programming language has specific rules for the construction of names—some languages limit the number of characters, some allow dashes, and so on—but there are other general guidelines:

- Use meaningful names. A data field named SOME-DATA or a module named FIRST-MODULE makes a program cryptic. You will forget the purpose of these identifiers within your own programs. All programmers occasionally use short nondescriptive names such as X or VAL in a quick program written to test a procedure or as an array subscript. But in most cases, data and module names should be meaningful.
- Usually, use pronounceable names. A variable name like PZF is neither pronounceable nor meaningful. However, a name that looks meaningful when you write it, like PREPAREAD, may mean "Prepare ad" to you, but is "Prep a read" to others. Look at your names critically to ensure they are pronounceable. Very standard abbreviations do not have to be pronounceable. Anyone in business would interpret SSN as a Social Security number.
- Be judicious in your use of abbreviations. You may save a few keystrokes when creating a module called GET-STAT, but is its purpose to find the state in which a city is located, output some statistics, or determine the status of some flag variables? Similarly, is a variable named FN meant to hold a first name, file number, or something else?
- Usually, avoid digits in a name. Zeroes get confused with the letter "O" and lowercase "1"s are misread as the numeral "l". Of course, use your judgment: BUDGET-FOR-2002 is probably not going to be misinterpreted.
- Use the system your language allows to separate words in long, multiword variable names. For example, if the programming language you will use allows dashes or underscores, then a method name like PREPARE-AD or PREPARE_AD is easier to read then PREPAREAD. If you use a language that is case sensitive, like C++ or Java, then use initializeData instead of initializedata or INITIALIZEDATA.
- Consider including a form of the verb *to be*, such as *is* or *are*, in names for variables that are intended to hold a status. For example, use IS-FINISHED as a flag variable that holds a "Y" or "N" to indicate whether a file is exhausted. The name FINISHED is likely to be confused with a module that executes when a program is done.

When you begin to write programs, the process of determining what data variables and modules you will need and what to name them all may seem overwhelming. The design process is crucial, however. When you acquire a first programming job assignment, the design process may very well have been completed already. Most likely, your first assignment will be to write, or make modifications to, one small member module of a much larger application. The more the original programmers stuck to these guidelines, the better the original design is, and the easier your job of modification will be.

# TERMS AND CONCEPTS

source code                                    implementation hiding

 # SUMMARY

- As your programs become larger and more complicated, the need for good planning and design increases.

- Most modern programming languages allow you to store program components in separate files. The statement you use to access the files varies from language to language, but is usually a verb such as *include*, *import*, or *copy*. Using this technique allows you to call modules more easily from several locations within any one program, or from many programs.

- When you store components in separate files you can provide other programmers with only the compiled (machine-language) version of your code, not the source code, or readable statements. Storing your program or module statements in a separate, non-readable, compiled file is an example of implementation hiding, or hiding the details of how the program or module works.

- An often overlooked element in program design is the selection of good data and module names. Guidelines include using meaningful, pronounceable, nonabbreviated names. Usually, you should avoid digits in a name, and use the system your language allows to separate words in long, multiword variable names. Consider including a form of *to be*, such as *is* or *are*, in names for variables that are intended to hold a status.

 # EXERCISES

1. Critically review at least two programs you flowcharted or wrote pseudocode for earlier in this course. Identify the places where you should choose different module and variable names.

2. Exchange flowcharts or pseudocode with another student. Suggest at least two new names for variables or modules in his or her logic.

**After studying Section B, you should be able to:**

- Describe how to organize modules
- Reduce module coupling
- Increase module cohesion
- Maintain good programming habits

# Coupling and Cohesion

## Organizing Modules

When you begin to design computer programs, it is difficult to decide how much to put into a module or subroutine. For example, a process that requires 40 instructions can be contained in a single module, two 20-instruction modules, twenty 2-instruction modules, or any other combination. In most programming languages, any of these combinations is allowed. That is, you can write a program that will execute and produce correct results no matter how you divide the individual steps into modules. However, placing either too many or too few instructions in a single module makes a program harder to follow and reduces flexibility. When you are deciding how to organize your program steps into modules, you should adhere to two general rules:

- Reduce coupling.
- Increase cohesion.

## Reducing Coupling

**Coupling** is a measure of the strength of the connection between two program modules; it is used to express the extent to which information is exchanged by subroutines. Coupling is either tight or loose depending on how much one module depends on information from another. **Tight coupling**, when there is much dependence between modules, makes programs more prone to errors; there are many data paths to keep track of, many chances for bad data to pass from one module to another, and many chances for one module to alter information needed by another module. **Loose coupling** occurs when modules do not depend on others. In general, you want to reduce coupling as much as possible because connections between modules make them more difficult to write, maintain, and reuse.

Imagine four cooks wandering in and out of the kitchen preparing a stew. If each is allowed to add seasonings at will without the knowledge of the other cooks, you could end up with a culinary disaster. Similarly, if four payroll program modules are allowed to alter your gross pay figure "at will" without the "knowledge" of the other modules, you could end up with a financial disaster. A program in which several modules have access to your gross pay figure has modules that are tightly coupled. A superior program would control access to the payroll figure by controlling its passage to modules that need it.

You can evaluate whether coupling between modules is loose or tight by looking at the intimacy between modules and the number of parameters that are passed between modules.

- Tight coupling: The least intimate situation is one in which modules have access to the same globally defined variables; these modules have tight coupling. When one module changes the value stored in a variable, other modules are affected.

- Loose coupling: The most intimate way to share data is passing a copy of needed variables from one module to another. That way, the sharing of data is always purposeful—variables must be explicitly passed to and from modules that use them. The loosest (best) subroutines and functions pass single parameters rather than many variables or entire records, if possible.

Usually, you can determine that coupling is occurring at one of several levels. **Data coupling** is the loosest type of coupling; therefore it is the most desirable. Data coupling is also known as **simple data coupling** or **normal coupling**. Data coupling occurs when modules share a data item by passing parameters. For example, a module that determines a student's eligibility for the dean's list might receive a copy of the student's grade-point average to use in making the determination.

**Data-structured coupling** is similar to data coupling, but an entire record is passed from one module to another. For example, consider a module that determines whether a customer applying for a loan is creditworthy. You might write a module that receives the entire customer record and uses many of its fields in order to determine whether the customer should be granted the loan. If you need many of the customer fields—such as salary, length of time on the job, savings account balance, and so on—then it makes sense to pass a customer's record to a module. Figure 14-3 shows an example of such a module.

```
CHECK-CREDIT (record CUST-REC)
    declare variables — — — — ⌐local char CREDIT-IS-OK
    CREDIT-IS-OK = "Y"          └
    if CUST-SALARY < 300.00 then
        CREDIT-IS-OK = "N"
    if CUST-TIME-ON-JOB < 2 then
        CREDIT-IS-OK = "N"
    if CUST-SAVING-BAL < 1000.00 then
        CREDIT-IS-OK = "N"
RETURN(CREDIT-IS-OK)
```

**Figure 14-3:** Module that determines customer creditworthiness

In the CHECK-CREDIT module, an entire record (CUST-REC), rather than any single data field, is passed to the module. The coupling could have been made looser by writing three separate modules: one to check salary, one to check time on the job, and one to check savings balance. However, since so many of the fields in the customer's record are needed, in this case it is very appropriate to pass the entire record to the module.

**Control coupling** occurs when a main program (or other module) passes a parameter to a module, controlling the module's actions or telling it what to do. For example, Figure 14-4 shows a module that receives a user's choice and calls one of several other modules.

```
SELECT-FUNCTION (num USER-CHOICE)
     if USER-CHOICE = 1 then
          perform ADD-A-RECORD-TO-FILE
     else if USER-CHOICE = 2 then
          perform DELETE-A-RECORD-FROM-FILE
     else if USER-CHOICE = 3 then
          perform PRINT-RECORDS
     else
          perform ILLEGAL-CHOICE
RETURN
```

**Figure 14-4:** SELECT-FUNCTION module

Of course, this kind of coupling is appropriate at times, but the implication is any module that calls SELECT-FUNCTION is aware of how SELECT-FUNCTION works. After all, an appropriate choice had to be made and passed to SELECT-FUNCTION. The program that uses SELECT-FUNCTION probably prompts the user for a choice and passes that choice to SELECT-FUNCTION. Therefore the calling program must know how to phrase the prompt correctly in order to elicit an appropriate USER-CHOICE. This coupling is relatively tight. This is a problem, because if you make a change to the SELECT-FUNCTION—for example, by adding a new option or changing the order of the existing options—then all the programs and other modules that use SELECT-FUNCTION will have to know about the change. If they don't, their prompts will offer incorrect choices, and they won't be sending the appropriate USER-CHOICE to the module. Once you have to start keeping track of all the modules and programs that might call a module, the opportunity for errors in a system increases dramatically.

**External coupling** and **common coupling** occur, respectively, when two or more modules access the same global variable or record. When data can be modified by more than one module, programs become harder to write, read, and modify. That's because if you make a change in a single module, many other modules may be affected. For example, if one module increases a field that holds the year from two digits to four, then all other modules that use the year will have to be altered before they can operate correctly. For another example, if one module can increase your gross pay figure by 10 percent based on years of service and another module can increase your pay by 20 percent based on annual sales, it makes a difference which module operates first. It's possible that a third module won't work when the salary increases over a specified limit. If you avoid external or common coupling and pass variables instead, you can control how and when the modules receive the data.

Pathological coupling occurs when two or more modules change one another's data. An especially confusing case occurs when MODULE-ONE changes data in MODULE-TWO, MODULE-TWO changes data in MODULE-THREE, and MODULE-THREE changes data in MODULE-ONE. This makes programs extremely difficult to follow and should be avoided at all costs.

# Increasing Cohesion

Analyzing coupling lets you see how modules connect externally with other modules and programs. You also want to analyze a module's **cohesion**, which refers to how the internal statements of a module or subroutine serve to accomplish its purposes. Highly cohesive modules are ones in which all the operations are related or "go together." Such modules are usually more reliable than those that have low cohesion; they are considered stronger, and they make programs easier to write, read, and maintain.

### Functional Cohesion

**Functional cohesion** occurs when all of the operations in a module contribute to the performance of only one task. Functional cohesion is the highest level of cohesion; you should strive for functional cohesion in all functions you write. For example, a module that calculates gross pay appears in Figure 14-5. The module receives two parameters, HOURS and RATE, and computes gross pay including time-and-a-half for overtime. This module is highly functionally cohesive because each of its instructions contributes to one task—computing gross pay. If you can write a sentence describing what a module does and use only two words—for example, "Compute gross," "Cube value," or "Print record"—the module is probably functionally cohesive.

```
GROSS-PAY (num HOURS, num RATE)
    declare variables — — — — —┐local num GROSS
    if HOURS <= 40 then         └
          GROSS = HOURS * RATE
    else
          GROSS = (40 * RATE) + (HOURS - 40) * (RATE * 1.5)
RETURN(GROSS)
```

**Figure 14-5:** GROSS-PAY module

You may work in a programming environment where there is a rule such as, "No module will be longer than can be printed on one page" or "No module will have more than 30 lines of code." What the rule-maker is trying to achieve is more cohesion, but this is an arbitrary way of going about it. It's possible for a 2-line module to have low cohesion and—although less likely—a 40-line module to have high cohesion. Because good functionally cohesive modules perform only one task, they tend to be short. However, the issue is not size. If it takes 20 statements to perform one task within a module, then the module is still cohesive.

## Sequential Cohesion

**Sequential cohesion** takes place when a module performs operations that must be carried out in a specific order on the same data. Sequential cohesion is a slightly weaker type of cohesion than functional cohesion because the module may perform a variety of tasks, but the tasks are linked together because they use the same data, often transforming it in a series of steps.

For example, Figure 14-6 shows a module that computes a customer's bill based on several factors. The customer is charged either $25 or $35 per item, depending on the item ordered. This per-item charge is multiplied by the quantity ordered. Then the customer receives a 5 percent discount if the order is for over 100 items, and an additional 10 percent discount if the customer has patronized the business since 1996 or before. If the customer is an Illinois resident, sales tax is added, and if the customer is not located in the immediate zip code, a $10 delivery charge is added.

```
COMPUTE-BALANCE-DUE (record CUST-ORDER)
    declare variables- — — — —｜local num BALANCE
    if CUST-ITEM-NUM = 1001 then
          BALANCE = 25.00
    else BALANCE = 35.00
    BALANCE = BALANCE * CUST-QUANTITY
    if CUST-QUANTITY > 100 then
          BALANCE = BALANCE * .95
    if CUST-ORIGIN-DATE <= 1996 then
          BALANCE = BALANCE * .90
    if CUST-STATE = "IL" then
          BALANCE = BALANCE * 1.06
    if CUST-ZIP-CODE not = 60014 then
          BALANCE = BALANCE + 10.00
RETURN(BALANCE)
```

**Figure 14-6:** COMPUTE-BALANCE-DUE module

The steps in this module are sequentially cohesive because they occur in a specific order on the same data. It is important that the quantity ordered is tested before the length of patronage—the results will differ if these tests are not made in the correct order. Similarly, if delivery charges are not taxable, then the tax must be computed before a delivery charge is added to the balance. Of course, each of these calculations could be diverted into its own module; very often, you can break a sequentially cohesive module down into more functionally cohesive units. But for practical purposes, a sequentially cohesive module is an acceptable programming form. If you find yourself writing a sentence describing what a module does and you repeatedly use the same noun, the module is probably sequentially cohesive. For instance, if you find yourself describing a module by writing "Input the year, make sure it is a valid year, determine if it is a leap year, and print the year," the module is performing a series of actions on the year and is sequentially cohesive.

## Communicational Cohesion

**Communicational cohesion** occurs in modules that contain statements that perform tasks that share data. The tasks are not related, just the data are. If the tasks must be performed in order, the module is sequentially cohesive. If the tasks are not performed in any sequential order but just use the same data, the module is communicationally cohesive; this is considered a weaker form of cohesion than functional or sequential cohesion. For example, consider a module that produces a score that rates prospective customers on their likelihood of buying your product. Assume you have a product that appeals to high-income, older, married people. Figure 14-7 shows a DETERMINE-CUSTOMER-SCORE module that adds a point to a customer's score for each of the factors that contributes to the likelihood the customer will buy the product.

```
DETERMINE-CUSTOMER-SCORE (record CUST-RECORD)
      declare variables- — — — —|local num SCORE = 0
      if CUST-INCOME > 30000 then
            SCORE = SCORE + 1
      if CUST-AGE > 40 then
            SCORE = SCORE + 1
      if CUST-MARITAL-STATUS = "M" then
            SCORE = SCORE + 1
RETURN(SCORE)
```

**Figure 14-7:** DETERMINE-CUSTOMER-SCORE module

The DETERMINE-CUSTOMER-SCORE module in Figure 14-7 is communicationally cohesive because the steps involved share data; the value SCORE is adjusted repeatedly throughout the module. Other examples of modules that have communicational cohesion are ones that validate a value by performing several tests (Is the value positive? Is it less than 100? Is it a perfect square?) and ones that perform several different operations on the same data based on an input value. For example, Figure 14-8 shows a module that takes one of several actions based on a transaction code.

```
PERFORM-TRANSACTION (num CUST-BALANCE, num TRANSACTION-AMT, char CODE)
      if CODE = "A" then
            CUST-BALANCE = CUST-BALANCE + TRANSACTION-AMT
      else if CODE = "S" then
            CUST-BALANCE = CUST-BALANCE - TRANSACTION-AMT
      else if CODE = "D" then
            CUST-BALANCE = CUST-BALANCE - TRANSACTION-AMT * .9
RETURN(CUST-BALANCE)
```

**Figure 14-8:** PERFORM-TRANSACTION module

Since the same data (CUST-BALANCE) is manipulated in different fashions, the PERFORM-TRANSACTION module is communicationally cohesive. The data items are shared, but the actions on the data are different. More cohesion can be obtained by writing three functionally cohesive modules, perhaps named ADD-TRANSACTION-TO-BALANCE, SUBTRACT-TRANSACTION-FROM-BALANCE, and APPLY-DISCOUNT-AND-SUBTRACT-FROM-BALANCE.

## Temporal, Procedural, Logical, and Coincidental Cohesion

**Temporal cohesion** takes place when the tasks in a module are related by time. That is, the tasks are placed together because of *when* they must take place—for example, at the beginning of a program. The prime examples of temporally cohesive modules that you have seen are HOUSEKEEPING and FINISH modules.

**Procedural cohesion** takes place when, as with sequential cohesion, the tasks of a module are done in sequence. However, unlike sequential cohesion, the tasks in procedural cohesion do not share data. Main program modules are often procedurally cohesive; they consist of a series of steps that must be performed in sequence, but perform very different tasks, like HOUSEKEEPING, MAIN-LOOP, and FINISH-UP. A main module can also be called a **dispatcher module**, because it dispatches messages to a sequence of more cohesive modules. If you sense that a module you have written has only procedural cohesion (that is, it consists of a series of steps that use unrelated data), you probably want to turn it into a dispatcher module. You accomplish this by changing the module so that it calls other modules in which the diverse tasks take place. Each of the new modules can be functionally, sequentially, or communicationally cohesive.

**Logical cohesion** takes place when a member module performs one or many tasks depending on a decision, whether the decision is in the form of a case structure or a series of if statements. The actions performed may go together logically (that is, perform the same type of action), but they don't work on the same data. Like a module that has procedural cohesion, a module that has only logical cohesion should probably be turned into a dispatcher. If you can write a sentence describing what a module does and you use "if" and the same verb repeatedly with different objects, the module is probably logically cohesive. For example, "If code is 1, read a record from the floppy disk drive; if code is 2, read a record from the hard drive; otherwise read a record from the keyboard" is a sentence that indicates that the module being described is logically cohesive. This module should be modified so that the code dispatches processing to one of three record-reading modules.

**Coincidental cohesion,** as the name implies, is based on coincidence. The operations in a module just happen to have been placed together. Obviously, this is the weakest form of cohesion and is not desirable. However, if you modify programs written by others, you may see examples of coincidental cohesion. Perhaps the program designer did not plan well, or perhaps an originally well-designed program was modified to reduce the number of modules, and now there are a number of unrelated statements grouped in a single module.

Coincidental cohesion is almost an oxymoron—cohesion that is simply coincidental is really no cohesion at all.

There is a time and a place for shortcuts. If you need a result from spreadsheet data in a hurry, you can type in two values and take a sum rather than creating a formula with proper cell references. If a memo must go out in five minutes, you don't have to change fonts or add clip art with your word processor. Similarly, if you need a quick programming result, you may very well use cryptic variable names, tight coupling, and coincidental cohesion. When you create a professional application, however, you will want to keep professional guidelines in mind.

## Maintaining Good Programming Habits

When you learn a programming language and begin to write lines of program code, it is easy to forget the principles you have learned in this text. Having some programming language knowledge and a keyboard at your fingertips can lure you into the process of typing lines of code before you think things through. But every program you write will be a better program if you plan before you code. If you maintain the habits of first drawing flowcharts or writing pseudocode that you have learned here, your future programming projects will go more smoothly. If you walk through your program logic on paper (called **desk-checking**) before starting to type statements in C, COBOL, Visual Basic, or Java, your programs will run correctly sooner. If you plan ahead to create high cohesion and loose coupling, you will be rewarded with programs that are easier to get up and running and to maintain.

 **T E R M S    A N D    C O N C E P T S**

coupling

tight coupling

loose coupling

data coupling

simple data coupling

normal coupling

data-structured coupling

control coupling

external coupling

common coupling

pathological coupling

cohesion

functional cohesion

sequential cohesion

communicational cohesion

temporal cohesion

procedural cohesion

dispatcher module

logical cohesion

coincidental cohesion

desk-checking

# S U M M A R Y

- You can write a program that will execute and produce correct results no matter how you divide the individual steps into modules. However, placing either too many or too few instructions in a single module makes a program harder to follow and reduces flexibility.

- In general, when you are deciding how to organize your program steps into modules, you should adhere to two general rules: reduce coupling and increase cohesion.

- Coupling is a measure of the strength of the connection between two program modules; it is used to express the extent to which information is exchanged by subroutines.

- Coupling is either tight or loose depending on how much one module depends on information from another.

- Tight coupling, when there is much dependence between modules, makes programs more prone to errors; loose coupling occurs when modules do not depend on others.

- You can evaluate whether coupling between modules is loose or tight by looking at the intimacy between modules and the number of parameters that are passed between modules.

- Data coupling is the loosest type of coupling; therefore it is the most desirable. Data coupling is also known as simple data coupling or normal coupling. Data coupling occurs when modules share a data item by passing parameters.

- Data-structured coupling is similar to data coupling, but an entire record is passed from one module to another.

- Control coupling occurs when a main program (or other module) passes a parameter to a module, controlling it or telling it what to do.

- External coupling and common coupling occur, respectively, when two or more modules access the same global variable.

- Pathological coupling occurs when two or more modules change one another's data.

- Cohesion refers to how well the operations in a module relate to one another.

- Functional cohesion occurs when all of the operations in a module contribute to the performance of only one task. Functional cohesion is the highest level of cohesion.

- Sequential cohesion takes place when a module performs operations that must be carried out in a specific order on the same data.

- Communicational cohesion occurs in modules that contain statements that perform tasks that share data. The tasks are not related, just the data are.

■ Temporal cohesion takes place when the tasks in a module are related by time.

■ Procedural cohesion takes place when, as with sequential cohesion, the tasks of a module are done in sequence. However, unlike those in sequential cohesion, the tasks in procedural cohesion do not share data.

■ Main program modules are often procedurally cohesive; a main module can also be called a dispatcher module.

■ Logical cohesion takes place when a member module performs one or many tasks depending on a decision.

■ Coincidental cohesion is based on coincidence; the operations in a module just happen to have been placed together.

■ If you maintain good program planning by drawing flowcharts or writing pseudocode and desk-checking your logic, your programming projects will be more successful.

# E X E R C I S E S

1. Critically review programs for which you have drawn flowcharts or written pseudocode earlier in this course. Identify at least one example of each of the following:
   a. tight coupling
   b. loose coupling
   c. data coupling
   d. simple data coupling
   e. normal coupling
   f. data-structured coupling
   g. control coupling
   h. external coupling
   i. common coupling
   j. pathological coupling

2. Critically review programs for which you have drawn flowcharts or written pseudocode earlier in this course. Identify at least one example of each of the following:
   a. functional cohesion
   b. sequential cohesion
   c. communicational cohesion
   d. temporal cohesion
   e. procedural cohesion
   f. dispatcher module
   g. logical cohesion
   h. coincidental cohesion

# A Difficult Structuring Problem

In Chapter 2 you learned that any logical problem can be solved by using only the three standard structures—sequence, selection, and looping. Often it is a simple matter to modify an unstructured program to make it adhere to structured rules. Sometimes, however, it is a challenge to structure a more complicated program. Still, no matter how complicated, large, or badly structured a problem is, the same tasks can *always* be accomplished in a structured manner.

Consider the flowchart segment in Figure A-1. Is it structured?

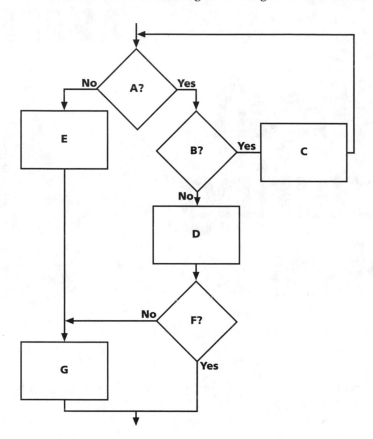

**Figure A-1:** Unstructured flowchart

No, it's not. Let's straighten it out. You can use the "spaghetti" method to enforce structure. Start at the beginning with the decision labeled A, shown in Figure A-2. This must represent the beginning of either a selection or a loop, because a sequence would not contain a decision.

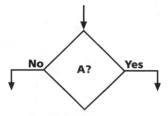

**Figure A-2:** Structuring Step 1

If you follow the logic on the "No" or left side of the question, you can pull up on the left branch of the decision. You get process E, followed by G, followed by the end, as shown in Figure A-3.

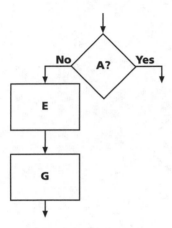

**Figure A-3:** Structuring Step 2

Now continue on the right or "Yes" side of decision A. When you follow the flowline, you encounter a decision symbol, labeled B. Pull on B's left side, and a process, D, comes up next. See Figure A-4.

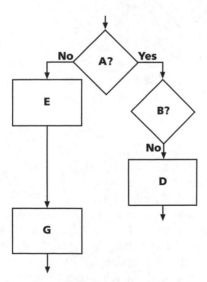

**Figure A-4:** Structuring Step 3

After D, a decision labeled F comes up. Pull on its left side and get a process, G, and then the end. When you pull on F's right side, you simply reach the end, as shown in Figure A-5.

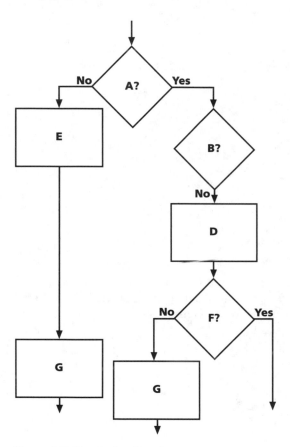

**Figure A-5:** Structuring Step 4

The biggest problem in structuring the original flowchart segment lies on the right side of the B decision. Pull up and get process C, as shown in Figure A-6. This looks like a loop because it doubles back on itself, up to Decision A. However, the rules of a structured loop say that it must have the appearance shown in Figure A-7: a question, followed by a structure, returning right back to the question. If the arrow coming out of C returned right to B, there would be no problem; but as it is, Question A must be repeated. The spaghetti technique says if things are tangled up, start repeating them. So bring another A decision down after C, as Figure A-6 shows.

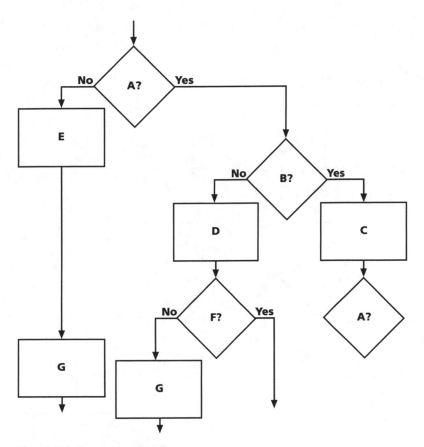

**Figure A-6:** Structuring Step 5

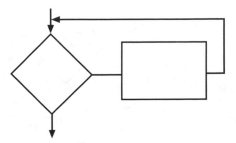

**Figure A-7:** A structured loop

Now, on the right side of A, B repeats. On the right side of B, C repeats. After C, A occurs. On the right side of A, B occurs. On the right side of B, C occurs. After C, A occurs again. Soon you should realize that you will repeat these same steps forever. See Figure A-8.

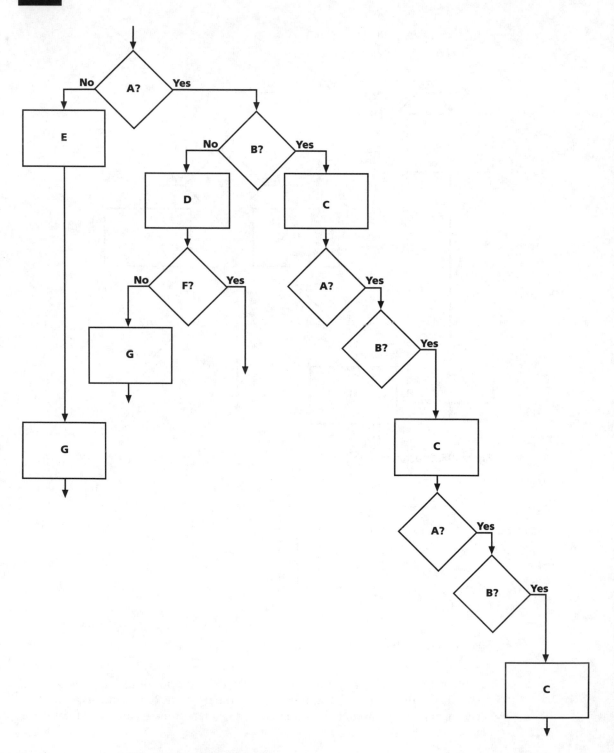

**Figure A-8:** Structuring Step 6

Sometimes, in order to make a program segment structured, you have to add an extra flag variable to get out of an infinite mess. You can create a flag variable named GO-BACK-TO-A and set the value of GO-BACK-TO-A to "Yes" or "No," depending on whether it is appropriate to "go back" to Step A. When A is no, the GO-BACK-TO-A flag should be set to "No" because when A is No, you never want to go back to Question A again. See Figure A-9.

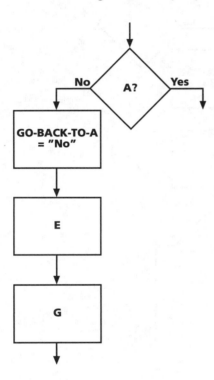

**Figure A-9:** Structuring Step 7

Similarly, when B is No, you never want to go back to A again, either. Figure A-10 shows that you set GO-BACK-TO-A to "No" when the answer to B is No.

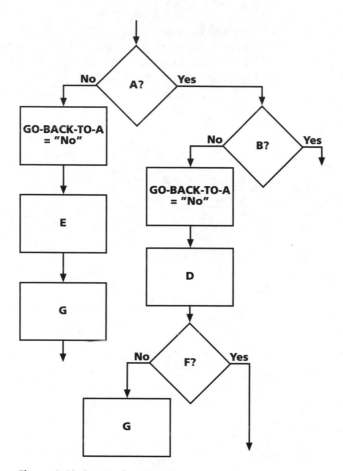

**Figure A-10:** Structuring Step 8

When the B decision result is Yes, however, you *do* want to go back to A. So when B is Yes, perform the process for C and set the GO-BACK-TO-A flag equal to "Yes" as shown in Figure A-11.

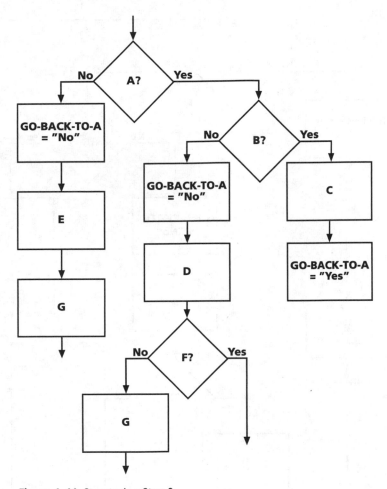

**Figure A-11:** Structuring Step 9

Now all paths of the flowchart can come together at the bottom with one final question: Is GO-BACK-TO-A equal to "Yes"? If it isn't, exit; but if it is, extend the flowline to go back to A! (See Figure A-12.)

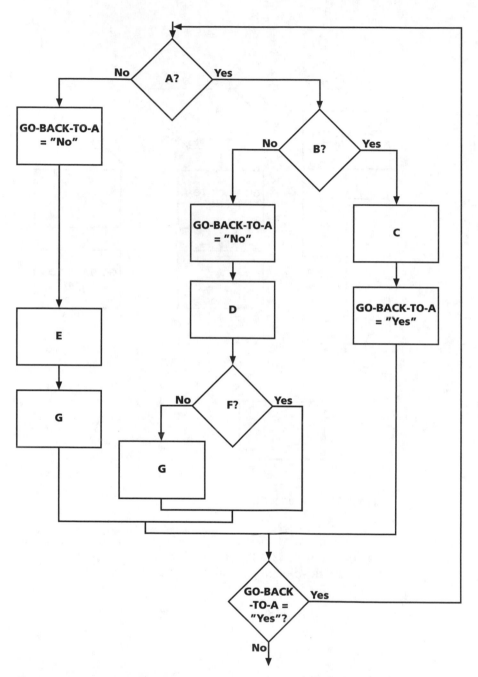

**Figure A-12:** Structuring Step 10

Is this flowchart segment structured now? There is so much information here that it is hard to tell. You may be able to see the structure more clearly if you create a module named A-THROUGH-G. If you create the module shown in Figure A-13, then the original flowchart segment can be drawn as in Figure A-14.

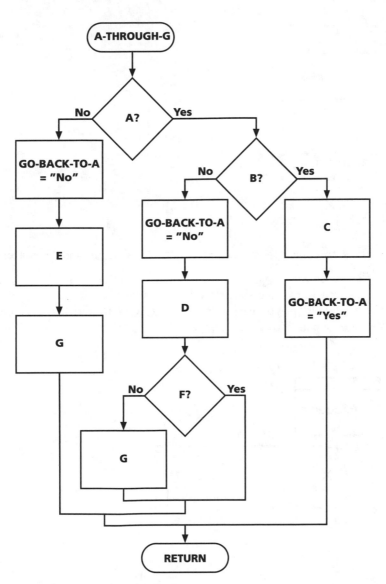

**Figure A-13:** A-THROUGH-G module

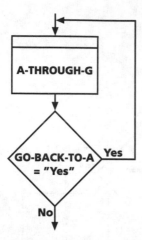

**Figure A-14:** Original segment using A-THROUGH-G module and do until loop

Now you can see that flowchart segment is a do until loop. If you prefer to use a while loop, you can redraw Figure A-14 to perform a sequence followed by a while loop as shown in Figure A-15.

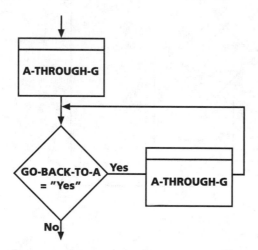

**Figure A-15:** Original segment using A-THROUGH-G module and while loop

It has taken some effort, but any logical problem can be made to conform to structured rules. It may take extra steps, including using some flag variables, but every logical problem can be solved using the three structures.

# Using a Large Decision Table

In Chapter 5 you learned to use a simple decision table. Real life problems often require many decisions; a complicated decision process is represented in the following situation. Suppose your employer sends you a memo outlining a year-end bonus plan with complicated rules. Appendix B will walk you through the process of solving this problem by using a large decision table.

```
To: Programming staff

From: The boss

I need a report listing every employee and the
bonus I plan to give him or her. Everybody gets
at least $100. All the employees in Department 2
get $200, unless they have more than 5 depen-
dents. Anybody with more than 5 dependents gets
$1000 unless they're in Department 2. Nobody
with an ID number greater than 800 gets more
than $100 even if they're in Department 2 or
have more than 5 dependents.

P.S. I need this by 5 o'clock.
```

Drawing the flowchart or writing the pseudocode for the MAIN-LOOP for this task may seem daunting. You can use a decision table to help you manage all the decisions, and you can begin to create one by listing all the possible conditions. They are:

- EMP-DEPT = 2
- EMP-DEPEND > 5
- EMP-ID-NUM > 800

Next, determine how many possible Boolean value combinations there are for the conditions. In this case, there are eight possible combinations, shown in Figure B-1. An employee can be in Department 2, have over five dependents, and have an ID number greater than 800. Another employee can be in Department 2, have over five dependents, but have an ID number that is 800 or less. Since each condition has two outcomes and there are three conditions, there are 2 * 2 * 2 , or eight possibilities. Four conditions would produce 16 possible outcome combinations, five would produce 32, and so on.

| Condition | Outcome | | | | | | | |
|---|---|---|---|---|---|---|---|---|
| EMP−DEPT = 2 | T | T | T | T | F | F | F | F |
| EMP−DEPEND > 5 | T | T | F | F | T | T | F | F |
| EMP−ID−NUM > 800 | T | F | T | F | T | F | T | F |

**Figure B-1:** Possible outcomes of bonus conditions

Next, list the possible outcome values for the bonus amounts. If you declare a numeric variable named BONUS by placing the statement num BONUS in your list of variables at the beginning of the program, then the possible outcomes can be expressed as:

- BONUS = 100
- BONUS = 200
- BONUS = 1000

Finally, choose one required outcome for each possible combination of conditions, as shown in Figure B-2. Place Xs in the BONUS = 100 row each time EMP-ID-NUM > 800 is true, no matter what other conditions exist, because the memo from the boss said, "Nobody with an ID number greater than 800 gets more than $100 even if they're in Department 2 or have more than 5 dependents."

| Condition | Outcome | | | | | | | |
|---|---|---|---|---|---|---|---|---|
| EMP-DEPT = 2 | T | T | T | T | F | F | F | F |
| EMP-DEPEND > 5 | T | T | F | F | T | T | F | F |
| EMP-ID-NUM > 800 | T | F | T | F | T | F | T | F |
| BONUS = 100 | X | | X | | X | | X | |
| BONUS = 200 | | | | | | | | |
| BONUS = 1000 | | | | | | | | |

**Figure B-2:** Decision table for bonuses, 1

Place an X in the BONUS = 1000 row under all remaining columns in which EMP-DEPEND > 5 is true unless the EMP-DEPT = 2 condition is true, because the memo stated, "Anybody with more than 5 dependents gets $1000 unless they're in Department 2." Only the sixth column in Figure B-3 meets these criteria.

| Condition | Outcome | | | | | | | |
|---|---|---|---|---|---|---|---|---|
| EMP-DEPT = 2 | T | T | T | T | F | F | F | F |
| EMP-DEPEND > 5 | T | T | F | F | T | T | F | F |
| EMP-ID-NUM > 800 | T | F | T | F | T | F | T | F |
| BONUS = 100 | X | | X | | X | | X | |
| BONUS = 200 | | | | | | | | |
| BONUS = 1000 | | | | | | X | | |

**Figure B-3:** Decision table for bonuses, 2

Place Xs in the BONUS = 200 row for any remaining columns in which EMP-DEPT = 2 is true and EMP-DEPEND > 5 is false because "All the employees in Department 2 get $200, unless they have more than 5 dependents." Column 4 in Figure B-4 satisfies these criteria.

| Condition | Outcome | | | | | | | |
|---|---|---|---|---|---|---|---|---|
| EMP-DEPT = 2 | T | T | T | T | F | F | F | F |
| EMP-DEPEND > 5 | T | T | F | F | T | T | F | F |
| EMP-ID-NUM > 800 | T | F | T | F | T | F | T | F |
| BONUS = 100 | X | | X | | X | | X | |
| BONUS = 200 | | | | X | | | | |
| BONUS = 1000 | | | | | | X | | |

**Figure B-4:** Decision table for bonuses, 3

Finally, fill any unmarked columns with an X in the BONUS = 100 row because, according to the memo, "Everybody gets at least $100." The only columns remaining are the second column and the last column on the right.

| Condition | Outcome | | | | | | | |
|---|---|---|---|---|---|---|---|---|
| EMP-DEPT = 2 | T | T | T | T | F | F | F | F |
| EMP-DEPEND > 5 | T | T | F | F | T | T | F | F |
| EMP-ID-NUM > 800 | T | F | T | F | T | F | T | F |
| BONUS = 100 | X | X | X | | X | | X | X |
| BONUS = 200 | | | | X | | | | |
| BONUS = 1000 | | | | | | X | | |

**Figure B-5:** Decision table for bonuses, 4

The decision table is complete. When you count the Xs, you'll find there are eight possible outcomes. Take a moment and confirm that each bonus is the appropriate value based on the specifications in the original memo from the boss. Now you can start to plan the logic. If you choose to use a flowchart, you start by drawing the path to the first outcome, which occurs when EMP-DEPT = 2, EMP-DEPEND > 5 and EMP-ID-NUM > 800 are all true, and which corresponds to the first column in the decision table. See Figure B-6.

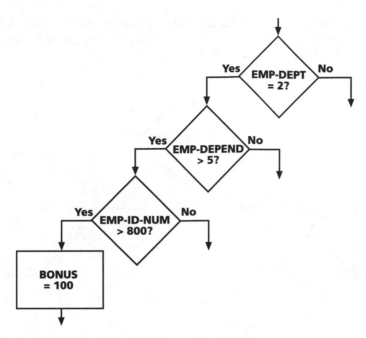

**Figure B-6:** Flowchart for bonus decision, Part 1

Add the "false" outcome to the EMP-ID-NUM > 800 decision, which corresponds to the second column in the decision table. See Figure B-7.

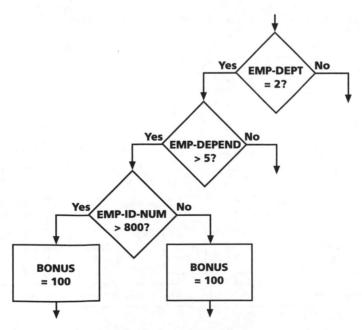

**Figure B-7:** Flowchart for bonus decision, Part 2

Add the "false" outcome when the EMP-DEPEND > 5 decision is No and the EMP-ID-NUM > 800 decision is Yes, which is represented by the third column in the decision table. See Figure B-8.

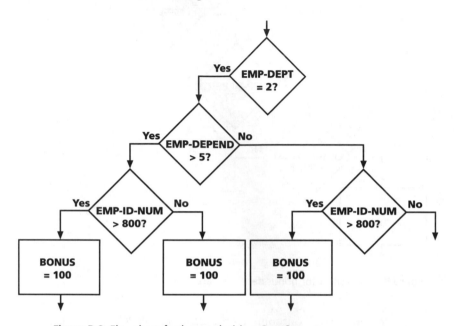

**Figure B-8:** Flowchart for bonus decision, Part 3

Continue until you have drawn all eight outcomes, as shown in Figure B-9.

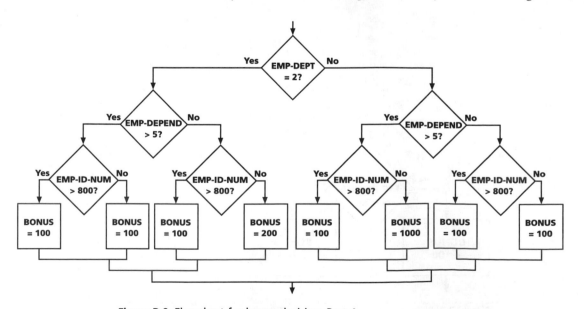

**Figure B-9:** Flowchart for bonus decision, Part 4

Next eliminate any decision that doesn't make any difference. For example, if you look at the far left side of Figure B-9, you see that when EMP-DEPT is 2 and EMP-DEPEND is greater than 5, the outcome of `EMP-ID-NUM > 800` does not matter; the BONUS value is 100 either way. You might as well eliminate the selection. Similarly, on the far right, the question EMP-ID-NUM makes no difference. The result is Figure B-10. The pseudocode appears in Figure B-11.

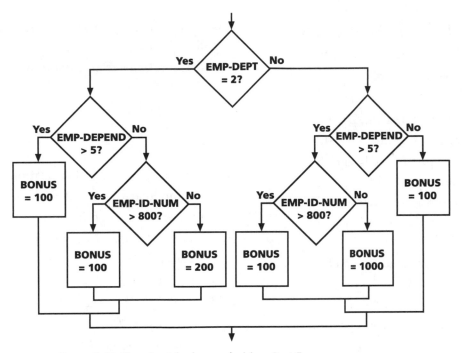

**Figure B-10:** Flowchart for bonus decision, Part 5

```
if EMP-DEPT = 2 then
      if EMP-DEPEND > 5 then
            BONUS = 100
      else
            if EMP-ID-NUM > 800 then
                  BONUS = 100
            else
                  BONUS = 200
else
      if EMP-DEPEND > 5 then
            if EMP-ID-NUM > 800 then
                  BONUS = 100
            else
                  BONUS = 1000
      else
            BONUS = 100
```

**Figure B-11:** Pseudocode for bonus decision

# Index

## Special Characters

## A

# R

# S